The Journals of the Lewis and Clark Expedition, Volume 4

April 7–July 27, 1805

Sponsored by the Center for
Great Plains Studies,
University of Nebraska-Lincoln
and the American
Philosophical Society, Philadelphia

A Project of the Center for
Great Plains Studies,
University of Nebraska-Lincoln
Gary E. Moulton, Editor
Thomas W. Dunlay, Assistant Editor

The Journals of the Lewis & Clark Expedition

Volume 4, April 7–July 27, 1805

University of Nebraska Press

Lincoln and London

The preparation and publication of this volume
were assisted by grants from
the National Endowment for the Humanities.

The paper in this book meets the minimum
requirements of American National Standard for
Information Sciences – Permanence of Paper for
Printed Library Materials, ANSI z39.48-1984.

Library of Congress Cataloging-in-Publication Data
(Revised for volume 4)
Lewis, Meriwether, 1774–1809.
The Journals of the Lewis and Clark expedition.
"The Journals of the Lewis & Clark Expedition" –
Vol. 2 – , t.p.
"Sponsored by the Center for Great Plains Studies,
University of Nebraska—Lincoln, and the American
Philosophical Society, Philadelphia." – t.p.
Bibliography: v.2, p. 568-589.
Includes index.
Contents: v.1. Atlas of the Lewis & Clark Expedition
– v.2. August 30, 1803-August 24, 1804 – –
v.4. April 7-July 27, 1805.
1. Lewis and Clark Expedition (1804-1806) – Collected
works.   2. West (U.S.) – Description and travel—To 1848
– Collected works.   3. United States – Exploring
expeditions – Collected works.   4. Lewis, Meriwether,
1774-1809.   5. Clark, William, 1770-1838.
I. Clark, William, 1770-1838.   II. Moulton, Gary E.
III. University of Nebraska – Lincoln. Center for Great
Plains Studies.   IV. American Philosophical Society.
V. Title: Journals of the Lewis & Clark Expedition.
F592.4   1983   917.8'042   82-8510
ISBN 0-8032-2861-9 (v.1)   ISBN 0-8032-2877-5 (v.4)

Contents

Preface

Again it is a pleasure to acknowledge the help of persons who have assisted in the development of this new edition of the journals. The individuals named in previous volumes have been a continuing source of help. Persons who have helped with this particular volume include Robert N. Bergantino (geology), Butte, Montana, and Lawrence L. Loendorf (archaeology), Grand Forks, North Dakota.

Beginning with this volume, the annotation makes extensive use of United States Geological Survey (USGS) maps. Bergantino graciously supplied the project with a set of USGS maps (1° x 2°, 1:250,000) on which he had plotted Lewis and Clark's route, camps, and points of observation through Montana. We used those maps principally for obtaining modern place names and did not cite them in notes. Since these maps did not always provide sufficient detail, we turned to other USGS maps (30° x 60°, 1:100,000), and these were cited in the notes; they are also listed in the "Sources Cited," at the end of this volume. We were also aided by three special sources. In July 1979, Bob Saindon prepared a special supplement for the *Glasgow* (Montana) *Courier* titled "Lewis and Clark in Northeast Montana." This material was especially helpful for the expedition's trip between the Yellowstone and Musselshell rivers. The Bureau of Land Management has developed a set of maps for the Missouri River Breaks region, from James Kipp State Park to Fort Benton, Montana. Titled "Upper Missouri National Wild and Scenic River," these maps locate Lewis and Clark camps and other historic features on a modern projection. In 1984 Bergantino produced a special map of "The Great Falls Portage of Lewis and Clark, 1805–1806." In addition to aiding our annotation, it was also used in preparing this volume's map of the area. None of the three sources are cited specifically in the notes.

EDITORIAL SYMBOLS AND ABBREVIATIONS

[roman]	Word or phrase supplied or corrected.
[roman?]	Conjectural reading of the original.
[*italics*]	Editor's remarks within a document.
[*Ed: italics*]	Editor's remarks that might be confused with *EC, ML, NB, WC,* or *X*.
[*EC: italics*]	Elliott Coues's emendations or interlineations.
[*ML: italics*]	Meriwether Lewis's emendations or interlineations.
[*NB: italics*]	Nicholas Biddle's emendations or interlineations.
[*WC: italics*]	William Clark's emendations or interlineations.
[*X: italics*]	Emendations or interlineations of the unknown or an unidentified person.
⟨roman⟩	Word or phrase deleted by the writer and restored by the editor.

SPECIAL SYMBOLS OF LEWIS AND CLARK

α	Alpha
$\angle$	Angle
☽	Moon symbol
☞	Pointing hand
★	Star
☉	Sun symbol
♍	Virgo

COMMON ABBREVIATIONS OF LEWIS AND CLARK

Altd., alds.	altitude, altitudes
Apt. T.	apparent time
d.	degree
do.	ditto
h.	hour
id., isd.	island
L. L.	lower limb
L., Larb., Lard., Lbd., or Ld. S.	larboard (or left) side
Lad., Latd.	latitude
Longtd.	longitude
m., mts.	minute, minutes
M. T.	mean time
mes., mls., ms.	miles
obstn.	observation
opsd.	opposite
pd., psd.	passed
pt.	point
qde., quadt., qudt.	quadrant
qtr., qutr.	quarter
s.	second
S., St., Star., Starbd., Stb., or Stbd. S.	starboard (or right) side
sext., sextn., sextt.	sextant
U. L.	upper limb

Note: abbreviations in weather entries are explained at the presentation of the first weather data, following the entry of January 31, 1804.

Introduction to Volume 4

Fort Mandan, North Dakota, to Three Forks of Missouri River, Montana

April 7–July 27, 1805

On April 7, 1805, the permanent party of the Lewis and Clark expedition set out up the Missouri River from Fort Mandan in present day North Dakota. They had spent the winter among the Mandan and Hidatsa Indians, waiting for the river's ice to break up and make travel possible. On the same day that they headed upriver, their keelboat which had brought them as far as the Mandan villages set off downriver for St. Louis with most of their French boatmen and a squad of soldiers under Corporal Richard Warfington. The boat carried dispatches and ethnological and natural history specimens which the captains were sending back to President Thomas Jefferson—the first fruits of the expedition.

The Corps of Discovery was now entering an area where there had been no previous white exploration, although they were informed about the country as far as the Continental Divide from the Mandans and Hidatsas. They also had with them the Shoshone woman Sacagawea, through whom they hoped to make friendly contact with her people living along the divide. Beyond that point they could only hope that with Indian assistance and guidance they could make a portage of the Rocky Mountains to some navigable stream flowing into the Columbia River, and thus reach the Pacific.

They would spend the rest of the spring and summer toiling their way up the Missouri to its headwaters in their two pirogues and six canoes. On April 25 Lewis with four men reached the Yellowstone River, near the present North Dakota-Montana boundary. Two days later, after taking astronomical readings to fix the position of the site, they passed on into Montana. The journey across Montana, unlike the earlier stages of the trip, brought no encounters with Indians. The party observed signs of Assiniboine and Blackfeet encampments, but the people themselves were absent. It may be, however, that Indians did observe the group's passage without making themselves known. In place of meetings with Indians, however, the party began a series of combats with grizzly bears. At first they had thought that their superior weaponry would give them an advantage over these animals—one not possessed by the Indians. Instead, the subsequent encounters led them to feel some of the same awe and respect for the bear that the Indians did.

Other natural phenomena posed even greater dangers. The severe spring winds sometimes made it impossible to navigate safely on the river, thus impeding their progress. On May 14 a pirogue turned on its side in a squall of wind, nearly causing the loss of its contents and passengers, including Sacagawea and her baby. Aside from the potential human tragedy, the loss of the supplies in the pirogue might have made it impossible for the expedition to continue; fortunately the quick action of boatman Pierre Cruzatte righted the craft and saved the situation.

As they moved west the country grew increasingly arid and rugged. Small mountain ranges in the distance came into view which the captains assumed to be part of the Rockies. To the north and south they were viewing the present Bears Paw, Little Rocky, and Judith mountains. In late May the travelers entered the Breaks of the Missouri, an area of colorful and impressive geological formations, including the fantastically sculpted White Cliffs, which prompted Lewis to pen a romantic description of these "seens of visionary enchantment." Clark named one major stream in the area for a young woman, Julia Hancock, who would later become his wife and today it retains that name, the Judith. The captains were also beginning to notice new species not seen on the lower Missouri. Ponderosa pine began to appear as did quaking aspen, sagebrush, and new varieties of willows and cottonwood trees. They were also taken with the abundance of currants and gooseberries. While the expedition's fisherman Silas Goodrich caught goldeye and cutthroat trout, others saw new animals such as the prairie rattlesnake, the Montana horned owl, and the thirteen-lined ground squirrel.

After nearly two months of travel, on June 2, the Corps arrived at the mouth of a major fork of the Missouri which they named the Marias River, after a cousin of Lewis's. This stream posed a dilemma, for none of the information given them by the Mandans and Hidatsas had referred to this stream. The problem was to determine which fork was the true Missouri, which would lead them to the Continental Divide. To make the wrong decision and take the wrong river might cause such delay as to leave them stranded in the mountains in winter, with the likelihood that the expedition would fail altogether. Matters were not helped by the fact that, while the captains believed that the river coming from the southwest was the Missouri, virtually all their men were sure that the other fork was the one to be followed. The captains led reconnaissances a short distance up each stream, without reaching any satisfactory conclusion. Finally they decided to set off up the southwest fork, with Lewis going ahead with a few men in the hope of finding an identifiable landmark soon enough to determine if they were in error.

On June 13 Lewis found the evidence that proved they were on the right river; the Hidatsas had told them of the Great Falls of the Missouri, the point at which the river emerged from the mountains. As his little group walked upstream, Lewis heard a roaring and saw clouds of spray that could only come from the falls. His relief was great, reflected in his ecstatic description of the beauty of the "sublime" spectacle, but the presence of the five cascades and intervening rapids presented a new problem, for the canoes and supplies must now be portaged around this obstacle. This task would consume an entire month of their precious time.

A survey of the area showed that a portage of about eighteen miles would be necessary to skirt the falls. To transport the heavy canoes and goods to their upper portage camp they constructed crude carriages out of cottonwood, the wheels being rounded slabs of the trunks. The men had to pull heavy loads across ground roughened by the dried tracks of buffalo and infested with prickly pear cactus, all of which tormented their moccasined feet. The exertion was so great that at every rest stop they fell down and went immediately to sleep. Some of the men were exempted from this labor to hunt for the party's food, but they had to contend with the numerous grizzly bears. Heavy rain showers drenched everyone, and large hailstones injured several. During one downpour Clark, surveying the falls with Charbonneau, Sacagawea, her baby, and York, was nearly swept into the Missouri by a flash flood coming down the gully in which the little group had taken refuge.

At the upper portage camp Lewis labored on a collapsible boat of his own design, whose dismantled frame the party had transported across the continent for use when heavier boats had to be left behind. The frame could be bolted together and covered with animal skins. Unfortunately, tar was required to make the invention waterproof, and there were no pine trees near the area to provide it. Attempts to contrive a substitute were unsuccessful; the boat leaked too badly to be useful. The captains decided that Clark should go ahead several miles upriver where there were some sizable cottonwood trees and build two more dugout canoes.

On July 15 the party set out from the canoe-building camp, after more than three months of travel from Fort Mandan. First Lewis and then Clark forged ahead of the main party looking for the Shoshones, for it was now vital to find these Indians to obtain horses and guides for the mountain crossing which increasingly appeared likely. The party moved through the deep canyon which they called the "Gates of the Rocky Mountains," a name which remains today. They were now within the mountains, and shallow waters and rapids would make navigation increasingly difficult. On July 25 Clark with four men reached the Three Forks of the Missouri, of which the Hidatsas had told them. Lewis with the main party reached the forks two days later, and the captains decided to name the three streams the Jefferson, the Madison, and the Gallatin, after the president and his secretaries of state and treasury. There was still no contact with the Shoshones, although various signs of their presence were evident. Sacagawea was now recognizing familiar landmarks. A meeting with her people was now their most urgent concern.

The Journals of the Lewis and Clark Expedition, Volume 4

April 7–July 27, 1805

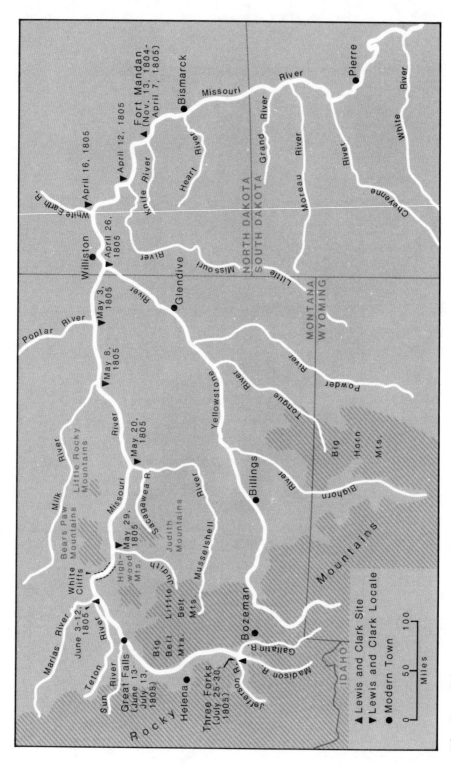

The Expedition's Route, April 7–July 27, 1805

Chapter Eleven

From Fort Mandan to the Yellowstone

April 7–27, 1805

[Lewis]   Fort Mandan April 7th 1805.[1]

Having on this day at 4 P. M. completed every arrangement necessary for our departure, we dismissed the barge and crew[2] with orders to return without loss of time to S. Louis, a small canoe with two French hunters accompanyed the barge; these men had assended the missouri with us the last year as engages. The barge crew consisted of six soldiers and two [blank] Frenchmen; two Frenchmen and a Ricara Indian also take their passage in her as far as the Ricara Vilages, at which place we expect Mr. Tiebeau [Tabeau] to embark with his peltry who in that case will make an addition of two, perhaps four men to the crew of the barge. We gave Richard Warfington, a discharged Corpl., the charge of the Barge and crew, and confided to his care likewise our dispatches to the government, letters to our private friends, and a number of articles to the President of the United States. One of the Frenchmen by the Name of [NB?: Joseph][3] Gravline an honest discrete man and an excellent boat-man is imployed to conduct the barge as a pilot; we have therefore every hope that the barge and with her our dispatches will arrive safe at St. Louis. Mr. Gravlin who speaks the Ricara language extreemly well, has been imployed to conduct a few of the Recara Chiefs to the seat of government who have promised us to decend in the barge to St. Liwis with that view.—

Meriwether Lewis. Portrait by Charles B. J. F. de Saint-Mémin,
1807, courtesy Corcoran Gallery of Art, Washington, D.C.

William Clark. Portrait by Charles B. J. F. de Saint-Mémin,
1810, courtesy Corcoran Gallery of Art, Washington, D.C.

At same moment that the Barge departed from Fort Mandan, Capt. Clark embaked with our party and proceeded up the river.[4] as I had used no exercise for several weeks, I determined to walk on shore as far as our encampment of this evening; accordingly I continued my walk on the N. side of the River about six miles, to the upper Village of the Mandans, and called on the Black Cat or Pose cop'se há, the great chief of the Mandans;[5] he was not at home; I rested myself a minutes, and finding that the party had not arrived I returned about 2 miles and joined them at their encampment on the N. side of the river opposite the lower Mandan village.[6] Our party now consisted of the following Individuals. Sergts. John Ordway, Nathaniel Prior, & Patric Gass; Privates, William Bratton, John Colter, Reubin, and Joseph Fields, John Shields, George Gibson, George Shannon, John Potts, John Collins, Joseph Whitehouse, Richard Windsor, Alexander Willard, Hugh Hall, Silas Goodrich, Robert Frazier, Peter Crouzatt, John Baptiest la Page, Francis Labiech, Hue McNeal, William Werner, Thomas P. Howard, Peter Wiser, and John B. Thompson.—

Interpreters, George Drewyer and Tauasant Charbono also a Black man by the name of York, servant to Capt. Clark, an Indian Woman wife to Charbono with a young child, and a Mandan man who had promised us to accompany us as far as the Snake Indians with a view to bring about a good understanding and friendly intercourse between that nation and his own, the Minetares and Ahwahharways.

Our vessels consisted of six small canoes, and two large perogues. This little fleet altho' not quite so rispectable as those of Columbus or Capt. Cook[7] were still viewed by us with as much pleasure as those deservedly famed adventurers ever beheld theirs; and I dare say with quite as much anxiety for their safety and preservation.   we were now about to penetrate a country at least two thousand miles in width, on which the foot of civillized man had never trodden; the good or evil it had in store for us was for experiment yet to determine, and these little vessells contained every article by which we were to expect to subsist or defend ourselves. however as this the state of mind in which we are, generally gives the colouring to events, when the immagination is suffered to wander into futurity, the picture which now presented itself to me was a most pleasing one. entertaing ⟨now⟩ as I do, the most confident hope of succeading in a voyage which had formed a da[r]ling project of mine for the last ten years ⟨of my life⟩, I could but esteem this moment of my ⟨our⟩ departure as among the most happy of my life. The party are in excellent health and sperits, zealously attatched to the enterprise, and anxious to proceed; not a whisper of murmur or discontent to be heard among them, but all act in unison, and with the most perfect harmony. I took an early supper this evening and went to bed. Capt. Clark myself the two Interpretters and the woman and child sleep in a tent of dressed skins. this tent is in the Indian stile, formed of a number of dressed Buffaloe skins sewed together with sinues.[8] it is cut in such manner that when foalded double it forms the quarter of a circle, and is left open at one side where it may be attatched or loosened at pleasure by strings which are sewed to its sides to the purpose. to erect this tent, a parsel of ten or twelve poles are provided, fore or five of which are attatched together at one end, they are then elivated and their lower extremities are spread in a circular manner to a width proportionate to the demention of the lodge, in the same position orther poles are leant against those, and the leather is then thrown over them forming a conic figure.—

[Clark]   7th of *April Satturday 1805*[9]

a windey day, The Interpreter we Sent to the Villages returned with Chief of the Ricara's & 3 men of that nation   this Chief informed us that he was Sent by his nation to Know the despositions of the nations in this neighbourhood in respect to the recara's Settleing near them, that he had not yet made those arrangements, he request that we would Speek to the Assinniboins, & Crow Inds. in their favour, that they wished to follow our directions and be at peace with all, he viewed all nations in this quarter well disposed except the Sioux. The wish of those recaras appears to be a junction with the Mandans & Minetarras in a Defensive war with the Sioux who rob them of every Spece [species] of property in Such a manner that they Cannot live near them any longer. I told this Chief we were glad to See him, and we viewed his nation as the Dutifull Children of ⟨his⟩

a Great father who would extend his protection to ⟨them⟩ all those who would open their ears to his good advice, we had already Spoken to the Assinniboins, and Should Speeke to the Crow Indians if we Should See them &c. as to the Sioux their Great father would not let them have any more good Guns &c. would take Care to prosu Such measurs as would provent those Sioux from Murding and taking the property from his duty-full red Children &c.— we gave him a certificate of his good Conduct & a Small Medal, a Carrot of Tobacco and a String of Wompom— he requested that one of his men who was lame might decend in the boat to their nation and returned to the Mandans well Satisfied—

The name of this Chief of War is *Kah-kah, we to*—Raven brave.[10]

This Cheif delivered us a letter from Mr. Taboe. informing us of the wish of the Grand Chiefs of the Ricarras to visit their Great father and requesting the privolage of put'g on board the boat 3000 w of Skins &c. & adding 4 hands and himself to the party. this preposeal we Shall agree to, as that addition will make the party in the boat 15 Strong and more able to defend themselves from the Seoux &c.

[Clark]   *Fort Mandan* April 7th 1805[11]

Sunday, at 4 oClock P M, the Boat, in which was 6 Soldiers 2 frenchmen & an Indian, all under the command of a corporal who had the charge of dispatches, &c.—and a Canoe with 2 french men, Set out down the river for St. Louis. at the same time we Sout out on our voyage up the river in 2 perogues and 6 canoes, and proceded on to the 1st villg. of Mandans & Camped on the S. S.— our party consisting of Sergt. Nathaniel Pryor Sgt. John Ordway Sgt. Pat: Gass, William Bratten, John Colter Joseph & Reubin Fields, John Shields George Gibson George Shannon, John Potts, John Collins, Jos: Whitehouse, Richard Windser, Alexander Willard, Hugh Hall, Silas Gutrich, Robert Frazure, Peter Crouzat, John Baptiest la page, Francis Labich, Hugh McNeal, William Werner, Thomas P. Howard, Peter Wiser, J. B. Thompson and my Servent york, George Drewyer who acts as a hunter & interpreter, Shabonah and his *Indian Squar* to act as an Interpreter & interpretress for the snake Indians—one Mandan & Shabonahs infant. *Sah-kah-gar we â*[12]

1. Here begins Lewis's notebook journal Codex D, running to May 23, 1805. It contains his first known daily journal-keeping since September 17, 1804, except for entries in Clark's Codex C in February 1805. See the Introduction and Appendix C, vol. 2. From this point we have complete journals by Lewis to August 26, 1805.

2. In their entries for this date the captains provide a complete list of their permanent party bound for the Pacific. For the party returning downriver, however, there is no such definite information. Corporal Richard Warfington, in charge of the party, was definitely along, as were the two dishonorably discharged men, John Newman and Moses Reed. So were Warfington's squad, probably consisting now of Privates John Boley, John Dame, Ebenezer Tuttle, and Isaac White. Just possibly the mysterious John Robinson, or Robertson, was present instead of Boley, Tuttle, or White. See Appendix A, vol. 2, and June 12, 1804, above. Newman, Reed, Boley, Tuttle, Dame, and White probably make up the six soldiers Lewis mentions. Joseph Gravelines was present as an interpreter, and as Lewis indicates there was one Arikara. The difficulty arises with the anonymous "Frenchmen" on the keelboat and accompanying the boat in a canoe. The two in the canoe are not readily identifiable. Lewis refers to two French boatmen working the boat, and two more going as far as the Arikaras, who may or may not have been expedition *engagés*. One of those on the boat was probably Baptiste Deschamps, the boss of the boatmen. Etienne Malboeuf, François Rivet, and Peter Pinaut are other possibilities. The lack of record as to which boatmen left the party in the fall of 1804 complicates matters further. This lack of information concerning these men presumably reflects the captains' own lack of interest in the "hirelings." Clarke (MLCE), 145–46; Jackson (LLC), 1:237 n. 7.

3. "Joseph" appears to be added to a blank space and is written in red, perhaps by Biddle.

4. Ordway says they left at 5:00 p.m.

5. Black Cat is identified in notes for October 28, 1804.

6. On the starboard shore opposite Mitutanka village, in McLean County, North Dakota, some three miles below Stanton. *Atlas* maps 29, 33, 46, 55; MRC map 52.

7. Captain James Cook of the British Navy, the most famous explorer of his time, made three voyages (1768–79), in which he greatly increased European knowledge of the Pacific. Jefferson's library included Cook's journals of his last voyage, published in 1784, and Lewis was evidently familiar at least with the portions of it dealing with the Northwest coast. Jackson (TJ), 45–46, 55–56.

8. Lewis's spelling of "sinews." The tent is obviously a plains Indian tipi, later referred to by the captains as a "leather lodge." It was apparently Biddle who wrote "Qu" in red across this passage.

9. The last daily entry in Clark's Codex C.

10. Apparently the captains did not meet Kakawita (*kaakaawiítA*, "raven man") when they were at the Arikara villages in October. He was an important war chief and a rival to Kakawissassa. Ronda (LCAI), 48–49, 52–53, 65. It was probably Gravelines who was sent to the villages. See April 6, 1805.

11. Here begins Clark's notebook journal Voorhis No. 1, which runs to July 3, 1805. On the flyleaf of the journal is a note by Lewis. The first line consists of unidentified courses.

The remainder seems to be a reminder of information to be gathered about Indians when inquiries could be made. The use of the word "Kooskooske," a possible Nez Perce name for the Clearwater River in Idaho, and of "Lewis's River" (the Salmon and Snake rivers as named by the captains), shows that Lewis must have made the note some time after the dates of the main text of the journal (April 7–July 3, 1805). Possibly Lewis wrote the note at Fort Clatsop or elsewhere to be filled in when he could ask the Indians, not having had time on the trip west. It reads thus:

N. 42½° W.— N. 78° W. 102 poles. N. 12° E

Names of Indian nations & their places of residence	No. of Lodges	Probable No. of Souls
Flatheads		
of the Kooskooske—		
of Lewis's river above the Kooskooske—	120—	
of Lewis's river below the mouth of the Kooskooske—		

12. Sacagawea's name may have been added as an afterthought, or perhaps later, after Clark came to know her better. The underscore for "Indian Squar" also appears to be an addition. See the entry of November 4, 1804, where she is discussed.

[Lewis]

April 8th Set out early this morning, the wind blew hard against us from the N. W. we therefore traveled very slowly. I walked on shore, and visited the *black Cat,* took leave of him after smoking a pipe as is their custom, and then proceeded on slowly by land about four miles where I wated the arrival of the party, at 12 Oclock they came up and informed me that one of the small canoes was behind in distress. Capt Clark returned foud she had filled with water and all her loading wet. we lost half a bag of bisquit, and about thirty pounds of powder by this accedent; the powder we regard as a serious loss, but we spread it to dry immediately and hope we shall still be enabled to restore the greater part of it. this was the only powder we had which was not perfectly secure from geting wet. we took dinner at this place, and then proceed on to oure encampment, which was on the S. side opposite to a high bluff.[1] the Mandan man came up after we had encamped and brought with him a woman who was extreemly solicitous to accompany one of the men of our party, this however we positively refused to permit.

Courses distances and references for Apl. 8th[2]

From the upper point on an island (⟨which was⟩ being the point to which Capt. Clark took his last course when he assended the river in surch of a place for winter quarters 1st November last)[3] to a point of wood land Stard side, passing a high bluff on the Lard.   N 40° W. 3½

[Clark]   8th of *April Monday 1805*

Set out verry early   wind hard a head from the N. W.   proceeded on passed all the villages the inhabitents of which flocked down in great numbers to view us, I took my leave of the great Chief of the Mandans who gave me a par of excellent mockersons, one Canoe filed with water every thing in her got wet.   ⅔ of a barrel of powder lost by this accedent.

From the upper part of an island just below Morparperyoo-
patoo's camp to a point of wood land on the Stad. Side
passing a high bluff on the Lad. containing many horizontal narrow Stratas of Carbonated wood, some of which
are Sixty feet above the Surface of the water[4]   N. 40° W. 3½

Camped on the S. S. opsd. a high bluff   an Indian Joined us, also an Indian woman with a view to accompany us, the woman was Sent back   the man being acquainted with the Countrey we allowed him to accompanie us

1. In McLean County, North Dakota, a mile or so below the Garrison Dam. Mattison (GR), 25; *Atlas* maps 29, 33, 46, 55; MRC map 52.
2. The courses also appear on *Atlas* map 33 in Clark's hand.
3. Actually October 30, 1804. The island appears on *Atlas* maps 29, 33, 46, 55.
4. See geology note for April 9.

[Lewis]   *Tuesday April 9th*[1]

Set out as early as it was possible to see this morning and proceed about five miles where we halted and took beakfas—   the Indian man who had promised us to accompany us as far as the Snake Indians, now informed us of his intention to relinquish the journey, and accordingly returned to his village.   we saw a great number of brant passing up the river, some of them were white, except the large feathers in the first and second joint of the wing which are black.   there is no other difference between them and the common gray brant but that of their colour—   their note and habits are the same, and they are freequently seen to associate together. I have not yet positively determined whether they are the same, or a different species.—[2]   Capt Clark walked on shore to-day and informed me on his return, that passing through the prarie he had seen an anamal that precisely resembled the burrowing squrril, accept in point of size, it being only about one third as large as the squirrel, and that it also burrows.[3] I have observed in many parts of the plains and praries the work of an anamal of which I could never obtain a view.[4]   their work resembles that of the salamander common to the sand hills of the States of South Carolina and Georgia; and like that anamal also it never appears above the ground.   the little hillocks which are thrown up by these anamals have much the appearance of ten or twelve pounds of loose earth poared out of a vessel on the surface of the plain.   in the state they leave them you can discover no whole through which they throw out this earth; but by removing the loose earth gently you may discover that the soil has been broken in a circle manner for about an inch and a half in diameter, where it appears looser than the adjacent surface, and is certainly the place through which the earth has been thrown out, tho' the operation is performed without leaving any visible aperture.—   the Bluffs of the river which we passed today were upwards of a hundred feet high, formed of a mixture of yellow clay and sand—   many horizontal stratas of carbonated wood, having every appearance of pitcoal at a distance; were seen in the the face of these bluffs.   these stratas are of unequal thicknesses from 1 to 5 feet, and appear at different elivations above the water some of them as much as eighty feet.   the hills of the river are very broken and many of them have the apearance of having been on fire at some former period.   considerable quantities of pumice stone and lava appear in many parts of these hills where they are broken and washed down by the rain and melting snow.[5]   when we halted for dinner the squaw busied herself in serching for the wild artichokes[6] which the mice collect and deposit in large hoards.   this operation she performed by penetrating the earth with a sharp stick about some small collections of drift wood.   her labour soon proved successful, and she procurrd a good quantity of these roots.   the flavor of this root resembles that of the Jerusalem Artichoke, and the stalk of the weed which produces it is also similar, tho' both the root and stalk are much smaller than the Jarusalem Artichoke.   the root is white and of an ovate form, from one to three inches in length and usually about the size of a man's finger. one stalk produces from two to four, and somitimes six of these roots.—

at the distance of 6 miles passed a large wintering or hunting camp of the Minetares on the Stard. side. these lodges about thirty in number are built of earth and timber in their usual stile. 2¼ miles higher we passed the entrance of Miry Creek,[7] which discharges itself on the Stard. side. this creek is but small, takes it's rise in some small lakes near the Mouse river and passes in it's course to the Missouri, through beatifull, level, and fertile plains, intirely destitute of timber.— Three miles above the mouth of this creek we passed a hunting camp of Minetares[8] who had prepared a park and were wating the return of the Antelope; which usually pass the Missouri at this season of the year from the Black hills on the South side, to the open plains on the north side of the river; in like manner the Antelope repasses the Missouri from N. to South in the latter end of Autumn, and winter in the black hills, where there is considerable bodies of woodland. we proceed on 11½ miles further and encamped on the N. side[9] in a most beatifull high extensive open bottom

	The courses and distances of this day are as follow[10]	miles
N. 20° W.	to a Stard. point opposte to a bluff	1
N.	to a Stard. point do. do. do.	½
N. 80 E.	to a sand point on Lard. side	1 ½
N.	to a Lard. point[11]	½
N. 18 W.	to a handsome elivated plain on Lard. Sd.	1
N. 22 E.	to a point of willows on Lard. side opposite to a wintering camp of the Minetares	1 ½
N. 20 W.	to the mouth of Miry creek Stard. side, passing a small run[12] and a hill called snake den	2 ¼
W.	to a point on Lard side	1
S. 75 W.	to a point on Stard opposite to a camp of Minetares, and lower pot. of a high bluff	4
N. 65 W.	to the upper point point of woo[d]land on Std Sd.	3
S. 45 W.	to a point of timber on the Lard. side	2

S. 30 W.	to a sand point on the Stard side	1 ¼
S. 78 W.	to a point of woodland on the Lard side	4
		23 ½ [13]

[Clark]   9th *of April Tuesday 1805.*

Set out this morning verry early under a gentle breeze from the S. E.   at Brackfast the Indian deturmined to return to his nation. I saw a Musquetor to day [14]   great numbers of Brant flying up the river, the Maple, & Elm has buded & Cotton and arrow wood beginning to bud. [15] I saw in the prarie an animal resembling the Prarie dog or Barking Squirel & burrow in the Same way, this animal was about ⅓ as large as the barking Squirel. But fiew resident birds or water fowls which I have Seen as yet   at 6 miles passed an old hunting camp of *Menitarrees* on the S. S.   2 ½ miles higher passed the mouth of Miry Creek on the S. S.   passed a hunting Camp of Minetarees on the S. S. waiting the return of the Antilope, Saw Great numbers of Gees feedin in the Praries on the young grass, I saw flowers in the praries to day, juniper grows on the Sides of the hills, & runs on the ground [16]   all the hills have more or Less indefferent Coal in Stratias at different hites from the waters edge to 80 feet.   those Stratias from 1 inch to 5 feet thick.   we Campd. on the S. S. above some rocks makeing out in the river in a butifull ellivated plain.

Course distance & refferences for the 9th

N. 20° W.	1	mile on the S. pt opsd. a Bluff
N	½	mile on the S. pt. do.
N. 80° E	1 ½	miles to a sand pt. on the L. S.
N.	½	a mile to the L. pt.
N. 18° W.	1	mile to a handsom elivated plain on L. S.
N. 22° E	1 ½	miles to a pt. of willows on the L. S. opposit a Wintering camp of the Menetarras.
N. 20° W.	2 ¼	miles to the mouth of Miry Creek; passd. a hill call Snake house & Small run S. S.
West	1	mile to a pt. on the Larboard Side

S. 75° W.	4	miles to a pt. on the S. S. opsd. a Bluff and a camp of Miniterras.
N. 65° W.	3	miles to the upper part of the timber S. S.
S. 45° W.	2	miles to a pt. of timber on the L. S.
S. 30 W	1 ¼	miles to a Sand pt. on the S. S.
S. 78° W.	4	miles to a pt. of wood on the L. S
	23 ½	

1. Someone drew vertical lines through the natural history material in this entry, apparently in red.

2. Lewis here makes a distinction between the blue phase and white phase of the snow goose, *Chen caerulescens* [AOU, 169], a distinction recognized by ornithologists only recently when the blue became a subspecies of the white. Holmgren, 28; AOU, 67. The majority of the brant were probably *Branta bernicla* [AOU, 173].

3. Probably Richardson's ground squirrel, *Spermophilus richardsonii.* Burroughs, 102; Jones et al., 137–41.

4. It is not completely clear if this animal was considered by Lewis to be the same as the one Clark saw, mentioned just above. Its workings, as described, seem to be those of the northern pocket gopher, *Thomomys talpoides;* they never did obtain a specimen. The "salamander" mentioned for comparison is a rodent, not an amphibian, probably *Geomys pinetis,* the southeastern pocket gopher. Cutright (LCPN), 130; Burroughs, 107; Jones et al., 166–69.

5. The Sentinel Butte Formation extends for more than 100 miles along the Missouri River between Knife and Little Knife Rivers. Lignite coal (Lewis's carbonated wood) is common in this formation and occasionally catches fire, baking and fusing the overlying clay or shale into rocks that superficially resemble rocks of volcanic origin. The burnt hills are probably hills that exhibit these products, but the term may also refer to the burnt sienna or umber colors of some of the sandstones because it is used on October 5, 1804, and May 26, 1805, in places where there is insufficient coal to have produced this appearance.

6. *Helianthus tuberosus* L., Jerusalem artichoke. The species is near its northwestern distributional limit in McLean County, North Dakota. Barkley, 380; Heiser, 171. Artichokes were not apparently gathered in the way Lewis described. He may be confusing the method Indians used to gather the hog peanut, *Amphicarpa bracteata* (L.) Fern. Gilmore (UPI), 43–44. See also October 11, 1804, and May 12, 1805. The collecting mice are probably the meadow mouse or vole, *Microtus pennsylvanicus.* Burroughs, 118, 322 n. 26; Jones et al., 221–25.

7. Now Snake Creek, in McLean County; much of it is now under Snake Creek Reservoir, a branch of the Garrison Reservoir (Lake Sakakawea). It is "Bourbeaux" or "Muddy Creek" on *Atlas* map 29. *Atlas* maps 33, 46, 55; MRC map 52.

8. Both these camps are clearly marked on *Atlas* maps 46 and 55.

9. Now inundated by Garrison Reservoir, the site was in McLean County above Douglas Creek and a few miles southwest of Garrison. Mattison (GR), 31–32; *Atlas* maps 33, 46, 55; MRC map 53.

10. These courses are also on *Atlas* map 33, in both captains' hands.

11. *Atlas* map 33 says "Stard."

12. Later Wolf Creek, in McLean County. It appears, nameless, just below Snake (Miry) Creek on *Atlas* maps 29, 33, 46, 55. On the first map apparently Maximilian has labeled it "Snake R Creek." MRC map 52.

13. *Atlas* map 33 has an incorrect total of 23¾.

14. Probably *Aedes vexans*.

15. Other than the boxelder there are no maple species native to this area of North Dakota; Clark probably meant *Acer negundo* L., boxelder, which is of the maple genus and flowers in early spring as described. The elm is *Ulmus americana* L., American elm; the cottonwood is *Populus deltoides* Bartr. ex Marsh. ssp. *monilifera* (Ait.) Eckenwalder, plains cottonwood; arrow wood is *Cornus sericea* L., red osier dogwood. Little, 96-E, 196-N, 149-W; Barkley, 101, 205; Kartesz & Kartesz, 169.

16. Probably in reference to the two species of juniper in the area, *Juniperus scopulorum* Sarg., Rocky Mountain red cedar, an upright tree found on hillsides, and *J. horizontalis* Moench, creeping juniper, a low, dwarf species. Barkley, 13, 12.

[Lewis]   *Wednesday April 10th 1805.*

Set out at an early hour this morning   at the distance of three miles passed some Minetares who had assembled themselves on the Lard shore to take a view of our little fleet. Capt Clark walked on shore today, for several hours, when he returned he informed me that he had seen a gang of Antelopes[1] in the plains but was unable to get a shoot at them   he also saw some geese and swan.[2]   the geese are now feeding in considerable numbers on the young grass which has sprung up in the bottom praries— the Musquetoes were very troublesome to us today. The country on both sides of the missouri from the tops of the river hills, is one continued level fertile plain as far as the eye can reach, in which there is not even a solitary tree or shrub to be seen except such as from their moist situations or the steep declivities of hills are sheltered from the ravages of the fire. at the distance of 12 miles from our encampment of last night we arrived at the lower point of a bluff on the Lard side; about 1½ miles down this bluff from this point, the bluff is now on fire and throws out considerable quantities of smoke which has a strong sulphurious smell.[3]   the appearance of the coal in the blufs continues as yesterday.   at 1 P. M. we overtook three french hunters who had set out a few days before us with a view of traping beaver; they had taken 12 since they left Fort Mandan. these people avail themselves of the protection which our numbers will enable us to give them against the Assinniboins who sometimes hunt on the Missouri and intend ascending with us as far as the mouth of the Yellow stone river and continue there hunt up that river. this is the first essay of a beaver hunter of any discription on this river. the beaver these people have already taken is by far the best I have ever seen. the river bottoms we have passed to-day are wider and possess more timber than usual—the courant of the Missouri is but moderate, at least not greater than that of the Ohio in high tide; it's banks are falling in but little; the navigation is therefore comparitively with it's lower portion easy and safe.— we encamped this evening on a willow point, Stard. side just above a remarkable bend in the river to the S. W. which we called the little bason.—[4]

	Courses and distances of this day.[5]	miles
S. 45. W.	to a point of timbered land on the Std. Sid	3
W.	to a point of timbered land on the Lard. sid.	3
S. 72 W.	to a tree in a bend on the Stard. side	2
S. 32 W.	to a point of woods on the Stard side	4
W.	on the Stad point	½
N. 40 W.	on the Stard point	½
N. 50 E.	to a point on the Lard side, opposite to a low bluff	2
S. 52 W.	to a point on the Stard. side opposite to a bluf, above which a small creek falls in.	3 ½
		18 ½

[Clark]   *10th of April Wednesday* 1805

Set out verry early. the morning cool and no wind proceeded on passed a camp of Inds. on the L. S. this day proved to be verry worm, the Misquetors troublesom. I Saw Several Antilope on the S. S. also gees & Swan, we over took 3 french men Trappers The countrey to day as usial except that the points of Timber is larger than below, the Coal Continue to day, one man Saw a hill on fire at no great distance from the river, we camped on the S. S. just above a remarkable bend in the river to the S W, which we call the little *bason.*

Course Distance & reffurences the 10th

S. 45° W.	3	miles to a pt. of timbered land on the S. S.
West	3	miles to a pt. of timbered land on the L. S.
S 72° W.	2	miles to a tree in an elevated plain in the bend to the S. S.
S. 32° W.	4	miles to a pt. of wood on the S. S.
West	½	a mile on the S. point.
N. 40° W.	½	a mile on the S. point.
N. 50° E	2	miles to a pt. on the L. S. opsd. a low bluff.
S 52° W	3 ½	miles to a pt. on the S. S. opsd. a bluff above which a Small
	18 ½	creek falls in [6]

1. The pronghorn, *Antilocapra americana.*

2. The geese are probably Canada geese, *Branta canadensis* [AOU, 172]; the swans could be either *Cygnus buccinator* [AOU, 181], trumpeter swan, or *C. columbianus* [AOU, 180], tundra, or whistling, swan. Someone drew vertical lines through the next sentence, apparently in red.

3. This area, in Mercer County, North Dakota, is on the fringe of the Badlands. Prairie fires and spontaneous combustion of methane in the coal, itself, occasionally cause coal beds to burn. These fires sometimes burn for many years. There is very little sulphur in the Sentinel Butte Formation, but it is sufficient to be recognized as sulphur dioxide when burned.

4. Just above the later site of Fort Berthold, in McLean County, North Dakota, and now under Garrison Reservoir. Mattison (GR), 38; *Atlas* maps 33, 46, 55; MRC map 53.

5. Also given on *Atlas* map 33, in Clark's hand.

6. Nameless on *Atlas* maps 33, 46, 55, this stream may be later Little Beaver, or Pretty, Creek, in Mercer County. MRC map 54.

[Lewis]   *Thursday April 11th*

Set out at an early hour; I proceeded with the party and Capt Clark with George Drewyer walked on shore in order to procure some fresh meat if possible.   we proceeded on abot five miles, and halted for breakfast, when Capt Clark and Drewyer joined us; the latter had killed, and brought with him a deer which was at this moment excepable as we had had no fresh meat for several days.   the country from fort Mandan to this place is so constantly hunted by the Minetaries that there is but little game we halted at two P. M. and made a comfortable dinner on a venison stake and beavers tales with the bisquit which got wet on the 8th inst. by the accidant of the canoe filling with water before mentioned. the powder which got wet by the same accedent, and which we had spread to dry on the baggage of the large perogue, was now examined and put up; it appears to be almost restored, and our loss is therefore not so great as we had at first apprehended.— the country much the same as yesterday. on the sides of the hills and even the banks of the rivers and sandbars, there is a white substance t[h]at appears in considerable quantities on the surface of the earth, which tastes like a mixture of common salt and glauber salts. many of the springs which flow from the base of the river hills are so strongly impregnated with this substance that the water is extreemly unpleasant to the taste and has a purgative effect.—[1] saw some large white cranes pass up the river—[2] these are the largest bird of that genus common to the country through which the Missouri and Mississippi pass. they are perfectly white except the large feathers of the two first joints of the wing which are black. we encamped this evening on the Stard. shore just above the point of woodland which formed to extremity of the last course of this day.[3] there is a high bluff opposite to us, under which we saw some Indians, but the river is here so wide that we could not speake to them; suppose them to be a hunting party of Minetares.— we killed two gees today.

The couses and distances of this day[4]		*miles*
S. 85 W.	to the upper point of a bluff on Lard. Sd.	2
N. 38 W.	to a point on the Lard. shore oppot. a bluff	3
S. 30 W.	to the upper part of a timbered bottom on the Lard. side. a large sand bar making out from the Stard side 1 ½ miles wide	2
N. 52 W.	to a red knob in a bend to the Stad side near the upper part of a timbered bottom	5
S. 70 W.	to a point of timbered land on the Stard. Sid.	6
W.	on the Stard. point	1
		19

[Clark]   *11th of April Thursday 1805*

Set out verry early   I walked on Shore, Saw fresh bear tracks, one deer & 2 beaver killed this morning   in the after part of the day killed two gees; Saw great numbers of Gees Brant & Mallard Some White Cranes Swan & guls,[5] the plains begin to have a green appearance, the hills on either side are from 5 to 7 miles asunder and in maney places have been burnt, appearing at a distance of a redish brown choler, containing Pumic Stone & *lava*, Some of which rolin down to the base of those hills—   In maney of those hills forming bluffs to the river we procieve Several Stratums of bituminious Substance which resembles *Coal*;[6] thoug Some of the pieces appear to be excellent Coal it resists the fire for Some[time], and consumes without emiting much flaim.

The plains are high and rich   Some of them are Sandy Containing Small pebble, and on Some of the hill Sides large Stones are to be Seen—[7] In the evening late we observed a party of *Me ne tar ras* on the L. S. with horses and dogs loaded going down, those are a part of the Menetarras who camped a little above this with the Ossinniboins at the mouth of the little Missouri all the latter part of the winter   we Camped on the S. S. below a falling in bank.   the river raise a little.

Course distance &c the 11th

S. 85° W.	2	miles to the upper part of a Bluff in a bend to the Larboard Side.
N. 38° W.	3	miles to a point on the L. S. opsd. a bluff
S. 30° W.	2	miles to the upper part of a timbered bottom on the L. S. a large Sand bar makeing out from the S. S. 1½ miles
N 52° W.	5	miles to a red knob in a bend to the S. S. near the upper part of wood bottom.
S. 70° W.	6	miles to a timbered point on the S. S.
West	1	mile on the S. point.
	19	

1. These salts are an admixture of sodium sulphate, sodium bicarbonate, and magnesium sulphate. Sodium chloride is not especially common. Ground water dissolves the salts from the formations through which it passes. Evaporation of this water where it is

discharged produces salt crystals and salt crusts. Someone drew vertical lines through this passage and the next about cranes, apparently in red.

2. The whooping crane, *Grus americana* [AOU, 204], now an endangered species. Cutright (LCPN), 129.

3. In McLean County, North Dakota, a few miles below the mouth of the Little Missouri River. The entire area is now inundated by Garrison Reservoir. Mattison (GR), 39–40; *Atlas* maps 33, 46, 55; MRC map 54.

4. Also given on *Atlas* map 33, in Clark's hand.

5. The mallard is *Anas platyrhynchos* [AOU, 132], while the gulls could be any of a number of species of *Larus*.

6. Some of the shale beds of the Sentinel Butte Formation contain much organic material and appear black. Inorganic material dominates so that the carbonaceous shale either burns poorly or not at all.

7. Glacial till overlies bedrock on the plains here. It generally contains more clay than sand, but sand is locally abundant. The large stones are glacial erratics.

[Lewis]   *Friday April the 12th 1805.*

Set out at an early hour. our peroge and the Canoes passed over to the Lard side in order to avoid a bank which was rappidly falling in on the Stard. the red perogue contrary to my expectation or wish passed under this bank ⟨with⟩ by means of her toe line where I expected to have seen her carried under every instant. I did not discover that she was about to make this attempt untill it was too late for the men to reembark, and retreating is more dangerous than proceeding in such cases; they therefore continued their passage up this bank, and much to my satisfaction arrived safe above it. this cost me some moments of uneasiness, her cargo was of much importance to us in our present advanced situation— We proceeded on six miles and came too on the lower side of the entrance of the little Missouri on the Lard shore in a fine plain where we determined to spend the day for the purpose of celestial observation.[1] we sent out 10 hunters to procure some fresh meat. at this place made the following observations.—

Point of Observation No. 1.

Observed ☉'s Magnetic Azimuth with Circumfert   S. 88° E.

	h	m	s
Time by Chronometer A. M.	8	20	25
Altitude by Sextant	52°	20′	45″

⊙'s Magnetic Azimuth by Circumferenter		S. 87° E.
Time by Chronometer		8° 25′ 11″
Altitude by Sextant		53° 55′ 30″

Observed equal altitudes of the with ⊙ Sextant.

	h	m	s		
A. M.	8	30	11	P. M.	the P. M. observation
″		31	52.5		was lost in consequence
″		33	3.1		of the Clouds.

Altd. by Sextant at the time of observation   55° 28′ 45″

Observed Meridian altitude of the ⊙'s U. L. with Octant by the back observation   81° 25′ 15″

Latitude deduced from this observation [*blank*]

Remarks

The artifil. Horizon recommended by Mr. A. Ellicott, in which water forms the reflecting surface, is used in all observations which requirs the uce of an Artificial horizon, except when expressly mentioned to the contrary.—

The altitude of any object in the fore observation as here entered is that deduced immediately from the graduated limb of the instrument, and is of course the double altitudes of the object observed.—

The altitudes of objects observed by the back observation, with Octant as here entered, is that shewn by the graduated limb of the Instrument at the time of observation, and is the compliment of 180° of the double altitude of the object observed.—

Error of Sextant Subtractive	—°	8′	45″
Error of Octant fore observation	2°	—′	—″ x
Error of do. in back observation addtve.	2°	40′	— x

The night proved so cloudy that I could make no further observations. George Drewyer shot a Beaver this morning, which we found swiming in the river a small distance below the entrance of the little Missouri.   the beaver being seen in the day, is a proof that they have been but little hunted, as they always keep themselves closly concealed during the day where they are so.—   found a great quantity of small onions[2] in the plain where we encamped; had some of them collected and cooked, found them agreeable. the bulb grows single, is of an oval form, white, and about the size of a small bullet; the leaf resem[bles] that of the shive, and the hunters returned this eving with one deer only. the country about the mouth of this river had been recently hunted by the Minetares, and the little game which they had not killed and frightened away, was so extreemly shy that the hunters could not get in shoot of them.

The little Missouri disembogues on the S. side of the Missouri 1693 miles from the confluence of the latter with the Mississippi. it is 134 yards wide at it's mouth, and sets in with a bould current but it's greatest debth is not more than 2½ feet. it's navigation is extreemly difficult, owing to it's rapidity, shoals and sand bars. it may however be navigated with small canoes a considerable distance. this river passes through the Northern extremity of the black hills where it is very narrow and rapid and it's banks high an perpendicular. it takes it's rise in a broken country West of the Black hills with the waters of the yellow stone river, and a considerable distance S. W. of the point at which it passes the black hills. the country through which it passes is generally broken and the highlands possess but little timber. there is some timber in it's bottom lands, which consists of Cottonwood red Elm, with a small proportion of small Ash and box alder.[3] the under brush is willow, red wood, (sometimes called red or swamp willow—) the red burry, and Choke cherry—[4] the country is extreamly broken about the mouth of this river, and as far up ⟨and⟩ on both sides, as we could observe it from the tops of some elivated hills, which stand betwen these two rivers, about 3 miles from their junction. the soil appears fertile and deep, it consists generally of a dark rich loam intermixed with a small proportion of fine sand. this river in it's course passed near the N. W. side of the turtle mountain, which is said to be no more than 4 or 5 leagues distant from it's entrance in a straight direction, a little to the S. of West.— this mountain and the knife river have therefore been laid down too far S. W.[5] the colour of the water, the bed of the river, and it's appearance ⟨of this river⟩ in every respect, resembles the Missouri; I am therefore induced to believe that the texture of the soil of the country in which it takes it's rise, and that through which it passes, is similar to the country through which the Missouri passes after leaving the woody country, or such as we are now in.— on the side of a hill not distant from our camp I found some of the dwarf cedar of which I preserved a specimen (See No. 2).[6] this plant spreads it's limbs alonge the surface of the earth, where they are sometimes covered, and always put forth a number of roots on the under side, while on the upper there are a great number of small shoots which with their leaves seldom rise higher than 6 or eight inches. they grow ⟨very⟩ so close as perfectly to conceal the eath. it is an evergreen; the leaf is much more delicate than the common Cedar, and it's taste and smell the same. I have often thought that this plant would make very handsome edgings to the borders and walks of a garden; it is quite as handsom as box,[7] and would be much more easily propegated.— the appearance of the glauber salts and Carbonated wood still continue.

Couse and distance of this day was[8]   m

N. 80° W.   to the entrance of the little Missouri   4 ½[9]

[Clark]   12th *April* ⟨*Wednesday*⟩ *Friday 1805*

a fine morning   Set out verry early, the murcery Stood 56° above o. proceeded on to the mouth of the Little Missouri river and formed a Camp in a butifull elivated plain on the lower Side for the purpose of takeing Some observations to fix the Latitude & Longitude of this river. this river falls in on the L. Side and is 134 yards wide and 2 feet 6 Inches deep at the mouth, it takes its rise in the N W extremity of the black mountains, and through a broken countrey in its whole course washing the N W base of the Turtle Mountain which is Situated about 6 Leagues S W of its mouth, one of our men Baptiest[10] who came down this river in a canoe informs me that it is not navagable, he was 45 days descending.

One of our men Shot a beaver Swimming below the mouth of this river.

I walked out on the lower Side of this river and found the countrey hilley the Soil composed of black mole & a Small perportion of Sand containing great quantity of Small peable Some limestone, black flint, & Sand Stone[11]

I killed a Hare[12] Changeing its Colour Some parts retaining its long white fur & other parts assumeing the Short grey, I Saw the Magpie in pars, flocks of Grouse, the old field lark & Crows,[13] & observed the leaf of the wild Chery half grown,[14] many flowers are to be seen in the plains, remains of Minetarra & Ossinneboin hunting Camps are to be Seen on each Side of the two Missouris

The wind blew verry hard from the S. all the after part of the day, at 3 oClock P M. it became violent & flowey accompanied with thunder and a little rain. We examined our canoes &c found Several mice which had already commenced cutting our bags of corn & parched meal, the water of the little Missouri is of the Same texture Colour & quallity of that of the Big Missouri the after part of the day so Cloudy that we lost the evening observation.

Course & Distance of the 12th

N. 80° W.   4 ½   miles to the mouth of the Little Missouri River on the S. S.

1. The mouth of the Little Missouri may have shifted over the years; in any case, the site, perhaps in Dunn County, North Dakota, is under Garrison Reservoir. It is misplaced on *Atlas* map 55. The point of observation, No. 1, is shown nearby on the maps. *Atlas* maps 33, 46; MRC map 54.

2. *Allium textile* A. Nels. & Macbr., white wild onion. Barkley, 537. Someone drew a vertical line through this passage, apparently in red.

3. The small ash is *Fraxinus pennsylvanica* Marsh var. *subintegerrima* (Vahl) Fern., green ash. Little, 130-W.

4. The willow is sandbar, or coyote, willow, *Salix exigua* Nutt. ssp. *interior* (Rowlee) Cronq.; red wood (also called *bois roche*, arrow wood, and other similar names) is red osier dogwood; "red burry" is *Sheperdia argentea* (Pursh) Nutt., buffaloberry; and "Choke cherry" is *Prunus virginiana* L. Barkley, 103, 205, 203, 148; Cutright (LCPN), 127 n. 5.

5. Turtle Mountain is the present Killdeer Mountains, in Dunn County. (See above, January 13, 1805.) Lewis has deduced from information received from Jean Baptiste Lepage that the Knife and Little Missouri rivers had been placed too far to the southwest on Clark's Fort Mandan map (*Atlas* maps 32a, 32b, 32c). Lepage informed them that the latter river touched the base of the mountain on the northwest. David Thompson had located Turtle Mountain quite accurately on his 1798 map of the Missouri bend area, a copy of which they had with them, so now, knowing the relationship of the rivers to the mountain range, it became apparent that they must revise their assumed courses for the two rivers. *North Dakota Guide*, 304; Allen (PG), 87–93, 255–57. The passage is an interlineation and may be a later interpolation.

6. Perhaps the creeping juniper that Clark noticed on April 9, here more certain. Here Lewis provides an indication of the plant specimens that he was preserving, labeling this one number 2. These items were cached at White Bear Islands and later found to be com-

pletely destroyed. See Cutright (LCPN), 127, 165, 312, 369. Someone drew a vertical line through this passage, apparently in red.

7. *Buxus sempervirens* L., common box. Bailey, 623.

8. Also given on *Atlas* map 33, in Clark's hand.

9. *Atlas* map 33 says 4¼ miles, disagreeing with both captains' journals.

10. Jean Baptiste Lepage (see above, November 3, 1804), probably the source of much of their information on the Little Missouri.

11. The soil is weathered glacial till. The rocks have been brought here by glacial ice.

12. A white-tailed jackrabbit, *Lepus townsendii*, described by Clark on September 14, 1804, and by Lewis in more detail on February 28, 1806. The species was then unknown to science. Burroughs, 121–22.

13. Clark's magpie is the black-billed magpie, *Pica pica* [AOU, 475], the "old field lark" is probably the western meadowlark, *Sturnella neglecta* [AOU, 501.1], and the crow is *Corvus brachyrhynchos* [AOU, 488]. Lewis describes the meadowlark on June 22, 1805. Holmgren, 31.

14. The familiar choke cherry.

[Lewis]   *Saturday April 13th*

Being disappointed in my observations of yesterday for Longitude, I was unwilling to remain at the entrance of the river another day for that purpose, and therefore determined to set out early this morning; which we did accordingly; the wind was in our favour after 9 A. M. and continued favourable untill three 3 P. M.   we therefore hoisted both the sails in the White Perogue, consisting of a small squar sail, and spritsail, which carried her at a pretty good gate, untill about 2 in the afternoon when a suddon squall of wind struck us and turned the perogue so much on the side as to allarm Sharbono who was steering at the time, in this state of alarm he threw the perogue with her side to the wind, when the spritsail gibing was as near overseting the perogue as it was possible to have missed.   the wind however abating for an instant I ordered Drewyer to the helm and the sails to be taken in, which was instant executed and the perogue being steered before the wind was agin plased in a state of security.   this accedent was very near costing us dearly.   beleiving this vessell to be the most steady and safe, we had embarked on board of it our instruments, Papers, medicine and the most valuable part of the merchandize which we had still in reserve as presents for the Indians.   we had also embarked on board ourselves, with three men who could not swim and the squaw with the young child, all of whom, had the perogue overset, would most probably have perished, as the waves were high, and the perogue upwards of 200 yards from the nearest shore; however we fortunately escaped and pursued our journey under the square sail, which shortly after the accident I directed to be again hoisted. our party caught three beaver last evening; and the French hunters 7. as there was much appearance of beaver just above the entrance of the little Missouri these hunters concluded to remain some days; we therefore left them without the expectation of seeing them again.— just above the entrance of the Little Missouri the great Missouri is upwards of a mile in width, tho' immediately at the entrance of the former it is not more than 200 yards wide and so shallow that the canoes passed it with seting poles. at the distance of nine miles passed the mouth of a creek on the Stard. side which we called onion creek[1] from the quantity of wild onions which grow in the plains on it's borders. Capt. Clark who was on shore informed me that this creek was 16 yards wide a mile & a half above it's entrance, discharges more water than creeks of it's size usually do in this open country, and that there was not a stick of timber of any discription to be seen on it's borders, or the level plain country through which it passes. at the distance of 10 miles further we passed the mouth of a large creek;[2] discharging itself in the center of a deep bend. of this creek and the neighbouring country, Capt Clark who was on shore gave me the following discription "This creek I took to be a small river from it's size, and the quantity of water which it discharged. I ascended it 1 ½ miles, and found it the discharge of a pond or small lake, which had the appearance of having formerly been the bed of the Missouri. several small streems discharge themselves into this lake.   the country on both sides consists of beautifull level and elivated plains; asscending as they recede from the Missouri; there were a great number of Swan and gees in this lake and near it's borders I saw the remains of 43 temperary Indian lodges, which I presume were those of the Assinniboins who are now in the neighbourhood of the British establishments on the Assinniboin river—" This lake and it's discharge we call *goos* Egg from the circumstance of Capt Clark shooting a goose while on her nest in the top of a lofty cotton wood tree, from which we afterwards took one egg. the wild gees frequently build their nests in this manner, at least we have already found several in trees, nor have we as yet seen any

on the ground, or sand bars where I had supposed from previous information that they most commonly ⟨lay⟩ deposited their eggs.—[3] saw some
Buffaloe and Elk at a distance today but killed none of them.   we found a
number of carcases of the Buffaloe lying along shore, which had been
drowned by falling through the ice in winter and lodged on shore by the
high water when the river broke up about the first of this month.   we saw
also many tracks of the white bear of enormous size,[4] along the river
shore and about the carcases of the Buffaloe, on which I presume they
feed.   we have not as yet seen one of these anamals, tho' their tracks are
so abundant and recent.   the men as well as ourselves are anxious to
meet with some of these bear.   the Indians give a very formidable account of the strengh and ferocity of this anamal, which they never dare to
attack but in parties of six eight or ten persons; and are even then frequently defeated with the loss of one or more of their party.   the savages
attack this anamal with their bows and arrows and the indifferent guns
with which the traders furnish them, with these they shoot with such
uncertainty and at so short a distance, [*NB: unless shot thro' head or heart
wound not mortal*] that they frequently mis their aim & fall a sacrefice to
the bear.   two Minetaries were killed during the last winter in an attack
on a white bear.   this anamall is said more frequently to attack a man on
meeting with him, than to flee from him. When the Indians are about to
go in quest of the white bear, previous to their departure, they paint themselves and perform all those supersticious rights commonly observed when
they are about to make war uppon a neighbouring nation. Oserved more
bald eagles on this part of the Missouri than we have previously seen.[5]   saw
the small hawk, frequently called the sparrow hawk, which is common to
most parts of the U States.[6]   great quantities of gees are seen feeding in
the praries.   saw a large flock of white brant or gees with black wings pass
up the river; there were a number of gray brant with them; from their
flight I presume they proceed much further still to the N. W.—   we have
never been enabled yet to shoot one of these birds, and cannot therefore
determine whether the gray brant found with the white are their brude
of the last year or whether they are the same with the grey brant common
to the Mississippi and lower part of the Missouri.—   we killed 2 Antelopes today which we found swiming from the S. to the N. side of the

river; they were very poor.— We encamped this evening on the Stard. shore in a beautifull plain, elivated about 30 feet above the river.[7]

The courses and distances of this day are as follow.—[8]   *miles*

N. 18° W.	to a point of wood on the L. side, point on the Lard. at 1 ½ miles	7 ½
N. 10° W.	to the upper point of a Low bluff on the Stad. pass a creek on Stard. side.	5
N. 45 W.	to a point of Woodland on Lard. side	4
N. 28 W.	to a point of Woodland Stard. side	3
S. 35 W.	to a point of Woodland on Std. side, passed a creek on Stard. side— near the commencement of this course also, two points on the Lard. side, the one at a mile, and the other ½ a mile further, also a large sand bar in the above the entrance of the creek.	4
		23 ½

Note our encampment was one mile short of the extremity of the last course.—

[Clark]   13th of *April Satturday* 1805

Set out this morning at 6 oClock, the Missouri above the mouth of Little Missouri widens to nearly a mile containing a number of Sand bars   this width &c. of the River Continues Generally as high as the Rochejhone River.

Cought 3 beaver this morning, at 9 miles passd. the mouth of a Creek on the S. S. on the banks of which there is an imence quantity of wild onions or garlick, I was up this Creek ½ a m. and could not See one Stick of timber of any kind on its borders, this creek is 16 yds wide ½ a mile up it and discharges more water than is common for Creeks of its Size.   at about 10 miles higher we pass a Creek about 30 yards wide in a deep bend to the N W. This creek I took to be a Small river from its Size & the quantity of water which it discharged, I assended it 1 ½ mes and found it the discharge of a pond or Small Lake which has appearance of haveing been once the bead of the river, Some Small Streams discharge themselves into this Lake.   the Countery on both Side is butifull elevated plains assending in Some parts to a great distance near the aforesaid Lake (which we call Goose egg L from a Circumstance of my Shooting a goose on her neast on Some Sticks in the top of a high Cotton wood tree in which there was one egg) We Saw 8 buffalow at a distance, We also Saw Several herds of Elk at a distance which were verry wild, I Saw near the Lake the remains of 43 lodges, which has latterly been abandond I Suppose them to have been Ossinniboins and now near the british establishments on the Ossinniboin River tradeing. we camped on the S. S. in a butifull Plain. I observe more bald Eagles on this part of the Missouri than usial also a Small Hawk Killed 2 Antelopes in the river to day

Course distance &c. the 13th of April 1805

N. 18° W	7 ½	miles to a point of wood on the L. S. passd a point on the L. S. at 1 ½ miles
N. 10° W.	5	miles to the upper point of a low bluff on the S. S. passed a Creek on the S. S. (1)
N. 45° W.	4	miles to a point of wood land on L. S.
N. 28° W.	3	miles to a point of wood land on S. S. the river makeing a Deep bend to the N W.
S 35° W.	4 / 23 ½	miles to a point of wood on the S. S. passed a creek (2) on the S. S. near the commencement of this course, also two points on the L. S one at a mile & the other ½ a mile further, also a large Sand bar in the middle of the river above the mouth of the Creek—

emence numbers of Geese to be seen pared &c. a Gange of brant pass one half of the gange white with black wings or the large feathers of the 1s & 2d joint the remds. of the comn. color. a voice much like that of a goos & finer &c.

1. Former Lucky Mound Creek (a corruption of the French *L'eau qui monte*, "water that rises"), in McLean County, North Dakota, also known as Rising Water or Pride Creek; it is today's Deepwater Creek. Mattison (GR), 44; *Atlas* maps 33, 46, 55; MRC map 55.

2. Shell Creek, now inundated, in Mountrail County, North Dakota; the actual source is much higher than the captains thought. The lake, "Goose Egg Lake" on *Atlas* maps 33, 46, 55, is also under Garrison Reservoir. Mattison (GR), 45; MRC map 55.

3. Nesting in trees is contrary to the habits of the Canada goose in the East. Nineteenth-

century ornithologists challenged the captains' statement, but Coues confirmed this behavior, which provided protection from such predators as wolves and badgers, from observations in the same region. See also May 3, 1805. Coues (HLC), 1:269–70 n. 27; Cutright (LCPN), 128. Someone drew a vertical line through this passage, apparently in red.

4. The bear is the grizzly, *Ursus horribilis;* a specimen was taken on April 29, 1805.

5. Bald eagles, *Haliaeetus leucocephalus* [AOU, 352].

6. The sparrow hawk, otherwise the American kestrel, *Falco sparverius* [AOU, 360]. Holmgren, 30.

7. In Mountrail County, in what was later called Fort Maneury Bend, now under Garrison Reservoir. Mattison (GR), 45; *Atlas* maps 33, 46, 55; MRC map 55.

8. Also given on *Atlas* map 33, in both captains' hands.

[Lewis]   *Sunday April 14th 1805.*

One of the hunters saw an Otter[1] last evening and shot at it, but missed it. a dog came to us this morning, which we supposed to have been lost by the Indians who were recently encamped near the lake that we passed yesterday. the mineral appearances of salts, coal and sulpher, together with birnt hills & pumicestone still continue.—[2] while we remained at the entrance of the little Missouri, we saw several pieces of pumice stone floating down that stream, a considerable quanty of which had lodged ⟨and collected⟩ against a point of drift wood a little above it's entrance. Capt. Clark walked on shore this morning, and on his return informed me that he had passed through the timbered bottoms on the N. side of the river, and had extended his walk several miles back on the hills; in the bottom lands he had met with several uninhabited Indian lodges built with the boughs of the Elm, and in the plains he met with the remains of two large encampments of a recent date, which from the appearance of some hoops of small kegs, seen near them we concluded that they must have been the camps of the Assinniboins, as no other nation who visit this part of the missouri ever indulge themselves with spirituous liquor. of this article the Assinniboins are pationately fond, and we are informed that it forms their principal inducement to furnish the British establishments on the Assinniboin river with the dryed and pounded meat and grease which they do. they also supply those establishments with a small quantity of fur, consisting principally of the large and small wolves and the small fox skins.[3]   these they barter for small kegs of rum which they generally transport to their camps at a distance from the establishments, where they revel with their friends and relations as long as they possess the means of intoxication, their women and children are equally indulged on those occasions and are all seen drunk together.   so far is a state of intoxication from being a cause of reproach among them, that with the men, it is a matter of exultation that their skill and industry as hunters has enabled them to get drunk frequently.   in their customs, habits, and dispositions these people very much resemble the Siouxs from whom they have descended. The principal inducement with the British fur companies, for continuing their establishments on the Assinniboin river, is the Buffaloe meat and grease they procure from the Assinniboins, and Christanoes, by means of which, they are enabled to supply provision to their engages on their return from rainy Lake to the English river and the Athabaskey country[4] where they winter; without such resource those voyagers would frequently be straitened for provision, as the country through which they pass is but scantily supplied with game, and the rappidity with which they are compelled to travel in order to reach their winter stations, would leave therm but little leasure to surch for food while on their voyage.

The Assinniboins have so recently left this neighbourhood, that the game is scarce and very shy.   the river continues wide, and not more rapid than the Ohio in an averge state of it's current.   the bottoms are wide and low, the moister parts containing some timber; the upland is extreemly broken, chonsisting of high gaulded nobs[5] as far as the eye can reach on ether side, and entirely destitute of timber.   on these hills many aromatic herbs are seen; resembling in taste, smel and appearance, the sage, hysop, wormwood, southernwood,[6] and two other herbs which are strangers to me; the one resembling the camphor in taste and smell, rising to the hight of 2 or 3 feet;[7] the other about the same size, has a long, narrow, smooth, soft leaf of an agreeable smel and flavor; of this last the Atelope is very fond; they feed on it, and perfume the hair of their foreheads and necks with it by rubing against it.[8]   the dwarf cedar and juniper is also found in great abundance on the sides of these hills.   where the land is level, it is uniformly fertile consisting of a dark loam intermixed with a proportion of fine sand. it is generally covered with a short grass resembling very much the blue grass.—[9] the miniral appearances still continue; considerable quantities of bitumenous water, about the colour of strong lye trickles down the sides of the hills; this water partakes of the taste of glauber salts and slightly of allumn.—[10] while the party halted to take dinner today Capt Clark killed a buffaloe bull; it was meagre, and we therefore took the marrow bones and a small proportion of the meat only. near the place we dined on the Lard. side, there was a large village of burrowing squirrels. I have remarked that these anamals generally celect a South Easterly exposure for their residence, tho' they are sometimes found in the level plains.— passed an Island, above which two small creeks fall in on Lard side; the upper creek largest, which we called Sharbono's Creek[11] after our interpreter who encamped several weeks on it with a hunting party of Indians. this was the highest point to which any whiteman had ever ascended; except two Frenchmen [*NB: one of whom Lepage was now with us— See at Mandan*] who having lost their way had straggled a few miles further, tho' to what place precisely I could not learn.— I walked on shore above this creek and killed an Elk, which was so poor that it was unfit for uce; I therefore left it, and joined the party at their encampment on the Stard shore a little after dark. on my arrival Capt Clark informed me that he had seen two white bear pass over the hills shortly after I fired, and that they appeared to run nearly from the place where I shot. the lard. shore on which I walked was very broken, and the hills in many places had the appearance of having sliped down in masses of several acres of land in surface.— we saw many gees feeding on the tender grass in the praries and several of their nests in the trees; we have not in a single instance found the nest of this bird on or near the ground. we saw a number of Magpies their nests and eggs. their nests are built in trees and composed of small sticks leaves and grass, open at top, and much in the stile of the large blackbird comm to the U' States. the egg is of a bluish brown colour, freckled with redish brown spots. one of the party killed a large hooting owl.[12] I observed no difference between this burd and those of the same family common to the U' States, except that this appeared to be more booted and more thickly clad with feathers.—

The courses and distances of the 14th April.[13]   miles

S. 45 W.	to the mouth of a small creek at the upper part of a timbered botrom	2 ½
W.	to a point of Woodland on the Lard. side	3 ½
N. 85 W.	to a point on the Stard. opposite to a bluff	2
N. 80 W.	to a point on Stard opposite to a bluff on Lad.	1 ¾
W.	to the lower point of an Island which from the circumstance of our arriving at it on sunday—we called Sunday Island.[14] the river washes the base of the hills on both sides of this Island	1
N. 70 W.	to a point of woodland on the Stard. Side the Island and it's sandbar occupy ½ the distance of this course pass— two small creeks on the Lard Side, the upper one the largest, called Sharbono's creek.	3 ¼

miles 14

Point of Observation No. 2.

On the Stard. shore ¼ of a mile above the extremity of the third course of this day observed Meridian Altd. ☉'s L. L. with Octant by the back Obst. 81° 34′ —″ Latitude deduced from this Observatn. [*blank*]

Point of Observation No. 3.

At our encampment of this evening on the Sd. Sid. observed time and distance of ☽'s Western limb from Regulus, with Sextant. ★ West.—

	Time			Distance		
	h	m	s			
P. M.	10	47	2	72°	20′	30″
	″	51	10	″	21	
	″	53	19	″	21	45
	″	56	2	″	23	
	″	58	58	″	24	15

	Time			Distance		
	h	m	s			
P. M.	11	2	2	72°	25′	45″
	″	4	27	″	27	15
	″	7	55	″	29	

"	10	19	"	30	
"	12	12	"	31	15

Observed time and distance of ☽ from α Aquilae with Sextant. ★ East.—

		Time			Distance	
	h	m	s			
P. M.	11	22	7	82°	16′	45″
	"	27	7	"	16	15
	"	30	23	"	15	30
	"	32	27	"	15	15
	"	34	39	"	15	15

		Time			Distance	
	h	m	s			
P. M.	11	36	47	82°	14′	30″
	"	39	34	"	14	
	"	43	2	"	13	15
	"	46	8	"	13	30
	"	48	16	"	13	

[Clark]   14th *of April Sunday 1805*.

a fine morning, a dog came to us this morning   we Suppose him to be left by the Inds. who had their camps near the Lake we passd. yesterday not long Sence, I observed Several Single Lodges built of Stiks of [c]otten timber in different parts of the bottoms.   in my walk of this [day] which was through the wooded bottoms and on the hills for several miles back from the river on the S. S. I Saw the remains of two Indian incampments with wide beeten tracks leading to them.   those were no doubt the Camps of the Ossinnaboin Indians (a Strong evidence is hoops of Small Kegs were found in the incampments)   no other nation on the river above the *Sioux* make use of Spiritious licquer, the Ossinniboins is said to be pasionately fond of Licquer, and is the principal inducement to their putting themselves to the trouble of Catching the fiew wolves and foxes which they furnish, and recive their [liquor] always in small Kegs. The Ossinniboins make use of the Same kind of Lodges which the Sioux and other Indians on this river make use of—   Those lodges or tents are made of a number of dressed buffalow Skins ⟨dressed⟩ Sowed together with Sinues & deckerated with the tales, & Porcupine quils, when open it forms a half circle with a part about 4 Inches wide projecting about 8 or 9 Inches from the center of the Streight Side for the purpose of attaching it to a pole to it the hight they wish to raise the tent, when the[y] errect this tent four poles of equal length are tied near one end, those poles are elevated and 8 10 or 12 other poles are anexed forming a Circle at the ground and lodging in the forks of the four attached poles, the tents are then raised, by attach the projecting part to a pole and incumpassing the poles with the tent by bringing the two ends together and attached with a Cord, or laied as high as is necessary, leaveing the lower part open for about 4 feet for to pass in & out, and the top is generally left open to admit the Smoke to pass— The ⟨Countrey⟩ Borders of the river has been So much hunted by those Indians who must have left it about 8 or 10 days past and I prosume are now in the neighbourhood of British establishments on the Osinniboin; the game is Scerce and verry wild. The River Continues wide and the current jentle not more rapid than the ⟨waters⟩ Current of the Ohio in middle State— The bottoms are wide and low and the moist parts of them Contain Som wood such as cotton Elm & Small ash, willow rose bushes &c. &c. &. next to the hills Great quantity of wild Isoop,[15] the hills are high broken in every direction, and the mineral appearance of Salts Continue to appear in a greater perportion, also Sulpher, Coal & bitumous water in a Smaller quantity, I have observed but five burnt hills, about the little Missouri, and I have not Seen any pumey stone above that River I Saw Buffalow on the L. S. Crossed and dureing the time of dinner killed a Bull, which was pore, we made use of the best of it, I Saw a village of Burrowing dogs on the L. S. passed a Island above which two Small Creeks falls in on the L. S. the upper of which is the largest and we call Shabonas Creek after our interpreter who incamped several weeks on this Creek and is the highest point on the Missouri to which a white man has been previous to this time. Capt. Lewis walked out above this creek and killed an Elk which he found So meager that it was not fit for use, and joined the boat at Dusk at our Camp on the S. S. opposit a high hill Several parts of which had Sliped down. on the Side of those hills we Saw two white bear running from the report of Capt. Lewis Shot, those animals assended those Steep hills with Supprising ease & verlocity. they were too far to discover their prosise Colour & Size— Saw Several gees nests on trees, also the nests & egs of the Magpies, a large grey owl killed, booted & with ears &c.

Course distance &c. the 14th of April

S. 45° W.	2 ½	miles to the mouth of a Small Creek at the upper part of a wood bottom in a bend to L. S.
West	3 ½	miles to a point of wood land on the L. S.
N. 85° W.	2	miles to a point on the S. S. opposit a bluff
N. 80° W	1 ¾	ms. to a point on S. S. passd. a bluff on the L. S.
West	1	mile to a small Island opsd. the *upper point* the river washes the base of the hill on both Sides, which we call Sunday Isld. &c.
N. 70° W.	3 ¼	miles to a pt. of wood land on the S. S. the lsland & its Sand
	14	bars Occupy half the distance. passed 2 Small Creeks on the L. S. the upper the largest

1. *Lutra canadensis.* Burroughs, 75–76.

2. These rocks of the Sentinel Butte Formation contain very little sulphur. Perhaps the yellowish color of some of the sands and sandstones has suggested its presence.

3. The large wolves are *Canis lupus*, gray wolf, and the small wolves are *C. latrans*, coyote, both described by Lewis on May 5, 1805. The skins are probably those of the swift fox, *Vulpes velox* described by Lewis on July 6 and 8, 1805. Jones et al., 250–59.

4. Rainy Lake is between Minnesota and Ontario; English River runs into the Winnipeg River in western Ontario; Lake Athabaska is in northern Alberta and Saskatchewan. The canoe transport system of the North West and Hudson's Bay companies tied all these places together by water, and the canoemen lived during their trips on the pemmican furnished by the plains tribes.

5. The noun "gall" was used in Virginia for bare or eroded patches of ground. A variant spelling is gaule. The "nobs" are knobs, or rounded hills. McJimsey, 73, 86.

6. Coues interprets this passage as meaning that there is one plant which resembles all four named, presumably a type of sagebrush, *Artemisia* sp. Coues (HLC), 1:272–73 n. 32. These four plants were cultivated garden species known to Lewis and introduced from Europe: *Salvia officinalis* L., garden sage; *Hyssopus officinalis* L., hyssop; *Artemisia vulgaris* L., wormwood or common mugwort; and *A. abrotanum* L., southernwood. All are shrubby or evergreen and have aromatic, volatile oils released from the crushed leaves. Fernald, 1236, 1241, 1522. Someone drew a vertical line through this and the next few natural history passages, apparently in red.

7. *Artemisia tridentata* Nutt. ssp. *wyomingensis* Beetle & Young, big sagebrush. Barkley, 339; Shultz, 33.

8. *Artemisia cana* Pursh ssp. *cana*, silver sagebrush. Barkley, 337; Booth & Wright, 251; Shultz, 16.

9. Probably *Poa secunda* Presl., western, or Sandberg, bluegrass. Weaver & Albertson, 306.

10. Ground water in this area is commonly highly mineralized with salts and occasionally iron. Ground water often acquires an oily sheen after passing through beds of lignite coal.

11. Formerly Indian, now Bear Den, Creek, entering the Missouri near the Dunn-McKenzie county line. The camp for the day was on the opposite shore, a little above the creek mouth, in Mountrail County, North Dakota. Mattison (GR), 49; *Atlas* maps 34, 47, 56; MRC map 56.

12. The great horned owl, *Bubo virginianus* [AOU, 375]. Perhaps a subspecies, the Montana horned owl, *B. v. occidentalis*, and probably noted here for the first time. Cutright (LCPN), 129. Someone drew a vertical line through this and the previous passage on the magpie, apparently in red.

13. Also given on *Atlas* map 34, in both captains' hands.

14. Sunday Island was still on the map in the 1890s; it would now be under Garrison Reservoir. *Atlas* maps 34, 47, 56; MRC map 56.

15. The wild hyssop is that identified by Lewis as an unfamiliar herb; it is the first one, big sagebrush.

[Lewis]   *Monday April 15th 1805.*

Set out at an early hour this morning. I walked on shore, and Capt. Clark continued with the party it being an invariable rule with us not to be both absent from our vessels at the same time. I passed through the bottoms of the river on the Stard. side.   they were partially covered with timber & were extensive, level and beatifull.   in my walk which was about 6 miles I passed a small rivulet of clear water making down from the hills, which on tasting, I discovered to be in a small degree brackish.   it possessed less of the glauber salt, or alumn, than those little streams from the hills usually do.—   in a little pond of water fromed by this rivulet where it entered the bottom, I heard the frogs crying for the first time this season;[1] their note was the same with that of the small frogs which are common to the lagoons and swam[p]s of the U States.—   I saw great quantities of gees feeding in the bottoms, of which I shot one.   saw some deer and Elk, but they were remarkably shy. I also met with great numbers

41

of Grouse or *prarie hens*[2] as they are called by the English traders of the N. W.   these birds appeared to be mating; the note of the male is kuck, kuck, kuck, coo, coo, coo.   the first part of the note both male and female use when flying.   the male also dubbs [*EC: drums*] [*NB: with his wings*] something like the pheasant, but by no means as loud.   after breakfast Capt. Clark walked on the Std. shore, and on his return in the evening gave me the following account of his ramble.[3] "I assended to the high country, about 9 miles distant from the Missouri.   the country consists of beatifull, level and fertile plains, destitute of timber   I saw many little dranes, which took their rise in the river hills, from whence as far as I could see they run to the N. E."   these streams we suppose to be the waters of Mous river a branch of the Assinniboin which the Indians informed us approaches the Missouri very nearly, about this point. "I passed," continued he, ["]a Creek about 20 yards wide,[4] which falls into the Missouri; the bottoms of this creek are wide level and extreemly fertile, but almost entirely destitute of timber.   the water of this creek as well as all those creeks and rivulets which we have passed since we left Fort Mandan was so strongly impregnated with salts and other miniral substances that I was incapable of drinking it. I saw the remains of several camps of the Assinniboins; near one of which, in a small ravene, there was a park which they had formed of timber and brush, for the purpose of taking the Cabrie or Antelope.   it was constructed in the following manner.   a strong pound was first made of timbers, on one side of which there was a small apparture, sufficiently large to admit an Antelope; from each side of this apparture, a curtain was extended to a considerable distance, widening as they receded from the pound.—"   we passed a rock this evening standing in the middle of the river, and the bed of the river was formed principally of gravel.   we encamped this evening on a sand point on Lard. side.[5]   a little above our encampment the river was confined to a channel of 80 yards in width.—

Courses and distances of the 15th April.[6]		*miles*
N.	to a point of wood on Lard. side, opposite to a high hill	2
N. 18 W.	to a point of wood on the Stard. side opposite to the lower point of an Island in a Lard. bend of the river	5

N. 20 E	to a bluff point on Stard passed the upper part of the Island at 2 miles	3 ¼
N. 30 E.	to a point of woodland on Lard. side.	2 ½
N. 10 W.	on the Lard. point	½
N. 15 W.	on the Lard. point	¼
N. 12 W.	to the lower part of a bluff on the Stad. side, passing a creek on Stard	1 ½
N. 52 W.	to a high bluff on the Stad. side	2
N. 75 W.	to a point of woodland on the Stard Sid	3
N. 16 W.	to a point of Woodland on Lard. side	3

miles 23

Point of Observation No. 4.

Apl. 15th 1805.

On the Stad. shore, one mile above the extremity of the 2cd course of this day, I took two altitudes of the Sun with Sextant and artificial horizon.—

	Time			*Altitudes*		
	h	m	s			
A. M.	9	9	33	69°	20′	45″
	10	3	28	84	24	15

Chronometer to fast at the time of observation on mean time

[Clark]   15th of *April Monday 1805*

Set out at an early hour, Captn Lewis walked on Shore and Killed a goose, passed a Island in a bend to the L. S. the wind hard from the S. E. after brackfast I walked on Shore and assended to the high Countrey on the S. S. and off from the Missouri about three miles the countrey is butifull open fertile plain the dreans take theer rise near the Clifts of the river and run from the river in a N E derection as far as I could See, this is the part of the River which Mouse river the waters of Lake Winnipec approaches within a fiew miles of ⟨the⟩ Missouri, and I believe those dreans lead into that river. we passed a creek about 20 yds. wide on the S. S. the bottoms of this Creek is extensive & fertile, the water of

43

this as also, all the Streams which head a fiew miles in the hills discharge water which is black & unfit for use (and can Safely Say that I have not Seen one drop of water fit for use above fort Mandan except Knife and the little Missouris Rivers and the Missouri, the other Streams being So much impregnated with mineral as to be verry disagreeble in its present State.[)]   I saw the remains of Several Camps of ossinniboins, near one of those camps & at no great distance from the mouth of the aforesid Creek, in a hollow, I saw a large Strong pen made for the purpose of Catching the antelope, with wings projecting from it widining from the pen

Saw Several gangs of Buffalow and Some elk at a distance, a black bear[7] Seen from the Perogues to day—   passed a rock in the Middle of the river, Some Smaller rocks from that to the L. Shore, the dog that came to us yesterday morning continues to follow us, we camped on a Sand point to the L. S.

Course distance &c. the 15th of April

North	2	m. to a pt. of wood on the Ld. Sid. a high hill on the Sd. Sid.
N. 18° W.	5	miles to a point of wood on the Sd. Sid. opsd. the lower point of an Island L. Bend
N. 20° E	3 ¼	miles to a Bluff point on the Sd. Sid. passed the upper part of the Island at 2 miles
N. 30° E.	2 ½	miles to a point of wood land on the L. Side
N. 10° W	½	a mile on the Lad. point
N. 15° W.	¼	of a mile on the L. pt. here the waters of Mous river is near
N. 12° W.	1 ½	miles to the lower part of a Bluff on the Sd. Side passing a Creek on the S. Side. Goat pen Creek
N. 52° W.	2	miles to a high Bluff on the Sd. Side
N. 75° W.	3	miles to a pt. of wood land on the S. Side
N. 16° W.	3	miles to a point of woods on the L. S.
	23	

1. Probably the striped chorus frog, *Pseudacris triseriata.* Benson (HLCE), 88.

2. The sharp-tailed grouse, *Tympanuchus phasianellus* [AOU, 308], which Lewis com-

pares to a pheasant, the ruffed grouse, *Bonasa umbellus* [AOU, 300], with which he was already familiar. Coues (HLC), 1:274 n. 15; Burroughs, 211–13. Someone drew a vertical line through this passage, apparently in red.

3. Clark's route is marked by a dotted line on *Atlas* map 47 and incompletely on *Atlas* map 56.

4. Clark named it Goat Pen Creek on *Atlas* maps 34, 47, 56, after the Indian pen, or pound, for catching pronghorns which he found on it. It is now the Little Knife River, in Mountrail Country, North Dakota. Mattison (GR), 51–52; MRC map 56.

5. In McKenzie County, North Dakota, a site now under Garrison Reservoir. *Atlas* maps 34, 47, 56; MRC map 47.

6. Also given on *Atlas* map 34, in both captains' hands.

7. *Ursus americanus.* Cf. Lewis's entry of May 22, 1805. Burroughs, 52.

[Lewis]   *Tuesday April 16th 1805.*

Set out very early this morning. Capt. Clark walked on Shore this morning, and killed an Antelope, rejoined us at ½ after eight A. M.— he informed me that he had seen many Buffaloe Elk and deer in his absence, and that he had met with a great number of old hornets nests[1] in the woody bottoms through which he had passed.— the hills of the river still continue extreemly broken for a few miles back, when it becomes a fine level country of open fertile lands   immediately on the river there are many fine leavel extensive and extreemly fertile high plains and meadows. I think the quantity of timbered land on the river is increasing.   the mineral appearances still continue. I met with several stones today that had the appearance of wood first carbonated and then petrefyed by the water of the river, which I have discovered has that effect on many vegitable substances when exposed to it's influence for a length of time.[2]   I believe it to be the stratas of Coal seen in those hills which causes the fire and birnt appearances frequently met with in this quarter.   where those birnt appearances are to be seen in the face of the river bluffs, the coal is seldom seen, and when you meet with it in the neighbourhood of the stratas of birnt earth, the coal appears to be presisely at the same hight, and is nearly of the same thickness, togeter with the sand and a sulphurious substance which ususually accompanys it.[3]   there was a remarkable large beaver caught by one of the party last night.   these anamals are now very abundant. I have met with several trees which have been felled by them

20 Inches in diameter. bark is their only food; and they appear to prefer that of the Cotton wood and willow; as we have never met with any other species of timber on the Missouri which had the appearance of being cut by them.— we passed three small creeks on the Stard. side.[4] they take their rise in the river hills at no great distance. we saw a great number of geese today, both in the plains and on the river— I have observed but few ducks, those we have met with are the Mallard and blue winged Teal.[5]

Courses and distances of 16th April.[6]

S. 80° W.	to a point of woodland on the Stard. side	3
N. 36 W.	to a point of woodland on the Lard. side	2 ½
S. 60 W.	to a point of wood on the Stad. side, opposite to a bluff which commences 1 mile below on the Lard. side	3 ½
N. 25 W.	to a point of woodland on the Lard. side	2 ½
S. 70 W.	to a point of woodland on the Lard. side, passing a point of wood and large sand bar on the Stard. side	6
S 65 W.	along the Lard point of woods to our encampment of this evening	½
		miles 18

Note. The distances we are obliged to pass around the sand bars is much greater than those here stated from point to point.—

[Clark]   16th *of April Tuesday 1805*

Wind hard from the S. E I walked on Shore and Killed an antilope which was verry meagre, Saw great numbers of Elk & some buffalow & Deer, a verry large Beaver Cought this morning. Some verry handsom high planes & extensive bottoms, the mineral appearances of Coal & Salt together with Some appearance of Burnt hils continue. a number of old hornets nests Seen in every bottom more perticularly in the one opposit to the place we camped this night—[7] the wooded bottoms are more extensive to day than Common. passed three Small Creeks on the S. S. to day which take their rise in the hills at no great distance, Great numbers of Gees in the river & in the Plains feeding on the Grass.

Course Distance &c. April 16th

S. 80° W.	3	miles to a point of wood land on the Sd. Side.
N. 36° W.	2 ½	miles to a point of wood land on the L. Side
S. 60° W	3 ½	miles to a point of wood on the Sd. Side opsd. a bluff which commences 1 mile below on the Larboard Side.
N. 25° W.	2 ½	miles to a pt. of wood land on the L. Side.
S. 70° W.	6	miles to a point of Wood land on the L. Side, passing a point of wood land on the Sd. Side, passing a large Sand bar Sd.
S 65° W.	½	a mile along the L. Point of wood.
	18	

1. Perhaps the baldfaced hornet, *Dolichovespula maculata.* Werner et al., 57.

2. The party is passing through country underlain by the Paleocene Bullion Creek (Tongue River) Formation, but the petrified (silicified) wood comes from the overlying Sentinel Butte Formation. It has either been washed downstream by the river or has rolled down the river hills to the bottoms. The petrified wood comes from trees that grew during the Paleocene. The water of the Missouri River contains salts that might help retard spoilage or decay of vegetable matter, but it has no petrification properties.

3. The Bullion Creek Formation also contains lignite coal. When the coal burns, it is largely destroyed, but as the overlying clay or shale are baked and fused, they collapse into the area formerly occupied by the coal. Thus, they occupy approximately the same level as the unburned coal. The sulphurous substance may be yellow-colored sand or sandstone, but there is very little sulphur in this formation.

4. The first is evidently White Earth River, in Mountrail County, North Dakota, a more significant stream than indicated on *Atlas* maps 34, 47, 56, where it and the second creek appear nameless. This is not the stream the captains called White Earth River (see below, April 21, 1805). The last stream, "Hornet Creek" on Clark's maps, is probably Beaver Creek, in Williams County. Mattison (GR), 54; MRC map 57.

5. The blue-winged teal, *Anas discors* [AOU, 140].

6. Also given on *Atlas* map 34, in Lewis's hand.

7. In McKenzie County, North Dakota, a little above Beaver Creek on the other side. Mattison (GR), 54; *Atlas* maps 34, 47, 56; MRC map 57.

[Lewis]   *Wednesday April 17th 1805.*

A delightfull morning, set out at an erly hour.   the country though which we passed to day was much the same as that discribed of yesterday;

there wase more appearance of birnt hills, furnishing large quanties of lava and pumice stone,[1] of the latter some pieces were seen floating down the river. Capt. Clark walked on shore this morning on the Stard. side, and did not join us untill ⟨near sunset⟩ half after six in the evening. he informed me that he had seen the remains of the Assinniboin encampments in every point of woodland through which he had passed. we saw immence quantities of game in every direction around us as we passed up the river; consisting of herds of Buffaloe, Elk, and Antelopes with some deer and woolves. tho' we continue to see many tracks of the bear we have seen but very few of them, and those are at a great distance generally runing from us; I thefore presume that they are extreemly wary and shy; the Indian account of them dose not corrispond with our experience so far. one black bear passed near the perogues on the 16th and was seen by myself and the party but he so quickly disappeared that we did not shoot at him.— at the place we halted to dine on the Lard. side we met with a herd of buffaloe of which I killed the fatest as I concieved among them, however on examining it I found it so poar that I thought it unfit for uce and only took the tongue; the party killed another which was still more lean. just before we encamped this evening we saw some tracks of Indians who had passed about 24 hours; they left four rafts of tim[ber] on the Stard. side, on which they had passed. we supposed them to have been a party of the Assinniboins who had been to war against the rocky mountain Indians, and then on their return. Capt. Clark saw a Curlou today.[2] there were three beaver taken this morning by the party. the men prefer the flesh of this anamal, to that of any other which we have, or are able to procure at this moment. I eat very heartily of the beaver myself, and think it excellent; particularly the tale, and liver. we had a fair wind today which enabled us to sail the greater part of the distance we have travled, encamped on the Lard shore the extremity of the last course[3]

Courses and distances of the 17th[4]

S. 70 W.	to a point of willows on the Stard. side	3
S. 75 W.	along the Stard. point, opposite to a bluff	½
N. 75 W.	to a wood in a bend on the Std. side	3

N. 50 W.	to a point of woodland Stard. side	3 ½
S. 60⁵ W.	to a point of woodland on Stard. side opposite to a bluff on Lard, just above which, a creek falls in on the Lard. about 10 yards wide.	¾
N. 80 W.	to a willow point on the Lard. side.	3 ¼
S. 85 W.	to a point of woodland Lard. opposite to a bluff on Stard. side	3 ¾
West	Along the Lard. point, opposite to a high bluff above which a small run falls in	1
S. 40 W.	along the same point of woodland Lard. side	1
S. 30 W.	along the Lard side to a willow point	¼
S. 14 W.	to the upper part of the high timber on the stard. side	4
S. 28 W.	to a point of woodland on the Lard. side where we en- camped for the night	2

Miles 26

[Clark] 17th *of April Wednesday 1805*

a fine morning   wind from the S E. Genly   to day handsom high extencive rich Plains on each Side, the mineral appearances continue with
greater appearances of Coal, much greater appearance of the hills haveing been burnt, more Pumice Stone & Lava washed down to the bottoms
and some Pumice Stone floating in the river, I walked on the S. S. Saw
great numbs. of Buffalow feeding in the Plains at a distance   Capt. Lewis
killed 2 Buffalow buls which was near the water at the time of dineing,
they were So pore as to be unfit for use. I Saw Several Small parties of
antelopes large herds of Elk, Some white wolves, and in a pond (formed
on the S. S. by the Missouries Changeing its bead) I Saw Swan Gees &
different kinds of Ducks in great ⟨quantity⟩ numbers also a Beaver house.
Passed a Small Creek on the S. S. & Several runs of water on each Side,
Saw the remains of Indian camps in every point of timbered land on the
S. S.   in the evining a thunder gust passed from the S W, without rain,
about Sunset Saw Some fresh Indians track and four rafts on the shore
S. S. Those I prosume were Ossinniboins who had been on a war party
against the Rockey Mountain Indians—   Saw a Curlow, Some verry large

49

beaver taken this morning.   those animals are made use of as food and preferred by the party to any other at this Season

Course distance &c. 17th of April 1805

S. 70° W.	3	miles to a point of willows on the S. Sd.
S 75° W.	½	miles on the Sd. Side opposed a Bluff
N. 75° W.	3	miles to a wood in a bend to the Sd. Side
N. 50° W	3 ½	miles to a point of wood Land Sd. Side
S 60° W	¾	of a mile to a pt. of wood land on the S. Sd. opposit to a Bluff on the Ld. Side just above which a creek falls in on the Labd. about 10 yds. wide.
N. 80° W.	3 ¼	miles to a willow point on the L. Sd. a Lake & creek Std. Halls Strand lake
S. 85° W.	3 ¾	miles to a L. pt. of wood land opposit to a bluff on the Starboard Side.
West	1	mile along the L. pt. of wood land, a high bluff on the S. S above which a run falls in burnt hills
S. 40° W.	1	mile along the same point of wood land Lard. S.
S. 30° W.	¼	of a mile on the Lad. Side of a willow point.
S. 14° W.	4	miles to the upper part of a high timber on the Starboard Side.
S. 28° W.	2	miles to a point of wood land on the L. Side where we camped for the night.
mls.	26	

note The distance we are obliged to go round Sand bars &c. is much greater than those called for in the courses from point to point &c.

1. Here Lewis is passing through country underlain by the Bullion Creek Formation until late in the day, when he again enters country underlain by the Sentinel Butte Formation; both formations contain lignite coal.

2. Probably the long-billed curlew, *Numenius americanus* [AOU, 264], and if so, a bird new to science. Cutright (LCPN), 125.

3. In McKenzie County, North Dakota. Mattison (GR), 57; *Atlas* maps 34, 47, 56; MRC map 58.

4. Also given on *Atlas* map 34, in Lewis's hand.

5. *Atlas* map 34 says 65°, in opposition to both captains' journals.

[Lewis]   *Thursday April 18th 1805.*

A fine morning, set out at an early hour.   one Beaver caught this morning by two traps, having a foot in each; the traps belonged to different
individuals, between whom, a contest ensued, which would have termi-
nated, most probably, in a serious rencounter had not our timely arrival at
the place prevented it.   after breakfast this morning, Capt. Clark walked
on Stad. shore, while the party were assending by means of their toe lines, I
walked with them on the bank; found a species of pea bearing a yellow
flower, and now in blume; it seldom rises more than 6 inches high, the leaf
& stalk resembles that of the common gardin pea, the root is pirenial.[1]
(See specimen of vegitables No. 3.) I also saw several parsels of buffaloe's
hair hanging on the rose bushes,[2] which had been bleached by exposure
to the weather and became perfectly white.   it every appearance of the
wool of the sheep, tho' much finer and more silkey and soft. I am confident that an excellent cloth may be made of the wool of the Buffaloe.
the Buffaloe I killed yesterday had cast his long hare, and the poil[3] which
remained was very thick, fine, and about 2 inches in length. I think this
anamal would have furnished about five pounds of wool.   we were detained today from one to five P. M. in consequence of the wind which blew
so violently from N. that it was with difficulty we could keep the canoes
from filling with water altho' they were along shore; I had them secured
by placing the perogues on the out side of them in such manner as to
break the waves off them.   at 5 we proceed, and shortly after met with
Capt. Clark, who had killed an Elk and a deer and was wating our arrival.   we took the meat on board and continued our march untill nearly
dark when we came too on the Stard side under a boald welltimbered
bank which sheltered us from the wind which had abated but not yet
ceased.   here we encamped,[4] it being the extremity of the last course of
this day.—

Courses and distances of the 18th April.[5]

South	to a sand point on the Stard. side	3
N. 75° W.	to a point of Woodland on Lard. side	2 ½
N. 85 W.	along the Lard. point	½

S. 25 E.	to a sand point Stard. side	2
S. 60 W.	to a willow point Stard. side	1
S. 65 W.	along the Stard. shore to a point of timbered land, oppo-site to a bluff on Lard.	½
N. 25 W.	to a copse of wood on stard side, in a bend	2
S. 50. W.	to a point of timbered land on Stard side where we en-camped for the night	1 ½

miles 13

Point of Observation No. 5.

On the Stard. shore at the extremity of the fifth course of this day—

Observed meridian Altd. of ⊙'s L. L. with Octant by the back observation 79° 12′ 00″

Latitude deduced from this observatn. [*blank*]

[Clark]   18th *of April Thursday 1805*

Set out at an early hour   one Beaver & a Musrat[6] Cought this morn-ing, the beaver cought in two traps, which like to have brought about a missunderstanding between two of the party &c.   after brackfast I as-sended a hill and observed that the river made a great bend to the South, I concluded to walk thro' the point about 2 miles and take Shabono, with me, he had taken a dost of Salts &c.   his Squar followed on with his child, when I Struck the next bend of the [river] could See nothing of the Party, left this man & his wife & Child on the river bank and went out to hunt, Killed a young Buck Elk, & a Deer, the Elk was tolerable meat, the Deer verry pore, Butcherd the meat and Continued untill near Sunset before Capt Lewis and the party Came up, they were detained by the wind, which rose Soon after I left the boat from the N W. & blew verry hard untill verry late in the evening.   we Camped on the S. S. in an excellent harbor, Soon after We came too, two men went up the river to Set their beaver traps   they met with a Bear and being without their arms thought pro-dent to return &c.   the wild Cheries are in bloom,[7] Great appearance of Burnt hills Pumice Stone &c.   the Coal & Salt appearance Continued,[8] the water in the Small runs much better than below,—   Saw Several old

Indian Camps, the game, Such as Buffalow Elk, antelopes & Deer verry plenty

Course distance &c. 18th of April

South	3	miles to a point on the Std. Side
N. 75° W.	2 ½	miles to a wood point on the L. Side
N. 85° W.	½	a mile along the Lad Side
S. 25° E	2	miles to a Sand point on the Sd. Side
S. 60° W.	1	mile to a pt. of Willows on the Sd. Side
S. 65° W	½	mile along the Sd. pot. to a point of timbered land opsd. a Bluff on the Lard. Side
N. 25° W	2	miles to a Copse of woods on the Sd. Side
S. 50° W.	1 ½	miles to the upper part of a wood on the Stad. Side & Camped
miles	13	

1. *Thermopsis rhombifolia* Nutt., golden pea. Barkley, 184. Someone drew a vertical line through this passage, apparently in red.

2. *Rosa woodsii* Lindl., western wild rose. Ibid., 151.

3. Probably meant for "pile." Criswell, 66.

4. This camp, where they remained until April 20, was in Williams County, North Dakota. *Atlas* map 56 shows it as the camp of April 19 only. Mattison (GR), 57; *Atlas* maps 34, 47; MRC map 58.

5. Also given on *Atlas* map 34, in both captains' hands.

6. *Ondatra zebethicus*. Jones et al., 230–34.

7. Probably *Prunus americana* Marsh., wild plum, one of the earliest flowering shrubs. Barkley, 146.

8. The party is still passing through country underlain by the Sentinel Butte Formation which is capped with glacial till.

[Lewis]   *Friday April 19th 1805.*

The wind blew So hard this morning from N. W. that we dared not to venture our canoes on the river.— Observed considerable quantities of dwarf Juniper on the hill sides (see specimen No. 4) it seldom rises higher then 3 feet.— the wind detained us through the couse of this day, tho' we were fortunate in having placed ourselves in a safe harbour. the party killed one Elk and a beaver today. The beaver of this part of the Missouri are larger, fatter, more abundant and better clad with fur than those of any other part of the country that I have yet seen; I have remarked also that their fur is much darker.—

[Clark]   19th *of April Friday 1805*

   a blustering windey day   the wind So hard from the N, W. that we were fearfull of ventering our Canoes in the river, lay by all day on the S. Side in a good harber, the Praries appear to green, the cotton trees bigin to leave, Saw some plumb bushes in full bloom, those were the plumb bushes which I have Seen for Some time. Killed an Elk an a Beaver to day—   The beaver of this river is much larger than usial, Great deal of Sign of the large Bear,—

[Lewis]   *Saturday April 20th 1805.*

   The wind continued to blow tolerably hard this morning but by no means as violently as it did yesterday; we determined to set out and accordingly departed a little before seven. I walked on shore on the N. side of the river, and Capt Clark proceeded with the party.   the river bottoms through [*NB: ⟨copy this for Dr Barton⟩*] which I passed about seven miles were fertil and well covered with Cottonwood some Box alder, ash and red Elm.   the under brush, willow, rose bushes Honeysuccle, red willow, goosbury, currant and servicebury[1] & in the open grounds along the foot of the river hills immence quantities of the hisop.   in the course of my walk I killed two deer, wounded an Elk and a deer; saw the remains of some Indian hunting camps, near which stood a small scaffold[2] of about 7 feet high on which were deposited two doog slays with their harnis. underneath this scaffold a human body was lying, well rolled in several dressed buffaloe skins and near it a bag of the same materials containg sundry articles belonging to the disceased; consisting of a pare of mockersons, some red and blue earth, beaver's nails, instruments for dressing the Buffalo skin, some dryed roots, several platts of the sweet grass, and a small quantity of Mandan tobacco.—[3]   I presume that the body, as well as the bag containing these articles, had formerly been placed on the scaffold as is the custom of these people, but had fallen down by accedent.   near the scaffold I saw the carcase of a large dog not yet decayed, which I supposed had been killed at the time the human body was left on the scaffold; this was no doubt the reward, which the poor doog had met with for performing the [*blank*]—friendly office to his mistres of transporting her corps to the place of deposit. it is customary with the Assinniboins, Mandans, Minetares &c who scaffold their dead, to sacrefice the favorite horses and doggs of their disceased relations, with a view of their being servicable to them in the land of sperits. I have never heard of any instances of human sacrefices on those occasions among them.—

The wind blew so hard that I concluded it was impossible fror the perogues and canoes to proceed and therefore returned and joined them about three in the evening. Capt. Clark informed me that soon after seting out, a part of the bank of the river fell in near one of the canoes and had very nearly filled her with water.[4] that the wind became so hard and the waves so high that it was with infinite risk he had been able to get as far as his present station. the white perrogue and several of the canoes had shiped water several times but happily our stores were but little injured; those which were wet we put out to dry and determined to remain untill the next morning.[5] we sent out four hunters who soon added 3 Elk 4 gees and 2 deer to our stock of provisions.[6] the party caught six beaver today which were large and in fine order. the Buffaloe, Elk and deer are poor at this season, and of cours are not very palitable, however our good health and apetites make up every necessary deficiency, and we eat very heartily of them.— encamped on Stard side; under a high well timbered bank.

	Courses and Distances of this day[7]	miles
South	to the upper part of a timbered bottom at a bluff on the Lard. side	1 ½
West	to a point of high timber on the Stad. sid. passing over a large sand point on Sd. side	1 ½
N. 45° W.	to a large tree in a bend on stard side opposite a large sand point	1 ½
S. 45° W.	to a point of low willows on Stard. side	2
		Miles 6 ½

[Clark]   20th *of April Satturday 1805*

wind a head from the N W.   we Set out at 7 oClock proceeded on, Soon after we Set out a Bank fell in near one of the Canoes which like to have filled her with water, the wind became hard and waves So rought that we proceeded with our little Canoes with much risque, our Situation was Such after Setting out that we were obliged to pass round the 1st Point or lay exposed to the blustering winds & waves, in passing round the Point Several canoes took in water as also our large Perogue but without injuring our Stores & much I proceeded on to the upper part of the 1st bend and came too at a butifull Glade on the S. S., about 1 mile below Capt Lewis who had walked thro the point, left his Coat & a Deer on the bank which we took on board,—.   a Short distance below our Camp I Saw Some rafts on the S. S. near which, an Indian woman was Scaffeled in the Indian form of Deposing their dead, & fallen down   She was or had been raised about 6 feet inclosed in Several robes tightly laced around her, with her dog Slays, her bag of Different coloured earths paint Small bones of animals beaver nales and Several other little trinkets, also a blue jay,[8] her dog was killed and lay near her. Capt. Lewis joined me Soon after I landed & informed me he has walked Several miles higher, & in his walk killed 2 Deer & wounded an Elk & a Deer, our party ⟨killed⟩ Shot in the river four beaver & cought two, which were verry fat and much admired by the men, after we landed they killed 3 Elk 4 Gees & 2 Deer   we had Some of our Provisions & which got a little wet aired, the wind Continued So hard that we were Compelled to delay all day. Saw Several buffalow lodged in the drift wood which had been drouned in the winter in passing the river; Saw the remains of 2 which had lodged on the Side of the bank & eate by the bears.

Course distance &c. 20th of April 1805.

South	1 ½	miles to the upper part of a timbered bottom at a bluff on the Lad. Side
West	1 ½	miles to a high timber on the Sd. Side passing over a large Sand point on S. S.
N. 45° W.	1 ½	mile to a tree in a Glade in a bend to the Starboard Side a Sand pt. opsd.

S. 45° W.   2   miles to a point of low willows on the Sd. Side.

    6 ½

This morning was verry cold, Some Snow about 2 oClock from flying clouds, Some frost this morning & the mud at the edge of the water was frosed

1. Lewis's underbrush can be identified as: sandbar, or coyote, willow; western wild rose; honeysuckle is either *Lonicera dioica* L. var. *glaucescens* (Rydb.) Butters, wild honeysuckle, or *Symphoricarpos occidentalis* Hook., western snowberry; red willow is red osier dogwood; gooseberry is either *Ribes oxyacanthoides* L., hawthorn gooseberry, or *R. setosum* Lindl., bristly, or redshoot, gooseberry; currant is either *R. americanum* Mill., wild black currant, or *R. odoratum* Wendl. f., buffalo currant; and serviceberry is *Amelanchier alnifolia* Nutt., juneberry or serviceberry. Barkley, 103, 151, 327–28, 205, 134–37; Cutright (LCPN), 127. Someone, apparently Biddle, drew a red vertical line through this passage.

2. Marked on *Atlas* maps 47 and 56.

3. *Hierochloe odorata* (L.) Beauv., sweetgrass, an important ceremonial item of plains tribes. Barkley, 497; Gilmore (UPI), 14. The tobacco is *Nicotiana quadrivalvis* Pursh, Indian tobacco. Gilmore (SCAT); Cronquist et al., 72.

4. Ordway notes that he was in this canoe.

5. In Williams County, North Dakota. *Atlas* map 56 misidentifies this camp as that of April 17. Mattison (GR), 57; *Atlas* maps 34, 47; MRC map 58.

6. Ordway notes, "Drewyer Shot a beaver."

7. Also given on *Atlas* map 34, in Clark's hand.

8. *Cyanocitta cristata* [AOU, 477], not mentioned in Lewis's entry as among the burial items.

[Lewis]   *Sunday April 21st 1805.*

Set out at an early hour this morning. Capt Clark walked on shore; the wind tho' a head was not violent. the country through which we passed is very simelar in every rispect to that through which we have passed for several days.— We saw immence herds of buffaloe Elk deer & Antelopes. Capt Clark killed a buffaloe and 4 deer in the course of his walk today; and the party with me[1] killed 3 deer, 2 beaver, and 4 buffaloe calves. the latter we found very delicious. I think it equal to any veal I ever tasted. the Elk now begin to shed their horns. passed one large and two small creeks on the Lard. side, tho' neither of them discharge any water at present. the wind blew so hard this evening that we were obliged to halt several hours. we reached the place of incampment after dark, which was on the Lard. side a little above *White earth* river[2] which discharges itself on the Stard. side.   immediately at the mouth of this river it is not more than 10 yards wide being choked up by the mud of the Missouri; tho' after leaving the bottom lands of this river, or even sooner, it becomes a boald stream of sixty yards wide and is deep and navigable.   the course of this river as far as I could see from the top of *Cut bluff*, was due North.   it passes through a beatifull level and fertile vally about five miles in width. I think I saw about 25 miles up this river, and did not discover one tree or bush of any discription on it's borders.   the vally was covered with Elk and buffaloe.   saw a great number of gees today as usual, also some swan and ducks.—

	Courses and Distances of this day.[3]	*mils*
S. 18° E.	to a sand point Std. opposite to a bluf Lard.	1 ½
N. 75 W.	to a point of high timber on Std. opposite a blff.	½
N. 40 W.	to a willow point on Lard. opposite to a bluff.	3 ½
N. 60 W.	to a point of woodland on Stard. side, oposite to a bluff, just below which on the Lard. side a creek falls in.	4 ½
N. 25 E.	to a point of wood land on Lard. opposite to a high bluff	2
N. 10 W.	to the upper part of a bluff Stard. and in a Stard. bend.	2
S.[4] 50 W.	to the upper point of the timbered bottom on Lard. side below a high bluff point which we called *Cut bluff*, at 1 mile pass White Earth river on Stard.	2 ½
		16 ½

[Clark] 21st of *April Sunday 1805*

Set out early   the wind gentle & from the N. W.   the river being verry Crooked, I concluded to walk through the point, the Countrey on either Side is verry Similar to that we have passed, Saw an emence number of Elk & Buffalow, also Deer Antelopes Geese Ducks & a fiew Swan, the Buffalow is about Calveing   I killed a Buffalow & 4 Deer in my walk to day, the party killed 2 deer 2 beaver & 4 Buffalow Calves, which was verry good veele. I Saw old Camps of Indians on the L. Side, we passed 1 large & 2 Small Creeks on the L. Side   neither of them discharge any water into the river, in the evening the wind became verry hard a head, we made

Camp at a late hour which was on the L. Side a little above the mouth of *White Earth* River which falls in on the Stad Side and is 60 yds. wide, several Mes. up

	miles	Corse distance &: 21st of Apl.
S 18° E	1 ½	me. to a Sand pt. S. S. opsd. a bluff on the L. S.
N. 75° W	½	to a pt. of high timber on the S. Sd. opsd. a Bluff
N. 40° W	3 ½	to a willow pt. L. Sd. opsd. a Bluff on the S. Sd.
N. 60° W	4 ½	to a pt. of wood land on the S. Sd. opsd. a bluff just below which a creek falls in on the L. S.
N. 25° E	2	to a pt. of wood land on the L. Sd. opposd. to a high bluff on the Stard. Side
N. 10° W	2	to the upper part of a low bluff on the S. Sd. opsd. to a pt. of timber on the L. Side
N 50° W	2 ½	miles to the upper part of a timber at a high Short bluff on the Lard. Side, passd white earth river at ½ mile on the Sd Side
miles	16 ½	

1. Including Potts and Drouillard, according to Ordway, each of them killing a buffalo calf.

2. Not to be confused with the present White Earth River, which they passed on April 16 without naming it. The present stream is Little Muddy River or Creek, in Williams County, North Dakota. The camp was in McKenzie County, nearly opposite present Williston. Mattison (GR), 58; *Atlas* maps 34, 47, 56; MRC map 59. The words "White earth" may be a later interpolation as are the same words in the last course of the course and distance table for this day.

3. Also given on *Atlas* map 35, in both captains' hands.

4. Clark has "N." in his journal entry; *Atlas* map 35 agrees with Lewis.

[Lewis] *Monday April 22cd 1805.*

Set out at an early hour this morning; proceeded pretty well untill breakfat, when the wind became so hard a head that we proceeded with difficulty even with the assistance of our toe lines. the party halted and Cpt. Clark and myself walked to the white earth river which approaches the Missouri very near at this place, being about 4 miles above it's entrance. we found that it contained more water than streams of it's size generally do at this season. the water is much clearer than that of the

Missouri. the banks of the river are steep and not more than ten or twelve feet high; the bed seems to be composed of mud altogether. the salts which have been before mentioned as common on the Missouri, ⟨and⟩ appears in great quantities along the banks of this river, which are in many places so thickly covered with it that they appear perfectly white. perhaps it has been from this white appearance of it's banks that the river has derived it's name. this river is said to be navigable nearly to it's source, which is at no great distance from the Saskashawan, and I think from it's size ⟨and⟩ the direction which it seems to take, and the latitude of it's mouth, that there is very good ground to believe that it extends as far North as latitude 50°.—[1] this stream passes through an open country generally.— the broken hills of the Missouri about this place exhibit large irregular and broken masses of rocks and stones; some of which tho' 200 feet above the level of the water seem at some former period to have felt it's influence, for they appear smoth as if woarn by the agetation of the water. this collection consists of white & grey gannite, a brittle black rock, flint, limestone, freestone, some small specimens of an excellent pebble and occasionally broken stratas of a stone which appears to be petrefyed wood, it is of a black colour, and makes excellent whetstones. Coal or carbonated wood pumice stone lava and other mineral apearances still continue.[2] the coal appears to be of better quality; I exposed a specimen of it to the fire and found that it birnt tolerably well, it afforded but little flame or smoke, but produced a hot and lasting fire.— I asscended to the top of the cutt bluff this morning, from whence I had a most delightfull view of the country, the whole of which except the vally formed by the Missouri is void of timber or underbrush, exposing to the first glance of the spectator immence herds of Buffaloe, Elk, deer, & Antelopes feeding in one common and boundless pasture. we saw a number of bever feeding on the bark of the trees alonge the verge of the river, several of which we shot, found them large and fat. walking on shore this evening I met with a buffaloe calf which attatched itself to me and continued to follow close at my heels untill I embarked and left it. it appeared allarmed at my dog which was probably the cause of it's so readily attatching itself to me. Capt Clark informed me that he saw a large drove of buffaloe pursued by wolves today, that they at length caught a calf which was unable to keep up with the herd.   the cows only defend their young so long as they are able to keep up with the herd, and seldom return any distance in surch of them.—

	Courses and distances of 22cd of April 1805[3]	miles
N. 60° W.	to a point of woodland on the Lard. side	2 ½
W.	along the woodland on Lard. shore	1
S. 70 W.	to the lower point of a bluff in a bend on stard. side	1
S. 20 W.	to the upper part of the stard. bluff	2
S. 60 E.	to a point of woods in a bend on Stard.	1
S. 30 E.	to a willow point on the Stard. side.	2
N. 65 E.	to an object in a bend on Lard. where we encamped for the evening[4]	1 ½

Miles 11

Point of Observation No. 6.

April 22cd 1805.

On the Lard shore one mile above the *cut bluff*

Observed time and distance of ⊙'s and ☽'s nearest limbs, with Sextant, the ⊙ East.—

		Time			*Distance*		
		h	m	s			
A. M.	10	44	3	84°	20′	45″
	″	46	16	″	20	30
	″	48	8	″	20	
	″	49	28	″	19	45
	″	50	24	″	19	30
	″	51	27	″	19	30
	″	52	35	″	19	
	″	53	40	″	18	45

		Time			*Distance*		
		h	m	s			
A. M.	11	1	54	84°	15′	—″
	″	4	25	″	14	
	″	6	8	″	13	45
	″	7	2	″	12	45

"	8	3	"	12	45
"	9	4	"	12	37½
"	10	20	"	12	30
"	12	40	"	12	

Observed equal altitudes of the with ⊙ Sextant

	h	m	s			h	m	s
A. M.	11	21	49		P. M.	5	13	38
	"	23	38			"	15	31
	"	25	29			"	17	20

Altitude by Sextant at the time of observation   77° 52' 45"

[Clark]   22nd *of April Monday 1805*

a verry cold morning Some frost, we Set out at an early hour and proceeded on verry well untill brackfast at which time the wind began to blow verry hard ahead, and Continued hard all day   we proceeded on with much dificuelty with the assistance of the toe Ropes. Capt. Lewis & my Self walked to the [*blank*] River which is near the Missouri four miles above its mouth, this river is 60 yards wide and contains a greater perportion of water at this time than is Common for Rivers of its Size   it appears navagable as fur as any of the party was, and I am told to near its Source in morrasses in the open Plains, it passes (as far as we can See which is 6 or 7 Leagus) thro' a butifull extinsive vallie, rich & fertile and at this time Covered with Buffalow, Elk & antelopes, which may be Seen also in any other direction in this quarter—   this river must take its rise at no great distance Easte of the Saskashawan, and no doubt as far N. as Latd. 50°.

Some of the high plains or the broken Revien of the river contains great quantity of Pebble Stones of various Sizes, The Stratum of Coal is much richer than below, the appearances of Mineral & burnt hills Still continue

the river riseing a little, Saw an emence number of beaver feeding on the waters edge & Swiming Killed Several, Capt. Lewis assended a hill from the top of which he had a most inchanting prospect of the Countrey around & the meanderings of the two rivers, which is remarkable Crooked—   a buffalow calf which was on the Shore alone followed Cap

Lewis Some distance,— I observed a large drove of buffalow prosued by wolves the wolves cought one of their Calves in my view, those animals defend their young as long as they Can keep up with the drove

	miles	*Course & Distance 22nd of April*
N. 60° W.	2 ½	to a point of wood land on the Ld. Side
West	1	along the wood on the Ld. point
S. 70° W.	1	to the lower point of a bluff in a bend to the Starboard Side
S. 20° W.	2	to the upper part of the Said bluff on the Starboard Side
S. 60° E	1	to a wood in a bend to the Sd. Side
S. 30° E	2	to a willow point on the Sd. Side
N. 65° E	1 ½	to an object in a bend to the L. S. and Camped
	11	

1. A highly optimistic estimate, based on a hope of finding an American entryway into the Canadian fur regions and extending the Louisiana Purchase in that direction. The Little Muddy rises in Williams County, North Dakota. Even the real White Earth River would not have matched their hopes, probably based on Indian information. Allen (PG), 242.

2. The broken hills (breaks) were formed when the Missouri River cut a new course along the southern and western edges of glacial ice. The large rocks are glacial erratics. Most of these rocks have been derived from the Canadian Shield and from lower Paleozoic formations just west of it. The day's camp was near the contact between the Sentinel Butte and Bullion Creek formations; coal is more abundant in the latter formation.

3. Also given on *Atlas* map 35, in Clark's hand.

4. In McKenzie County, North Dakota, a few miles above Williston. Mattison (GR), 58; *Atlas* maps 34, 47, 56; MRC map 59.

[Lewis] *Tuesday April 23rd*

Set out at an early hour this morning. about nine A. M. the wind arose, and shortly after became so violent that we were unabled to proceed, in short it was with much difficulty and some risk that I was enabled to get the canoes and perogues into a place of tolerable safety, there being no timber on either side of the river at this place. some of the canoes shiped water, and wet several parsels of their lading, which I directed to be opened and aired   we remained untill five in the evening when the wind abating in some measure, we reloaded, and proceeded.   shortly after we were joined by Capt. Clark who had walked on shore this morning, and passing through the bottom lands had fallen on the river some miles above ⟨us⟩, and concluding that the wind had detained us, came down the river in surch of us.   he had killed three blacktaled, or mule deer,[1] and a buffaloe Calf, in the course of his ramble.   these hard winds, being so frequently repeated, become a serious source of detention to us.—   incamped on the Stard. side.—[2]

Courses and distances of the 23rd April[3]		miles
S. 25° E.	to a point of timbered land on Stard.—	2 ½
S.	along this Stard. point of woodland. a high bluff opposite	1
S. 78 W.	to a cops of woods, under a hill on Stard in a bend	4
S. 14 E.	to a point of high timber in a Lard. bend passing the extremity of a little bay Std.	4 ½
S. 25 W.	to a point of woodland on the Lard. side.	1 ½
		13 ½

[Clark]   23rd *of April 1805*

a cold morning   at about 9 oClock the wind as usial rose from the N W and continued to blow verry hard untill late in the evening   I walked on Shore after brackfast   in my walk on the S side passed through extensive bottoms of timber intersperced with glades & low open plains, I killed 3 mule or black tail Deer, which was in tolerable order, Saw Several others, I also killed a Buffalow Calf which was verry fine, I Struck the river above the Perogus which had Come too in a bend to the L. S. to Shelter from the wind which had become violently hard, I joined Capt Lewis in the evening & after the winds falling which was late in the evening we proceeded on & encamped on the S. S. The winds of this Countrey which blow with Some violence almost every day, has become a Serious obstruction in our progression onward, as we Cant move when the wind is high with[out] great risque, and [if] there was no risque the winds is generally a head and often too violent to proceed

Course & Distance 23d April

S. 25° E	2 ½	miles to a point of timbered land on the Starboard Side
South	1	mile on the Sd. point, of wood land a high Bluff opposit.
S. 78° W.	4	miles to a Copse of woods under a hill to the Sd Side in a bend
S 14° E.	4 ½	miles to a point of high timber in a larboard bend, passing the enterence of a little bay to S. S.
S. 25° W.	1 ½	miles to a point of woods on the Ld. Side
Miles	13 ½	

1. Evidently the first written use of the term "mule deer" for *Odocoileus hemionus*, an expedition discovery. See above, September 16, 1804. Cutright (LCPN), 83–84. Other references to deer in this chapter are to *O. virginianus*, white-tailed deer.

2. The campsite, where they remained until April 25, in Williams County, North Dakota, appears on *Atlas* map 56 as that for April 24 only. *Atlas* maps 34, 47; MRC map 59.

3. Also given on *Atlas* map 35, in both captains' hands.

[Lewis]   *Wednesday April 24th*

The wind blew so hard during the whole of this day, that we were unable to move.   notwithstanding that we were sheltered by high timber from the effects of the wind, such was it's violence that it caused the waves to rise in such manner as to wet many articles in the small canoes before they could be unloaded.   we sent out some hunters who killed 4 deer & 2 Elk, and caught some young wolves of the small kind.— Soar eyes is a common complaint among the party. I believe it origenates from the immence quantities of sand which is driven by the wind from the sandbars of the river in such clouds that you are unable to discover the opposite bank of the river in many instances.   the particles of this sand are so fine and light that they are easily supported by the air, and are carried by the wind for many miles, and at a distance exhibiting every appearance of a collumn of thick smoke.   so penitrating is this sand that we cannot keep any article free from it; in short we are compelled to eat, drink, and breath it very freely.[1]   my pocket watch, is out of order, she will run only a few minutes without stoping. I can discover no radical defect in her works, and must therefore attribute it to the sand, with which, she seems plentifully charged, notwithstanding her cases are double and tight.

[Clark]   24th *of April Wednesday 1805*

The wind rose last night and continued blowing from the N. & N W. and Sometimes with great violence, untill 7 oClock P. M, Several articles wet in the Perogues by their takeing water &c.   as the wind was a head we could not move to day   Sent out hunters, they killed 4 Deer 2 Elk & cought Some young wolves of the Small kind, The party complain much of the Sand in their eyes, the Sand is verry fine and rises in clouds from the Points and bars of the river, I may Say that dureing those winds we eat Drink & breeth a prepotion of Sand.

1. The fine alkalai dust and the constant glare of the sun on the water may have been responsible for the sore eyes. Venereal disease may also have been a factor. Chuinard (OOMD), 158, 279.

[Lewis]   *Thursday April 25th 1805.*

The wind was more moderate this morning, tho' still hard; we set out at an early hour.   the water friezed on the oars this morning as the men rowed.   about 10 oclock A. M. the wind began to blow so violently that we were obliged to lye too.   my dog had been absent during the last night, and I was fearfull we had lost him altogether, however, much to my satisfaction he joined us at 8 Oclock this morning. The wind had been so unfavorable to our progress for several days past, and seeing but little prospect of a favourable chang; knowing that the river was crooked, from the report of the hunters who were out yesterday, and beleiving that we were at no very great distance from the Yellow stone River; I determined, in order as mush as possible to avoid detention, to proceed by land with a few men to the entrance of that river and make the necessary observations to determine it's position, which I hoped to effect by the time that Capt. Clark could arrive with the party; accordingly I set out at 11 OCk. on the Lard. side, accompanyed by four men.[1]   we proceeded about four miles, when falling in with some buffaloe I killed a yearling calf, which was in good order; we soon cooked and made a hearty meal of a part of it, and re-

newed our march   our rout lay along the foot of the river hills.   when we
had proceeded about four miles, I ascended the hills from whence I had
a most pleasing view of the country, perticularly of the wide and fertile
vallies formed by the missouri and the yellowstone rivers, which occasionally unmasked by the wood on their borders disclose their meanderings
for many miles in their passage through these delightfull tracts of country. I could not discover the junction of the rivers immediately, they being
concealed by the woods, however, sensible that it could not be distant I
determined to encamp on the bank of the Yellow stone river which made
it's appearance about 2 miles South of me.   the whol face of the country
was covered with herds of Buffaloe, Elk & Antelopes; deer are also abundant, but keep themselves more concealed in the woodland.   the buffaloe Elk and Antelope are so gentle that we pass near them while feeding,
without apearing to excite any alarm among them, and when we attract
their attention, they frequently approach us more nearly to discover what
we are, and in some instances pursue us a considerable distance appar-
enly with that view.—   in our way to the place I had determined to encamp, we met with two large herds of buffaloe, of which we killed three
cows and a calf.   two of the former, wer but lean, we therefore took their
tongues and a part of their marrow-bones only. I then proceeded to the
place of our encampment with two of the men, taking with us the Calf
and marrowbones, while the other two remained, with orders to dress
the cow that was in tolerable order, and hang the meat out of the reach
of the wolves, a precaution indispensible to it's safe keeping, even for a
night.   we encamped on the bank of the yellowstone river, 2 miles South
of it's confluence with the Missouri.—[2]   On rejoining Capt. Clark, the
26th in the evening, he informed me, that at 5 P. M. after I left him the
wind abated in some measure and he proceeded a few miles further and
encamped.[3]

The courses and distances of this day (25th) being as follow.—[4]		*miles*
N. 68° W.	to a point of woodland on Lard. side	2 ½
West	to a tree in a low plain, in a bend on Std.	1 ¼
South	to the upper part of a low bluff in a bend on Stard. side	1 ½

East	to a point of timbered land on Stard. side.	2 ½
S. 28° E.	along the Stard. point, opposite a bluff	¾
S. 20 W.	along the Stard. point opposite a bluff	1
N. 65 W.	to the upper part of a timbered bottom in a bend on Stard. side	3
S. 72 W.	to the lower point of some timber in a bend on Stard. side	1 ¾ [5]

miles 14 ¼ [6]

[Clark]   25th *of April Thursday 1805*

The wind was moderate & ahead this morning, we Set out at an early hour   The morning cold, Some flying Clouds to be Seen, the wind from the N: ice collected on the ores this morning, the wind increased and became So violent about 1 oClock we were obliged to lay by our Canoes haveing taken in Some water, the Dog which was lost yesterday, joined us this morning.

finding that the winds retarded our progression for maney days past, and no apparance of an alteration, and the river being Crooked that we could never have 3 miles fair wind, Capt. Lewis concluded to go by land as far as the Rochejhone or yellow Stone river, which we expect is at no great distance by land and make Some Selestial observations to find the Situation of its mouth, and by that measure not detain the Perogues at that place any time for the purpose of makeing those necessary observations   he took 4 men & proceeded on up the Missouri on the L. Side, at 5 oClock the wind luled and we proceeded on and incamped.

Course Distance &c. 25th of April

N. 68° W.	2 ½	miles to point of wood land on the Larboard Side
West	1 ½	miles to a tree in a bend to the Std. Side in a low plain
South	1 ½	miles to the upper part of a low bluff in a bend to the Sd Side
East	2 ½	miles to a point of timbered land on the Starboard Side.
S. 28° E.	¾	on the Std. point. Bluff opsed.
S 20° W.	1	mile on the Std point bluff opsd.

N. 65° W	3	miles to the upper part of a timbered bottom in a bend to the S. Sd.
S. 72° W.	1 ¾	mile to the lower part of some timber in a bend to the S. Side
	14 ¼	

1. Including Ordway, by his own testimony, and Drouillard and Joseph Field, from later evidence in the captains' journals.

2. The Yellowstone meets the Missouri in McKenzie County, North Dakota, a little east of the Montana state line. The actual mouth has shifted over the years. *Atlas* maps 35, 48, 56; MRC map 59.

3. In Williams County, North Dakota, in the vicinity of Glass Bluffs, on the opposite side. The bluffs may have received their name from their glassy appearance, although some locals believe they are named after Hugh Glass, the fur trapper. Mattison (GR), 59; *Atlas* maps 35, 48, 56, MRC map 59.

4. Also given on *Atlas* map 35, in Clark's hand.

5. *Atlas* map 35 has 2¾.

6. *Atlas* map 35 gives an incorrect total of 14.

[Lewis]   *Friday April 26th 1805.*

This morning I dispatched Joseph Fields up the yellowstone river with orders to examine it as far as he could conveniently and return the same evening; two others were directed to bring in the meat we had killed last evening, while I proceeded down the river with one man[1] in order to take a view of the confluence of this great river with the Missouri, which we found to be two miles distant on a direct line N. W. from our encampment.   the bottom land on the lower side of the yellowstone river near it's mouth for about one mile in width appears to be subject to inundation; while that on the opposite side of the Missouri and the point formed by the junction of these rivers is of the common elivation, say from twelve to 18 feet above the level of the water, and of course not liable to be overflown except in extreem high water, which dose not appear to be very frequent   there is more timber in the neighbourhood of the junction of these rivers, and on the Missouri as far below as the White earth river, than there is on any part of the Missouri above the entrance of the Chyenne river to this place.   the timber consists principally of Cottonwood, with some small elm, ash and boxalder.[2]   the under growth on the sandbars and verge of the river is the small leafed willow; the low bottoms, rose bushes which rise to three or four fe[e]t high, the redburry, servicebury, and the red-wood; the high bottoms are of two discriptions either timbered or open; the first lies next to the river and it's under brush is the same with that of the low timbered bottoms with the addition of the broad leafed willow, Goosbury, choke cherry, purple currant; and honeysuckle bushis; the open bottoms border on the hills, and are covered in many parts by the wild hyssop which rises to the hight of two feet. I observe that the Ante-lope, Buffaloe Elk and deer feed on this herb; the willow of the sandbars also furnish a favorite winter food to these anamals as well as the growse, the porcupine, hare, and rabbit.[3] about 12 Olock I heard the discharge of several guns at the junction of the rivers, which announced to me the arrival of the paty with Capt Clark; I afterwards learnt that they had fired on some buffaloe which they met with at that place, and of which they killed a cow and several Calves; the latter are now fine veal. I dispatched one of the men to Capt Clark requesting him to send up a canoe to take down the meat we had killed and our baggage to his encampmt, which was accordingly complyed with. after I had completed my observations in the evening I walked down and joined the party at their encampment on the point of land fromed by the junction of the rivers;[4] found them all in good health, and much pleased at having arrived at this long wished for spot, and in order to add in some measure to the general pleasure which seemed to pervade our little community, we ordered a dram to be issued to each person; this soon produced the fiddle, and they spent the evening with much hilarity, singing & dancing, and seemed as perfectly to forget their past toils, as they appeared regardless of those to come. in the evening, the man I had sent up the river this morning returned, and reported that he had ascended it about eight miles on a streight line; that he found it crooked, meandering from side to side of the valley formed by it; which is from four to five miles wide. the corrent of the river gentle, and it's bed much interrupted and broken by sandbars; at the distance of five miles he passed a large Island well covered with timber, and three miles higher a large creek falls in on the S. E. side[5] above a high bluff in which there are several stratas of coal.[6] the country bordering on this river as far as he could percieve, like that of the Missouri, consisted of open plains. he saw several of the bighorned anamals in the couse of his walk;[7] but they were so shy that he could not get a shoot at them; he found a large horn of one of these anamals which he brought with him. the bed of the yellowstone river is entirely composed of sand and mud, not a stone of any kind to be seen in it near it's entrance. Capt Clark measured these rivers just above their confluence; found the bed of the Missouri 520 yards wide, the water occupying 330. it's channel deep. the yellow-stone river including it's sandbar, 858 yds. of which, the water occupyed 297 yards; the depest part 12 feet; it was falling at this time & appeard to be nearly at it's summer tide.— the Indians inform that the yellowstone river is navigable for perogues and canoes nearly to it's source in the Rocky Mountains, and that in it's course near these mountains it passes within less than half a day's march of a navigable part of the Missouri. it's ex-treem sources are adjacent to those of the Missouri, river platte, and I think probably with some of the South branch of the Columbia river.[8] the first part of its course lies through a mountanous rocky country tho' well timbered and in many parts fertile; the middle, and much the most exten-sive portion of the river lies through a delightfull rich and fertile country, well covered with timber, intersperced with plains and meadows, and well watered; it is some what broken in many parts. the lower portion con-sists of fertile open plains and meadows almost entirely, tho' it possesses a considerable proportion of timber on it's borders. the current of the upper portion is extreemly rappid, that of the middle and lower portions much more gentle than the Missouri. the water of this river is turbid, tho' dose not possess as much sediment as that of the Missouri. this river in it's course recieves the waters of many large tributary strams principally from the S. E. of which the most considerable are the Tongue and big-horn rivers [*NB: & Clark's fork*] the former is ⟨much⟩ [*NB: rather*] the [*NB: smallest— next in size Clarkes fork, and the Big horn the largest by much.*] ⟨largest, and heads with the river Platte and Bighorn river, as dose the latter with the Tongue river and the river Platte⟩.—[9] a suficent quantity of limestone may be readily procured for building near the junction of the Missouri and yellowstone rivers. I could observe no regular stratas of it, tho' it lies on the sides of the river hills in large irregular masses, in considerable quantities; it is of a light colour, and appears to be of an excellent quality.—[10]

The courses and distances of the 26th as the party ascended the Missouri, are as follow—[11]

		miles
S. 45 E.	to a point of woodland on the Stard. side	2 ½
S. 40 W.	along the Stad. point, opposite a bluff	1 ½
N. 75 W.	to the commencement of the wood in a bend on Stard. side	3
South	to the point of land formed by the junction of the Missouri and yellow stone rivers	1

Miles 8

Point of Observation No. 7.

April 26th 1805.

On the Lard. bank of the yellowstone river 2 miles S. E. of it's junction with the Missouri observed Equal altitudes of the ☉ with Sextant and artificial horizon.—

	h	m	s			h	m	s	
A. M.	9	41	13		P. M.	6	49	3	Altd. given by Sextant at
	"	42	52			"	50	41	the time of observation
	"	44	31			"	52	17	48° 57′ 45″

h   m   s

Chronometer too fast mean time— [*blank*]

☞ the clouds this morning prevented my observing the moon with α Aquilae; and as the moon was not again observable untill the 1st of May, I determined not to wait, but reather to relinquish for the present the obtaining the necessary data to fix the longitude of this place.—

Observed Meridian altitude of ☉'s L. L. with Octant by the back observation   73° 47′

Latitude deduced from this observation. [*blank*]

[Clark]   26th *of April Friday 1805*

last night was verry Cold. the Thermometer Stood at 32 abov o this morning. I Set out at an early hour, as it was cold I walked on the bank, & in my walk Shot a beaver & 2 Deer, one of the Deer in tolerable order, the low bottom of the river is generaly Covered with wood willows & rose bushes, red berry, wild Cherry & red or arrow wood intersperced with glades The timber is Cottonwood principally, Elm Small ash also furnish a portion of the timber, The Clay of the bluffs appear much whiter than below, and Contain Several Stratums of Coal, on the hill Sides I observe pebbles of different Size & Colour—[12] The river has been riseing for Several days, & raised 3 inches last night, at 12 oClock arrived at the forks of the Roche Johne & Missouri and formed a Camp on the point Soon after George Drewyer Came from Capt Lewis & informed me that he was a little way up the Roche johne and would join me this evining, I Sent a canoe up to Capt Lewis and proceeded measure the width of the [rivers], and find the debth. The Missouri is 520 yards wide above the point of yellow Stone and the water covers 330 yards; the YellowStone River is 858 yards wide includeing its Sand bar, the water covers 297 yards and the deepest part is 12 feet water, it is at this time falling, the Missouri rising The Indians inform that the yellow Stone River is navagable for Perogues to near its Source in the Rocky Mountains, it has many tributary Streams, principally on the S. E. Side, and heads at no great distance from the Missouri, the largest rivers which fall into it is Tongue river which heads with the waters of River Platt,[13] and Big horn river which also heads with Platt & Tongue R   the current of this river is Said to be rapid near its mouth it is verry jentle, and its water is of a whitish colour ⟨tolerably Cl⟩ much Clearer of Sediment than the Missouri. the Countrey on this river is Said to be broken in its whole Course & Contains a great deel of wood, the countrey about its mouth is verry fine, the bottoms on either Side is wooded with Cotton wood, ash, Elm &c. near the banks of the river back is higher bottoms and Covered with red berry, Goose berry & rose bushes &. interspersed with Small open Glades, and near the high land is Generally open rich bottoms— at our arrival at the forks I observed a Drove of Buffalow Cows & Calves on a Sand bar in the point, I directed the men to kill the fattest Cow, and 3 or 4 Calves, which they did and let the others pass, the Cows are pore, Calves fine veele.

Course & Distance 26th of April

S. 45° E	2 ½	miles to a point of wood land on the Starboard Side
S. 40° W.	1 ½	miles on the S. pt. a bluff opposit
N. 75° W	3	miles to the commencement of a wood bottom in a bend to the Std. Side
South	1 ⎯⎯ 8	mile to the junction of Rochejhone or yellow Stone River & the Missouri

Capt Lewis joined me in the evening after takeing equal altitudes a little way up the YellowStone river   the Countrey in every direction is plains except the moist bottoms of the river, which are covered with Some indifferent timber Such as Cotton wood Elm & Small ash, with different kind of Srubs & bushes in the forks   about 1 mile from the point at which place the 2 rivers are near each other a butifull low leavel plain Commences, and extends up the Missourie & back, this plain is narrow at its commencement and widens as the Missouri bends north, and is bordered by an extencive wood land for many miles up the yellow Stone river, this low plain is not Subject to over flow, appear to be a few inches above high water mark and affords a butifull commanding Situation for a fort[14] near the commencement of the Prarie, about [*blank*] miles from the Point & [*blank*] yards from the Missouri a Small lake is Situated,[15] from this lake the plain rises gradually to a high butifull Countrey, the low Plain continues for Some distance up both rivers on the Yellow Stone it is wide & butifull   opsd. the point on the S. Side is Some high timbered land, about 1 ½ miles below on the Same Side a little distance from the water is an elivated plain—   Several of the party was up the yellow Stone R Several miles, & informed that it meandered throught a butifull Countrey Joseph Fields discovered a large Creek falling into the Yellowstone River on the S E Side 8 miles up near which he Saw a big horn animal, he found in the Prarie the horn of one of those animals which was large and appeared to have laid Several years   I Saw maney buffalow dead on the banks of the river in different places Some of them eaten by the white bears & wolves all except the Skin & bones, others entire, those animals either drounded in attempting to Cross on the ice dureing the winter or Swiming across to bluff banks where they Could not get out & too weak to return   we Saw several in this Situation.

emence numbers of antelopes in the forks of the river, Buffalow & Elk & Deer is also plenty   beaver is in every bend. I observe that the Magpie Goose duck & Eagle all have their nests in the Same neighbourhood, and it is not uncommon for the Magpie to build in a few rods of the eagle, the nests of this bird is built verry Strong with Sticks Covered verry thickly with one or more places through which they enter or escape, the Goose I make no doubt falls a pray to those vicious eagles

1. Probably Drouillard, whom Lewis sent down to meet Clark.

2. Someone drew a vertical line through this passage, apparently in red.

3. The porcupine is the yellow-haired porcupine, *Erethizon dorsatum epixanthum;* the hare is the white-tailed jackrabbit; and the rabbit may be the eastern cottontail, *Sylvilagus floridanus,* or less probably Nuttall's cottontail, *S. nuttallii.* Burroughs, 119–23; Jones et al., 103–9. Lewis's description of the willows in this area is not entirely clear. The "small leafed willow" (also called the "willow of the sandbars") is certainly the sandbar, or coyote, willow. The "broad leafed willow" could possibly be the diamond willow, *Salix rigida* Muhl. (variety uncertain), but based on Lewis's ecological description of "high [timbered] bottoms" is more likely to be the peach-leaved willow, *S. amygdaloides* Anderss. However, this latter willow is not an underbrush species as noted by Lewis, but a small tree commonly found in open floodplains along the Missouri. Barkley, 102–5.

4. In McKenzie County, North Dakota; shifts of the Missouri and the mouth of the Yellowstone make determination of the exact spot difficult. Mattison (GR), 65; *Atlas* maps 35, 48, 56; MRC map 60.

5. Undoubtedly the Joseph Fields Creek of *Atlas* maps 48 and 56, now Charbonneau Creek, in McKenzie County.

6. This is the Bullion Creek Formation (Tongue River Member of the Fort Union Formation in Montana usage).

7. Field may have been seeing Audubon's mountain sheep, *Ovis canadensis auduboni*, an extinct subspecies of *O. canadensis* of which the explorers had already heard, and which they were to encounter and describe later (see May 25, 1805). It is difficult to determine in this region, where both varieties occurred, which one the men saw. Some authorities have argued against the separate classification of *O. c. auduboni*. Cutright (LCPN), 134, 444; Jones et al., 340–43.

8. Most of this would be from Indian information. The Yellowstone, the Gallatin and Madison forks of the Missouri, and the Snake, the greatest tributary of the Columbia, do all rise on the Yellowstone Plateau of northwest Wyoming, the closest actual approxima-

tion to the pyramidal height of land of pre-Lewis and Clark conjectural geography. The sources of the North and South Platte are in the Colorado Rockies. Allen (PG), 260.

9. The interlined material and corrections (with much crossing out) are by Biddle and are based on Clark's journey down the Yellowstone in 1806.

10. The masses of limestone are glacial erratics derived from lower Paleozoic formations near Lake Winnipeg, Canada, more than 150 miles to the northeast.

11. Also given on *Atlas* map 35, in Clark's hand.

12. The Bullion Creek Formation is usually less drab or dull-colored than the Sentinel Butte Formation. The pebbles were either brought here by glacial ice or are higher terrace deposits of the Yellowstone River.

13. The sources of the Powder River, one of the main tributaries of the Yellowstone, rise in Central Wyoming near some tributaries of the North Platte.

14. See below, April 27, 1805.

15. Not marked on *Atlas* maps 35, 48, or 56. Probably present Nohly Lake, Richland County, Montana.

[Lewis]   Saturday April 27th 1805.

Previous to our seting out this morning I made the following observations.

Point of observation No. 8.

Suns magnetic azimuth by Circumferentor	N. 81° E.

	h	m	s
Time by Chronometer A. M.	9	27	14
Altitude by sextant	44°	56′	30″

Sun's magnetic azimuth by Circumft.	N. 82° E.

	h	m	s
Time by Chronometer A. M.	9	34	29
Altitude by Sextant	47°	22	

Sun's Magnetic azimuth by Circumftr.	N. 83° E.

	h	m	s
Time by Chronometer A. M.	9	42	17
Altitude by Sextant	49	56	30

This morning I walked through the point formed by the junction of the rivers; the woodland extends about a mile, when the rivers approach each other within less than half a mile; here a beatifull level low plain commences and extends up both rivers for many miles, widening as the rivers recede from each other, and extending back half a mile to a plain about 12 feet higher than itself; the low plain appears to be a few inches higher than high water mark and of course will not be liable to be over-flown; tho' where it joins the high plain a part of the Missouri when at it's greatest hight, passes through a channel of 60 or 70 yards wide and falls into the yellowstone river. on the Missouri about 2½ miles from the en-trance of the yellowstone river, and between this high and low plain, a small lake is situated about 200 yards wide extending along the edge of the high plain parallel with the Missouri about one mile. on the point of the high plain at the lower extremity of this lake I think would be the most eligible site for an establishment.[1] between this low plain and the Yellowstone river their is an extensive body of timbered land extending up the river for many miles. this site recommended is about 400 yards distant from the Missouri and about double that distance from the river yellowstone; from it the high plain, rising very gradually, extends back about three miles to the hills, and continues with the same width between these hills and the timbered land on the yellowstone river, up that stream, for seven or eight miles; and is one of the hadsomest plains I ever be-held. on the Missouri side the hills sircumscribe it's width, & at the dis-tance of three miles up that river from this site, it is not more than 400 yards wide. Capt Clark thinks that the lower extremity of the low plane would be most eligible for this establishment; it is true that it is much nearer both rivers, and might answer very well, but I think it reather too low to venture a permanent establishment, particularly if built of brick or other durable materials, at any considerable expence; for so capricious, and versatile are these rivers, that it is difficult to say how long it will be, untill they direct the force of their currents against this narrow part of the low plain, which when they do, must shortly yeald to their influence; in such case a few years only would be necessary, for the annihilation of the plain, and with it the fortification.— I continued my walk on shore; at 11 A. M. the wind became very hard from N. W. insomuch that the perogues and canoes were unable either to proceede or pass the river to me; I was under the necessity therefore of shooting a goose and cooking it for my dinner. the wind abated about 4. P. M. and the party proceeded tho' I could not conveniently join them untill night. altho' game is very abundant and gentle, we only kill as much as is necessary for food. I believe that two good hunters could conveniently supply a regiment with provisions. for several days past we have observed a great number of buffaloe lying dead on the shore, some of them entire and others partly devoured by the wolves and bear. those anamals either drownded during the winter in attempting to pass the river on the ice during the winter or by swiming acrss at present to bluff banks which they are unable to ascend, and feeling themselves too weak to return remain and perish for the want of food; in this situation we met with several little parties of them.— beaver are very abundant, the party kill several of them every day. The Eagles, Magpies, and gees have their nests in trees adjacent to each other; the magpye particularly appears fond of building near the Eagle, as we scarcely see an Eagle's nest unaccompanyed with two or three Magpies nests within a short distance.— The bald Eagle are more abundant here than I ever observed them in any part of the country.

Courses and distances 27th Aprile 1805.[2]   Miles

N.[3] 9° E.	to the upper part of the timber on Lard. in the point, the same being the commencement of the low plain, at which the Missouri and yellowstone rivers are about 250 yards distant.	1
West	to the lower part of the timber in the bend on Lard. side	1
N. 32 W.	to a point of the timbered bottom on Lard. opposite to a low bluff, between two points of wooded bottom ½ a mile distant from each other; a beautifull plain back. several high open situations between the woodlands on the Stard. side	3
West	to a point of small willows on the Stard side, opposite a low white bluff bordering a beautifull rising plain; some woodland below this bluff on the Lard. side, and a thick wooded bottom on Stard. side. on this course the river is wide, and crouded with sandbars. a little below the low bluff on the Lard. side, a timbered bottom commences;	

here the country rises gradually from the river on the
Lard. side [4]

<u>3</u>

Miles 8

[Clark]   27th *of April Satturday 1805*

after take the azmuth of the Sun & brackfasting we Set out   wind moderate & a head, at 11 oClock the wind rose and continued to blow verry
hard a head from the N. W. untill 4 oClock P M, which blew the Sand off
the Points in Such clouds as almost Covered us on the opposit bank, at 4
I Set out from my unpleasent Situation and proceeded on, Capt. Lewis
walked on Shore in the Point to examine & view the Countrey and could
not get to the boats untill night, Saw great numbers of Goats or antilopes,
Elk, Swan Gees & Ducks, no buffalow to day   I Saw Several beaver and
much Sign, I Shot one in the head which imediately Sunk, altho the game
of different kinds are in abundance we Kill nothing but what we can make
use of

Course distance the 27th of April

N. 9° E	1	mile to the upper part of the wood in the point and Commence-ment of a butifull elivated plain at which place the Yellow Stone river is about 250 yards distant from the Missouri
West	1	mile to the lower part of the timber in a bend to the Lard Side back of which and on the river below is high bottom, and the upper plains are not So high as below and butifull as far as Can be Seen
N. 32° W	3	miles to a point of the timbered bottom on the Lad Side op-posit a low bluff between two points of wooded bottom ½ a mile distant from each a butifull plain back, Several high open Situations between the wood land in the S. bend.
West	<u>3</u>	miles to a point of Small Willows on the Sd. Side opposit a low white bluff bordering a butifull riseing Plain, Some woodland below this bluff on the L. S. and a thick wooded bottom on the S. Side in this course the river is wide and crouded with Sand bars a little above the low bluff on the L. S. a timbered bottom commences. here the countrey runs gradually from the river on the L. S.
	miles 8 =	

79

1. Lewis was considering a site for a military and fur-trading post; Clark's proposed location is marked on *Atlas* maps 35, 48, and 56; Lewis's site would be about one mile west. The American Fur Company's Fort Union (1828), the Sublette and Campbell post Fort William (1832), and the military post of Fort Buford (1866), were all built, not in the point as Lewis proposed, but on the north side of the Missouri, in Williams County, North Dakota, probably to avoid the flooding which Lewis noted. Mattison (GR), 59–60; MRC map 60.

2. Also given on *Atlas* map 35, in Clark's hand.

3. *Atlas* map 35 says "S," which is correct but in opposition to both captains' journals.

4. Their first camp in present Montana was in Roosevelt County, about a mile below and opposite the village of Nohly, Richland County. *Atlas* maps 35, 48, 56; MRC map 60.

Chapter Twelve

From the Yellowstone to the Musselshell (Part 1)

April 28–May 5, 1805

[Lewis]   *Sunday April 28th 1805.*

Set out this morning at an early hour; the wind was favourable and we
employed our sails to advantage. Capt Clark walked on shore this morning,[1] and I proceeded with the party.   the country through which we
passed today is open as usual and very broken on both sides near the river
hills, the bottoms are level fertile and partially covered with timber.   the
hills and bluffs exhibit their usual mineral appearances, some birnt hills
but no appearance of Pumicestone; coal is in great abundance and the
salts still increase in quantity; the banks of the river and sandbars are incrusted with it in many places and appear perfectly white as if covered
with snow or frost.—[2]   the woods are now green, tho' the plains and
meadows appear to abate of the verdure those below exhibited some days
past.   we past three small runs today.   two falling in on the Stard. and
one on the Lard. side,[3] they are but small afford but little water and head
a few miles back in the hills.   we saw great quantities of game today; consisting of the common and mule deer, Elk, Buffaloe, and Antelopes; also
four brown bear, one of which was fired on and wounded by one of the
party but we did not get it; the beaver have cut great quantities of timber;

saw a tree nearly 3 feet in diameter that had been felled by them. Capt. Clark in the course of his walk killed a deer and a goose; & saw three black bear; he thinks the bottoms are not so wide as they have been for some days past.—

	Courses and distances 28th of April.[4]	miles
North	to a point of timber on Lard. side.	2 ¼
N. 40° W.	to the upper part of the point on Lard. opposite to a high rugged bluf	1
S. 56 W.	to a high bluff on the Lard. side just above a timbered bottom, and opposite a point of woodland on Stard. side	2 ¾
S. 85 W.	to the center of a bend on Lard. side.	1
N. 25 W.	to a point of timbered land on Lard. passing a point on Stard. side at 1 ¼ mes.	3
N. 18 W.	to the lower point of the timber in a bend on Stard. side	2
S. 4 W.	to a point of woodland on Stard. side.	4
S. 10 W.	to a high bluff point on Lard. side, the river making a considerable bend to S. E.	2
N. 80 W.	to a point of woodland on the Lard. side	2
N. 45 W.	to a high bluff point on the Stard. side.	1
S. 80 W.	to a point of woodland on Stard. side.	3

Miles 24

[Clark]   28th *of April Sunday 1805*

a fine day   river falling, wind favourable from the S. E. and moderate, I walked on Shore to view the Countrey, from the top of the high hills, I beheld a broken & open Countrey on both Sides, near the river Some verry handsom low plains, I killd. a Deer & a goose, Saw three black bear great numbers of Elk antelopes & 2 Gangues of Buffalow, the hills & Bluffs Shew the Straturs of Coal, and burnt appearances in maney places, in and about them I could find no appearance of Pumice Stone, the wood land have a green appearance, the Plains do not look So green as below, The bottoms are not So wide this afternoon as below   Saw four bear this evening, one of the men Shot at one of them. The Antilopes are nearly

1. Aspect of the Missouri River, April 28, 1805, Voorhis no. 1

red, on that part which is Subject to change i' e' the Sides & ⅔ of the back from the head, the other part as white as Snow, 2 Small runs fall in on the S. Side and one this evening on the Lard Side those runs head at a fiew miles in the hills and discharge but little water, the Bluffs in this part as also below Shew different Straturs of Coal or carbonated wood, and Coloured earth, such as dark brown, yellow a lightish brown, & a dark red &c.

	miles	*Course & distance the 28th of April*[5]
N.	2 ¼	to a point of timber on the Lad Side
N. 40° W.	1	to the upper part of the point on the L. Side opposit is a high ruged Bluff on the S. S.
S. 56° W.	2 ¾	To a high bluff on the Ld Side opposit to a point of woods & just above a wood
S. 85° W.	1	To the center of a bend on the Lad Side
N. 25° W.	3	To a point of timbered land on the Ld. Side passing a point on the Std. Side at 1 ¼ miles
N. 18° W.	2	To the lower point of a timber in a bend to the Starboard Side.
S. 4° W.	4	To a point of wood Land on the Sd Side
S. 10° W.	2	to a high bluff point on the L. Side the river making a considerable bend S. E.
N. 80° W.	2	to a point of wood land on the Lard Side

N. 45° W.	1	to a high Bluff pt. on the Std Side
S. 80° W.	3	To a point of wood land on the Std Side
	24	

1. Accompanied by Charbonneau, according to Ordway.

2. The party is passing through country underlain by the Paleocene Tongue River Member of the Fort Union Formation; lignite coal is abundant in it. The increased amounts of salts result from increased aridity of climate and increased seasonal discharge of ground water.

3. One of those on the starboard would be Little Muddy Creek, in Roosevelt County, Montana. The one from the south in Richland County would be Otis Creek, near which they camped. *Atlas* maps 35, 48, 56; MRC map 60.

4. Also given on *Atlas* map 35, in both captains' hands.

5. At this point in Voorhis No. 1 is a small sketch (fig. 1), presumably representing some aspect of the river.

[Lewis]   *Monday April 29th 1805.*

Set out this morning at the usual hour; the wind was moderate; I walked on shore with one man.[1]   about 8 A. M. we fell in with two brown or ⟨yellow⟩ [X: *White*] bear; both of which we wounded; one of them made his escape, the other after my firing on him pursued me seventy or eighty yards, but fortunately had been so badly wounded that he was unable to pursue so closely as to prevent my charging my gun; we again repeated our fir and killed him.[2]   it was a male not fully grown, we estimated his weight at 300 lbs. not having the means of ascertaining it precisely. The legs of this bear are somewhat longer than those of the black, as are it's tallons and tusks incomparably larger and longer.   the testicles, which in the black bear are placed pretty well back between the thyes and contained in one pouch like those of the dog and most quadrupeds, are in the yellow or brown bear placed much further forward, and are suspended in seperate pouches from two to four inches asunder; it's colour is yellowish brown, the eyes small, black, and piercing; the front of the fore legs near the feet is usually black; the fur is finer thicker and deeper than that of the black bear.   these are all the particulars in which this anamal appeared to me to differ from the black bear; it is a much more furious and formidable anamal, and will frequently pursue the hunter when wounded. it is asstonishing to see the wounds they will bear before they can be put to death. the Indians may well fear this anamal equiped as they generally are with their bows and arrows or indifferent fuzees, but in the hands of skillfull riflemen they are by no means as formidable or dangerous as they have been represented. game is still very abundant we can scarcely cast our eyes in any direction without percieving deer Elk Buffaloe or Antelopes. The quantity of wolves appear to increase in the same proportion; they generally hunt in parties of six eight or ten; they kill a great number of the Antelopes at this season; the Antelopes are yet meagre and the females are big with young; the wolves take them most generally in attempting to swim the river; in this manner my dog caught one drowned it and brought it on shore; they are but clumsey swimers, tho' on land when in good order, they are extreemly fleet and dureable. we have frequently seen the wolves in pursuit of the Antelope in the plains; they appear to decoy a single one from a flock, and then pursue it, alturnately relieving each other untill they take it. on joining Capt Clark he informed me that he had seen a female and faun of the big-horned anamal; that they ran for some distance with great aparent ease along the side of the river bluff where it was almost perpendicular; two of the party fired on them while in motion without effect. we took the flesh of the bear on board and proceeded. Capt. Clark walked on shore this evening, killed a deer, and saw several of the bighorned anamals. there is more appearance of coal today than we have yet seen, the stratas are 6 feet thick in some instances; the earth has been birnt in many places, and always appears in stratas on the same level with the stratas of coal.[3] we came too this evening in the mouth of a little river, which falls in on the Stard. side. This stream is about 50 yards wide from bank to bank; the water occupyes about 15 yards. the banks are of earth only, abrupt, tho' not high— the bed, is of mud principally. Capt Clark, who was up this streeam about three miles, informed me that it continued about the same width, that it's current was gentle and it appeared navigable for perogus it meanders through an extensive, fertile, and beautifull vally as far as could bee seen about N. 30° W. there was but one solitary tree to be seen on the banks of this river after it left the bottom of the Missouri. the water of this river is clear, with a brownish yelow tint. here the highlands receede from the Missouri, leaving the vally formed by the river from seven to eight miles wide, and reather lower then usual.— This stream my friend Capt. C. named Marthas river[4] ⟨in honor of Miss M F—⟩

	Courses and distances of the 29th of April[5]	Miles
N. 45° W.	to a point of woodland on Lard. side opposite to a high bluff on Stard.	3
West	to a point of woodland Stard. opposite to a bluff	2
N. 80 W.	along the Stard. point opposite a high sharp bluff	1 ½
N. 45 W	to a point of woodland Lard. opposite to a bluff	2
N. 55 W.	to a point of woodland Lard. opposite to a bluff	3
N. 65 W.	to a bluff point on Stard. side	1 ¼
S. 30 W.	to the upper point of the high timber on the Lard. side in a bend of the river	3
S. 85 W.	to a point of woodland on Stard. opposite a bluff	1 ¼
N. 55 W.	to a commencement of a bluff on Stard. Side, passing a sand point at 2 ½ miles on Lard. side	3 ½
S. 75 W.	to a point of woodland on Lard. passing the poit. of a sandbar on Stard., the river making a deep bend to the South	1 ½
S. 75 W.	to the entrance of a Marthys[6] river in a bend on Stard. where we encamped for the night. this stream we call [*blank*]	3
		25

[Clark]   *29th of April Monday 1805*

Set out this morning at the usial hour.   the wind is moderate & from the N E   had not proceeded far eer we Saw a female & her faun of the Bighorn animal on the top of a Bluff lying, the noise we made allarmed them and they came down on the Side of the bluff which had but little Slope being nearly purpindicular, I directed two men to kill those ana-mals, one went on the top and the other man near the water   they had two Shots at the doe while in motion without effect, Those animals run & Skiped about with great ease on this declivity & appeared to prefur it to the leavel bottom or plain. Capt Lewis & one man walkd on Shore and he killed

86

a yellow Bear & the man with him wounded one other, after getting the flesh of the bear on bord which was not far from the place we brackfast, we proceeded on   Saw 4 gangus of buffalow and great numbers of Antelopes in every direction   also Saw Elk and Several wolves, I walked on Shore in the evening & killed a Deer which was So meager as to be unfit for use   The hills Contain more Coal, and has a greater appearance of being burnt that below, the burnt parts appear on a parrilel with the Stratiums of Coal, we Came too in the mouth of a Little river on the S. S. which is about 50 or 60 yards from bank to bank, I was up this Stream 3 miles it continues its width and glides with a gentle Current, its water is about 15 yards wide at this time, and appears to be navagable for Canoes &c.   it meanders through a butifull & extencive vallie as far as can be Seen about N 30° W. I saw only a Single tree in this fertile vallie   The water of the River is clear of a yellowish Colour, we call this river Martheys river in honor to the Selebrated M. F

Here the high land widen from five to Eight miles and much lower than below, Saw Several of the big horn animals this evening. The Wolves distroy great numbers of the antilopes by decoying those animals Singularly out in the plains and prosueing them alternetly, those antelopes are Curious and will approach any thing which appears in motion near them &c.

	miles	*Course & Distance the 29th of April*
N. 45° W	3	to a point of wood land on the Ld. Side opsd. to a high Bluff on the Stard Side
West	2	to a wood land on the Std Side opsd. a Bluff
N 80° W.	1 ½	on the Std point, a high Sharp bluff
N. 45° W.	2	to a point of wood land on the L. Side, a high bluff opposit on the S. S.
N. 55° W	3	to a point of timbered land on the Lard Side a Bluff on the S. Side
N. 65° W	1 ¼	to a Bluff point on the Stard. Side.
S 30° W.	3	to the upper point of a high timber on the L. Side in a lard bend of the river
S. 85° W	1 ¼	to a pt. of timber on Stard. Sd. opsd. a bluff

N 55° W	3 ½	the commencement of a bluff on S. S. passg a Sand pt. at 2 ½ miles on the Lard. S.
S 75° W.	1 ½	to a point of wood land on the passing a Sand bar the river makeing a Deep bend to the South
N. 75° W.	3	to the enterence of a river on the Stard Side in a bend, where we encamped for the night.
	25	

1. Lewis's route and the site of the encounter with the bears appear on *Atlas* maps 48 and 57.

2. Their first actual specimen of the grizzly bear from which Lewis wrote the first scientific description of the species. He is inexplicably wrong about the testicles. See also, May 5, 1805. Cutright (LCPN), 140–42.

3. The lower part of the Tongue River Member of the Fort Union Formation contains abundant lignite coal. This area is part of the Culbertson and Girard coal (lignite) fields.

4. Present Big Muddy Creek, in Roosevelt County, Montana, the eastern boundary of the Fort Peck Indian Reservation (Sioux and Assiniboine). After the name are the crossed out words "in honour of Miss M F"; this would be the "Selebrated M. F" referred to by Clark, below, whose identity remains obscure. Camp was just above the creek in Roosevelt County. *Atlas* maps 48 and 57; MRC map 61.

5. Also given on *Atlas* map 35, in both captains' hands.

6. "Marthys" may have been a later interpolation.

[Lewis]   *Tuesday April 30th 1805.*

Set out at sunrise.   the wind blew hard all last night, and continued to blow pretty hard all day, but not so much, as to compell us to ly by.   the country as usual is bare of timber; the river bottoms are level and fertile and extensive, but possess but little timber and that of an indifferent quality even of it's kind; principally low cottonwood, either too small for building, or for plank or broken and dead at top and unsound in the center of the trunk.   saw great quantities of game as usual.   Capt. Clark walked on shore the greater part of the day, ⟨the Interpreter, Charbono and his Indian woman attended him.⟩   past some old Indian lodges built of drift wood; they appear to be of antient date and not recently inhabited. I walked on shore this evening and killed a buck Elk, in tolerable order; it appeared to me to be the largest I had seen, and was therefore induced to measure it; found it five feet three inches from the point of the hoof, to the top of the sholders; the leg and hoof being placed as

nearly as possible in the same position they would have been had the anamal been standing.—

	Courses and distances of 30th April[1]	miles
S. 15° W.	to a point of timbered land on the Stard side passing a sand point at ¾ of a me. Lard.	2 ½
S. 22 W.	to the upper point of the high timber in the center of a bend Lard side at the commencement of a bluff	1 ½
S. 85 W.	to a point of timbered land on Stard side opposite to a bluff.	1
S. 75 W.	to a point of timber at the upper part of a bluff in a bend on Lard. side	½
N. 40 W.	to the point of a sandbar on the Lard. side, passing a willow point at two miles and a large sandbar on Stard.	5
S. 40 W.	to a point of woodland on Stard. opposite to a bluff on Lard. the river making a considerable bend on Lard. side	3 ½
N. 70 W.	to a point of woodland on the Lard. side, passing, at the commencement of this course, a large sand Island in the Lard. bend.	3
S. 25 W	to the upper part of the high timber on the Lard. side.	2 ½
West	to a point of high timber on the Lard. side, a large sand island in the bend to the Stard. side.	3 ½
N. 80 W.	to a point of high woods on the Lard. side opposite to which we encamped on a sandbar Stard. side	1[2]

Miles 24

[Clark]   30th *of April Tuesday 1805*

The wind blew hard from the N E all last night, we Set out at Sunrise
the wind blew hard the greater part of the day and part of the time
favourable, we did not lie by to day on account of the wind   I walked
on Shore to day our interpreter & his Squar followed, in my walk the
Squar found & brought me a bush Something like the Current,[3] which
She Said bore a delicious froot and that great quantites grew on the Rocky
Mountains, this Srub was in bloom has a yellow flower with a deep Cup,
the froot when ripe is yellow and hangs in bunches like ⟨graps⟩ Cheries,
Some of those berries yet remained on the bushes. The bottoms above

the mouth of the last river is extensive level & fertile and covered with in-different timber in the points, the up land appear to rise gradually, I saw Great numbers of Antelopes, also Scattering Buffalow, Elk, Deer, wolves, Gees, ducks & Grows— I Killed 2 Gees which we dined on to day— Capt Lewis walked on Shore and killed an elk this evening, and we Came too & camped on the S. S.[4] the Countrey on both Sides have a butifull appearance.

	miles	Course & Distance the 30th of April
S. 15° W.	2 ½	to a point of timbered land on the Sd Side passed a Sand point at ¾ of a mile L. S.
S 22° W.	1 ½	to the upper point of the high timber on the Ld. Side in a bend a Bluff on the Lard.
S 85° W.	1	to a point of timbered land on the Std. Side opposit to a bluff on the Lard Side
S 75° W	½	to a point of timber at the upper part of a bluff in a bend to the Lard Side
N. 40° W.	5	to a point of a Sand bar on the Lard Side passing a Willow point at 2 miles, and a large Sand bar on S. S.
S 40° W.	3 ½	to a point of wood land on Std. Side opposit to a Bluff on the L. Side the [river] makeing a considerable bend L. S
N. 70° W.	3	to a point of wood land on the Lard. Side passing at the commencement of this course a large Sand Island in the Lard. bend.
S. 25° W.	2 ½	miles to the upper part of a high timber on the Lard. Side
West	3 ½	to a point of high timber on the Lard Side a large Sand Island in the bend to the Std. Side.
N. 80° W	1	to a point of high woods on the Larboard Side
	24	

1. Also given on *Atlas* map 35, in both captains' hands.

2. On *Atlas* map 36 this last course has been combined with the one above as "West 4¼."

3. The Missouri, or buffalo, currant (see April 20, 1805). The species commonly has both yellow or purple to black fruits on different shrubs. Fernald, 751; Barkley, 134–35; Booth & Wright, 107; Hitchcock & Cronquist, 202; Kartesz & Kartesz, 435. Botanists

recognize three closely related currant species along the upper Missouri. *Ribes odoratum* (the one noticed) is more eastern, principally in South Dakota and eastern Montana, while *R. aureum* Pursh, golden current, is primarily in western Montana. The two species apparently come together in central Montana along the Missouri River. Thus, Sacagawea considered the currant near the mouth of the Yellowstone River (*R. odoratum*) the same as the one from the Rocky Mountains (*R. aureum*). The two species differ mainly in flower length. In addition, a third species, the wild black currant (*R. americanum*), occurs in eastern and western Montana and may occur on the Missouri River in central Montana as well. The latter has black fruits while the other two species have fruits which vary from yellow or orange, to purple or black.

4. In Richland County, Montana, in the neighborhood of present Brockton, Roosevelt County. *Atlas* maps 35, 48, 57; MRC map 62.

[Lewis and Clark]   [*Weather, April 1805*][1]

Day of the month	State of thermometer at ☉ rise	Weather	Wind at ☉ rise	State of Thermometer at 4 P. M.	Weather	Wind at 4 P. M.	State of the River raised or falln.	fet	Inch
April 1st	33 a[2]	c	N. W.	43 a	c. a. t. l. r. & H.[3]	W	f		1 1
2cd	28 a	c a r	N. W	38 a	f. a. c.	W.	f		5
3rd	24 a	f.	N.	44 a	f.	W.[4]	f		4
4th	36 a	f.	S.	55 a	f.	N. W.	f		4
5th	30 a	f.	N. W.	39 a	f.	N.[5]	f		2
6th	19 a	f.	N.	48 a	c.	N. W.	f		1
7th	28 a	f.	W.	64 a	f.	S. W.	r		2[6]
8th	19 a	f.	N. W.	56 a	f.	N. W.	f		2
9th	38 a	f.	S. E.	70 a	f	S. W.	f		½
10th	42 a	f	E	74 a	f	S W.	r		⅛
11th	42 a	f	N W	76 a	f	W.	f		½
12th	56 a	f	N. W.	74 a	car T&L	W.	r		⅛
13th	58 a	f	S. E.	80 a	f	S. E.	f		1
14th	52 a	c	S E	82 a	f	S. W.	f		¾
15th	51 a	f	E	78 a	f	S W.	f		½
16th	54 a	f	S E	78 a	f	S.	f		½
17th	56 a	f	N. E.	74 a	c	S. W.	f		½
18th	52 a	f	N. E.	64 a	c	N.			
19th	45 a[7]	c	N. W.	56 a	c	N. W.			
20th	40 a	c	N W	42 a	c a s	N W			
21st	28 a	f	N W	40 a	c	N. W.	f		½
22nd	34 a	f a c	W.	40	f	N W	r		2

23rd	34 a	f	W.	52	c	N. W.	r	2
24th	40 a	f	N.	56	f	N	r	1
25th	36 a	f.	N	52 a	f	N W	r	2
26th	32 a	f	S	63 a	f	S E	r	3
27th	36 a	f	S W	64 a	f	N W	f	2
28th	44 a	f	S. E.	63 a	f	S E	f	1½
29th	42 a	f	N E	64 a	f	E	f	1½
30th	50 a	f	N. W.	58 a	f	S E	f	½

[*Remarks*][8]

1st   ice ceases to run   A fine refreshing shower of rain fell about 2 P. M.   this was the first shower of rain that we had witnessed since the fifteenth of September 1804 tho' it several times has fallen in very small quantities, and was noticed in this diary of the weather.   the cloud came from the west, and was attended by hard [*EC: thun*]der and Lightning. I have observed that all thunderclouds in the Western part of the continent, proceed from the westerly quarter, as they do in the Atlantic States.   the air is remarkably dry and pure in this open country, very little rain or snow ether winter or summer.   the atmosphere is more transparent than I ever obseved it in any country through which I have passed.

2cd   rained hard and without intermission last night

3rd   frost last night[9]

4th   Observed a flock of brant passing up the river today; the wind blew very ha[r]d as it dose frequently in this quarter; there is sarcely any timber to brake the wind from the river, & the country on both sides being level plains, wholy destitute of timber, the wind blows ⟨over them⟩ with astonishing violence.   in this open country the winds form a great obstruction to the navigation of this river particularly with small vessels, which can neither ascend or descend should the wind be the least violent.—

6th   This day a flock of *cherry* or *cedar* birds[10] were seen, one of the men killed, several of them which gave me an opportunity of ex-

amining them. they are common in the United States; usually
ascociate in large flocks and are frequently distructive to the
chery orchards, and in winter in the lower parts of the states of
Virginia & Maryland feed on the buries of the Cedar. they are
a small bluish brown bird, crested with a tuft of dark brown
feathers with a narrow black stripe passing on each side of the
head underneath the eye from the base of the upper beak to the
back of the head. it is distinguished more particularly by some
of the shorter feathers of the wing, which are tiped with a red
spots that have much the appearance at a little distance of seal-
ing wax. all the birds that we believe visit this country have now
returned.—

7th   Visited by a Ricara Chief   wind very high. set out on our voyage
at 5 P. M. encampt a 4 me. S. S.

8th   the Kildee, and large Hawk have returned.[11] buds of the Elm
swolen and appear red—[12] the only birds that I obseved during
the winter at Fort Mandan was the Missouri Magpie, a bird of the
Corvus genus, the raven in immence numbers,[13] the small [*EC:
wood*] woodpecker or *sapsucker*[14] as they are sometimes called,
⟨and⟩ the [*EC: beau*] beautifull eagle, or *calumet bird,* so called
from the circumstance of the natives decorating their pipe-stems
with it's plumage and the Prairie Hen or grouse.—[15]

9th   the Crow has also returned   saw the first today. & the corvus
bird disappears   the Musquitoes revisit us, saw several of them.
Capt. Clark brought me a flower in full blo. it is a stranger
to me.— the peroque ⟨shakes with⟩ is so unsteady that I can
scarcely write

10th   The prarie lark, bald Eagle, & the large plover have returned.[16]
the grass begins to spring, and the leaf buds of the willow to
appear.— Chery birds disappear.

11th   The lark wood pecker,[17] with yellow wings, and a black spot on the
brest common to the U' States has appeared, with sundry small
birds.— many plants begin to appear above the ground.— saw

a large white gull today— the Eagle is now laying their eggs, and the gees have mated.— the Elm, large leafed, willow and the bush which bears a red berry, called by the engages *greas de buff* are in blume—[18]

12th   small shower from the W. attended with hard wind.

13th   The leaves of the Choke cherry are about half grown; the Cotton wood is in blume   the flower of this tree resembles that of the aspen in form, and is of a deep perple colour.—[19]

15th   several flocks of white brant with black wings pass us today, their flight was to the N. W.   the trees now begin to assume a green appearance, tho' the earth at the debth of about three feet is not yet thawed, which we discovered by the banks of the river, falling in ⟨to the river⟩ and disclosing a strata of frozen eath.—

16th   saw the first leather winged bat.[20]   it appeared about the size of those common to the U' States.

17th   thunder Shower passed above us from S. W. to N. E.   ⟨no⟩ rain where we were.[21]

18th   Wind very violent   a heavy dew this morning.   which is the first and only one we have seen since we passed the council bluffs last summer.   there is but little dew in this open country.—   saw a flock of pillecan[22] pass from S. W. to N. E.   they appeared to be on a long flight.—

19th   wind violent.   The trees have now put forth their leaves.   the goosbury, current, servisbury, and wild plumbs are in blume.

20th   wind violent.

21st   wind violent   white frost last night—   the earth friezed along the water's edge.—

22nd   wind very hard greater part of the day—

23d   Do   Do   Do   saw the first robbin.[23]   also the brown Curloo.

24th   do.   this morning.

25th   do.   until 5 oClock P M

27th wind very hard from 11 to 4 oClock

28th Vegetation has progressed but little since the 18th in short the change is scarcely perceptible.

1. Tabled weather observations by both captains are found for the whole of April 1805 in Lewis's Codex Fe and Clark's Codex I. They are accompanied in each case by remarks in both the margins of the tables and separately. There are similar observations and remarks in Clark's Codex C through April 7, 1805, the date of departure from Fort Mandan, when Codex C was apparently sent down the Missouri with the keelboat. Lewis's Weather Diary has observations and marginal remarks through April 9, but lacks the 4:00 p.m. temperature, weather, and wind observations. It would thus appear that Lewis took the Weather Diary with him up the Missouri, although there is no clear reason why he did not continue to use it after April 9. (See Appendix B, vol. 2.) Significant differences in the tabled observations between the four sources are noted. The table given here follows Lewis in Codex Fe.

2. Clark in Codex C has "38 a."

3. Clark in Codex C appears to have "c. a t. c. h. & r."

4. Clark in Codex I has "N."

5. Clark in Codex C has "N W."

6. Clark in Codex C has "½."

7. Clark in Codex I has "54 a."

8. The two captains have remarks for the month of April in both the margins of the weather tables and in separate sections in Lewis's Codex Fe and Clark's Codex I. Clark has marginal and separate remarks to April 7 in Codex C; Lewis has marginal remarks to April 9 in his Weather Diary. All these have been colated, basically following Lewis in Codex Fe, to provide the fullest coverage without duplication. Coues penciled in some words in Codex Fe that were partially missing due to paper damage.

9. Lewis in the Weather Diary has also "a white frost & Some ice on the edge of river visit by Mr. la rock & MacKinzey, pack up Sundry articles."

10. *Bombycilla cedrorum* [AOU, 619], cedar waxwing.

11. The killdeer, *Charadrius vociferus* [AOU, 273], already known to science. Burroughs, 225. The hawk could be any of a number of species in the area.

12. In the Weather Diary Lewis calls it the "bitter elm."

13. The common raven, *Corvus corax* [AOU, 486], known to science and not described further.

14. Maybe either the hairy woodpecker, *Picoides villosus* [AOU, 393], or the downy woodpecker, *P. pubescens* [AOU, 394], although Holmgren suggests the yellow-bellied sapsucker, *Sphyrapicus varius* [AOU, 402]. Burroughs, 240–41; Holmgren, 33.

15. The calumet bird is the golden eagle, *Aquila chrysaetos* [AOU, 349]; prairie hen is the sharp-tailed grouse.

16. Perhaps the horned lark, *Eremophila alpestris* [AOU, 474]. Reid & Gannon, 19. The plover is the black-bellied plover, *Pluvialis squatarola* [AOU, 270].

17. The northern or common flicker, *Colaptes auratus* [AOU, 412]; here a yellow-shafted subspecies. Burroughs, 241; Holmgren, 34.

18. Clark in Codex I says "Small leaf willows . . . in blum."

19. Lewis compares the plains cottonwood to the quaking aspen, *Populus tremuloides* Michx. Fernald, 521–22. The purple color refers to the color of elongate male catkins or flowers of both species.

20. The bat may be any one of a number of species.

21. Clark has this under date of April 16 in Codex I, but with a pointing hand from April 17.

22. The American white pelican, *Pelecanus erythrorhynchos* [AOU, 125].

23. Probably the ubiquitous American robin, *Turdus migratorius* [AOU, 761].

[Lewis]   *Wednesday May 1st 1805.*

Set out this morning at an early, the wind being favourable we used our sales which carried us on at a good pace untill about 12 OCk. when the wind became so high that the small canoes were unable to proceed   one of them which seperated from us just befor the wind became so violent, is now lying on the opposite side of the river,[1] being unable to rejoin us in consequence of the waves, which during those gusts run several feet high.   we came too on the Lard. shore in a handsome bottom well stocked with cottonwood timber; here the wind compelled us to spend the ballance of the day.[2]   we sent out some hunters who killed a buffaloe, an Elk, a goat and two beaver.   game is now abundant.   the country appears much more pleasant and fertile than that we have passed for several days; the hills are lower, the bottoms wider, and better stocked with timber, which consists principally of cottonwood, not however of large size; the under-growth willow on the verge of the river and sandbars, rose bushes, red willow and the broad leafed willow in the bottom lands; the high country on either side of the river is one vast plain, intirely destitute of timber, but is apparently fertile, consisting of a dark rich mellow looking lome. John Shields sick today with the rheumatism. Shannon killed a bird of the plover kind.[3]   weight one pound.   it measured from the tip of the toe, to the extremity of the beak, 1 foot 10 Inches; from tip to tip of wings when extended 2 F. 5 I.; Beak 3⅝ inches; tale 3⅛ inches; leg and toe 10 Ins.—   the eye black, piercing, prominent and moderately large.   the legs are flat thin, slightly imbricated and of a pale sky blue colour, being covered with feathers as far as the mustle extends down it, which is about half it's length. it has four toes on each foot, three of which, are connected by a web, the fourth is small and placed at the heel about the ⅛ of an inch up the leg. the nails are black and short, that of the middle toe is extreemly singular, consisting of two nails the one laping on or overlaying the other, the upper one somewhat the longest and sharpest. the tale contains eleven feathers of equal length, & of a bluish white colour. the boddy and underside of the wings, except the large feathers of the 1st & 2cd joints of the same, are white; as are also the feathers of the upper part of the 4th joint of the wing and part of those of the 3rd adjacent thereto, the large feathers of the 1st or pinion and the 2cd joint are black; a part of the larger feathers of the 3rd joint on the upper side and all the small feathers which cover the upper part of the wings are black, as are also the tuft of long feathers on each side of the body above the joining of the wing, leaving however a stripe of white betwen them on the back. the head and neck are shaped much like the grey plover, and are of a light brickdust ⟨colour⟩ brown; the beak is black and flat, largest where it joins the head, and from thence becoming thiner and tapering to a very sharp point, the upper chap being ⅛ of an inch the longest ⟨and⟩ turns down at the point and forms a little hook. the nostrils, which commence near the head are long, narrow, connected, and parallel with the beak; the beak is much curved, the curvature being upwards in stead of downwards as is common with most birds; the substance of the beak precisely resembles whalebone at a little distance, and is quite as flexable as that substance their note resembles that of the grey plover, tho' is reather louder and more varied, their habits appear also to be the same, with this difference; that it sometimes rests on the water and swims which I do not recollect having seen the plover do. this bird which I shall henceforth stile the *Missouri plover,* generally feeds about the shallow bars of the river; to collect it's food which consists of [*blank*], it immerces it's beak in the water and throws it's head and beak from side to side at every step it takes.

Courses and distances of this day[4]

N. 88 W.	to the upper point of some high timber in a bend on the Stard. side	1 ½

South	to the upper point of a timbered bottom Lard. Sd.	2
S. 26° W.	to a bluff on the Lard. side	1 ½
S. 60° W	to a single tree on a point Lard. side	1
West	to a point of woodland Lard. side	2
S. 60° W.	to a point of woodland just beneath the upper point of an elivated plane on Stard. side. one mile short of which we encamped on the Lard.	2
		10

[Clark]   *May the 1st Wednesday 1805*

We Set out at Sun rise under a Stiff Breeze from the East, the morning Cool & Cloudy.   one man J. Shields Sick with rhumetism—   one of the men (Shannon) Shot a Gull or pleaver, which is about the Size of an Indian hen, with a Sharp pointed bill turning up & 4 Inches long, the head and neck of a light brown, the breast, the underfeathers of the 2nd and 3d joint of the wings, the Short feathers on the upper part of the 3rd joint of the wings, down the back the rump & tail white. The large feathers of the 1st joints of the wing the upper feathers of the 2d joints of the wings, on the body on the joints of the wing and the bill is black.—   the legs long and of a Skie blue. The feet webed &c. This fowl may be properly Stiled the Missouri Pleaver—   the wind became verry Hard and we put too on the L. Side, as the wind Continued with Some degree of violence and the waves too high for the Canoes we were obliged to Stay all day

	miles	*Course & Distance 1st of May*
N. 88° W.	1 ½	to the upper point of Some high timber in a bend to the Std. Side
South	2	to the upper part of a timber Ld Side
S. 26° W.	1 ½	to a Bluff on the Lard Side
S 60° W	1	to a Single tree on a point the Ld Side
West	2	to a point wood land Lard Side
S. 60° W.	2	to a wood at the upper part of an elivated plain on the S. Side, one mile Short of which we camped
	10	

[Lewis]   *May 1st 1805.*[5]

Shannon killed a bird of the plover kind the weight one pound.— eye black percing and prominent [*EC: avocet (Recurvirostra)*]

Measure	F.	Inchs
from the tip of the toe to the extremity of the beak	1	10
from tip to tip of wing when extended	2	5
length of beak		3 ⅝
length of tale		3 ⅛
length of leg ⟨thy,⟩ and toe		10

the legs are flat, of pale skye blue colour and but slightly imbricated. the second joint, as low as the mustle extends is covered with feathers which is about half it's length. it has three toes on a foot connected by a web. there is also a small toe on each foot placed about the eighth of an inch up the leg behind. the nails are black and short and those of the middle toes ar singular—there being two nails on each the one above the other the upper one the longest and sharpest.— the tale contains eleven feathers of the same length of a bluish white colour. the body and under side of the wings except the large feathers of the 1 & 2cd joints of the wings are white, as are also the feathers of the upper part of the 4th joint of the wing. and some of those of the 3rd adjoining.— the large feathers of the pinion or first ⟨joint⟩ & the second joint ⟨and a part of those of the third on the⟩ are black; a part of the larger feathers of the third-joint on the upper side and all the smaller feathers which cover the upper part of these joints ar black; as are also the tuft of long feathers on each side of the body above the joining of the wing, leaving however a stripe of white between them on the back. the head and neck are shaped much like the grey plover, and is a light ⟨yellowish⟩ brickdust brown. the beak is black and flat, largest where it joins the head and from thence tapering every way gradually to a very sharp point the upper beak being ⅛ of an inch the longest turning down at the point. the nostrils are parrallal with the beak and are long narrow and connected. the beak is curvated and invirted; the Curvature being upwards in stead of downwards as those of most birds are— the substance of the beak is as flexable as whalebone and ⟨to all appe⟩ at a little distance precisely resembles that substance. their note is like that of the common whistling or grey plover tho' reather louder, and more varied, and their habits are the same with that bird so far as I have been enabled to learn, with this difference however that this bird some-times lights in the water and swims.— it generally feads about the shal-low bars of the river; to collect it's food, it immerces it's beak in the water, and thows it's head and beak from side to side at every step it takes.

1. In this canoe, Whitehouse tells us, were he and another man who were "obledged to lay out all night without any blanket."

2. In Roosevelt County, Montana, in the vicinity of the later Elkhorn Point. *Atlas* maps 35, 48, 57; MRC map 62.

3. An American avocet, *Recurvirostra americana* [AOU, 225], already known to science. The plover used for comparison is probably the lesser golden-plover, *Pluvialis dominica* [AOU, 272]. Burroughs, 225, 228–29. Someone drew a vertical line through this passage, apparently in red.

4. Also given on *Atlas* map 36, in both captains' hands.

5. Lewis's zoological note from Codex Q; the bird is the American avocet as identified above for this day.

[Lewis]   *Thursday May 2ed 1805*

The wind continued violent all night nor did it abate much of it's vio-lence this morning, when at daylight it was attended with snow which continued to fall untill about 10 A. M. being about one inch deep, it formed a singular contrast with the ⟨trees and other⟩ vegitation which was considerably advanced. some flowers had put forth in the plains, and the leaves of the cottonwood were as large as a dollar. sent out some hunters[1] who killed 2 deer 3 Elk and several buffaloe; on our way this evening we also shot three beaver along the shore; these anamals in conse-quence of not being hunted are extreemly gentle, where they are hunted they never leave their lodges in the day, the flesh of the beaver is esteemed a delecacy among us; I think the tale a most delicious morsal, when boiled it resembles in flavor the fresh tongues and sounds of the codfish,[2] and is usually sufficiently large to afford a plentifull meal for two men. Joseph Fields one of the hunters who was out today found several yards of scarlet cloth which had been suspended on the bough of a tree near an old in-dian hunting cam[p], where it had been left as a sacrefice to the deity by the indians, probably of the Assinniboin nation, it being a custom with them as well as all the nations inhabiting the waters of the Missouri so far as they are known to us, to offer or sacrefice in this manner to the deity watever they may be possessed off which they think most acceptable to him, and very honestly making their own feelings the test of those of the deity offer him the article which they most prize themselves. this being the most usual method of weshiping the great sperit as they term the deity, is practiced on interesting occasions, or to produce the happy eventuation of the important occurrances incident to human nature, such as relief from hungar or mallady, protection from their enemies or the delivering them into their hands, and with such as cultivate, to prevent the river's overflowing and distroying their crops &c. screfices of a similar kind are also made to the deceased by their friends and relatives. the are was very piercing this evening the [water] friezed on the oars as they rowed. the wind dying at 5 P. M. we set out.—

Courses and distance 2cd May[3]

S. 70° E.	to the upper point of the timber on the Lard. side in a bend passing a point of timber on the Lard. side at ¼ of a mile	2
S. 10° E.	to a point of woodland on the Stard. side	½
S. 30° W.	to a point of low timber on the Lard side, a little above which on the Stard. side we encamped, having passed some ⟨extensive⟩ wider fertile bottoms and beatifull high level plains	2
		4 ½

every thing which is incomprehensible to the indians they call *big medicine,* and is the opperation of the presnts and power of the *great sperit.* this morning one of the men shot the indian dog that had followed us for several days, he would steal their cooked provision.

[Clark]   *May 2nd Thursday 1805*

The wind blew verry hard all the last night, this morning about Sunrise began to Snow, (The Thermomtr. at 28 abov o) and Continued untill about 10 oClock, at which time it Seased, the wind Continued hard untill about 2 P. M. the Snow which fell to day was about 1 In deep, a verry extroadernaley Climate, to behold the trees Green & flowers Spred on

the plain, & Snow an inch deep.   we Set out about 3 oClock and proceeded on about five ½ miles and encamped on the Std Side,[4] the evening
verry cold, Ice freesing to the Ores, I Shot a large beaver & Drewyer three
in walking on the bank, the flesh of those animals the party is fond of
eating &c.

Course & distance 2d May

S. 70° E.   2   miles to the upper point of the timber on the Lard Side in a
                        bend, passing a point of timber on the L. S. at a quarter of
                        a mile

S. 10° E   ½   mile to a point of wood Land on the Starboard Side

S. 30° W   2   miles to a point of Low timber on the Lard Side a little
            _____   above which on the Starboard Side we encamped
            4 ½

2 deer and 3 Elk killed

1. Including Drouillard, as Clark notes, and Joseph Field.
2. Lewis's codfish is probably the Atlantic cod, *Gadus morhua.* Nelson, 154. Sounds is a
term for the air bladder of a fish.
3. Also given on *Atlas* map 36, in Lewis's hand.
4. In Richland County, Montana, in the vicinity of the crossing of Montana Highway
251. *Atlas* maps 36, 48, 57; MRC map 62.

[Lewis]   *Friday May 3rd 1805.*

   The morning being very could we did not set out as early as usual; ice
formed on a kettle of water ¼ of an inch thick.   the snow has melted generally in the bottoms, but the hills still remain covered.   on the lard side
at the distance of 2 miles we passed a curious collection of bushes which
had been tyed up in the form of a faciene[1] and standing on end in the
open bottom   it appeared to be about 30 feet high and ten or twelve feet
in diameter, this we supposed to have been placed there by the Indians,
as a sacrefice for some purpose. The wind continued to blow hard from
the West but not so strong as to compel us to ly by.   Capt. Clark walked
on shore and killed an Elk which he caused to be butched by the time I
arrived with the party, here we halted and dined being about 12 OCk. our

usual time of halting for that purpose. after dinner Capt. Clark pursued his walk, while I continued with the party, it being a rule which we had established, never to be absent at the same time from the party. the plains or high lands are much less elivated than they were, not being more than from 50 to 60 feet above the river bottom, which is also wider than usual being from 5 to 9 ms. in width; traces of the ancient beds of the river are visible in many places through the whole extent of this valley. since the hills have become lower the appearance of the stratas of coal burnt hills and pumice stone have in a great measure ceased;[2] I saw none today. we saw vast quantities of Buffaloe, Elk, deer principally of the long tale kind, Antelope or goats, beaver, geese, ducks, brant and some swan. near the entrance of the river mentioned in the 10th course of this day, we saw an unusual number of Porcupines from which we determined to call the river after that anamal, and accordingly denominated it *Porcupine river*.[3] this stream discharges itself into the Missouri on the Stard. side 2000 miles above the mouth of the latter, it is a beatifull bold runing stream, 40 yards wide at it's entrance; the water is transparent, it being the first of this discription that I have yet seen discharge itself into the Missouri; before it enters a large sand bar through which it discharges itself into the missouri it's banks and bottom are formed of a stiff blue and black clay;[4] it appears to be navigable for canoes and perogues at this time and I have no doubt but it might be navigated with boats of a considerable size in high water. it's banks appear to be from 8 to ten feet high and seldom overflow; from the quantity of water furnished by this river, the appearance of the country, the direction it pursues, and the situation of it's entrance, I have but little doubt but it takes it's source not far from the main body of the Suskashawan river,[5] and that it is probably navigable 150 miles; perhaps not very distant from that river. should this be the case, it would afford a very favorable communication to the Athebaskay country, from whence the British N. W. Company derive so large a portion of their valuable furs.— Capt. Clark who ascended this river several miles and passed it above where it entered the hills[6] informed me on his return that he found the general width of the bed of the river about one hundred yards, where he passed the river the bed was 112 yards wide, the water was knee deep and 38 yard in width; the river which he could observe from the rising grounds for about 20 miles, bore a little to the East of North.   there was a considerable portion of timber in the bottom lands of this river. Capt Clark also met with limestone on the surface of the earth in the course of his walk.[7]   he also saw a range of low mountains at a distance to the ⟨N⟩ W of ⟨West⟩ N , their direction being N. W.   the country in the neighbo[rhood] of this river, and as far as the eye can reach, is level, fertile, open and beatifull beyond discription. ¼ of a mile above the entrance of this river a large creek falls in which we called *2000 mile creek*.[8]   I sent Rubin Fields to examine it, he reported it to be a bold runing stream, it's bed 30 yards wide.   we proceeded about 3 miles abov this creek and encamped on the Stard. shore.[9]   I walked out a little distance and met with 2 porcupines which were feeding on the young willow which grow in great abundance on all the sandbars; this anamal is exceedingly clumsy and not very watchfull I approached so near one of them before it percieved me that I touched it with my espontoon.—[10]   found the nest of a wild goose among some driftwood in the river from which we took three eggs.   this is the only nest we have met with on driftwood, the usual position is the top of a broken tree, sometimes in the forks of a large tree but almost invariably, from 15 to 20 feet or upwards high.—

Courses and distances May 3rd 1805[11]		*miles*
N. 50° W.	to a point of high timber in a bend Stard.	¾
S. 65° W.	to a point of high timber in the center of a ⟨Lard⟩ bend on Lard side	2 ¼
N. 40 W.	to a point of woodland Star. side	1
N. 55° W.	to some dead timber in a stard bend	2 ½
South	to the upper part of the high timber in a bend on the Lard. side.	3
S. 80° W.[12]	to a point of woodland Stard. side	½
S. 85° W.	to the commencement of the timber on the Lard. side in a bend	1 ¼
North	to the upper part of the high timber in a bend on the Stard., passing a sand point at ½ mile on Lard.	1 ½
S. 65° W.	to a point of woodland on the Lard. side.	½

S. 75° W.	to a point of woodland on the Stard. side, at the entrance of a large river on the Stard. side, called Porcupine R.	1 ¾
S. 45° W.	to the high timber on the lard. side, passing the entrance of 2000 mile Creek at ¼ of a mile on Lard. side	3
N. 40° W.	to some high timber on the Stard side, just above an old channel of the river on the Stard. where we encampd.	½

miles 18 ½

[Clark]   *May 3rd Friday 1805*

we Set out reather later this morning than usial owing to weather being verry cold, a frost last night and the Thermt. Stood this morning at
26 above 0 which is 6 Degrees blow freeseing— the ice that was on the
Kittle left near the fire last night was ¼ of an inch thick. The Snow is all or
nearly all off the low bottoms, the Hills are entireley Covered.   three of
our party found in the back of a bottom 3 pieces of Scarlet one brace in
each, which had been left as a Sacrifice near one of their Swet houses, on
the L. S. we passed to day a curious collection of bushes tied up in the
shape of *fascene* about 10 feet diamuter, which must have been left also by
the natives as an offering to their medison which they Convinced protected or gave them relief near the place, the wind Continued to blow
hard from the West, altho not Sufficently So to detain us, I walked on
Shore and killed an Elk & had him bucchured by the time the Perogus
Came up which was the usial time of dineing. The high lands are low and
from 8 to 9 miles apart and there is evident marks of the bead of the river
having been changed frequently but little appearance of the Coal & burnt
hills to day— Great numbers of Buffalow, Elk, Deer, antilope, beaver,
Porcupins, & water fowls Seen to day, Such as, Geese, ducks of dift. kinds,
& a fiew Swan— I continued my walk on Shore after dinner, and arrived at the mouth of a river on the St. Side, which appeared to be large,
and I concluded to go up this river a few miles to examine it   accordingly
I Set out North 1 mile thro wood or timbered bottom, 2 miles through a
butifull leavel plain, and 1 mile over a high plain about 50 feet higher
than the bottom & Came to the little river, which I found to be a butifull
clear Stream of about 100 yds. from bank to bank, (I ⟨Stoped⟩ waded this
river at the narrowest part and made it 112 Steps from bank to bank and

at this place which was a kind of fording place the water was near Knee deep, and 38 steps wide, the bottom of a hard stiff Black Clay,[)]   I observed a Great perportion of timber in the bottoms of this river as far as I could See which was to the East of N. 18 or 20 miles, it appears to be navagable at this time for Canoes, and from appearances must be navagable a long distance for Perogus & boats in high water. This river we call *Porcupine* from the great number of those anamals found about it's mouth.— a Short distance above about ¼ mile and on the Lard Side a large Creek falls in, which R. Fields went to examine & reports that it is a bold running Stream, 30 yds wide   as this Creek is 2000 miles up the Missouri we Call it the 2000 mile Creek, we proceeded on 3 miles & Camped on the S. S.   here I joined Capt Lewis who had in my absens walkd. on the upper Side of Porcupine River for Some distance—   This river from its Size & quantity of water must head at no great distance from the Saskashawan   on this river I Saw emence herds Elk & Buffalow & many deer & Porcupine. I also Saw the top of a mountain which did not appear verry high to the West of N. & bore N W.   I Saw on the high land limestone & pebble—   The Countrey about the mouth of this river and as far as the eye Can reach is butifull ⟨beyond⟩ open Countrey. The greater part of the Snow is melted.

	mile	*Course & Distance 3d of May 1805*
N. 50° W	¾	to a point of high timber on the Std. Side in a bend
S. 65° W.	2 ¼	to a point of high timber on the Ld. Sd. about the middle of a bend L. S.
N. 40° W	1	mile to a point of wood land Std. Side [13]
N. 55 W	2 ½	miles to Some dead timber in St. bend
South	3	to the upper part of a timber in a bend to the Lard Side
N. 80° W.	½	to a pt. of wood land Std. Side
S. 85° W.	1 ¼	to the commencement of a timber on the Lard. Side in a bend
North	1 ½	to the upper part of the high timber in a bend on the Stard Side passing a Sand point at ½ a mile
S 65° W.	½	to a point of wood Land on the Ld Side

S 75° W.	1 ¾	to a point of wood land on the Std Side at the mouth of a large river on the Std Side
S 45° W	3	m. to a high timber on the Lard Side passed the mouth of 2000 mile Creek at ¼ of a mile on the Lard Side
N. 40° W.	½	to Some high timber on the S. Side just above an old Channel of the river Std Side. encamped
	18 ½	

1. Fascine is a military term for a cylindrical bundle of sticks used to fill ditches, strengthen ramparts, and other such functions.

2. The Poplar dome brings late Cretaceous rocks of the Hell Creek Formation, Fox Hills Sandstone, and Bearpaw Shale to the surface here. The Bearpaw Shale is easily eroded to form a wide valley. These formations contain no coal near here. The old river channel is marked with dotted lines on *Atlas* maps 35, 49.

3. Present Poplar River, in Roosevelt County, Montana, with the town of Poplar at its mouth. *Atlas* maps 36, 49, 57; MRC map 62.

4. Glacial till and Bearpaw Shale form the banks and beds of Poplar River. Both materials weather to a dark, blue-gray clay.

5. Poplar River rises near the U.S.-Canadian border. Lewis expressed the same optimism about the source of the Little Muddy River on April 22, 1805; see above.

6. Clark's route is marked by a dotted line on *Atlas* map 57.

7. The limestone was brought to this area by glacial ice from lower Paleozoic formations near Lake Winnipeg, Canada.

8. Present Red Water Creek, in Richland County, Montana. *Atlas* maps 36, 49, 57; MRC map 62.

9. In McCone County, Montana, some three or four miles above the town of Poplar, in Roosevelt County. The mouths of Poplar River (Porcupine Creek) and Red Water (2,000 Mile) Creek, may have shifted over the years, making it hard to locate this camp. *Atlas* map 57 incorrectly shows the site directly opposite the mouth of 2,000 Mile Creek. *Atlas* maps 35, 49; MRC map 62.

10. A spontoon, or espontoon, was a spear, six feet or more in length, with a wooden shaft and metal blade, still in use in the late eighteenth century as a symbol of authority for infantry officers. Lewis must have considered it a useful implement to have carried it with him on the expedition. At various times it was used as weapon, walking staff, and rifle support. See below, June 7 and 14, 1805. Peterson, 98–100. Robert Taylor of Washington, D.C., called attention to this material.

11. Also given on *Atlas* map 36, in Lewis's hand.

12. The course is "N. 80 W." in Clark's entry and on *Atlas* map 36.

13. This course and the next are displaced below the total in Clark's entry, proper placement being indicated by an asterisk and pointing hand.

[Lewis] *Saturday May 4th 1805.*

We were detained this morning untill about 9 OCk. in order to repare the rudder irons of the red perogue which were broken last evening in landing; we then set out, the wind hard against us. I walked on shore this morning, the weather was more plesant, the snow has disappeared; the frost seems to have effected the vegetation much less than could have been expected   the leaves of the cottonwood the grass the box alder willow and the yellow flowering pea seem to be scarcely touched; the rosebushes and honeysuckle seem to have sustaned the most considerable injury. The country on both sides of the Missouri continues to be open level fertile and beautifull as far as the eye can reach which from some of the eminences is not short of 30 miles.   the river bottoms are very extensive and contain a much greater proportion of timber than usual; the fore part of this day the river was bordered with timber on both sides, a circumstance which is extreemly rare and the first which has occurred of any thing like the same extent since we left the Mandans, in the after part of the day we passed an extensive beautifull plain on the Stard. side which gradually ascended from the river. I saw immence quantities of buffaloe in every direction, also some Elk deer and goats; having an abundance of meat on hand I passed them without firing on them; they are extreemly gentle   the bull buffaloe particularly will scarcely give way to you. I passed several in the open plain within fifty paces, they viewed me for a moment as something novel and then very unconcernedly continued to feed. Capt. Clark walked on shore this evening and did not rejoin us untill after dark, he struck the river several miles above our camp[1] and came down to us.   we saw many beaver some which the party shot, we also killed two deer to-day.   much sign of the brown bear.   passed several old Indian hunting camps in the course of the day   one of them contained two large lodges which were fortifyed with old driftwood and fallen timber; this fortification consisted of a circular fence of timber lade horizontally ⟨and⟩ laping on and over laying each other to the hight of 5 feet.   these pounds are sometimes built from 20 to 30 feet in diameter and covered over with the trunks and limbs of old timber.   the usual construction of the lodges we have lately passed is as follows.   three or more strong sticks the thickness of a man's leg or arm and about 12 feet long are attatched together at one end by a with of small willows, these are then set on end and spread at the base, ⟨to⟩ forming a circle of ten twelve or 14 feet in diameter; sticks of driftwood and fallen timber of convenient size are now placed with one end on the ground and the other resting against those which are secured together at top by the with and which support and give the form to the whole, thus the sticks are laid on untill they make it as thick as they design, usually about three ranges, each piece breaking or filling up the interstice of the two beneath it, the whole forming a connic figure about 10 feet high with a small apperture in one side which answers as a door. leaves bark and straw are sometimes thrown over the work to make it more complete, but at best it affords a very imperfect shelter particularly without straw which is the state in which we have most usually found them.[2]

Courses and distances of the 4th of May.[3]

S. 80° W.	to a point of timber on the Stard. side	3
S. 72° W.	to a point of woodland on the Stard. side river wide and filled with sandbars	5
S. 50° W.	to the mouth of a small creek in a deep bend on Lard. side, a sand Island opposite	1 ½
N. 10° W.	to a point of woodland on the Lard. side passing a Stard. Stard. point at 1 ¼ miles	3
S. 45° W.	to a willow point on the Stard. side, the river making a considerable bend to the N. an open plain on the Stard.	4
S. 70° W.	to a point of timbered land on the Strd. where we encamped.	1 ½
		Miles 18

At noon the sun was so much obscured that I could not obtain his maridian Altitude which I much wished in order to fix the latitude of the entrance of Porcupine river. Joseph Fields was very sick today with the disentary had a high fever   I gave him a doze of Glauber salts, which operated very well, in the evening his fever abated and I gave him 30 drops of laudnum.—[4]

[Clark] *May 4th Satturday 1805*

The rudder Irons of our large Perogue broke off last night, the replace-ing of which detained us this morning untill 9 oClock at which time we Set out   the wind a head from the west, The Countrey on each Side of the Missouri is a rich high and butifull ⟨Containing⟩   the bottoms are extencive with a great deal of timber on them   all the fore part of this day the wood land bordered the river on both Sides, in the after part a butifull assending plain on the Std Side   we Camped on the Std. Side a little above   we passed a Small Creek on the L. Side near which I Saw where an Indian lodge had been fortified many year past. Saw great num-bers of anamals of different kinds on the banks, I Saw the black martin to day—[5] in the evening I walkd. on Shore on the Std Side & Struck the river Several miles above our Camp & did not get to Camp untill Some time after night—   we have one man Sick, The river has been falling for Several days passed; it now begins to rise a little; the rate of rise & fall is from one to 3 inches in 24 hours.

	miles	*Course & Distance the 4th* of May
S. 80° W.	3	to a point of timber on the Stard. Side.
S. 72° W.	5	to a point of wood land on the Std. Side river wide & maney Sand bars
S. 50° W	1 ½	to the mouth of a creek in a Deep bend to the Lard. Side. a Sand Isd. opsd.
N 10° W.	3	to a point of wood Land on the Lard. Side passing a point S Side 1 ¼ miles.
S 45° W.	4	to a willow point on the Stard. Side, the river makeing a considerable [bend] arround to the North an open plain
S. 70° W.	1 ½	to a point of timbered land on the Stard. Side, where we encamped
miles	18	

1. This camp was in Roosevelt County, Montana. On *Atlas* map 57 the usual camp sym-bol has been misplaced, while the legend "Encamped the 4th May 1805" is in approxi-mately the right place. *Atlas* maps 36, 49; MRC map 63.

2. Apparently a description of a Blackfeet war lodge, a structure which served Black-feet war parties as a fortification, shelter from the weather, base for scouting, supply base, and a place to leave messages. From this structure, Clark named "Indian Fort Creek," An-

telope, or later Nickwall, Creek in McCone County, Montana. Ewers (ILUM), 117–30; *Atlas* maps 36, 57; MRC map 63.

3. Also given on *Atlas* map 36, in both captains' hands.

4. Glauber's Salts is the crystalline decahydrate of sodium sulfate, used as a laxative; the theory behind administering it to a man with dysentery was that disease was caused by poisons in the body that had to be flushed out. Laudanum is a tincture of opium, which would help Field sleep.

5. The purple martin, *Progne subis* [AOU, 61].

[Lewis]   *Sunday May 5th 1805*

A fine morning   I walked on shore untill 8 A M when we halted for breakfast and in the course of my walk killed a deer which I carried about a mile and a half to the river, it was in good order.   soon after seting out the rudder irons of the white perogue were broken by her runing fowl on a sawyer, she was however refitted in a few minutes with some tugs of raw hide and nales.   as usual saw a great quantity of game today; Buffaloe Elk and goats or Antelopes feeding in every direction; we kill whatever we wish, the buffaloe furnish us with fine veal and fat beef, we also have venison and beaver tales when we wish them; the flesh of the Elk and goat are less esteemed, and certainly are inferior.   we have not been able to take any fish for some time past. The country is as yesterday beatifull in the extreme.—

saw the carcases of many Buffaloe lying dead along the shore partially devoured by the wolves and bear.   saw a great number of white brant also the common brown brant, geese of the common kind and a small species of geese which differ considerably from the common canadian goose; their neck head and beak are considerably thicker shorter and larger than the other in proportion to it's size, they are also more than a third smaller, and their note more like that of the brant or a young goose which has not perfectly acquired his notes, in all other rispects they are the same in colour habits and the number of feathers in the tale, they frequently also ascociate with the large geese when in flocks, but never saw them pared off with the large or common goose.[1] The white brant[2] ascociate in very large flocks, they do not appear to be mated or pared off as if they intended to raise their young in this quarter, I therefore doubt whether they reside here during the summer for that purpose.

this bird is about the size of the common brown brant or two thirds of the common goose, it is not so long by six inches from point to point of the wings when extended as the other; the beak head and neck are also larger and stronger; their beak ⟨and⟩ legs and feet are of a redish or fleshcoloured white. the eye is of moderate size, the puple of a deep sea green incircled with a ring of yellowish brown. it has sixteen feathers of equal length in the tale; their note differs but little from the common brant, their flesh much the same, and in my opinion preferable to the goose, the flesh is dark. they are entirely of a beatifull pure white except the large feathers of the 1st and second joints of the wings which are jut black. form and habits are the same with the other brant; they some-times ascociate and form one common flock. Capt [*X: we*] Clark found a den of young wolves in the course of his walk today and also saw a great number of those anamals; they are very abundant in this quarter, and are of two species[3] the small woolf or burrowing dog of the praries are the inhabitants almost invariably of the open plains; they usually ascociate in bands of ten or twelve sometimes more and burrow near some pass or place much frequented by game; not being able alone to take a deer or goat they are rarely ever found alone but hunt in bands; they frequently watch and seize their prey near their burrows; in these burrows they raise their young and to them they also resort when pursued; when a person approaches them they frequently bark, their note being precisely that of the small dog. they are of an intermediate size between that of the fox and dog, very active fleet and delicately formed; the ⟨years⟩ ears large erect and pointed the head long and pointed more like that of the fox; tale long ⟨and bushey⟩; the hair and fur also resembles the fox tho' is much coarser and inferior. they are of a pale redish brown colour. the eye of a deep sea green colour small and piercing. their tallons are reather longer than those of the ordinary wolf or that common to the atlantic states, none of which are to be found in this quarter, nor I believe above the river Plat.— The large woolf found here is not as large as those of the atlantic states. they are lower and ⟨heaver⟩ thicker made shorter leged. their colour which is not effected by the seasons, is a grey or black-ish brown and every intermediate shade from that to a creen [cream] col-oured white; these wolves resort the woodlands and are also found in the plains, but never take refuge in the ground or burrow so far as I have been able to inform myself. we scarcely see a gang of buffaloe without observing a parsel of those faithfull shepherds on their skirts in readiness to take care of the mamed & wounded. the large wolf never barks, but howls as those of the atlantic states do. Capt. Clark and Drewyer killed the largest brown bear this evening which we have yet seen. it was a most tremendious looking anamal, and extreemly hard to kill notwithstanding he had five balls through his lungs and five others in various parts he swam more than half the distance acoss the river to a sandbar & it was at least twenty minutes before he died; he did not attempt to attact, but fled and made the most tremendous roaring from the moment he was shot. We had no means of weighing this monster; Capt. Clark thought he would weigh 500 lbs. for my own part I think the estimate too small by 100 lbs. he measured 8 Feet 7½ Inches from the nose to the extremety of the hind feet, 5 F. 10½ Inch arround the breast, 1 F. 11 I. arround the middle of the arm, & 3 F. 11 I. arround the neck; his tallons which were five in number on each foot were 4⅜ Inches in length. he was in good order, we therefore divided him among the party and made them boil the oil and put it in a cask for future uce; the oil is as hard as hogs lard when cool, much more so than that of the black bear. this bear differs from the common black bear in several respects; it's tallons are much longer and more blont, it's tale shorter, it's hair which is of a redish or bey brown, is longer thicker and finer than that of the black bear; his liver lungs and heart are much larger even in proportion with his size; the heart particularly was as large as that of a large Ox. his maw was also ten times the size of black bear, and was filled with flesh and fish. his testicles were pendant from the belly and placed four inches assunder in seperate bags or pouches.— this animal also feeds on roots and almost every species of wild fruit.

The party killed two Elk and a Buffaloe today, and my dog caught a goat, which he overtook by superior fleetness, the goat it must be understood was with young and extreemly poor. a great number of these goats are devowered by the wolves and bear at this season when they are poor and passing the river from S. W. to N. E. they are very inactive and easily taken in the water, a man can out swim them with great ease; the

Indians take them in great numbers in the river at this season and in autumn when they repass to the S. W.—

Courses and distances of May 5th 1805.[4]

		mls.
S. 70° W.	to the willows on the lower point of an Island near the Stard. shore, opposite a low bluf	3
S. 72° W.	to some high timber on a projecting point on the Stard. side opposite a pot. Lard. passing the upper part of Isld. at 2 miles	2 ½
S. 30° W.	to a point of woodland on the Stard. opposite a low bluff on Lard. side	2 ½
N. 48° W.	to a point of woodland on the Lard side	2 ¼
N. 45° W.	to the extremity of the sand bar from the Lard. point	1 ¾
South	to a willow point on the Stard. side short of which we encamped on Stard.	5
		miles 17

Point of observation No. 9.

On the Lard. shore near the fourth course of this day, observed meridian Altitude of the ☉'s L. L. with Octant by the back observation to be 68° 47'. the latitude deduced from which is 45° 46' 5.6"— I do think this observation can be depended on as it was reather late before I could commence it, the sun was about to decline or perhaps had declined a few minutes.—

[Clark] 5th of May Sunday 1805

We Set out verry early and had not proceeded far before the rudder Irons of one of the Perogus broke which detained us a Short time Capt Lewis walked on Shore this morning and killed a Deer, after brackfast I walked on Shore Saw great numbers of Buffalow & Elk Saw also a Den of young wolves, and a number of Grown wolves in every direction, the white & Grey Brant is in this part of the Missouri I shot at the white brant but at So great a distance I did not kill, The Countrey on both sides is as yesterday, handsom & fertile— The river rising & Current Strong & in the evening we Saw a Brown or Grisley beare on a Sand beech, I went out with one man Geo. Drewyer & Killed the bear, which was verry large and a turrible looking animal, which we found verry hard to kill we

114

Shot ten Balls into him before we killed him, & 5 of those Balls through his lights ⟨before⟩ This animal is the largest of the Carnivorous kind I ever Saw we had nothing that could way him, I think his weight may be Stated at 500 [600?] pounds, he measured 8 feet 7½ In. from his nose to the extremity of the Toe, 5 feet 10½ in. arround the breast, 1 feet 11 Ins: around the middle of the arm, 3 feet 11 Ins. arround the neck his tallents was 4 Inches & ⅜ long, he was good order, and appeared verry different from the Common black bear in as much as his ⟨tallents⟩ [*X: talons or nails*] were blunt, his tail Short, his liver & lights much larger, his maw ten times as large and Contained meat or flesh & fish only— we had him Skined and divided, the oile tried up & put in Kegs for use. we Camped on the Stard Side,[5] our men killed three Elk and a Buffalow to day, and our Dog Cought an antilope a fair race, this animal appeared verry pore & with young.

Course & Distance 5th of May

S. 70° W.	3	miles to the willows on the lower point of an Island near the Sd. Side opposit a low bluff.
S. 72° W.	2 ½	miles to Some high timber on a projecting point on the Stad. Side opsd. a pt. L. S., passed the Isd. at 2 miles
S. 30° W.	2 ½	miles to a point of wood land on the Stard Side opsd. a low Bluff L. Side
N. 48° W	2 ¼	miles to a point of wood land on the Lard. Side
N. 45° W.	1 ¾	miles to the extremity of the Sand bar from the Lard point
South	5	miles to a willow point on the Stard. Side (Short of which we encamped[)]
miles	17	

1. Lewis notices snow geese and brant. His common goose is the Canada goose, used for comparing what was probably the lesser Canada, or tundra, goose, *Branta canadensis leucopareia* [AOU, 172.1], the cackling goose, *B. c. minima* [AOU, 172.2], or Hutchins's goose, *B. c. hutchinsii* [AOU, 172.3]. All are now grouped as a single species. Clark copied this passage verbatim in his entry for May 26, 1805. Lewis gives a bit more detail on March 6, 1806. Burroughs, 195–96; Holmgren, 30; Cutright (LCPN), 430. Someone drew vertical lines through this and the following natural history passage in this entry, perhaps in red.

2. The snow goose, noted in detail on March 8, 1806. Lewis was correct about their breeding habits; they breed in northern Alaska and arctic Canada.

3. The coyote and gray wolf. The latter probably *Canis lupus nubilis* and now extinct. Both may be Lewis and Clark discoveries. Burroughs, 84–89; Cutright (LCPN), 87, 440.

4. Also given on *Atlas* map 36, in both captains' hands, with an incorrect total of 16¼.

5. In McCone County, Montana, southeast of the present town of Wolf Point. Due to shifts in the river the camp is now apparently on the opposite side from Lewis and Clark's time and a mile or so from the river. The legend "Encamped 5th May 1805" is misplaced on *Atlas* map 57, but the conventional campsite symbol is in the right place. *Atlas* maps 36, 49; MRC map 63.

Chapter Thirteen

From the Yellowstone to the Musselshell (Part 2)

May 6–22, 1805

[Lewis]

Monday May 6th 1805.

The morning being fair and pleasant and wind favourable we set sale at an early hour, and proceeded on very well the greater part of the day; the country still continues level fertile and beautifull, the bottoms wide and well timbered comparitively speaking with other parts of the river; no appearance of birnt hills pumice stone or coal, the salts of tartar or vegitable salts continues to appear on the river banks, sand bars and in many parts of the plains most generally in the little revines at the base of the low hills.[1]   passed three streames today which discharged themselves on the Lard. side; the first of these we call little dry creek   it contained some water in standing pools but discharged none, the 2ed 50 yards wide no Water, we called it Big dry Creek, the 3rd is bed of a conspicuous river 200 yards wide which we called little dry river;[2] the banks of these streams are low and bottoms wide with but little timber, their beds are almost en-tirely formed of a fine brown sand intermixed with a small proportion of little pebbles, which were either transparent, white, green, red, yellow or brown.   these streams appeared to continue their width without diminu-tion as far as we could perceive them, which with rispect to the river was

117

many miles, they had recenly discharged their waters. from the appearance of these streams, and the country through which they passed, we concluded that they had their souces in level low dry plains, which probably is the character of the country for a great distance west of this, or to the vicinity of the black hills, that the country being low on the same leve[l] nearly and in the same parallel of latitude, that the rains in the spring of the year ⟨in a few days⟩ suddonly melts the snow at the same time and causes for a few days a vast quantity of water which finds it's way to the Missouri through those channels; by reference to the diary of the weather &c it will be percieved that there is scarcely any rain during the summer Autumn and winter in this open country distant from the mountains. Fields still continues unwell. saw a brown bear swim the river above us, he disappeared before we can get in reach of him; I find that the curiossity of our party is pretty well satisfyed with rispect to this anamal, the formidable appearance of the male bear killed on the 5th added to the difficulty with which they die when even shot through the vital parts, has staggered the resolution several of them, others however seem keen for action with the bear; I expect these gentlemen will give us some amusement shotly as they soon begin now to coppolate. saw a great quantity of game of every species common here. Capt Clark walked on shore and killed two Elk, they were not in very good order, we therefore took a part of the meat only; it is now only amusement for Capt. C. and myself to kill as much meat as the party can consum; I hope it may continue thus through our whole rout, but this I do not much expect. two beaver were taken in traps this morning and one since shot by one of the party. saw numbers of these anamals peeping at us as we passed out of their wholes which they form of a cilindric shape, by burrowing in the face of the abbrupt banks of the river.

Courses and distances May 6th 1805.[3]   miles

S. 30° W.	to a Stard. point opposite a low bluf, just above which little dry creek falls in on Lard.	1 ½
N. 45° W.	to a point of high timber in a bend on Stard. side at the mouth of Lackwater creek 25 yds. wide	1 ½
N. 40° W.[4]	to a point of high timber on Stard side.	3

S. 55° W.	to a point of woodland on the Lard. side	3
S. 70° W.[5]	to a point of woodland Stard. side, passing Big dry Creek at ½ m. on Lard.	2 ½
S. 55° W.	to a point of woodland on the Lard. the river making a deep bend to N. W.	2
S. 50° W.	to a point of woodland Stard side opposite a low bluf on Lard. side	1 ¼
S. 60° W.	to the entrance of a river 200 yds. wide on Lard Side in a bend, this we called little dry river it having no water	¾
North	to an object in center of a Stard. bend, a large sand Island on Lard. side	
S. 40° W.	to a willow point on the Stard. side opposite to a bluff on Lard. side	4
S. 80° W.	to a clump of high trees on the Stard side passing a point on Lard. at 2 m. on which we encamped for the night[6]	3

Miles 25

May 6th 1805.

Point of observation No. 10.[7]

On the Stard. side, at the extremity of the 3rd course of this day observed Equal altitudes of ☉ with Sextant.

	h	m	s		
A. M.	8	59	57 ⎫	lost by ⎱	Altd. by sext
	9	1	35 ⎬	Clouds ⎰	71° 16′ 15″
	"	3	15 ⎭		

At noon the sun being obscured by clouds I was unable to observe his Altitude; it continued cloudy the ballance of the day and prevented all further observation.

[Clark]   *May 6th Monday 1805*

a fine morning   wind from the N. E.   we Set out early and proceeded on verry well under Sail the greater part of the day, passed two Creeks & a River to day on the Lard. Side, neither of them discharged any water into the Missouri, they were wide and Continued their width for Some distance, the little water of those Creeks & the little river must wash ⟨in⟩

the low Country ⟨on bottoms⟩, I believe those Streams to be the Conveyance of the water of the heavy rains & melting Snows in the Countrey back &c. &c. I walked on Shore and Killed two Elk neither of which was fat, we saved the best of the meat, one beaver Shot to day.   the countrey on both Sides butifull no appearances of either *Coal* or pumice Stone & burnt hills, The Salts of Tarter or white aprs. of Salts are yet to be Seen.

	miles	*Course & Distance 6th of May*
S. 30° W.	1 ½	to the Std Side, at a point opsd. a low bluff[8] just above which on Lard. Little dry creek falls in 25.
N. 45° W.	1 ½	to a point of high timber in a bend to the Std. Side, at the Mo: of a Creek 25 yd.
N. 40° W.	3	to a point of high timber on the Std. Side
S. 55° W.	3	to a point of wood land on the Lad. Side
S. 70° W	2 ½	to a point of wood Land on the Std. Side passing a large creek on L. S. at ½ a mile Containing but little water
S. 55° W.	2	to a point of wood land on the Lard Side the river making a Deep bend to the N. W.
S. 50° W.	1 ¼	to a point of wood land on the Std. Side opposit a bluff on the Lard Side
S. 60° W.	¾	to the mouth of a river 200 yds wide in a bend to the Lard. Side, no water running in it at present
North	2 ½	to an object in the center of a Stard. bend, a large Sand Island on Ld pt.
S. 40° W.	4	to a willow point on the Std. Side opposit to a bluff on the Lard Side
S 80° W.	3	to a Clump of high trees on the Stard. Side, passing a point on the Lard Side at 2 miles on which we encamped
miles	25	

1. The late Cretaceous Hell Creek Formation, Fox Hills Sandstone, and Bearpaw Shale form the hills along the river. Glacial till is present mainly north of the river. These formations contain no coal here. The salts are sodium sulphate, sodium bicarbonate, and magnesium sulphate. They form where ground water, and sometimes surface water, evaporates.

2. Little Dry Creek is probably either Spring Creek or an unnamed creek west of it; Big Dry Creek, present Sand Creek; Little Dry River, present Prairie Elk Creek, all in McCone

County, Montana. Lackwater Creek, mentioned in the courses and distances, is now Wolf Creek, in Roosevelt County. *Atlas* maps 36, 49, 57; MRC maps 63, 64.

3. Also given on *Atlas* map 36, in both captains' hands.

4. Given as "S. 40 W." on *Atlas* map 36.

5. Given as "S. 78° W." on *Atlas* map 36.

6. In McCone County, a few miles southwest of the present town of Oswego. *Atlas* maps 36, 49, 57, MRC map 64.

7. The letters "Qu" are written in red over the first lines of this observation, perhaps by Biddle.

8. The rest of this course appears to be in Lewis's hand.

[Lewis]   *Tuesday May 7th 1805.*

A fine morning, set out at an early hour; the drift wood begins to come down in consequence of the river's rising; the water is somewhat clearer than usual, a circumstance I did not expect on it's rise.   at 11 A. M. the wind became so hard that we were compelled to ly by for several hours, one of the small canoes by the bad management of the steersman filled with water and had very nearly sunk; we unloaded her and dryed the baggage; at one we proceed on the wind having in some measure abated.   the country we passed today on the North side of the river is one of the most beautifull plains we have yet seen, it rises gradually from the river bottom to the hight of 50 or 60 feet, then becoming level as a bowling green.   extends back as far as the eye can reach; on the S. side the river hills are more broken and much higher tho' some little destance back the country becomes level and fertile.   no appearance of birnt hills coal or pumicestone, that of salts still continue.[1]   vegitation appears to have advanced very little since the 28th Ulto.—   we continue to see a great number of bald Eagles, I presume they must feed on the carcases of dead anamals, for I see no fishing hawks[2] to supply them with their favorite food.   the water of the river is so terbid that no bird wich feeds exclusively on fish can subsist on it; from it's mouth to this place I have neither seen the blue crested fisher[3] nor a fishing hawk.   this day we killed 3 Buffaloe 1 Elk & 8 beaver; two of the Buffaloe killed by Capt Clark near our encampment[4] of this evening wer in good order dressed them and saved the meat, the Elk I killed this morning, thought it fat, but on examineation found it so lean that we took the tongue marrowbones and Skin only.

	Courses and distances May 7th 1805.[5]	miles
South	to the point of a sandbar on Stard. side.	1 ½
North	to a point of woodland on the Lard. side opposite a low bluff on Stard. side	2
S. 75° W.	to some high timber in the center of a Std. bend	2
S. 10° W.	to the upper point of a sandbar Stard side	2 ¼
S. 40° W.	to the upper point of the high timber in the center of a Lard. bend	1 ¾
N. 45° W.	to the point of a sandbar Lard. side	2 ½
S. 15° W.	to the upper part of the high timber near the center of a Lard. bend, passed the upper part of a large sandbar on Stard. and encamped on Lard near the extremity of this course	3

Mls. 15

May 7th 1805

Point of Observation No. 11.

On the Lard. shore near the extremity of the 2ed course of this day observed Equal altitudes with Sextant.

	h	m	s			h	m	s	
A. M.	8	57	48.5		P. M.	4	23	2.5	Altitd by Sext. 70° 28' 15"
	"	58	27			"	24	40	
	9		6			"	25	21	

Point of Observation No. 12.

On the Lard. shore at the extremity of the 5th course of this day Observed Meridian altd. of ☉'s L. L. with Octant by the back observation   67° 16'

Latitude deduced from this observation   N. 47° 34' 11.6"

This observation was very satisfactory and may be depended on as accurate.—

May 7th 1805.

Point of Observation No. 13.

At our encampment of this evening observed time and distance of ☽'s Western limb from Spica ♍ with Sextant.—

Mean of a set of ten observations

	Time			Distance		
	h	m	s			
P. M.	10	33	47.5	36°	59'	52.5"

☞ I could not observe Pollux in consequence of the clouds.—

[Clark]   *May 7th Tuesday, 1805*

A fine morning   river rose 1 ½ Inches last night, the drift wood begin-ning to run   the water Something Clearer than usial, the wind became verry hard, and at 11 oClock one Canoe by bad Stearing filled with water, which detained us about 3 hours, had a Meridian altitude, the Latd. from which is *47° 36° 11" ⁶⁄₁₀* The Countrey on the North Side of the Missouri is one of the handsomest plains we have yet Seen on the river   the plain rises from the river bottom gradually. The Hills on the South Side is high & uneavin.   no appearance of Coal or burnt hills, that of Salts Still ap-pear; vegitation appears to be Slow, I walked on the bank to day and Shot 2 beaver, in the evening Killed two Buffalow in tolerable order which we Saved and Camped on the Lard Side.   8 beaver, 3 buffalow & an Elk killed to day

	miles	*Course & Distance the 7th of May*
South	1 ½	to the point of a Sand bar from the Starboard Side
North	2	to a point of wood land on the L S. opposit a low bluff on the Std. Side
S. 75° W.	2	to Some high timber in the Center of the bend to the Stard. Side
S. 10° W.	2 ¼	to the upper point of a Sand bar Std. Sd.
S. 40° W.	1 ¾	to the upper point of a high timber in a bend to the Lard Side
N. 45° W.	2 ½	to the point of a Sand bar Lard Side
S. 15° W.	3	to the upper part of a high timber in a bend to the Lard. Side, passed the upper part of a large Sand bar
miles	15	

1. The party continues to pass through country underlain by late Cretaceous forma-tions capped with glacial till.

2. The osprey, *Pandion haliaetus* [AOU, 364]. Burroughs, 208.

3. The belted kingfisher, *Ceryle alcyon* [AOU, 390], already known to science. Holmgren, 31; Burroughs, 237–38.

4. In either McCone or Valley County, Montana, a few miles southwest of the present town of Frazer. *Atlas* maps 36, 49, 58; MRC map 64.

5. Also given on *Atlas* map 36, in both captains' hands.

[Lewis]   *Wednesday May 8th 1805.*

Set out at an early hour under a gentle brieze from the East.   a black cloud which suddonly sprung up at S. E.   soon over shaddowed the horizon; at 8 A. M. it gave us a slight sprinke of rain, the wind became much stronger but not so much so as to detain us.   we nooned it just above the entrance of a large river which disimbogues on the Lard. [*NB?: Starbd*] side;[1] I took the advantage of this leasure moment and examined the river about 3 miles; I found it generally 150 yards wide, and in some places 200.   it is deep, gentle in it's courant and affords a large boddy of water; it's banks which are formed of a dark rich loam and blue clay are abbrupt and about 12 feet high.[2]   it's bed is principally mud. I have no doubt but it is navigable for boats perogues and canoes, for the latter probably a great distance.   the bottoms of this stream ar wide, level, fertile and possess a considerable proportion of timber, principally Cottonwood. from the quantity of water furnised by this river it must water a large extent of country; perhaps this river also might furnish a practicable and advantageous communication with the Saskashiwan river; it is sufficiently large to justify a belief that it might reach to that river if it's direction be such.   the water of this river possesses a peculiar whiteness, being about the colour of a cup of tea with the admixture of a tablespoonfull of milk.   from the colour of it's water we called it Milk river.   (we think it possible that this may be the river called by the Minitares *the river which scoalds at all others* or [*blank*][)] [*NB: This is Maria's river see aftd.*][3]   Capt Clark who walked this morning on the Lard. shore ascended a very high point opposite to the mouth of this river; he informed me that he had a perfect view of this river and the country through which it passed for a great distance (probably 50 or 60 Miles,) [*X: to see 60 miles would require a height of 1000 feet*][4] that the country was level and beautifull on both sides of the river, with large herds of Buffaloe distributed throughout:

that the river from it's mouth boar N. W. for 12 or 15 Miles when it forked, the one taking a direction nearly North, and the other to the West of N. West.[5]   from the appearance of the vallies and the timber on each of these streams Capt. C. supposed that they were about the same size.   great appearance of beaver on this river, and I have no doubt but what they continue abundant, there being plenty of cottonwood and willow, the timber on which they subsist. The country on the Lard. side of the river is generally high broken hills, with much broken, grey black and brown grannite scattered on the surface of the earth in a confused manner.[6] The wild Licquorice is found on the sides of these hills, in great abundance.[7]   at a little distance from the river there is no timber to be seen on either side; the bottom lands are not more than one fifth covered with timber; the timber as below is confined to the borders of the river.   in future it will be understood that there is no timber of any discription on the upland unless particularly mentioned; and also that one fifth of the bottom lands being covered with timber is considered a large proportion. The white apple[8] is found in great abundance in this neighbourhood; it is confined to the highlands principally. The *whiteapple,* so called by the French Engages, is a plant which rises to the hight of 6 or 9 Inchs. rarely exceeding a foot; it puts forth from one to four and sometimes more stalks from the same root, but is most generally found with one only, which is branched but not defusely, is cylindric and villose; the leafstalks, cylindric, villose and very long compared with the hight of the plant, tho' gradually diminish in length as they ascend, and are irregular in point of position; the leaf, digitate, from three to five in number, oval 1 Inch long, absolutely entire and cottony: the whole plant of a pale green, except the under disk of the leaf which is of a white colour from the cottony substance with which it is covered.   the radix a tuberous bulb; generally ova formed, sometimes longer and more rarely partially divided or brancing; always attended with one or more radicles at it's lower extremity which sink from 4 to 6 inches deep.   the bulb covered with a rough black, tough, thin rind which easily seperates from the bulb which is a fine white substance, somewhat porus, spungy and moist, and reather tough before it is dressed; the center of the bulb is penitrated with a small tough string or ligament, which passing from the bottom of the stem terminates in the extremity of the radicle, which last is also covered by a prolongation of the rind which invellopes the bulb: The bulb is usually found at the debth of 4 inches and frequently much deeper. This root forms a considerable article of food with the Indians of the Missouri, who for this purpose prepare them in several ways. they are esteemed good at all seasons of the year, but are best from the middle of July to the latter end of Autumn when they are sought and gathered by the provident part of the natives for their winter store. when collected they are striped of their rhind and strung on small throngs or chords and exposed to the sun or placed in the smoke of their fires to dry; when well dryed they will keep for several years, provided they are not permitted to become moist or damp; in this situation they usually pound them between two stones placed on a piece of parchment, untill they reducc it to a fine powder thus prepared they thicken their soope with it; sometimes they also boil these dryed roots with their meat without breaking them; when green they are generally boiled with their meat, sometimes mashing them or otherwise as they think proper. they also prepare an agreeable dish with them by boiling and mashing them and adding the marrow grease of the buffaloe and some buries, until the whole be of the consistency of a haisty pudding. they also eat this root roasted and frequently make hearty meals of it raw without sustaining any inconvenience or injury therefrom. The White or brown bear feed very much on this root, which their tallons assist them to procure very readily. the white apple appears to me to be a tastless insippid food of itself tho' I have no doubt but it is a very healthy and moderately nutricious food. I have no doubt but our epicures would admire this root very much, it would serve them in their ragouts and gravies in stead of the truffles morella.

We saw a great number buffaloe, Elk, common and *Black taled* deer, goats beaver and wolves. Capt C. killed a beaver and a wolf, the party killed 3 beaver and a deer. We can send out at any time and obtain whatever species of meat the country affords in as large quantity as we wish. we saw where an Indian had recently grained, or taken the hair off of a goatskin; we do not wish to see those gentlemen just now as we presume they would most probably be the Assinniboins and might be troublesome to us. Capt C. could not be certain but thought he saw the smoke and some Indian lodges at a considerable distance up Milk river.

Courses and distances of May 8th 1805.[9]

S. 88° W.	to a point of timbered land on the Stard. side opposite to a bluff of black earth	1 ½
N. 60 W.	on the Stard. side.	¼
North	to some high timber on the Lard. side	2
East	to the extremity of a sandbar from a Lard. point; passed a gulph on Stard.	1 ¼
N. 70° W.	to a point of timber on ⟨Stard⟩ Lard. side	2
S. 65° W.	to a point of timber on the Stard side	2
S. 55° W.	to a point on the Stard. side	2 ¼
S. 85° W.	to a point of timbered land on the Lard side, passing a projecting point in a bend on Stard side at 3 ½ miles	5 ¾
S. 74° W.	to a point of woodland on the Stard side passing a large river on the Stard side at ½ a mile— we call this Milk river.	4
N. 5° W.	to a sand point on the Lard. side	2 ½
N. 70° W.	to some high timber on the Lard. side opposite to a low bluff on Stard.	1 ½
S. 18° W.	to a point of high timber on the Stard side opposite to a bluff on the Lard side, short of which one mile, we en-camped on the Lard. side	3

Miles 28

[Clark]   *May the 8th Wednesday 1805*[10]

a verry black Cloud to the S W.   we Set out under a gentle breeze from the N. E.   about 8 oClock began to rain, but not Sufficient to wet, we passed the mouth of a large river on the Starboard Side 150 yards wide and appears to be navagable.   the Countrey thro which it passes as far as Could be seen from the top of a verry high hill on which I was, ⟨the Coun-try is⟩ a butifull leavil plain   this river forks about N W from its mouth 12 or 15 miles   one fork runs from the North & the other to the West of

N W.   the water of this river will justify a belief that it has its Sourse at a considerable distance, and waters a great extent of Countrey— we are willing to believe that this is the River the Minitarres Call the river which Scolds at all others

the Countrey on the Lard. Side is high & broken with much Stone Scattered on the hills, In walking on Shore with the Interpreter & his wife, the Squar Geathered on the Sides of the hills wild Lickerish, & the white apple as called by the angegies [*engagés*] and gave me to eat, the Indians of the Missouri make great use of the white apple dressed in different ways— Saw great numbers of Buffalow, Elk, antelope & Deer, also black tale deer beaver & wolves, I killed a beaver which I found on the bank, & a wolf. The party killed 3 Beaver 1 Deer   I saw where an Indian had taken the hair off a goat Skin a fiew days past— Camped early on the Lard. Side.[11] The river we passed today we call Milk river from the peculiar whiteness of it's water, which precisely resembles tea with a considerable mixture of milk.

	miles	*Course and Distance the 8th of May*
S. 88° W,	1 ½	to a point of timbered land on the Std. Side opsd. a bluff of black earth L
N. 60° W	¼	on the Starboard Side
North	2	to the high timber on the Lard. Side
East	1 ¼	to the extremity of a Sand bar from the Lard point passed a Gulf
N. 70° W.	2	to a point of timber Lard. Side
S. 65° W.	2	to a point of timber on the Stard. Side
S. 55° W.	2 ¼	to a point on the Stard. Side
S. 85° W	5 ¾	to a point of timbered land on the Lard Side, passing a projected point in a bend to Stard Side at 3 ½ miles
S. 74° W.	4	to a point of wood land on the Stard. Side passed a large river on the Std. Side at ½ a mile
N 5° W.	2 ½	to a Sand point on the Lard Side
N. 70° W.	1 ½	to some high timber on the Ld. Side opposit a low bluff on the S. S.

S. 18° W.   3
    miles 28
        =

to a point of high trees on the Starbord Side opposit a bluff on the Lard Side, we Camped one mile Short on the L. Side

1. Milk River, which still bears the name Lewis and Clark gave it; it rises in the mountains of Glacier National Park, in northwestern Montana, flows through southern Alberta, then returns to the United States and enters the Missouri in Valley County, Montana. They concluded, correctly, that this was the "River Which Scolds at All Others" of which the Indians had told them at Fort Mandan. See below, June 2 and 3, 1805. Saindon (RSO); *Atlas* maps 37, 49, 58; MRC maps 64, 65.

2. Milk River alluvium is derived from weathered glacial till and Bearpaw Shale; some sand comes from the Judith River Formation.

3. Biddle's interlinear note, indicating that the Marias River, not the Milk, was the "River Which Scolds at All Others," was an error on his part. The captains briefly considered this possibility (see below, June 3, 1805), but concluded that their first identification of this stream as the Milk was correct. Saindon (RSO).

4. It may have been Biddle who added the red parentheses around the words, "probably . . . miles"; it may have been Coues who penciled in the words, "to see . . . feet."

5. The first is present Porcupine Creek, in Valley County, the other Milk River. Porcupine Creek, and the Milk below the fork, form the western boundary of Fort Peck Indian Reservation. *Atlas* maps 37, 49, 58.

6. The hills south of the river are the Milk River Hills; they rise nearly 700 feet above the floodplain of the Missouri. The granite rocks are glacial erratics brought here from the Canadian Shield by glacial ice.

7. *Glycyrrhiza lepidota* (Nutt.) Pursh, wild liquorice. It is significant that this species, first described by Pursh in 1814 from the expedition's collection, was known to Lewis by its common name even though it was not found growing in the East. Clark indicated on this same day that Sacagawea gathered both this root as well as the breadroot (see next note), indicating that both plants were known and used by Indians of the area. The wild liquorice is related to the cultivated liquorice plant from Southern Europe and Asia, *G. glabra* L. Fernald, 914; Cutright (LCPN), 265; Pursh, 480; Bailey, 561. Someone drew a vertical line through this passage down through the material about the morella.

8. *Psoralea esculenta* Pursh, breadroot, scurf pea, pomme blanche. Lewis's detailed description of the plant lacks reference to the flowers and the plant was probably not yet in bloom. Based on the early flowering stage of the plant shown in Pursh's illustration, it must have been drawn from Lewis's collection of the previous year on the lower Missouri River. Fernald, 898; Barkley, 181; Cutright (LCPN), 91; Pursh, 475–76.

9. Also given on *Atlas* map 37, in both captains' hands.

10. Beginning with this entry and appearing occasionally in the remainder of this journal, Voorhis No. 1, are small symbols in the margin by the date line. They appear to be circles with lines coming out, like rays. Their meaning or significance is unknown.

11. Probably in Valley County, a mile or two above present Fort Peck Dam. *Atlas* maps 37, 49, 58; MRC map 65.

[Lewis]   *Thursday May 9th 1805.*

Set out at an early hour; the wind being favourable we used our sails and proceeded very well; the country in appearance is much as yester, with this difference that the land appears more fertile particularly of the Lard. hills which are not so stoney and less broken; the timber has also in some measure declined in quantity. today we passed the bed of the most extraordinary river that I ever beheld. it is as wide as the Missouri is at this place or ½ a mile wide and not containing a single drop of runing water; some small standing pools being all the water that could be perceived. it falls in on the Lard. side.[1] I walked up this river about three miles and ascended an eminence from which I could perceive it many miles; it's course about South for 10 or 12 miles, when it viered around to the E of S. E. as far as I could see. the valley of this river is wide and possesses but a scanty proportion of timber; the hills which border it are not very high nor is the country very broken; it is what may properly be designated a wavy or roling country intersperced with some handsom level plains. the bank are low and abbrupt, seldom more than 6 or eight feet above the level of the bed, yet show but little appearance of being overflown; they are of black or yellow clay or a rich sandy loam. the bed is entirely composed of a light brown sand the particles of which as well as that of the Missoury are remarkably fine.[2] this river I presume must extend back as far as the black hills and probably is the channel through which a great extent of plain country discharge their superfluous waters in the spring season. it had the appearance of having recently discharged it's waters; and from the watermark, it did not appear that it had been more than 2 feet deep at it's greatest hight. This stream (if such it can properly be termed) we called Big dry river. about a mile below this river on the same side a large creek falls in also dry at present.[3] The mineral salts and quarts appear in large quantities in this neighbourhood. the sand of the Missouri from it's mouth to this place has always possessed a mixture of granulated talk [talc] or I now think most probably that[4] it is this quarts.[5] Capt C. killed 2 bucks and 2 buffaloe, I also killed one buffaloe which proved to be the best meat, it was in tolerable order; we saved the best of the meat, and from the cow I killed we saved the necessary materials for making what our wrighthand cook Charbono calls the *boudin blanc,* [*NB: poudingue*] and immediately set him about preparing them for supper; this white pudding we all esteem one of the greatest delacies of the forrest, it may not be amiss therefore to give it a place. About 6 feet of the lower extremity of the large gut of the Buffaloe is the first mosel that the cook makes love to, this he holds fast at one end with the right hand, while with the forefinger and thumb of the left he gently compresses it, and discharges what he says *is not good to eat,* but of which in the squel we get a moderate portion; the mustle lying underneath the shoulder blade next to the back, and fillets are next saught, these are needed up very fine with a good portion of kidney suit [suet]; to this composition is then added a just proportion of pepper and salt and a small quantity of flour; thus far advanced, our skilfull opporater C—o seizes his recepticle, which has never once touched the water, for that would intirely distroy the regular order of the whole procedure; you will not forget that the side you now see is that covered with a good coat of fat provided the anamal be in good order; the operator sceizes the recepticle I say, and tying it fast at one end turns it inwards and begins now with repeated evolutions of the hand and arm, and a brisk motion of the finger and thumb to put in what he says is *bon pour manger;* thus by stuffing and compressing he soon distends the recepticle to the utmost limmits of it's power of expansion, and in the course of ⟨the opperation the⟩ it's longtudinal progress it drives from the other end of the recepticle a much larger portion of the [*blank*] than was prevously discharged by the finger and thumb of the left hand in a former part of the operation; thus when the sides of the recepticle are skilfully exchanged the outer for the iner, and all is compleatly filled with something good to eat, it is tyed at the other end, but not any cut off, for that would make the pattern too scant; it is then baptised in the missouri with two dips and a flirt, and bobbed into the kettle; from whence after it be well boiled it is taken and fryed with bears oil untill it becomes brown, when it is ready to esswage the pangs of a keen appetite or such as travelers in the wilderness are seldom at a loss for.—

we saw a great quantity of game today particularly of Elk and Buffaloe, the latter are now so gentle that the men frequently throw sticks and stones at them in order to drive them out of the way.   we also saw this evening emence quantities of timber cut by the beaver which appeared to have been done the preceeding year, in place particularly they had cut all the timber down for three acres in front and on nearly one back from the river and had removed a considerable proportion of it, the timber grew very thick and some of it was as large as a man's body.   the river for several days has been as wide as it is generally near it's mouth, tho' it is much shallower or I should begin to dispair of ever reaching it's source; it has been crouded today with many sandbars; the water also appears to become clearer, it has changed it's complexin very considerably. I begin to feel extreemly anxious to get in view of the rocky mountains.

I killed four plover[6] this evening of a different species from any I have yet seen; it resembles the grey or whistling plover more than any other of this family of birds; it is about the size of the yellow legged or large grey plover common to the lower part of this river as well as most parts of the Atlantic States where they are sometimes called the Jack curloo; the eye is moderately large, are black with a narrow ring of dark yellowish brown; the head, neck, upper part of the body and coverts of the wings are of a dove coloured brown, which when the bird is at rest is the predominant colour; the brest and belley are of a brownish white; the tail is composed of 12 feathers of 3 Ins. being of equal length, of these the two in the center are black, with traverse bars of yellowish brown; the others are a brownish white.   the large feathers of the wings are white tiped with blacked.   the beak is black, 2½ inches in length, slightly tapering, streight of a cilindric form and blontly or roundly pointed; the chaps are of equal length, and nostrils narrow. longitudional and connected; the feet and legs are smoth and of a greenish brown; has three long toes and a sho[r]t one on each foot, the long toes are unconnected with a web, and the short one is placed very high up the leg behind, insomuch that it dose not touch the ground when the bird stands erect.   the notes of this bird are louder and more various than any other of this family that I have seen.

Courses and distances of May 9th 1805.[7]		*miles*
N. 30° W.	to a clump of high trees on the Stard. side in a bend	2 ½
S. 15° W.	to the upper part of the Lard. point, passing over a large sand bar, at the upper point of a large ⟨sand bar is⟩ Island in a deep bend to the N.	2 ½
S. 5° W.	to a point of high timber on the Stard. side, opposite to a bluff point on Lard. side	3
S. 20° E.	to a willow point on the Stard. side	6
S. 10° E.	to the entrance of big Dry river on Lard. side.	1 ¼
S. 85° W.	to a bluff point on the Lard. side	1 ½
N. 60 W.	to a tree in the center of a bend on stard. passing over a sand point from Lard. side	3
South	to the upper part of a timbered bottom in a bend on Lard. side	1 ¾[8]
S. 60 W.	to the entrance of a small creek, in a bend on Stard. side called Werner's C. where we encamped for the night[9] ☞ [(]the water this Creek contained was principally backwater)	3

miles 24 ½

Point of Observation No. 14.

At our encampment of this evening, observed time and distance of ☽'s Western limb from Regulus, ★ West with Sextant.—

The mean result of a set of 10 obsertns.

	Time			*distance*
	h	m	s	
P. M.	10	6	13.4	43° 30° 15″

☞ It clouded up suddonly and prevented my takeing any observations with Antares.

[Clark]   *May 9th Thursday 1805*

a fine Day   wind from the East   we proceeded on verry well   the Countrey much the appearance which it had yesterday the bottom & high land rich black earth, Timber not so abondant as below, we passed the mouth of a river (or the appearance of a river) on the Lard. Side the bend of which as far as we went up it or could See from a high hill is as large as that of the Missouri at this place which is near half a mile   this river did not Contain one drop of running water, about a mile below this river a large Creeke joins the river L. S. which is also Dry—   Those dry Streams which are also verry wide, I think is the Conveyance of the melted Snow, & heavy rains which is ⟨Said to⟩ Probable fall in from the high moun-tanious Countrey which is Said to be between this river & the Yellow Stone river—   I walked on Shore the fore part of this day, & observed Great quantities of the Shining Stone which we view as *quarts*, I killed 2 Bucks & a Buffalow, Capt Lewis also killed one which verry good meat, I saw emunerable ⟨quantities⟩ herds of buffalow, & goats to day in every derec-tion—   The Missouri keeps its width which is nearly as wide as near its mouth, great number of Sand bars, the water not So muddy & Sand finer & in Smaller perpotion. Capt. Lewis killed 4 pleaver different from any I have ever before Seen, larger & have white breast & the underfeathers of the wings are white &c.

	miles	*Course & Distance 9th of May*
N. 30° W.	2 ½	to a clump of high trees on the Stard Side in a bend
S. 15° W.	· 2 ½	to the upper part of the Lard point, passing over a large Sand bar at the upper pt. of a willow Island in a deep bend to the N.
S. 5° W.	3	to a point of high timber on the Std. Side opsd. a bluff pt. on the Ld Side
S. 20° E,	6	to a willow point on the Std. Side
S. 10° E	1 ¼	to the enterance of a Great dry river on the Lard. Side.
S. 85° W.	1 ½	to a bluff point on the Lard. Side
N. 60° W.	3	to a tree in a bend to the Std. Side passing over a Sand pt. from L. S.
South	1 ¾	to the upper part of the timbered bottom on the Lad. Side in a bend
S 60° W	3	m to the mouth of a ⟨large⟩ Small creek in a bend to the
	m 24 ½	Stad Side in the mouth of which we came too for[10] the

night and called this creek Werner's Creek, the water it contained was principally backwater.

[Lewis]   *May 9th 1805.*[11]

I killed four plover [*EC: Symphemia Semipalmata*] this evening of a different kind from any I have yet seen. it resembles the grey or whistling plover more than any other of this family of birds, tho' it is much larger. it is about the size of the yellow leged plover common to the U' States, and called the jack curlooe by some. the legs are of a greenish brown; the toes, three and one high at the heel unconnected with a webb, the breast and belly of a brownish white; the head neck upper part of the body and coverts of the wings are of a dove colured brown which when the bird is at rest is the predomanent colour. the tale has 12 feathers of the same length ⟨nearly⟩ of which the two in the center are black with transverse bars of yellowish bron, the others are a brownish white. the large feathers of the wings are white tiped with black. the eyes are black with a small ring of dark yellowish brown— the beak is black, 2½ inches long, cilindrical, streight, and roundly or blountly pointed. the notes of this bird are louder and more various than of any other ⟨kind of⟩ species which I have seen.—

1. "Big Dry River" on *Atlas* maps 37, 49, 50, 58, it is still called Big Dry Fork, or Creek, in McCone and Garfield counties, Montana. Its lower reaches are now under Fort Peck Reservoir. Lewis's surprise reflects the unfamiliarity of Anglo-Americans of his time with large streams which are dry much of the year, as are so many in the West. MRC map 65.

2. Big Dry Creek derives its alluvium from the Fort Union Formation, Hell Creek Formation, and Fox Hills Sandstone. Sands in these formations are white, light yellow, or yellow-brown. The black clay comes from the Bearpaw Shale near the creek's mouth.

3. "Calf Brook" or "No Water Creek" on *Atlas* maps 37, 49, 58; present Bear Creek in McCone County. MRC map 65.

4. At this point, at the top of p. 99 in Codex D, Lewis drew a pointing hand and wrote, *"Turn over five leaves beginning at the center of the Page."* The entry for May 9 resumes at the top of p. 109. The intervening pages have entries from May 15 to May 19.

5. There is no talc in this portion of the Missouri River. The talc here is probably calcium, or sodium carbonate-rich, silt. The quartz is selenite (crystalline gypsum). It is common in the Bearpaw Shale and some crystals are quite large.

6. The willet, *Catoptrophorus semipalmatus* [AOU, 258], then new to science. Cutright (LCPN), 148, 431. The birds used for comparison are the lesser golden-plover and per-

haps the greater yellowlegs, *Tringa melanoleuca* [AOU, 254], Lewis's "Jack curloo." Someone drew a vertical line through this paragraph.

7. Also given on *Atlas* map 37, in both captains' hands.

8. Given as "2" on *Atlas* map 37, for a total mileage of of 24¾, in opposition to both captains' journals.

9. Present Duck Creek in Valley County, Montana, above Fort Peck. The campsite is in Valley County, a few miles above the town of Fort Peck, and would now be inundated by the Fort Peck Reservoir. *Atlas* maps 37, 50, 58; MRC map 65.

10. The remainder of the sentence appears to be in Lewis's hand.

11. Lewis's zoological note from Codex Q; the plovers are the willet noted above this day.

[Lewis] *Friday May 10th 1805.*

Set out at sunrise and proceeded but a short distance ere the wind became so violent that we were obliged to come too,[1] which we did on the Lard. side in a suddon or short bend of the river where we were in a great measure sheltered from the effects of the wind.   the wind continued violent all day, the clouds were thick and black, had a slight sprinkle of rain several times in the course of the day.   we sent out several hunters to scower the country, to this we were induced not so much from the want of provision as to discover the Indians whome we had reasons to believe were in the neighbourhood, from the circumstance of one of their dogs comeing to us this morning shortly after we landed; we still beleive ourselves in the country usually hunted by the Assinniboins, and as they are a vicious illy disposed nation we think it best to be on our guard, accordingly we inspected the arms and accoutrements the party and found them all in good order. The hunters returned this evening having seen no tents or Indians nor any fresh sign of them; they killed two Mule deer, one common fallow or longtailed deer, 2 Buffaloe and 5 beaver, and saw several deer of the Mule kind of immence size, and also three of the Bighorned anamals.   from the appearance of the Mule deer and the bighorned anamals we beleive ourselves fast approaching a hilly or mountainous country; we have rarely found the mule deer in any except a rough country; they prefer the open grounds and are seldom found in the woodlands near the river; when they are met with in the woodlands or river bottoms and are pursued, the[y] invariably run to the hills or open country as the

Elk do.   the contrary happens with the common deer   ther are several esscential differences between the Mule and common deer as well in form as in habits.   they are fully a third larger in general, and the male is particularly large; I think there is somewhat greater disparity of size between the male and female of this speceis than there is between the male and female fallow deer; I am convinced I have seen a buck of this species twice the volume of a buck of any other species.   the ears are peculiarly large; I measured those of a large buck which I found to be eleven inches long and 3½ in width at the widest part; they are not so delicately formed, their hair in winter is thicker longer and of a much darker grey, in summer the hair is still coarser longer and of a paleer red, more like that of the Elk; in winter they also have a considerable quantity of a very fine wool intermixed with the hair and lying next to the skin as the Antelope has.   the long hair which grows on the outer sides of the 1st joint of the hinder legs, and which in the common deer do not usually occupy more than 2 inches in them occupys from 6 to eight; their horns also differ, these in the common deer consist of two main beams from which one or more points project the beam graduly deminishing as the points procede from it, with the mule deer the horns consist of two beams which at the distance of 4 or 6 inches from the head divide themselves each into two equal branches which again either divide into two other equal branches or terminate in a smaller, ⟨one⟩ and two equal ones; having either 2 4 or 6 points on a beam; the horn is not so rough about the base as the common deer and are invariably of a much darker colour.   the most striking difference of all, is the white rump and tale.   from the root of the tail as a center there is a circular spot perfectly white, of abot 3 inches radius, which occupys a part of the rump and extremitys of the buttocks and joins the white of the belley underneath; the tail which is usually from 8 to 9 inches long, ⟨is covered⟩ for the first 4 or 5 inches from it's upper extremity is covered with sho[r]t white hairs, much shorter indeed than the hairs of the body; from hence for about one inch further the hair is still white but gradually becomes longer, the tail then terminates in a tissue of black hair of about 3 Inches long.   from this black hair of the tail they have obtained among the French engages the appelation of the

black taled deer, but this I conceive by no means characteristic of the anamal as much the larger portion of the tail is white.   the year and the tail
of this anamal when compared with those of the common deer, so well
comported with those of the mule when compared with the horse, that
we have by way of distinction adapted the appellation of the mule deer
which I think much more appropriate.   on the inner corner of each eye
there is a drane or large recepicle which seems to answer as a drane to the
eye which gives it the appearance of weeping, this in the common deer of
the atlantic states is scarcely perceptable but becomes more conspicuous
in the fallow deer, and still more so in the Elk; this recepticle in the Elk is
larger than in any of the pecora order with which I am acquainted.[2]

Boils and imposthumes have been very common with the party[3]   Bratton is now unable to work with one on his hand; soar eyes continue also to
be common to all of us in a greater or less degree.   for the imposthume I
use emmolient poltices, and for soar eyes a solution of white vitriol and
the sugar of lead in the proportion of 2 grs. of the former and one of the
latter to each ounce of water.[4]

Courses and distances May 10th 1805.[5]

South	to a naked point on the Stard side	1 ¼
S. 10° W.	to a point on the Lard. side opposite to a bluff on Lard.[6] water strong	1 ¾
N. 45° E.	to the upper part of some timber in a bend on Lard. side, where we encamped	1 ¼
		miles 4 ¼

Point of Observation No. 15.

On the Lard. shore about the middle of the 3rd course of this day.   took
Equal altitudes of with ☉ sextant.

	h	m	s					
A. M.	8	58	14	P. M.	lost by	}	Altd. of Sext.	
	"	59	48		the clouds		72 12 45	
	9	1	31					

[Clark] *May the 10th Friday 1805*

river fell ¾ of an inch last night, wind from the N. W, we proceeded on but a short distance e'r'e the wind became So violent we could not proceed came to on the Lard. Side in a Short bend, the wind Continued all day   Several times in the course of the day We had some fiew drops of rain from verry black Clouds, no thunder or lightning latterly, Soon after we landed a Dog came to us from the opposit Side, which induced a belief that we had not passd. the Assinniboin Indians, parties wer Sent on the hills in different derections to examine but Saw no tents or fresh Sign.   examined the arms &c. of the party found all in good order. Three mule deer, two Buffalow & 5 beaver killed, 3 of the mountain ram Seen.

Course & Distance the 10th of May 1805

South	1 ¼	miles to a naked point on the Stard. Side
S. 10° W.	1 ¾	miles to a point on the Lard Side opposit to a Bluff on the Stard. Side water Strong
N. 45° E.	1 ¼	to the upper part of Some timber in a bend to the Lard
	4 ¼	Side, at which place we camped

The mule Deer Described in Book No. 8[7]

1. In either Garfield or Valley County, Montana, on a site now inundated by Fort Peck Reservoir. *Atlas* maps 37, 50, 58; MRC map 65.

2. This paragraph, beginning with "they killed two Mule deer," has a vertical line drawn through it.

3. Chuinard suggests the effects of malnutrition and even mild scurvy, owing to the meat diet. Chuinard (OOMD), 24.

4. Perhaps a recipe of Benjamin Rush's, taken from his *Recipe Book* or given directly to Lewis. White vitriol is zinc sulphate and sugar of lead is lead acetate. Ibid., 364 & n. 4; Cutright (LCPN), 127.

5. Also given on *Atlas* map 37, in Clark's hand.

6. Starboard in Clark's entry and *Atlas* map 37.

7. A reference to a description of the mule deer in Clark's notebook journal Voorhis No. 2 (no. 8 in Clark's original numbering system), dated March 11, 1806.

[Lewis] *Saturday May 11th 1805.*

Set out this morning at an early hour, the courant strong; and river very crooked; the banks are falling in very fast; I sometimes wonder that some of our canoes or perogues are not swallowed up by means of these immence masses of earth which are eternally precipitating themselves into the river; we have had many hair breadth escapes from them but providence seems so to have ordered it that we have as yet sustained no loss in consequence of them. The wind blue very hard the forepart of last night but abated toward morning; it again arose in the after part of this day and retarded our progress very much.   the high lands are broken, the hills higher and approach nearer the river, tho' the soil of both hills and bottoms appear equally as furtile as below; it consists of a black look-ing lome with a moderate portion of sand; the hills and bluffs to the debth of 20 or thirty feet, seemed to be composed entirely of this loam; when thrown in the water it desolves as readily as loaf sugar and effervesses like marle.   great appearance of quarts and mineral salts, the latter appears both on the hills and bottoms, in the bottoms of the gullies which make down from the hills it lies incrusting the earth to the debth of 2 or 3 inches, and may with a fether be swept up and collected in large quantities, I pre-served several specimines of this salts.   the quarts appears most commonly in the faces of the bluffs.   no coal, burnt hills, or pumice stone.[1]   saw today some high hills on the Stard. whose summits were covered with pine. Capt Clark went on shore and visited them; he brought with him on his return som of the boughs of this pine it is of the pitch kind but I think the leaves somewhat longer than ours in Virginia.[2] Capt C. also in his walk killed 2 Mule deer a beaver and two buffaloe; these last he killed about 3 miles above where we encamped this evening in the expectation that we would reach that place, but we were unable to do so from the adverse winds and other occurrences, and he came down and joined us about dark.   there is a dwarf cedar growing among the pine on the hills; it rises to the hight thre sometimes 4 feet, but most generally spreads itself like a vine along the surface of the earth, which it covers very closely, puting out roots from the underside of the limbs; the leaf is finer and more delicate than the common red ceader, it's fruit and smell are the same with the red ceader.[3]   the tops of these hills which produce the pine and cedar is of a different soil from that just described; it is a light coloured poor sterile sandy soil, the base usually a yellow or white clay;[4] it produces scarcely any grass, some scattering tuffts of sedge[5] constitutes the greater part of it's grass. About 5 P. M. my attention was struck by one of the Party runing at a distance towards us and making signs and hollowing as if in distress, I ordered the perogues to put too, and waited untill he arrived; I now found that it was Bratton the man with the soar hand whom I had permitted to walk on shore, he arrived so much out of breath that it was several minutes before he could tell what had happened; at length he informed me that in the woody bottom on the Lard. side about 1 ½ below us he had shot a brown bear which immediately turned on him and pursued him a considerable distance but he had wounded it so badly that it could not overtake him; I immediately turned out with seven of the party in quest of this monster, we at length found his trale and persued him about a mile by the blood through very thick brush of rosbushes and the large leafed willow; we finally found him concealed in some very thick brush and shot him through the skull with two balls; we proceeded dress him as soon as possible, we found him in good order; it was a monstrous beast, not quite so large as that we killed a few days past but in all other rispects much the same   the hair is remarkably long fine and rich tho' he appears parshally to have discharged his winter coat; we now found that Bratton had shot him through the center of the lungs, notwithstanding which he had pursued him near half a mile and had returned more than double that distance and with his tallons had prepared himself a bed in the earth of about 2 feet deep and five long and was perfectly alive when we found him which could not have been less than 2 hours after he received the wound; these bear being so hard to die reather intimedates us all; I must confess that I do not like the gentlemen and had reather fight two Indians than one bear; there is no other chance to conquer them by a single shot but by shooting them through the brains, and this becomes difficult in consequence of two large muscles which cover the sides of the forehead and the sharp projection of the center of the frontal bone, which is also of a pretty good thickness.   the flece and skin were as much as two men could possibly carry.   by the time we returned the sun had set and I determined to remain here all night,[6] and directed the cooks to render the bear's oil and put it in the kegs which was done.   there was about eight gallons of it.—

the wild Hysop grows here and in all the country through which we

have passed for many days past; [*NB: Copy for Dr Barton*] tho' from big
Dry river to this place it has been more abundant than below, and a smaller
variety of it grows on the hills, the leaves of which differ considerably being
more deeply indented near it's extremity.[7]   the buffaloe deer and Elk feed
on this herb in the winter season as they do also on the small willow of the
sandbars.   there is another growth that begins now to make it's appearance in the bottom lands and is becoming extreemly troublesome; it is a
shrub which rises to the hight of from two to four feet, much branched,
the bark of the trunk somewhat rough hard and of light grey colour; the
wood is firm and stif, the branches beset with a great number of long,
shap, strong, wooddy looking thorns; the leaf is about ¾ or an inch long,
and one ⅛ of an inch wide, it is obtuse, absolutely entire, veinless fleshy
and gibbose; has no perceptable taste or smell, and no anamal appears to
eat it.   by way of designating when I mention it hereafter I shall call it the
fleshey leafed thorn[8]

Courses and distances May 11th 1805[9]

South	to the upper part of some high timber on the Lard. side passing over a sand pont Lard.	1 ½
S. 50° W.	to the upper part of the timber in a bend on Stard. side	1 ½
South	to the commencement of a wood on Stard side, opposite to a Lard. point	¾
S. 68° E.	to the upper part of the timber in a bend on Lard. side, passing over a sand bar from a Stard. point	1 ¾
S. 10° E.	to the upper part of a sand-bar on the Stard. side opposite to a bluff	1 ½
S. 85° W.	to some timber in the center of a bend on Stard. side, passing a sand point on Lard at ¾	2
S. 10° E.	to a point of woodland on the Lard. side	1
S. 40° E.	to the point of a sand-bar on Stard. oposite to a low bluf	2 ½
S. 80° W.	to a point of woodland on the Lard side, passing a point of woodland on Std. side at ½ a mile, a deep bend to the N. W.	1 ¼
S. 75° W.	to a high bluff point in a bend on Stard. ☞ S. W. from hence	

distant 3 Miles is a ridge of high lands covered with pine
which is the first we have yet seen on the Missouri   1

S. 25° E.   to the point of a sand-bar on the Stard. ½ below which we
             encamped on the Lad.   2 ¼

                                                              Miles 17

Point of Observation No. 16.

On the Lard. shore about the middle of the 4th course of this day observed
equal altitudes of ☉ with Sext.

	h	m	s			
	h	m	s			
A M.	8	15	33.8	P. M.	lost in consequence	Altd. by Sextant
"		17	7.5		of the intervention	58° 41′ 30″
"		18	43		of clouds	

Point of Observation No. 17.

On the Lard. shore at the middle of the 8th course of this day, observed Meridian altd. of ☉'s L. L. with Octant by the back observation 64° 51′

Latitude deduced from this observtn. [*blank*]

[Clark]   *May the 11th Satturday 1805.*

Wind hard fore part of last night   the latter part verry Cold a white
frost this morning, the river riseing a little and verry Crooked   the high
land is rugged and approaches nearer than below, the hills and bluff exhibit more mineral quats & Salts than below, the gullies in maney places
are white, and their bottoms one, two & 3 Inches deep of this mineral, no
appearance of either burnt pumice Stone or Coal, the Countrey hilley on
both Sides of a rich black earth, which disolves ⟨like loaf Sugar in water,⟩
This kind of Countrey Continues of the Same quallity for maney miles on
either Side, we observed Some hills which appeared to be timbered, I
walked to this timber and found it to pitch pine & Dwarf Cedar, we observe
in every derection Buffalow, Elk, Antelopes & Mule deer inumerable and
So jintle that we Could approach near them with great ease, I killed 2
Mule Deer for the benifit of their Skins for the party, and about the place
I expected the party would get to Camp I killed 2 fat Bulls for theire use,
in my absence they had killed a fine fat Yellow *bear* below which detained

them and they did not reach the place I expected, but had Camped on the Lard. Side about 2 miles below   on my return to the party I killed a fat Beaver   the wind blew verry hard from the S. W. all the after part of this day which retarded our progress verry much.   river rose 2 In

	miles	*Course & Distance the 11th of May*
South	1 ½	to the upper part of a high timber on the Stard Side passing over a Sand point from the Ld. Side
S. 50° W.	1 ½	to the upper part of the timbered in a bend to the Stard. Side.
South	¾	to the Commencement of a wood on the Std. Side opsd. a point on L. S.
S 68° E	1 ¾	to the upper part of the timber in a bend on the Lard. Side passing over a Sand bar from Stard point
S. 10° E	1 ½	to the upper part of a Sand bar on the Stard Side opposit a Bluff
S. 85° W.	2	to Some timber in the Center of a bend on the Stard. Side passing a Sand point on the Lard. at ¾ of a mile
S. 10° E,	1	to a point of wood land on the Lard Side
S. 40° E.	2 ½	to the point of a Sand bar on the Stard Side opposit a low bluff
S. 80° W.	1 ¼	to a point of wood land on the Lard Side passing a pt. of wood land on S. S. at ½ m. a Deep bend to N W.
S. 75° W	1	to a high bluff point in a bend to the Std. Side S W 3 miles is a ridge of high land covered with *pine* which is the first we have seen on Missouri
S 25 E	2 ¼	to the pt. of a Sand bar on the Stard. ½ a mile below which, we encamped
miles 17		

1. The soil here is derived from weathered late Cretaceous sandstone and shale. It does not dissolve in water but readily dissociates. Salts are especially common in the Bearpaw Shale. The "quartz" is selenite. There is no coal in the formations near the river.

2. Probably northeast of what is now The Pines Recreation Area, in Valley County, Montana, on the edge of Fort Peck Lake. The needles of this pine, *Pinus ponderosa* Laws., ponderosa pine, are indeed longer than the pitch-pine, *P. rigida* Mill., with which Lewis was familiar from Virginia. Little, 64-W, 71-E; Fernald, 57.

3. Someone drew a vertical line through this passage about the dwarf cedar.

4. These hills are capped by the Hell Creek Formation and the Fox Hills Sandstone or their weathered products. These formations contain abundant white, light yellow-white sand, sandstone, and siltstone.

5. Probably *Carex filifolia* Nutt., thread-leaved sedge, a drought tolerant sedge, commonly found in similar sites and a common plant of this area. Barkley, 440; Weaver & Albertson, 39.

6. In Garfield County, a site now inundated by Fort Peck Reservoir. *Atlas* maps 37, 50, 58; MRC map 66.

7. Perhaps *Artemisia nova* A. Nels., black sagebrush. If true, the presence of black sagebrush in the Piney Buttes of Garfield County extends its known range to the east. Shultz, 45. It was probably Biddle who drew a red line through this paragraph.

8. *Sarcobatus vermiculatus* (Hook.) Torr. in Emory, greasewood, then new to science. A salt tolerant species which indicates alkaline soil. Barkley, 69; Booth & Wright, 48; Cutright (LCPN), 137.

9. Also given on *Atlas* map 37, in both captains' hands.

[Lewis]   *Sunday May 12th 1805.*

Set out at an early hour, the weather clear and Calm; I walked on shore this morning for the benifit of exersize which I much wanted, and also to examine the country and it's productions, in these excurtions I most generally went alone armed with my rifle and espontoon; thus equiped I feel myself more than an equal match for a brown bear provided I get him in open woods or near the water, but feel myself a little diffident with respect to an attack in the open plains, I have therefore come to a resolution to act on the defencive only, should I meet these gentlemen in the open country. I ascended the hills and had a view of a rough and broken country on both sides of the river; on the North side the summits of the hills exhibit some scattering pine and cedar, on the South side the pine has not yet commenced tho' there is some cedar on the face of the hills and in the little ravines.   the choke cherry also grows here in the hollows and at the heads of the gullies; the choke Cherry has been in blume since the ninth inst.   this growth has freequently made it's appearance on the Missouri from the neighbourhood of the *Baldpated Prarie,* to this place   in the form of it's leaf colour and appearance of it's bark, and general figure of it's growth it resembles much the Morillar cherry,[1] tho' much smaller not generally rising to a greater hight than from 6 to 10 feet and ascociating in thick clusters or clumps in their favorit situations which is usually the heads of small ravines or along the sides of small brooks which flow from the hills. the flowers which are small and white are supported by a common footstalk as those of the common wild cherry are, the corolla consists of five oval petals, five stamen and one pistillum, and of course of the Class and order Pentandria Monogynia.[2] it bears a fruit which much resembles the wild cherry in form and colour tho' larger and better flavoured; it's fruit ripens about the begining of July and continues on the trees untill the latter end of September— The Indians of the Missouri make great uce of this cherry which they prepare for food in various ways, sometimes eating when first plucked from the trees or in that state pounding them ⟨and⟩ mashing the seed boiling them with roots or meat, or with the prarie beans[3] and white-apple; again for their winter store they geather them and lay them on skins to dry in the sun, and frequently pound them and make them up in small roles or cakes and dry them in the sun; when thus dryed they fold them in skins or put them in bags of parchment and keep them through the winter either eating them in this state or boiling them as before mentioned. the bear and many birds also feed on these burries. the wild hysop sage, *fleshey leaf thorn,* and some other herbs also grow in the plains and hills, particularly the arromatic herb on which the Antelope and large hare feed. The soil has now changed it's texture considerably; the base of the hills and river bottoms continue the same and are composed of a rich black loam while the summits of the hills and about half their hight downwards are of a light brown colour, poor sterile and intermixed with a coarse white sand.[4] about 12 OClock the wind veered about to the N. W. and blew so hard that we were obliged to Ly by the ballance of the day.[5] we saw great quantities of game as usual. the bottom lands still becomeing narrower.

Courses and distances May 12th 1805.[6]

S. 45° W.	to a point of high wood on the Stard. side passing a bluff on Lard. just above which a creek[7] 20 yards wide falls in on Lard Sd	1
S. 70° W.	to a point of cottonwood on the Lard. Sd.	2 ½

S. 30° W.	to the upper part of a point on the Lard Sd. opposite to a bluf on Stard. side	½
S. 22° E.	to a white tree in a bend on Lard. side	2
S. 40° W.	to a point on Stard. opposite to a bluiff on Lard;	1 ½
S. 60° W.	to the upper part of a timbered bottom in a bend on Stard. side	2 ½
S. 40° W.	to a point of woodland on the Lard. side, opposite to which pine Creek falls in on Stard side 20 yds. wide, little water[8]	1 ¾
S. 10° E.	to a willow point on the Stard. side	1 ½
S. 45° W.	Along the stard. side opposite to a bluff	1
N. 54° W.	to some timber in the center of a bend Std.	1 ½
S. 15° W.	to a point of woodland on the Lard. side opposit a bluff on Stard.	1
S. 10° W.	to a point of wood and on the Stard side opposite to a high bluff, the river making a deep bend to the S. E. in which there is a willow Island, opposite to the lower point of which we encamped on the Lard. side	2

Miles— 18 ¾

About sunset it began to rain, and continued to fall a few drops at a time untill midnight; the wind blew violently all night.—

[Clark]   *May 12th Sunday 1805.*

Set out at an early hour, the morning Clear and Calm, Capt. Lewis walked on Shore this morning   about 12 oClock the wind becam Strong from the E.   about half past one oClock the wind Shifted round to the N. W. and blew verry hard all the latter part of the day, which obliged us to Lay by— The Countrey is hilley & rugged and the earth of a lightish brown and but indifferent, Some Small Cedar is Scattered on the Sides of the hils & in the hollars, Some pine ridges is also to be Seen on the North Side, we observe great quantites of game as usual. I killed a beaver in the water, Saw Several Sitting on the bank near the waters edge

	mile	*Course & Distance 12th of May*
S. 45° W.	1	mile to a point of high wood on the Stard Side passing a Bluff on the Ld. Side above which a Creek 20 yds. wide falls in L. S.
S. 70° W.	2 ½	to a point of Cotton wood on the Lard Side
S. 30° W.	½	to the upper part of the point on the Lard Side opposit a bluff S. S.
S. 22° E.	2	to a white tree in a bend to the Ld. Sd.
S. 40° W.	1 ½	to the point on the Stard. Side opposit a Bluff on the L. S.
S 60° W.	2 ½	to the upper part of a timberd. bottom in a bend to the Std. Side
S. 40° W,	1 ¾	to a point of wood land on the Lard Side, opposit to which *Pine* Creek falls in on the Stard Side 20 yards wide
S. 10° E.	1 ½	to a willow point on the Stard Side
S. 45° W.	1	on the Stard Side opposit a Bluff
N. 54° W	1 ½	to Some timber in the center of the Stard Bend
S. 15° W.	1	to a point of wood land on the Lard Side opposit a Bluff
S. 10° W.	2	to a point of wood land on the Stard Side opposit a high
	18 ¾	Bluff on the Lard Side, the river making a deep bend to the S E in which there is a Willow Island, opposit the lower point of which we camped on the Lard. Side

about Sunset it began to rain, and rained very moderately only a fiew drops at a time for about half the night, wind Continued violent all night

1. *Prunus cerasus* L., sour cherry. The morello is a variety of sour, or pie, cherry. Bailey, 544. It may have been Biddle who drew a vertical line through the passage, beginning with "the choke cherry" to "end of September."

2. Another rare instance of Lewis using Latin terminology. In this case the term describes a subdivision of flowering plants which have five stamens and one pistil.

3. The hog peanut (see April 9, 1805). Barkley, 158; Gilmore (UPI), 43–44.

4. The Missouri River cuts across a preglacial drainage divide here. As the valley narrows, the Hell Creek Formation and Fox Hills Sandstone extend lower down toward the river. These lighter colored formations overlie the darker colored Bearpaw Shale.

5. In Garfield County, Montana, on a site now inundated by Fort Peck Reservoir. *Atlas* maps 37, 50, 58; MRC map 66.

6. Also given on *Atlas* map 37, in both captains' hands.

7. Perhaps later Catamount Creek, today's Sage Creek, in Garfield County. *Atlas* maps 37, 50, 58; MRC map 66; USGS map Fort Peck Lake East.

8. Later Seventh Point Coulee in Valley County, Montana; nameless on MRC map 66. *Atlas* maps 37, 50, 58; USGS map Fort Peck Lake East.

[Lewis]   *Monday May 13th 1805.*

The wind continued to blow so violently this morning that we did not think it prudent to set out.   sent out some hunters. At 1 P. M. the wind abated, and altho' the hunters had not all returned we set out; the courant reather stronger than usual and the water continues to become reather clearer, from both which I anticipate a change of Country shortly.   the country much the same as yesterday; but little timber in the bottoms and a scant proportion of pine an cedar crown the Stard. hills.   Capt C. who was on shore the greater part of the day killed a mule and a Common deer, the party killed several deer and some Elk principally for the bene- fit of their skins which are necessary to them for cloathing, the Elk skins I now begin to reserve for making the leather boat at the falls.   the hunt- ers joined us this evening; Gibson had wounded a very large brown bear but it was too late in the evening to pursue him.

Courses and distances May 13th 1805.[1]

S 35° W.	along the Stard. shore to a point of high timber opposite to a bluff, passing the entrance of two Creeks on Lard. 1st 18 2cd 30 yards wide neither discharging any water at present	1 ½
S. 50° W.	Along the Stard. point opposite to a high blf.	1
N. 75° W.	to a point of woodland on the Lard. side	2
S. 80° W.	Along the Lard. shore to a point of wood land near which we encamped on Lard. shore	2 ½

Miles 7

Point of Observation No. 18.

At our encampment of this evening on Lard. side observed time and distance of ☽'s Western limb from Antares; ★ East with Sextant.—

Mean of sundry Observations.

	Time			Distance		
	h	m	s			
P. M.	11	51	18.4	39°	10'	30"

[Clark]   *13th of May Monday 1805*

The wind Continued to blow hard untill one oClock P M. to day at which time it fell a little and we Set out and proceeded on verry well about 9 miles and Camped on the Lard Side.[2]   the countrey much the Same appearance as yesterday but little timber in the bottoms; Some Pine in places on the Stard. Hills. I killed two deer this evening one a mule deer & the other a common Deer, the party killed Several this morning all for the use of their Skins which are now good, one man Gibson wounded a verry large *brown bear,* too late this evening to prosue him—   We passed two Creeks in a bend to the Lard Side neither them had any water,[3]

	miles	*Course & Distance 13th of May 1805*
S. 35° W.	1 ½	along the Std. Shore to a point of high timber opposit a bluff, passing the enterence of two Creeks on the L. S. neither of which discharge any water at this time. 1st 18 2d 30 yds wide
S 50° W.	1	along the Std. point oppsd. a high bluff
N. 75° W.	2	to a point of wood land on the Lard. Side
S. 80° W	2 ½	along the Lard Shore to a point of wood land near which we incamped on the Lard Side
miles	7	

1. Also given on *Atlas* map 38, in Lewis's hand.

2. In Garfield County, Montana, on a site now inundated by Fort Peck Reservoir, about one or two miles above the former entrance of today's Crooked Creek (see below). *Atlas* maps 38, 50, 58; MRC map 66.

3. The first is today's Sheep Creek; the second is later Flirt Creek, today's Crooked Creek, both in Garfield County. *Atlas* maps 38, 50, 58; MRC map 66; USGS map Fort Peck Lake East.

[Lewis]   *Tuesday May 14th 1805.*

Some fog on the river this morning, which is a very rare occurrence; the country much as it was yesterday with this difference that the bottoms are somewhat wider; passed some high black bluffs. saw immence herds of buffaloe today also Elk deer wolves and Antelopes. passed three large creeks one on the Stard. and two others on the Lard. side,[1] neither of which had any runing water. Capt Clark walked on shore and killed a very fine buffaloe cow. I felt an inclination to eat some veal and walked on shore and killed a very fine buffaloe calf and a large woolf, much the whitest I had seen, it was quite as white as the wool of the common sheep. one of the party wounded a brown bear very badly, but being alone did not think proper to pursue him. In the evening the men in two of the rear canoes discovered a large brown bear lying in the open grounds about 300 paces from the river, and six of them went out to attack him, all good hunters; they took the advantage of a small eminence which concealed them and got within 40 paces of him unperceived, two of them reserved their fires as had been previously conscerted, the four others fired nearly at the same time and put each his bullet through him, two of the balls passed through the bulk of both lobes of his lungs, in an instant this monster ran at them with open mouth, the two who had reserved their fires discharged their pieces at him as he came towards them, boath of them struck him, one only slightly and the other fortunately broke his shoulder, this however only retarded his motion for a moment only, the men unable to reload their guns took to flight, the bear pursued and had very nearly overtaken them before they reached the river; two of the party betook themselves to a canoe and the others seperated an concealed themselves among the willows, reloaded their pieces, each discharged his piece at him as they had an opportunity they struck him several times again but the guns served only to direct the bear to them, in this manner he pursued two of them seperately so close that they were obliged to throw aside their guns and pouches and throw themselves into the river altho' the bank was nearly twenty feet perpendicular; so enraged was this anamal that he plunged into the river only a few feet behind the second man he had compelled take refuge in the water, when one of those who still remained on shore shot him through the head and finally killed him; they then took him on shore and butched him when they found eight balls had passed through him in different directions; the bear being old the flesh was indifferent, they therefore only took the skin and fleece,[2] the latter made us several gallons of oil; it was after the sun had set before these men come up with us, where we had been halted by an occurrence, which I have now to re-cappitulate, and which altho' happily passed without ruinous injury, I cannot recollect but with the utmost trepidation and horror; this is the upseting and narrow escape of the white perogue   It happened unfortu-nately for us this evening that Charbono was at the helm of this Perogue, in stead of Drewyer, who had previously steered her; Charbono cannot swim and is perhaps the most timid waterman in the world; perhaps it was equally unluckey that Capt. C. and myself were both on shore at that moment, a circumstance which rarely happened; and tho' we were on the shore opposite to the perogue, were too far distant to be heard or to do more than remain spectators of her fate; in this perogue [*blank with apparent erasures*] were embarked, our papers, Instruments, books medi-cine, a great part of our merchandize and in short almost every article indispensibly necessary to further the views, or insure the success of the enterprize[3] ⟨of the expedition⟩ in which we are now launched to the dis-tance of 2200 miles.   surfice it to say, that the Perogue was under sail when a sudon squawl of wind struck her obliquely, and turned her con-siderably, the steersman allarmed, in stead of puting her before the wind, lufted her up into it, the wind was so violent that it drew the brace of the squarsail out of the hand of the man who was attending it, and instantly upset the perogue and would have turned her completely topsaturva, had it not have been from the resistance mad by the oarning against the water; in this situation Capt. C and myself both fired our guns to attract the attention if possible of the crew and ordered the halyards to be cut and the sail hawled in, but they did not hear us; such was their confusion and consternation at this moment, that they suffered the perogue to lye on her side for half a minute before they took the sail in, the perogue then wrighted but had filled within an inch of the gunwals; Charbono still crying to his god for mercy, had not yet recollected the rudder, nor could the repeated orders of the Bowsman, Cruzat, bring him to his recollec-tion untill he threatend to shoot him instantly if he did not take hold of the rudder and do his duty, the waves by this time were runing very high, but the fortitude resolution and good conduct of Cruzat saved her; he ordered 2 of the men to throw out the water with some kettles that fortunately were convenient, while himself and two others rowed her as[h]ore, where she arrived scarcely above the water; we now took every article out of her and lay them to drane as well as we could for the evening, baled out the canoe and secured her; there were two other men beside Charbono on board who could not swim, and who of course must also have perished had the perogue gone to the bottom.   while the perogue lay on her side, finding I could not be heard, I for a moment forgot my own situation, and involluntarily droped my gun, threw aside my shot pouch and was in the act of unbuttoning my coat, before I recollected the folly of the attempt I was about to make, which was to throw myself into the river and indevour to swim to the perogue; the perogue was three hundred yards distant the waves so high that a perogue could scarcely live in any situation, the water excessively could, and the stream rappid; had I undertaken this project therefore, there was a hundred to one but what I should have paid the forfit of my life for the madness of my project, but this had the perogue been lost, I should have valued but little.—[4] After having all matters arranged for the evening as well as the nature of circumstances would permit, we thought it a proper occasion to console ourselves and cheer the sperits of our men and accordingly took a drink of grog and gave each man a gill of sperits.

Courses and distances of May 14th 1805[5]

S. 55° W.	Along the Stard.[6] side, water swift	1
S. 35 W.	Along the Lard. side, opposite the lower point of an island in a bend on Stard.	½
S 20° W.	Along the Lard. side passing the head of an Island opposite to which a large creek falls in on the Stard. side, or *Gibson's Creek*	½
S. 12° E.	to a point of timber on the Stard. side opposite to a high hill on Lard.	3
S. 20° W.	to a point of timbered land on the Stard. side, a bluff point of rocks on Lard. passing a creek on Lard. called Stick Lodge C.	2 ½
S. 80° W.	to a point of timbered land on the Lard passing a point of woodland Stard at 1 m	3

S. 85° W.	to a point of timbered land on the Lard passing a Large dry creek Lard. the Brown bear defeat.	2 ½
S. 62° W.	to a point of woodland on the Stard. side at which place our perogue had very nearly been lost	3 ½

Miles— 16 ½[7]

[Clark]   *14th of May Tuesday 1805*

A verry Clear Cold morning a white frost & some fog on the river   the Thermomtr Stood at 32 above 0, wind from the S. W.   we proceeded on verry well untill about 6 oClock a Squawl of wind Struck our Sale broad Side and turned the perogue nearly over, and in this Situation the Perogue remained untill the Sale was Cut down in which time She nearly filed with water—   the articles which floated out was nearly all caught by the Squar who was in the rear. This accident had like to have cost us deerly;[8] for in this perogue were embarked our papers, Instruments, books, medicine, a great proportion of our merchandize, and in short almost every article indispensibly necessary to further the views, or insure the success of the enterprize in which, we are now launched to the distance of 2,200 miles.   it happened unfortunately that Capt. Lewis and myself were both on shore at the time of this occurrence, a circumstance which seldom took place; and tho' we were on the shore opposit to the perogue were too far distant to be heard or do more than remain spectators of her fate; we discharged our guns with the hope of attracting the attention of the crew and ordered the sail to be taken in but such was their consternation and confusion at the instant that they did not hear us.   when however they at length took in the sail and the perogue wrighted; the bowsman Cruzatte by repeated threats so far brought Charbono the Sternman to his recollection that he did his duty while two hands bailed the perogue and Cruzatte and two others rowed her on shore were she arrived scarcely above the water.   we owe the preservation of the perogue to the resolution and fortitude of Cruzatte

The Countrey like that of yesterday, passed a Small Island and the enterence of ⟨two⟩ 3 large Creeks, one on the Stard. & the other 2 on the Lard Side, neither of them had any running water at this time—   Six good hunters of the party fired at a Brown or Yellow *Bear* Several times before they killed him, & indeed he had like to have defeated the whole party, he pursued them Seperately as they fired on him, and was near Catching Several of them   one he pursued into the river, this bear was large & fat would way about 500 wt; I killed a Buffalow, & Capt. Lewis a Calf & a wolf this evening.

	mile	*Course & Distance May 14th 1805*
S 55° W.	1	on the Lard Side Swift water
S 35° W	½	allong the Lard Side opsd. the lower point of an Isd. in a bind to Std. Side.
S. 20° W	½	allong the Lard. Side passed the hd. of the Isd. opsd. to which a large creek falls in on the Std. Side Gibsons Creek
S. 12° E,	3	to a point of timber on the Std. Side high hills on the Lard Side
S. 20° W	2 ½	to a point of timbered land on the Std Side, a bluff on Lard Side
S. 80° W	3	to a point of timbered land on the Lard. Side, passd. a point of wood land on the Std. Side at 1 mile
S. 85° W	2 ½	to a point of timbered land on Lard. Sd. Passt. Yellow Bear Defeat creek 40 yds. wide
S. 62° W	3 ½	to a point of wood land on the Stard Side, at which place one perogue like to have been lost & we camped[9]
	16 ½	

1. On *Atlas* maps 38, 50, 58, the three are Gibson's, Stick Lodge, and Brown Bear Defeated creeks. Presently they are Sutherland Creek, in Valley County, Montana, Hell Creek, and Snow Creek, in Garfield County. MRC map 67 shows a "Gibson Creek" and a "Stick Lodge Creek," but these appear to be upstream from the creeks the captains gave those names. Since Clark's route maps were not available until the twentieth century, nineteenth-century mapmakers probably guessed from Clark's 1814 map (*Atlas* map 126) and Biddle's *History*. Coues (HLC), 1 : 309; MRC maps 66, 67; USGS map Fort Peck Lake East; USGS map Fort Peck Lake West.

2. "Fleece" can refer to the fat on the sides of a buffalo's hump; here it evidently means a layer of fat under the skin that could be boiled down for oil. Criswell, 39.

3. Someone has drawn a dark, bold, vertical line through this passage, beginning with, "in this perogue."

4. Someone has scratched lightly through these words, apparently in red ink, beginning with, "but this had."

5. Also given on *Atlas* map 38, in both captains' hands.

6. "Lard." in Clark's entry and apparently on *Atlas* map 38.

7. At this point in Codex D, p. 129, Lewis has a pointing hand and has written, "Turn back 15 leaves, read from the 15th to the 19 of May inclusive and return to this place." The entry for May 15 is on p. 99 of Codex D and the entries continue in sequence, as he says, to May 19, on p. 106.

8. From here to the end of the paragraph the words are in Lewis's hand.

9. The campsite, now under Fort Peck Reservoir, is in Valley County, a few miles above present Snow Creek, Lewis and Clark's Brown Bear Defeat Creek. They remained there until May 16. *Atlas* maps 38, 50, 58; MRC map 67.

[Lewis]   *Wednesday May 15th*

as soon as a slight shower of rain passed over this morning, we spread the articles to dry which had got wet yesterday in the white perogue; tho' the day proved so cloudy and damp that they received but little benifit from the sun or air; we were enabled to put them in such a state as to prevent their sustaining further injury.   our hunters killed several deer, and saw three bear one of which they wounded.

[Clark]   *May 15th Wednesday 1805*

Our medisons, Instruments, merchandize, Clothes, provisions &c. &c. which was nearly all wet we had put out to air and dry.   the day being Cloudy & rainey those articles dried but little to day—   our hunters killed Several deer &c. and Saw three Bear one of which they wounded &c.

We see Buffalow on the banks dead, others floating down dead, and others mired every day, those buffalow either drown in Swiming the river or brake thro' the ice

[Lewis]   *Thursday May 16th*

The morning was fair and the day proved favorable to our operations; by 4 oClock in the evening our Instruments, Medicine, merchandize provision &c, were perfectly dryed, repacked and put on board the perogue. the loss we sustained was not so great as we had at first apprehended; our medicine sustained the greatest injury, several articles of which were intirely spoiled, and many others considerably injured; the ballance of our losses consisted of some gardin seeds, a small quantity of gunpowder, and a few culinary articles which fell overboard and sunk, the Indian woman to whom I ascribe equal fortitude and resolution, with any person on-board at the time of the accedent, caught and preserved most of the light articles which were washed overboard   all matters being now arranged for our departure we lost no time in seting out; proceeced on tolerably well about seven miles and encamped on the Stard. side.[1]   in the early part of the day two of our men fired on a panther,[2] a little below our en-campment, and wounded it; they informed us that it was very large, had just killed a deer partly devoured it, and in the act of concealing the bal-lance as they discovered him.   we caught two Antelopes at our encamp-ment in attempting to swim the river; these anamals are but lean as yet, and of course not very pleasant food. I walked on shore this evening and killed a buffaloe cow and calf, we found the calf most excellent veal.   the country on either side of the river is broken and hills much higher than usual, the bottoms now become narrow and the timber more scant; some scattering pine and cedar on the steep declivities of the hills.—   this morn-ing a white bear toar Labuiche's coat which he had left in the plains.—

Courses and distances May 16th[3]

S. 80° W.	to a point of woodland on the Lard. side passing a low bluff on Stard.	2 ½
S. 70° W.	to a point of woodland[4] on Stard. near which we encamped for the night	<u>4 ½</u>
		Miles 7

May 16th 1805.

Point of observation No. 19.

at our encampment of this morning on the Stard. side which we called Pan-ther camp observed meridian Altitude of ☉'s L L. with Octant by the back obser-vation   62° 3′ —″

Latitude deduced from this observation.   [*blank*]

[Clark]   *May 16th Thursday 1805*

a fair morning   our articles all out to Dry   at 4 oClock we had every thing that was Saved dry and on bord, our loss is Some medison, Powder,

Seeds, & Several articles which Sunk, and maney Spoiled had a medn. altitude which gave for Latd.   °   ′   ″ N.—   two of our men fired at a *panthr* a little below our Camp, this animale they say was large, had Caught a Deer & eate it half & buried the ballance.   a fiew antilope Swam the river near our Camp   two of them were Cought by the party in the river.   at half past 4 oClock we Set out and proceeded on verry well [*blank*] miles and incamped on the Std. Side   the Countrey as before hilley & broken verry Small proprotion of timber in the points, Some little pine & Ceader in the hills

Course & Distance May 16th

S. 80° W	2 ½	miles to a point of wood land on the Lard Side passing a low bluff on the Std. Side
S. 74° W	<u>4 ½</u>	miles to a ⟨naked⟩ wood point on the Stard. Side
	<u>7</u>	

Buffalow & Deer is yet plenty on the river in the small timbered bottoms   Capt Lewis walked out on the Std. Side and killed a Cow & Calf the calf was verry fine

1. Both captains' journals say they camped on the starboard, or north, side, in Phillips County, Montana. *Atlas* maps 38, 50, 58 clearly show the camp on the larboard, or south side of the Missouri, in Garfield County. Ordway and Whitehouse place the camp on the "S." (south) side. In any case, the site is now under Fort Peck Reservoir. MRC map 67.

2. The mountain lion, or cougar, *Felis concolor*, already known to science. Burroughs, 94–95.

3. Also given on *Atlas* map 38, in Clark's hand.

4. *Atlas* map 38 calls it a "naked point," as does an excised portion of Clark's course.

[Lewis]   *Friday May 17th*

Set out at an early hour, and proceeded on very well; we employed the toe line the greater part of the day; the banks were firm and shore board which favoured the uce of the cord. I find this method of asscending the river, when the shore is such as will permit it, the safest and most expeditious mode of traveling, except with sails in a steady and favourable breze. The country rugged, the hills high, their summits and sides partially covered with pine and cedar, and the river on either side washing their bases. it is somewhat singular that the lower part of these hills appear to be formed of a dark rich loam while the upper region about 150 feet is formed of a whiteish brown sand, so hard in many parts as to resemble stone; but little rock or stone of any kind to be seen in these hills.[1] the river is much narrower than usual, the bed from 200 to 300 yards only and possessing a much larger proportion of gravel than usual. a few scattering cottonwood trees are the only timber near the river; the sandbars, and with them the willow points have almost entirely disappeared. greater appearance than usual of the saline incrustations of the banks and river hills. we passed two creeks[2] the one on Stard. side, and the other just below our camp on the Lard. side;[3] each of these creeks afford a small quantity of runing water, of a brackish tast. the great number of large beds of streams perfectly dry which we daily pass indicate a country but badly watered, which I fear is the case with the country through which we have been passing for the last fifteen or twenty days. Capt Clark walked on shore this evening and killed an Elk; buffaloe are not so abundant as they were some days past. the party with me killed a female brown bear, she was but meagre, and appeared to have suckled young very recently. Capt. Clark narrowly escaped being bitten by a rattle-snake[4] in the course of his walk, the party killed one this evening at our encampment, which he informed me was similar to that he had seen; this snake is smaller than those common to the middle Atlantic States, being about 2 feet 6 inches long; it is of a yellowish brown colour on the back and sides, variagated with one row of oval spots of a dark brown colour lying transversely over the back from the neck to the tail, and two other rows of small circular spots of the same colour which garnis the sides along the edge of the scuta. it's bely contains 176 scuta on the belly and 17 on the tale. Capt Clark informed me that he saw some coal which had been brought down by the water of the last creek we passed; this creek also throws out considerable quantities of Driftwood, though there is no timber on it which can be perceived from the Missouri; we called this stream rattlesnake creek. Capt Clark saw an Indian fortifyed camp this evening, which appeared to have been recently occupyed, from which we concluded it was probable that it had been formed by a war party of the Menetares who left their vilage in March last with a view to attack the blackfoot Indians in consequence of their having killed some of their principal warriors the previous autumn.   we were roused late at night by the Sergt. of the guard, and warned of the danger we were in from a large tree that had taken fire and which leant immediately over our lodge.   we had the loge removed, and a few minutes after a large proportion of the top of the tree fell on the place the lodge had stood; had we been a few minutes later we should have been crushed to attoms.   the wind blew so hard, that notwithstanding the lodge was fifty paces distant from the fire it sustained considerable injury from the burning coals which were thrown on it; the party were much harrassed also by this fire which communicated to a collection of fallen timber, and could not be extinguished.

	Couses and distances, May 17th[5]	miles
S. 70° W.	to a point of woodland on Stard. side.	1 ½
S. 75 W.	to a point of woods on Stard. side	2
W.	along the Stard. point.	1 ½
N. 70 W.	to a point of woods on the Lard. side the hills approach the river on each side	2
S. 80 W	to a point of timber on the Stard. side oppsite the entrance of a small creek	3 ½[6]
N. 82 W.	to a clump of trees on the Lard side	2
West	along the Lard. side to a point opposite to the entrance of a large creek [EC: Brattons]	1
S. 70 W.	along the highland on Lard. side	1 ½
S. 50 W.	along the Lard. side	¼
S. 30 W.	along the Lard. side	¼
S. 10 W.	along the Lard. side	¼
South	along the Lard. side	¼
S. 15 E.	along the Lard. side	¼
S. 30 E.	along the Lard. side	½
S. 35 E.	along the Lard. side to the commencement of a bluff in a Lard. bend	¼
S. 2 W.	to a point of timber on the Stard. side, opposite to a bluff	½
S. 45 W.	to a point of timber on the Lard. side	½

S. 20 E.	to a point of timber on the Stard. side	¼
South	along the Stard. point	¾
S. 15 W.	along the Stard. point, passing the entrance of a large creek [*EC: Rattlesnake*] on Lard.⁷ side	¼
S. 80 W.	to a point of woodland on Lard. side, passing a bluff on Lard. side; here we encamped	1 ¼

miles— 20 ½

[Clark]   *May 17th Friday 1805*

a fine morning   wind from the N W.   mercury at 60° a 0.   river falling a little.   we Set out at an early hour and proceeded on verry well by the assistance of the Toe rope principally, the Countrey verry rugged & hills high and the river washing the base on each Side, Great appearance of the Salt Substance.   a fiew Cotton trees is the only timber which is Scattered in the bottoms & the hills contain a fiew Pine & Cedar, which is Scattered.   river much narrower than below from 2 to 300 yards wide, the bottoms muddey & hills rich earth except near their topes—   We passed 2 large Creeks to day one on the Starbd Side and the other just below our camp on the Lard. Side   each of those creeks has a little running water near their mouthes which has a brackish taste, I was nearly treading on a Small fierce rattle Snake different from any I had ever Seen &c.   one man the party killed another of the Same kind. I walked on Shore after dinner & killed an Elk—   the party in my absence Killed a female Brown or yellow Bear which was meagre   the appearances of the Hills & Countrey is as ⟨yesterday⟩ before mentioned except a greater appearance of the white appearance of Salts or tarter and Some Coal which has been thrown out by the floods in the last Creek—⁸   Buffalow & Deer is not plenty to day, *Elk* is yet to be Seen in abundance   we Camped in the upper part of a Small timbered bottom on the Lard. Side in which I Saw a fortified Indian Camp, which I Suppose is one of the Camps of a *Mi ne tar re* war party of about 15 men, that Set out from their village in March last to war against the Blackfoot Indians.

we were roused late at night and warned of the danger of fire from a tree which had Cought and leaned over our Lodge, we had the lodge moved   Soon after the Dry limbs & top of the tree fell in the place the

Lodge Stood, the wind blew hard and the dry wood Cought & fire flew in every direction, burnt our Lodge verry much from the Coals which fell on it altho at Some distance in the plain, the whole party was much disturbed by this fire which could not be extinguished &c

	miles	Course & Distance May 17th 1805 [9]
S. 70° W	1 ½	miles to a wooded point on the Std. Side
S. 75° W	2	miles to a wood on the Stard. Side
West	1 ½	miles along the Stard point
N. 70° W.	2	miles to a point of wood on the Lard. Side the hills approach the river on each Side
S. 80° W	3 ½	to a point of timber on the Stard. Side opposit the enterence of a Small Creek on the Lard. Side Brattens Creek
N. 82° W.	2	miles to a fiew trees on the Lard pt.
West	1	mile along the Lard. Side to a point opposit the enterance of a large Creek on the Stard. Side, but fiew Cotton trees in the Small bottoms and a fiew Scattering pine & cedar on the tops & Sides of the hills &c. I saw a *Morking bird* [10]
S 70° W.	1 ½	under the high land on the Lard Side
S. 50° W.	¼	allong the Larboard Side
S. 30° W.	¼	allong the Lard. Side
S. 10° W.	¼	allong the Lard. Side
South	¼	allong the Lard. Side
S. 15° E.	¼	allong the Lard. Side
S. 30 E.	½	along the Lard Side
S. 35° E	¼	allong the Lard. Side to the Commencement of a Bluff in a Lard bend
S. 2° W	½	to a point of timber on the Stard. Side opposit to a Bliff on the Lard Side
S. 45° W.	½	to a point of timber on the Lard. Side
S. 20° E.	¼	to a point of timber on the Stard. Side
South	¾	allong the Stard. point
S. 15° W.	¼	allong the Stard. point passed the enterence of a large creek on the Lard. Side

S. 80° W   1 ¼   to a point of wood land on the Lard. Side passing a bluff

           20 ½   on the Lard Side   here we incamped for the night

1. The Missouri River is bordered by the lighter colored Hell Creek Formation and Fox Hills Sandstone which overlie the darker-colored Bearpaw Shale. Except where the sand is locally cemented to stone, these formations are not especially indurated.

2. The first is "Rattle Snake Creek" on *Atlas* map 38 (the first draft), and "Bratton's River" on *Atlas* maps 50, 59. In this same entry Lewis says they named the second creek Rattlesnake Creek; it is Burnt Lodge Creek on the maps. They are later Timber Creek, in Phillips County, Montana, and Seven Blackfoot Creek, in Garfield County. Another dry creek, shown on the maps, is not mentioned in the captains' journals, except in courses and distances. MRC map 68.

3. A little upstream from the mouth of Seven Blackfoot Creek. *Atlas* maps 38, 50, 59; MRC map 68.

4. The prairie rattlesnake, *Crotalus viridus viridus*, a subspecies then new to science. Benson (HLCE), 90; Cutright (LCPN), 149. Someone drew a vertical line through part of this passage, from "this snake is smaller" to "17 on the tale."

5. Also given on *Atlas* map 38, in both captains' hands.

6. Lewis left out the next two courses, inserting them at the end and indicating the proper order by asterisks.

7. Given as "Stard." on *Atlas* map 38.

8. The presence of salts increases in late spring when ground water discharge is at its maximum and evaporation increases. These salts are from the Bearpaw Shale. Seven Blackfoot Creek is flanked by coal-bearing deposits of the Fort Union Formation (Tullock Member).

9. Clark left out the first seven courses of the day, then inserted them after the remaining courses, using asterisks to indicate the correct placement. The proper order is used here.

10. *Mimus polyglottos* [AOU, 703].

[Lewis]   *Saturday May 18th 1805.*

The wind blew hard this morning from the West.   we were enabled to employ our toe line the greater part of the day and therefore proceeded on tolerably well.   there are now but few sandbars, the river is narrow and current gentle.   the timber consists of a few cottonwood trees along the verge of the river; the willow has in a great measure disappeared.   in the latter part of the day the hills widened, the bottoms became larger, and contained more timber.   we passed a creek [*EC: Wisers*] on the Stard. side about three oclock, which afforded no water;[1] came too and en-camped on the Lard. side opposite to the lower point of a small Island,

two miles short of the extremity of the last course of this day.[2]   Capt
Clark in the course of his walk this evening killed four deer, two of which
were the black tailed or mule deer; the skins are now good, they have not
yet produced their young.—   we saw a number of buffaloe, Elk, deer
and Antelopes.—   the saline substance frequently mentioned continues
to appear as usual.—

	Courses and distances 18th of May.[3]	*Miles*
S. 66° W.	to a point of wood on the Stard. side, opposite to a high irregular hill on Lard. side	¾
N. 80 W.	along the Stard. side oposite a bluff	½
N. 45 W.	to a clump of trees of a Lard. point, opposite a high rugged bluff	1 ½
S. 80 W.	to a point of timber on the Lard. side	1 ½
S. 60 W.	to a point of timber on the Stard side oposite a bluff	½
S. 85° W.	to a point on Lard. side	2
S. 60 W.	along the Lard. shore	½
South	to a point of woodland on the Stard side oposite a bluff	1 ¼
S. 45 W.	along the Stard. point, to the extremity of a sandbar, oposite a bluff.	½
N. 20 W.	to a point of woodland on the Lard. side the river making a deep bend to the N.	2
N. 55 W.	to a large tree in the center of a Stard bend	1
S. 70 W.	to the point of a sandbar on the Lard. side, passing the entrance of a Creek [*EC: Wisers*] on Stard. at ½ a mile	1 ¼
S. 20 W.	to a point of woodland on the Stard side	1 ½
S. 35 W.	along the Stard. side opposite a bluff	½
N. 85 W.	to a point of woodland Lard. side the river making a deep bend to N. under a bluff	2 ¼
S. 60. W.	along the Lard. point	½
S. 5 W.	to a timbered point on Stard side passing a small Island, ¾ of a mile in length, commencing at 1 mile opposite to the lower point of this island on the Lard. side we encamped	3

Miles 21

[Clark]   *May 18th Satturday 1805*

A windey morning wind from the West   we proceeded on verry well with the assistance of the Toe Coard, river narrow but fiew Sand bars, & current jentle, but a few Cotton Trees Contained in the bottoms   willow is not common on the bears [bars] as usial   Some little on the Sides of the river is yet to be Seen, the after part of the day was Cloudy & at about 12 oClock it began to rain and continued moderately for about 1½ hours, not Sufficient to wet a man thro' his clothes; this is the first rain Since we Set out this Spring   The hills widen and the bottoms Contain more timber than for Several days past, we passed a Wisers Creek on the Std. Side about 3 oClock and Camped on the Lard Side opposit the lower point of a handsom little Island near the middle of the river. I walked on Shore and killed four Deer, 2 common & 2 mule deer, one of which had 3 fauns, 2 others had 2 each, those deer are fat, & their Skins tolerable good, which are now in demand with us for clothes Such as Legins & Mockersons, I Saw great numbers of Buffalows & Elk; Some of the party Shoot & Catch beaver every day & night

	miles	*Course & Distance 18th of May*
S. 66° W.	¾	to a point of wood on the Stard. Side opposit a high uneavin hill L. S.
N. 80° W.	½	allong the Stard. Side opposit a bluff
N. 45° W.	1 ½	to a fiew trees on a point on the Lard. Side opposit a rugged bluff
S. 80° W.	1 ½	to a point of timber on the Lard. Side
S. 60° W.	½	to a point of timber on the Stard Side oppised to a Bluff on the L. S.
S. 85° W.	2	to a point on the Lard Side
S. 60° W	½	along the Lard Shore
South	1 ¼	to a point of wood land on the Std. Side opposit a Bluff
S. 45° W.	½	along the Stard point to the extremity of a Sand bar, opposit a low bluff
N. 20° W.	2	to a point of wood land on the Lard Side the river makeing a deep bend to the North

N. 55° W.	1	to a large tree in the Center of the bend on the Stard. Side
S. 70° W.	1 ¼	to the point of a Sand bar on the Lard Side passing the enterence of a Wisers Creek on S. S. at ½ m
S. 20° W	1 ½	to a point of wood land on the Stard. Side
S. 35° W.	½	allong the Stard. point opposit a bluff L. S.
N. 85° W	2 ¼	to a point of wood land ⟨Stard⟩ Lard[4] Side the river make-ing a deep bend to the N. under. a bluff
S. 60° W.	½	allong the Lard point.
S. 5° W.	3	to a timbered point on the Stard Side, pass a Small Island of a mile in length, comeng. at 1 mile. opposit to the lower point of this Island on the Lard Side we Camped
miles	21	

1. Fourchette Creek, in Phillips County, Montana. *Atlas* maps 38, 50, 59; MRC map 68.

2. In Garfield County, Montana, about two miles upstream from the present Devils Creek Recreation Area. The small island opposite the camp, Kid Island on *Atlas* maps 38, 50, 59, may be the later Elk Island. The area is now under the Fort Peck Reservoir. MRC map 68.

3. Also given on *Atlas* map 38, in both captains' hands.

4. The correction to "Lard" appears to be in Lewis's hand.

[Lewis] *Sunday May 19th 1805.*

The last night was disagreeably could; we were unable to set out untill 8 oclock A. M. in consequence of a heavy fogg, which obscured the river in such a manner that we could not see our way; this is the first we have experienced in any thing like so great a degree; there was also a fall of due last evening, which is the second we have experienced since we have entered this extensive open country. at eight we set out and proceeded as yesterday by means of the cord principally, the hills are high and the country similar to that of yesterday. Capt Clark walked on shore with two of the hunters and killed a brown bear; notwithstanding that it was shot through the heart it ran at it's usual pace near a quarter of a mile before it fell. one of the party wounded a beaver, and my dog as usual swam in to catch it; the beaver bit him through the hind leg and cut the artery; it was with great difficulty that I could stop the blood; I fear it will yet prove fatal to him. on Capt. Clark's return he informed me that he had from the top of one of the adjacent hights[1] discovered the entrance of a large stream which discharged itself into the Missouri on the Lard. side distant 6 or seven miles; from the same place he also saw a range of Mountains, bearing W. distant 40 or 50 miles; they appeared to proceed in a S. S. W. direction; the N. N. E. extremity of these mountains appeared abrupt.[2]

This afternoon the river was croked, rappid and containing more saw-yers than we have seen in the same space since we left the entrance of the river Platte. Capt. C. in the course of his walk killed three deer and a beaver, I also walked on shore this evening a few miles and killed an Elk, a buck, and a beaver. the party killed and caught 4 other beaver & 3 deer.

Courses and distances May 19th 1805.[3]

S. 35° W.	To a point of woodland on the Lard. side opposite to a bluff	1 ¼
South	To a point of timber on the Stard. side opposite high hills on Lard. side	1 ½
S. 75° W.	To a point of woodland on Lard. side opposite to a bluff on Stard.	1
S. 20° W.	To a willow point on Stard. side the river making a deep bend to the E.	1 ½
S. 30° W.	Along the Stard. opposite to a bluff	1
S. 60° W.[4]	To a point of woodland Stard. side opposite to a bluff	2 ½
West	Along the Lard. shore opposite to a bluff	¾
S. 60° W.	Along the Lard. shore opposite to a bluff	½
S. 15° W.	To a point of woodland on Stard. side opposite to a bluff a deep bend to the South	3
S. 20° W.	To a point on the Lard. side.	1 ½
S. 45° W	To a point of high timher on the Lard. opposite to a bluff	¾
South	To a point of Willows on the Stard. Sd.	1 ¾
West	To a point of low willows on the Lard. side opposite to the lower point of a willow Island St. Side	1 ½
S. 45° W.	Along the Lard. point opposite to the upper point of the Island; a bluff on the Stard. side	½
S. 10° E.	Along the Lard. point opposite to a bluff, under which is a shoal Stard. S., rappid water	¼

N. 45° E.	To the point of a sandbar on the Stard. side passing re-markable strong water	½
S. 45° E.	To the timber on the Stard. point, opposite to a bluff on Lard. where we encamped for the night	½

Miles— 20 ¼

The men complain much of sore eyes and imposthumes.

[Clark]   *May 19th Sunday 1805*

a verry cold night, the murckery Stood at 38 at 8 oClock this morning, a heavy dew which is the 2d I have Seen this Spring. The fog (which was the first) was So thick this morning that we could not Set out untill the Sun was about 2 hours up, at which time a Small breeze Sprung up from the E. which Cleared off the fog & we proceeded on by means of the Cord   The hills are high & rugged the Countrey as yesterday—   I walked on Shore with two men   we killed a ⟨brown⟩ white or grey bear; not withstanding that it was Shot through the heart it ran at it's usial pace near a quarter of a mile before it fell.   Capt Lewis's dog was badly bitten by a wounded *beaver* and was near bleading to death—.   after killing the Bear I continued my walk alone, & killed 3 Deer & a Beaver; finding that the Perogues were below I assended the highest hill I could See, from the top of which I Saw the mouth of *M. Shell R*[5] & the meanderings of the Missouri for a long distance. I also Saw a high mountain in a westerley direction, bearing S. S W. about 40 or 50 miles distant, in the evening the river was verry Crooked and much more rapid & Containing more Sawyers than any which we have passed above the River Platte   Capt Lewis walked on Shore this after noon & killed an Elk, Buck & a Beaver, I kiled three Deer at dinner, the hunters killed three other Deer to day   Several beaver also killed. We Camped on the Stard Side in a bottom of Small Cotton wood[6]

	miles	*Course & Distance May 19th*
S 35° W.	1 ¼	to a point of wood land on the Lard Side opposit to a Bluff. S. S.
South	1 ½	to a point of timber on the Stard. Side opposit High hills on the Lard Side

S. 75° W.	1	to a point of wood land on the Lard. Side opposit to Bluff
S. 20° W.	1 ½	to a willow point on the Std. Side the river makeing a deep bend to the E.
S. 30° W.	1	along the Stard. Side opsd. a Bluff
S. 60° W	2 ½	to a point of wood land Stard Side opposit to a Bluff
West	¾	allong the Lard Shore opsd. to a bluff
S. 60° W.	½	along the Lard. Point opposit to a bluff
S. 15° W.	3	to a point of wood land on the Stard. Side opsd. a bluff a Deep bend to the South
S. 20° W.	1 ½	to a point on the Lard Side
S. 45° W.	¾	to a point of high timber on the Ld Side opposit to a bluff
South	1 ¾	to a point of willows on the Stard. Side
West	1 ½	to a point of low willows on the Lard Side opsd. the lower point of a willow Island S. S.
S. 45° W.	½	along the Lard point, opsd. the upper point of the Island, a Bluff on the Std Side
S 10° E.	¼	allong the Lard. point opsd. to a Bluff, under which is a Shoal S. S. rapid waters
N. 45° E.	½	to the point of a Sand bar on the Stard Side passing Swift water
S 45° E	½	to the timber on the Stard. point opposit to a Bluff on Lard. here we Camped for the night
miles	20 ¼	

1. The hill appears prominently on *Atlas* maps 38, 51, 59; it may be one on the bluffs (possibly Brandon or Mikey buttes) in the vicinity of later Horseshoe Point on the Missouri, which is now under Fort Peck Lake. The river Clark saw was the Musselshell. MRC map 68; USGS map Fort Peck Lake West.

2. The Little Rocky Mountains, in Phillips and Blaine counties, Montana. Allen (PG), 264–65.

3. Also given on *Atlas* map 38, in both captains' hands.

4. Given as "N. 60 W." on *Atlas* map 38.

5. The words "*M. Shell R*" appear to have been added to a blank space.

6. In either Phillips or Garfield County, Montana, at or near the later Long Point, now under Fort Peck Lake. The site appears on *Atlas* maps 38, 39, 51, but not on map 59— apparently an omission by the copyist. MRC map 69.

[Lewis]   *Monday May 20th 1805*

Set out at an early hour as usual, the banks being favourable and water strong we employed the toe rope principally; river narrow and croked; country much as that of yesterday; immence number of the prickley pears[1] in the plains and on the hills. At the distance of 2¼ miles passed the entrance of a large Creek, affording but little water; this stream we named *Blowing Fly Creek*,[2] from the immence quantities of those insects found in this neighbourhood, they infest our meat while roasting or boiling, and we are obliged to brush them off our provision as we eat. At 11 A. M. we arrived at the entrance of a handsome bold river which discharges itself into the Missouri on the Lard. side; this stream we take to be that called by the Minnetares the [*blank*] or Muscleshell River; if it be the same, of which I entertain but little doubt, it takes it's rise, by their information in the 1st Chain of the Rocky Mountains at no great distance from the Yellow stone river,[3] from whence in it's course to this place it passes through a high and broken country pretty well timbered, particularly on it's borders, and intersperced with handsome fertile plains and medows.   but from the circumstance of the same Indians informing us that we should find a well timbered country in the neighbourhood of it's mouth, I am induced to beleive that the timbered country of which they speak is similar to that we have passed for a day or two, or that in our view above, which consists of nothing more than a few scattering small scrubby pine and dwarf cedar on the summits of some of the highest hills nine tenths of the country being wholy destitute of timber of any kind, covered with a short grass, arromatic herbs and the prickley pear; the river bottom however, so far as we have explored it or 8 m. are well stocked with Cottonwood timber of tollerable size, & lands of excellent quality. We halted at thentrance of the river on the point formed by it's junction with the Missouri determining to spend the day,[4] make the necessary observations and send out some hunters to explore the country. The Muscle Shell river falls into the Missouri 2270 miles above it's mouth, and is 110 yards in width, it affords much more water than streams of it's width generally do below, it's courant is by no means rappid, and from appearances it might be navigated with canoes a considerable distance; it's bed is coarse sand and gravel principally with an occasion mixture of black mud; it's banks abbrupt and about 12 feet high yet never appear to overflow; the waters of this river is of a greenish yellow cast, much more transparent than the Missouri, which last is also much more transparent than below but still retains it's whiteish hue and a proportion of it's sedement. the Missouri opposite to this point is deep, gentle in it's courant, and 222 yards in width. The hunters returned this evening and informed us that the country continued much the same in appearance as that we saw where we were or broken, and that about five miles abe [*NB: above*] the mouth of shell river a handsome river of about fifty yards in width discharged itself into the shell river on the Stard. or upper side; this stream we called Sâh-câ-gar me-âh [*NB: Sah ca gah we a*] or bird woman's River, after our interpreter the Snake woman.[5] Shields also found a bould spring or fountain issuing from the foot of the Lard. hills about 4 miles up the Missouri; a fountain in this plain country is a great novelty; I have not seen a bould fountain of pure water except one since I left the Mandans; there [*NB: are*] a number of small ones but all without exception are impregnated with the salts which abound in this country, and with which I believe the Missoury itself considerably impregnated but to us in the habit of useing it not perceptible; the exception I make is a very fine fountain under the bluffs on the Lard. side of the Missouri and at a distance from the river about five miles below the entrance of the yellowstone River. The sands of the Missouri are not so abundant as they have been for some time past, being confined to the points only; the bed of the river principally mud and still too deep to use the seting pole. Capt. Clark walked out today and killed two deer and an Elk, the hunters killed 4 deer and elk and a buffaloe. I saw two large Owls[6] with remarkable long feathers on the sides of the head which resembled ears; I take them to be the large hooting owl tho: they are somewhat larger and their colours brighter than those common to the U' States.—

Courses and distances of May 20th 1805.[7]

South	Along the Stard. side to the upper part of a bluff (bad water)	½
S. 70° E.	to a sand point on the Stard. side	1

S. 20° W.	to some timber on a Stard. point	½
S. 10° E.	to the entrance of a large creek on Lard. 25 yds. wide, called blowing Fly Ck.	¼
South	to a point of timher on the Lard. side opposite to a bluff on Stard. side	1 ¼
S. 30 E.	to a willow point on the Stard. side opposite to a bluff on Lard. side	1 ¼
South	along the Stard. point opposite to a bluff	¼
West	to a point of woodland on the Lard. Sd. just below which Muscle shell R. discharges itself on the Lard. 2270 m. up	2

Miles 7

Point of Observation No. 20.

On the Lard. shore opposite to the extremity of the 5th course of this day, observed time and distance of ⊙'s, and ☽'s nearest limbs, with Sextant, the ⊙ East.

Mean of a set of 12 observations

	Time			Distance
	h	m	s	
A. M.	9	44	48	103° 3' 14"

Longitude deduced,— [*blank*]

Point of Observation No. 21.[8]

On the point of land formed by the junction of the Missouri and Muscle Shell river observed Equal Altitudes of ⊙, with Sextant.

	h	m	s					
A. M.	9	53	31	P. M.	lost			Altd. of Sextant
"		55	6		4	40	33	at the time of Obst.
"		56	44		4	42	10	81° 58' 15"

h m s

Chronometer too [*blank*] *on Mean time* [*blank*]

Observed Meridian Altd. of ⊙'s L. L. with Octant by the back observation 59° 50'

Latitude deduced from this Observation 47° 00' 24.6"

Observed also magnetic Azimuth of ⊙'s Center.

Azimuth by Circumferenter	Time by Chronometer			Altitude by Sextant		
		h	m	s		
1st S. 85 W.	A. M.	6	14	35	50°	—′ —″
2cd S. 82 W.	"	6	24	36	46	37 30
3rd S. 80 W.	"	6	34	42	43	15 30

The variation of the magnetical needle.   [*blank*]

[Clark]   *May 20th Monday 1805*

a fine morning   wind from the N E.   river falling a little   We Set out at 7 oClock and proceeded on verry well as usial by the assistance of the Cord   passed Some verry Swift water, river narrow and Crooked, at 11 oClock arrived at the mouth of *Shell* river on the Lard Side and formed a Camp for the present.   haveing passed a large Creek about 4 miles below on the Ld Side which we call Blowing fly Creek from the emence quantites of those insects which geather on our meat in Such numbers that we are oblige to brush them off what we eate.

muscle *Shell* River falls in on Lard Side 2270 miles up   Contains a greater perportion of water than Rivers of its Size below, I measured it and find it to be 110 yards wide, the water of a Greenish yellow Colour, and appers to be navagable for Small Craft, The *Minetarras* inform us that this river heads in the 1st of the rockey Mountains & passes through a broken Countrey.   its head at no great distance from the Yellow Stone River   The Countrey about this river as described yesterday   we took the Meredian altitude 59° 50′ 0″ back observation and found the Latd. to be 47° 0′ 24″

⟨The Distance of the Moon's Western Limb⟩

Observed time & Distance of Sun & Moons nearest limbs   the Sun East

	Time			Distance		
	h	m	s			
A M.	9	39	17	103°	5′	15
	"	40	26	103	4	45
	"	41	17	"	4	15
	"	42	45	"	4	0
	"	44	0	"	3	30

"	45	2	"	3	15
"	45	50	"	3	0
"	46	51	"	2	0
"	47	53	"	2	0
"	48	57	"	1	45
"	50	22	"	1	30

h m s

Cronomoter too fast mean time [*blank*]

observed Equal altitudes with Sextent

	H	M	S	
A M	9	53	31	
	"	55	6	
	"	56	44	altitude produced from this observation is 81° 58′ 15″
P M	"	"	"	
	4	40	33	
	4	42	10	

Took the Magnetick azmoth of the Sun

	Cours	*Time*			*Distance*		
		h	m	s			
P M	S 85° W	6	14	35	50°	00′	00″
	S 85° W	6	19	31	48	20	15
	S 82° W	6	24	38	46	37	30
	S 80° W	6	34	42	43	15	30

The Missouri at the mouth of Shell River is 222 yards wide with a Smoth Current   the Missouri water is not So muddey as below, but retains nearly its usial Cholour, and the Sands principally Confined to the points   I killed two Deer & an Elk, the hunters killed an Elk & Several deer mearly for their Skins to make Leagins,—   Sent men out in every derection, the Countrey generally verry broken Some leavel plains up the *Shell* river The bottoms of the *Shell* river is well timbered as also a Small river which falls into that river on the upper Side 5 miles above its mouth. The hills on the Lard. Contain Scattering Pine & Cedar.

	mile	*Course & Distance May 20th 1805*
South	½	allong the Stard. Side to the upper part of a Bluff (bad water[)]

S. 70° E	1	to Sand point on the Stard. Side
S. 20° W	½	to the timber on the Stard. point
S. 10° E	¼	to the enterence of a large Creek Lard Side
South	1 ¼	to the point of timber on the Lard Side opposit a Bluff S. S.
S. 30° E	1 ¼	to a willow point on the Stard Side opposit a bluff on the Lard Side
South	¼	allong the Std. Point opsd. a bluff
West	2	to a point of wood land on the Lard. Side below which the
miles 7		mouth of *Shell* river falls in on the Lard. Side *2270* up

1. *Opuntia polyacantha* Haw. var. *polyacantha,* plains prickly pear. Barkley, 49; Benson (CUSC), 382–88; Booth & Wright, 160.

2. Later Squaw Creek, in Garfield County, Montana. *Atlas* maps 39, 51, 59; MRC map 69. The blowing fly may be from either *Calliphoridae* or *Sacrophagidae* families. Someone drew a vertical line through this passage, from "this stream" to "we eat."

3. Musselshell River, here dividing Garfield and Petroleum counties, Montana, still bears the name the captains gave it, translating the Hidatsa name (see Chapter 10). It rises in the Castle Mountains in Meagher County, Montana, within one hundred miles of the Yellowstone River. *Atlas* maps 39, 43, 51, 59; MRC map 69.

4. In either Garfield or Petroleum County, on the upstream side of the Musselshell's earlier mouth, on a site now covered by Fort Peck Reservoir. *Atlas* maps 39, 43, 51, 59; MRC map 69.

5. The stream, in Petroleum County, was for many years called Crooked Creek; it has since been renamed Sacagawea River. *Atlas* maps 39, 51, 59; MRC map 69. Sacagawea herself is discussed at the entry of November 4, 1804. Thwaites gives the reading for Sacagawea's name as "Sâh-câ-ger we-âh" and attributes the interlineation to Biddle; Coues reads it as "Sâh-câ-gee-me-âh" and attributes the interlineation to Clark. The syllable "gar" could easily be read "ger," but Thwaites's reading of "we" for the fourth syllable is difficult to accept. The syllable might also be read with a capital "M." Thwaites (LC), 2:52; Coues (HLC), 1:317 n. 38. See also Anderson (SSS). Biddle made some other marks in red besides the bracketed material: he crossed out "Sâh-câ-gar me-âh" and placed parentheses around "or bird woman's River." Perhaps it also was he who drew vertical lines through passages from "which consists of" to "tollerable size" and "I saw two" to "U' States."

6. Probably the Montana horned owl; see above, April 14, 1805, and Burroughs, 208–9. Holmgren identifies it as the long-eared owl, *Asio otus* [AOU, 366]. Holmgren, 32.

7. Also given on *Atlas* map 39, in both captains' hands.

8. A nearly identical observation is found in Lewis's astronomy notebook (see Appendix C, vol. 2).

[Lewis]   *Tuesday May 21st 1805.*

A delightfull morning   set out at an early hour and proceeded on very well, imployed the chord principally; the shores are abbrupt and bould and composed of a black and yellow clay: see no extensive collection of pure sand, the bars are composed black mud and a small poportion of fine sand; [1] the courant still pretty strong.   the Missouri in it's course downward makes a suddon and extensive bend to receive the Muscle shell river, the point of country thus formed tho' high is still much lower than that surrounding it, thus forming a valley of wavey country which extends itself for a great distance in a Northerly direction; the soil is fertile, produces a fine turf of low grass and some herbs, also immence quantities of the Prickley pear, without a stick of timber of any discription.   the country on the South side is high broken and crowned with some scrubby pines and dwarf cedar; the leaf of this pine is much longer than the common pitch or red pine of Virginia, the cone is also longer and slimer, and the imbrications wider and thicker, and the whole frequently covered with rosin. Mineral appearances as usual.   the growse or praire hen are now less abundant on the river than they were below; perhaps they betake themselves to the open plains at a distance from the river at this season.—[2]

The wind which was moderate all the fore part of the day continued to encrease in the evening, and about dark veered about to N. W. and blew a storm all night, in short we found ourselves so invelloped with clouds of dust and sand that we could neither cook, eat, nor sleep; and were finally compelled to remove our lodge about eight oClock at night to the foot of an adjacent hill where we were covered in some measure from the wind by the hills.   several loose articles blown over board and lost.   our first station was on a bar on Stard. opposite the lower point of a small Island, which we now called windy Island.[3]   the bends of the river are short and suddon, the points covered with some cottonwood, larger willow, or broadleafed willow with an abundance of the wild rose and some small honeysuckle bushes constitute the undergrowth, the redwood is also found in small quantities. Capt. C walked on shore today and killed 2 Elk; the party killed several deer and a buffaloe Cow.—

Courses and distances of May 21st 1805[4]

West	To a point of timber on the Stard. side	1
N. 15° W.	Along the Stard. point opposite to a hill.	¼
N. 10° E.	To a point of timber on the Lard. side opposite to a bluff on Star. side	2
N. 30° W.	To the point of a timbered bottom on the Stard. side opposite to a bluff	1 ½
N. 20° E.	To a point of timber on the Lard. side opposite to a bluff	1 ½
N. 35° W.	to a point of woodland Lard. side	¼
N. 80° W.	To a point of woodland Stard. side	1 ¼
N. 45° W.	Along the Stard. shore opposite to a bluff.	¼
N. 15° E.	To a point of woodland Lard. side	1 ¼
N. 70° W.	To a point of woodland Stard. side	1
N. 30° W.	Along the Stard. shore	½
N. 10° W.	To the extremity of a willow bar on Lard. side	1 ¼
N. 60° W.	To a point of woodland Lard. side	1
S. 70° W.	To the commencement of a bluff in a bend on the Lard. side	2 ¼
N. 75° W.	To a point of woodland Stard. side	1
N. 30° W.	To a tree in the center of a Stard. bend.	2
S. 80° W.	To the lower point of a timbered bottom on the Stard. side, near which we encampd	2

Miles 20

Point of Observation No. 22.[5]

On the Lard. shore at the commencement of the 5th course of this day observed time, and distance of ☉'s and ☾'s nearest limbs with Sextant, ☉ East.

Mean of a set of 12 Observations.

	Time			Distance		
	h	m	s			
A. M.	9	25	35	91°	45′	19″

177

[Clark]   *May 21st Tuesday 1805.*

a butifull morning, wind from the West, river falling a little, we Set out
at an early hour and proceed on in the usial way by the assistance of the
Coard principally, but little use of the Oares & less with the poles as the
bottoms are muddey, we Se no great bodies of pure Sand the bars & points
are rich mud mixed with fine Sand. I walked on Shore Stard. Side   the
river makes a great bend to the South to receve Shell River, the boint for
many miles out in a Northerley direction is a rich uneaven valley Contain
Some Short grass, and Prickley pears without timber   The Countrey on
the South Side of the Missouri is high, Soil and mineral appearance as
usial, more Scattering pine & Cedar on the hills, the wind which blew
moderatly all the forepart of the day increassd and about Dark Shifted to
the N W. and Stormed all night, Several loose articles were blown over
board, our lodge & Camp which was on a Sand bar on the Std. Side &
⟨Sit⟩ opposite to the lower point of an Island we were obliged to move
under the hills, the dust & Sand blew in clouds. The bends of the river
are Short and points Covered with Cotton wood   under groth wild rose
bushes   I killed 2 Elk to day   Several Deer Killd. & a Buffalow Cow.

Course Distance May 21st 1805

West	1	mile to a point of timber on the Std. Side
N. 15° W	¼	allong the Std. point opsd. a Hill
N. 10° E	2	to a point of timber on the Lard Side opposit to a Bluff on the S. S.
N. 30° W.	1 ½	to the point of a timbered bottom on the Stard. Side opsd. to a Bluff
N. 20° E.	1 ¼	to a point of timber on the L. Side opsd. to a bluff
N 35° W.	¼	to a point of wood land Lard Side
N. 80° W.	1 ¼	to a point of wood land Stard Side
N. 45° W.	¼	allong the Stard. Shore opposit to a bluff on the L. S.
N. 15° E.	1 ¼	to a point of wood land Lard Side
N. 70° W.	1	to a point of wood land Stard. Side
N. 30° W	½	allong the Stard. Shore
N. 10° W.	1 ¼	to the extremity of a ⟨Sand⟩ willow bar on the Lard Side

N. 60° W.	1	to a point of wood land Lard. Side
S. 70° W.	2 ¼	to the Comencement of a bluff in a bend to the Lard Side.
N. 75° W.	1	to a point of wood land Stard. Side
N. 30° W.	2	to a tree in the center of the Std. bend
S. 80° W	2	to the lower point of timbered botm. on the Stard Side & Camped
miles 20		

1. The river hills are formed principally of Bearpaw Shale, but some of the summits contain the lighter colored Fox Hills Sandstone. The sand in the river bars probably comes from the Judith River Formation.

2. Someone drew a vertical line from "the soil is fertile" to here, and below on the passage, from "the bends" to "small quantities."

3. The two sites are in Phillips County, Montana, and are now inundated by Fort Peck Reservoir. Windy Island might be a small, nameless island appearing on MRC map 69. *Atlas* maps 39, 51, 59.

4. Also given on *Atlas* map 39, in both captains' hands.

5. A nearly identical observation is found in Lewis's astronomy notebook (see Appendix C, vol. 2).

[Lewis]   *Wednesday May 22cd 1805.*

The wind blew so violently this morning that we did not think it prudent to set out untill it had in some measure abated; this did not happen untill 10 A. M. when we proceeded principally by the toe lines   the bottoms somewhat wider than usual, the lands fertile or apparently so tho' the short grass and the scantey proportion of it on the hills would indicate no great fertility.   passed Windy Island on Lard. at 1 M.   5½ miles above passed a large Island in a bend on Stard. side, and three miles further on the same side passed the entrance of grows Creek 20 yds wide, affords but little water.[1]   this creek we named from seeing a number of the pointed tail praire hen near it's mouth,[2]   these are the fist we have seen in such numbers for some days. I walked on shore this morning   the country is not so broken as yesterday tho' still high and roling or wavy; the hills on Lard. side possess more pine than usual; some also on the Stard. hills. Salts and other mineral appearances as usual.   the river continues about the same width or from 200 to 250 yds. wide, fewer sandbars and the courant more gentle and regular; game not so abundant as below the Muscle

Shell river. I killed a deer in the course of my walk today. Capt. C. also walked out this evening and took a view of the country from a conspicuous point and found it the same as has been discribed.   we have caught but few fish since we left the Mandans, they do not bite freely, what we took were the white cat of 2 to 5 lbs.[3] I presume that fish are scarce in this part of the river. We encamped earlyer this evening[4] than usual in order render the oil of a bear which we killed. I do not believe that the Black bear common to the lower part of this river and the Atlantic States, exists in this quarter;[5] we have neither seen one of them nor their tracks which would be easily distinguished by it's shortness of tallons when compared with the brown grizly or white bear. I believe that it is the same species or family of bears which assumes all those colours at different ages and seasons of the year.—[6]

Courses and distances May 22cd 1805.[7]

S. 30° E.	To the lower point of an Island situated in a bend on Lard. side	¼
West	Along the Stard. side passing the upper point of the Island at ¾ of a mile high land Ld.	3
S. 70° W.	to a point of woodland on the Stard. passing under a bluff on Lard. opposite to an Island in a bend to the Stard.	3 ¼
N. 45° W.	To a point of timber on the Lard. side	2
West	To the mouth of a creek on the Stard. side in a deep bend to the Stard.	1
South	To a point of high wood on Stard. passing a Lard. point at ½ m. and over a willow bar from Std.	1 ½
S. 65° W.	Along the Stard. point, opposite to a bluff on Lard. covered with pine	¼
West	To a point of woodland on the Lard. side opposite to a bluff	1
S. 30° W.	To a willow point on the Stard. side	2
S. 60° W.	To a point of woodland on Stard. side, where we encamped; a bluff opposite.	2 ¼

Miles— 16 ½

[Clark]   *May 22nd Wednesday 1805*

The wind Continued to blow So violently hard we did not think it prudent to Set out untill it luled a little, about 10 oClock we Set out   the
morning Cold, passed a Small Island in the bend to the Lard Side, & proceeded on   at 5 miles higher passed a Island in a bend to the Stard Side,
and a Creek a Short distance above on the Stard Side 20 yds. w   Capt
Lewis walked out before dinner & Killed a Deer, I walked out after dinner and assended & but a few miles to view the Countrey, which I found
roleing & of a verry rich Stickey Soil produceing but little vegitation of
any kind except the prickley-piar, but little grass & that verry low.   a
great deal of Scattering *Pine* on the Lard Side & Some fur on the Stard.
Sd. The mineral productions as described in the proceeding days, game
not So abundant as below, the river Continue about the Same width, fewer
Sand bars & current more regular, river falls about an inch a day

We camped on the Stard. Side, earlier than we intend on account of
Saveing the oil of a bear which the party killed late this afternoon.

	mile	*Course & Distance May 22nd 1805*
S. 30° E.	¼	to the lower point of an Island Situated in a bend to the Lard Side
West	3	allong the Stard. Side passed the upper point of the Island at ¾ a high land on L. S.
S. 70° W.	3 ¼	to a point of wood land on the Stard. passing under a bluff Lard. opposit an Island in a bend to the Stard. Side
N. 45° W.	2	to a point of timber on the Lard. Side
West	1	to the mouth of a Creek on the Std. Side in a Deep bend to the Stard. Side
South	1 ½	to a point of high wood on Stard Side passed Lard pt. & over a willow bar from Std.
S. 65° W.	¼	allong the Stard. point opposit a Bluff Covered with pine on the Lard Side
West	1	to a point of woodland on the Lard. Side opposit to a bluff
S. 30° W.	2	to a willow point on the Stard. Side

S. 60° W.   2 ¼   to a point of wood land on Stard. side opposit a bluff.   we
            16 ½   encamped.

Maney of the Creeks which appear to have no water near ther mouths have Streams of running water higher up which rise & waste in the Sand or gravel.   the water of those Creeks are So much impregnated with the Salt Substance that it cannot be Drank with pleasure.

1. The large island is probably later Fort Island. Grouse Creek is probably later Beauchamp Creek in Phillips County, Montana. Although MRC map 69 shows a Grouse Creek farther on, it does not fit with the captains' courses and distances. *Atlas* maps 39, 51, 59.

2. The sharp-tailed grouse.

3. The white cat were channel catfish, *Ictalurus punctatus*. Lee et al., 446.

4. In Phillips County, just below present CK, or Kannuck, Creek (Lewis and Clark's Teapot Creek of May 23). *Atlas* maps 39, 51, 59; MRC map 69.

5. Lewis was not, in fact, beyond the range of the black bear. Burroughs, 52–53.

6. This sentence refers to the grizzly bear, which does indeed vary greatly in color, though it does not change with the seasons. See below, May 15 and 31, 1806.

7. Also given on *Atlas* map 39, in both captains' hands.

Chapter Fourteen

From the Musselshell to the Marias

May 23–June 7, 1805

[Lewis] *Thursday May 23rd 1805.*[1]

Set out early this morning, the frost was severe last night, the ice appeared along the edge of the water, water also freized on the oars.   at the distance of one mile passed the entrance of a creek 15 yds. wide on Stard. side, this we call Teapot Creek,[2] it affords no water at it's mouth but has runing water at some small distance above, this I beleive to be the case with many of those creekes which we have passed since we entered this hilley country, the water is absorbed by the earth near the river and of course appear dry; they afford but little water at any rate, and that is so strongly impregnated with these salts that it is unfit for uce; all the wild anamals appear fond of this water; I have tryed it by way of experiment & find it moderately pergative, but painfull to the intestens in it's opperation.   this creek runs directly towards some low mountains which lye N. W. of it and appear to be about 30 mes. distant, perhaps it heads in them. This range of mountains appear to be about 70 miles long runing from E to W. having their Eastern extremity about 30 mes.: distant in a northwardly direction from [*NB: Tea*] pot Island.—[3]   also passed two small creeks on Lard. and two others on Stard. all inconsiderable and dry at their entrances.   just above the entrance of Teapot Creek on the stard. there is a large assemblage of the burrows of the Burrowing Squirrel[4]   they generally seelect a south or a south Easterly exposure for their residence, and never visit the brooks or river for water; I am astonished how this anamal exists as it dose without water,[5] particularly in a country like this where there is scarcely any rain during ¾ of the year and more rarely any due [dew]; yet we have sometimes found their villages at the distance of five or six miles from any water, and they are never found out of the limits of the ground which their burrows occupy; in the Autumn when the hard frosts commence they close their burrows and do not venture out again untill spring, indeed some of them appear to be yet in winter quarters. passed 3 Islands the two first covered with tall cottonwood timber and the last with willows only. river more rappid, & the country much the same as yesterday. some spruce pine[6] of small size appears among the pitch pine, and reather more rock than usual on the face of the hills. The musquetoes troublesome this evening, a circumstance I did not expect from the temperature of the morning. The Gees begin to lose the feathers of their wings and are unable to fly. Capt Clark walked on shore and killed 4 deer and an Elk. We killed a large fat brown bear which took the water after being wounded and was carried under some driftwood where he sunk and we were unable to get him. Saw but few buffaloe today, but a great number of Elk, deer, some antelopes and 5 bear. The wild rose [*NB: copy for Dr Barton*] which is now in blume are very abundant, they appear to differ but little from those common to the Atlantic States, the leaves of the bushes and the bush itself appear to be of somewhat smaller size.[7]

Courses and distances of May 23rd 1805.[8]

N. 55° W.	To the entrance of a large creek at a bend, on the Stard. side, called Teapot Creek	1
S. 70° W.	To a point of woodland on the lard. side opst. blff	1 ¼
S. 50° W.	To a point of woodland on Stard. side	1 ¼
S. 55° W.	Along the stard. side opposite to a hill on which there is some pine	1 ½
West	To a tree in a bend on Stard. above a bluff	2
S. 45° W.	To the upper point of an Island in a bend on lard. side, opposite the center of this Isld. a small Creek falls in on the Stard. side	2

S. 75° W.	to the main Stard. point, opposite to a bluff Lard., just above which a small creek falls in	½
S. 85° W.	to the lower point of a timbered bottom, lying along a bluff in a bend on Stard. side	3
S. 10° W.	to the upper point of the timber in a bend on the Lard. opposite to a bluff	1 ½
N. 88° W.	To a point of woodland Stard. opposite to a bluff above which a creek falls in on Lard.	2
N. 15° W.	to a point of woodland Lard. opposite to a bluff	1 ¼
West	Along the Lard. point	¼
S. 60° W.	to a point of timbered land on Stard. side	1
N. 65° W.	to a point of timbered land passing a small Island, in a deep bend to the N. a bluff on Stard.	2
S. 65° W.	to a point of woodland Stard. opposite to a bluff	2
N. 75° W.	to the upper point of a bluff in a bend on Lard.	¼
N. 30° E.	to the upper point of a small Island in a deep bend to the North E.	1 ½
N. 40° W.	Along the Lard. shore to the point on Lard.	1 ½
S. 45° W.	to a point of wood in a bend on Lard. under a hill, opposite to which we encamped on the Stard. side [9]	1 ¼

Miles— 27

[Clark]   *May 23rd Thursday 1805*

a Severe frost last night, the Thrmotr. Stood at the freesing point this morning i e 32 a 0. wind S W. the water freeses on the oars. Ice on the edge of the river we Set out at an early hour and passed the mouth a Creek at 1 mile on the Stard. Side which heads in a mountain N W of its mouth 30 or [*illegible*] miles, the Countrey on each Side is as passed yesterday passed 2 Small Creeks on the Stard & 2 on the Lard. Side to day. a mountain which appears to be 60 or 70 miles long bearing E. & W is about 25 miles distant from this river on the Stard Side Notherley of Pot Island I walked on Shore and killed 4 deer & an Elk, & a beaver in the evening we killed a large fat Bear, which we unfortunately lost in the river, after being Shot took the water & was Carried under a drift   passed in course of this day three Islands, two of them Covered with tall timber & a 3rd with willows

The after part of this day was worm & the Misquitors troublesome. Saw but five Buffalow a number of Elk & Deer & 5 bear & 2 Antilopes to day. the river beginning to rise, and Current more rapid than yesterday, in maney places I saw Spruces on the hills Sides Stard. this evening.

	mile	*Course & Distance May 23rd*
N. 55° W.	1	to the enterence of a Creek in a bend to the Stard Side called Teapot C. 15 yds. wide
S 70° W.	1 ¼	to a point of wood land on Lard. opsd. a bluff
S 50° W.	1 ¼	to a point of wood land on Stard. Side
S. 55° W.	1 ½	allong the Stard. Side a hill opposit on which there is pine
West	2	to a tree in a bend to the Stard. above a bluff
S. 45° W	2	to the upper point of an Island in a bend to the Lard. Side opposit the Center of this Island a small Creek falls in on the Stard. Side
S. 75° W.	½	to the main Std. point opposit to a bluff Lard. just above which a Small Creek falls in
S. 85° W.	3	to the lower point of a timbered bottom allong a bluff in a bend on the Stard Side
S. 10° W.	1 ½	to the upper point of a timber in a bend on the Lard. opposit to a bluff.
N. 88° W.	2	to a point of wood land Stard. Side opsd. a bluff above which a Creek falls in Lard.
N. 15° W.	1 ¼	to a point of wood land Lard. opsd. a bluff
West	¼	along the Lard. point.
S 60° W.	1	to a point of timbered land on the Stard Side
N. 65° W.	2	to a pt. of timber Lard. passing a Small Island in a bend to the N. a bluff on Stard.
S. 65° W.	2	to a pt. of wood land Stard. opsd. a bluff
N. 75° W.	¼	to the upper point of a bluff in a bind to the Larboard Side

N. 30° E	1 ½	to the upper point of a Small Island in a deep bend to the N. E.
N. 40° W.	1 ½	allong the Lard. Shore to the point L. S.
N. 45 W.	1 ¼	to a point of wood in a bend on Lard. under a hill opposit
	27	to which we encamped on the S. S.

1. This entry ends the daily entries in Lewis's notebook Codex D.

2. Later CK, or Kannuck, Creek, in Phillips County, Montana. *Atlas* maps 39, 51, 59; MRC map 69. It was probably Biddle who marked Lewis's word "Teapot" by adding a red letter "o" over "pot."

3. Probably later Ryan Island; the small creeks are nameless on *Atlas* maps 39, 51, 59, and on MRC map 70. They include Sevenmile Creek in Phillips County, and Carroll Creek in Fergus County, Montana.

4. On *Atlas* maps 39, 51, 59, this prairie dog colony is shown above the mouth of North Mountain Creek (later Little Rocky, now Rock, Creek), which they passed the next day. MRC map 70.

5. Prairie dogs, *Cynomys ludovicianus*, like certain other arid-land rodent species, obtain water through their food and retain it better than most mammals. Lewis was apparently the first to report on this phenomenon in North America. Cutright (LCPN), 144–45.

6. *Pseudotsuga menziesii* (Mirb.) Franco, Douglas fir. This location is the northeastern-most limit of Douglas fir in the United States. A small population is known from the Piney Buttes area of Garfield County. It is more commonly found in the middle elevations of the Rocky Mountains much farther west in Montana. Little, 80-W.

7. It was probably Biddle who drew a red vertical line through this last sentence.

8. Also given on *Atlas* map 39, in both captains' hands.

9. A little below the mouth of Rock (North Mountain) Creek, in Fergus County. *Atlas* maps 39, 51, 59; MRC map 70.

Friday May 24th 1805.

[Lewis]   *Point of Observation N, 23.*[1]

On the Stard. point mentioned in the sixth course of this day, observed time and distance of ☉'s and ☽'s nearest limbs ☉ East.   with Sextant.—

		Time			Distance		
	h	m	s				
A M.	10	39	47		54°	38′	″
	″	41	35		″	37	30

by myself

"	49	23	"	35		
"	53	55	"	34	45	by Capt. Clark
"	55	23	"	32	15	
"	56	56	"	31		
A. M. 10	59	35	54	30	45	
11	3	55	"	28	15	by Capt. Clark
"	5	4	"	28		
"	8	17	"	27	15	
"	10	13	"	26	30	By Myself
"	11	30	"	25	45	

Friday May 24th 1805.[2]

The water standing in the vessels freized during the night ⅛ of an inch thick, ice also appears along the verge of the river. the folage of some of the cottonwood trees have been entirely distroyed by the frost and are again puting forth other buds. the high country in which we are at present and have been passing for some days I take to be a continuation of what the Indians as well as the French Engages call the Black hills. This tract of country so called consists of a collection of high broken and irregular hills and short chain of mountains sometimes 120 miles in width and again becomeing much narrower, but always much higher than the country on either side; they commence about the head of the Kanzas river and to the West of that river near the Arkansas, from whence they take their course a little to the W. of N. W. approaching the rockey Mountains obliquely, passing the river platte above the forks and intercepting the Yellowstone river near the big bend and passing the Missouri at this place and probably continuing to swell the country as far North as the Saskashawan river tho' they are lower here than they are discribed to the Sth. and may therefore probably terminate before they reach the Suskashawan. the black hills in their course nothwardly appear to approach more nearly to the Rocky Mountains.[3]

We set out at an early hour this morning and proceed on principally by the chord untill about 9 A. M. when a fine breeze sprung up from the S. E. and enabled us though the ballance of the day to employ our sails to advantage; we proceed at a pretty good pace notwithstanding the courant of the river was very strong. we passed two large and four small Islands; also several streams on either side; the first of these is a large Creek or small river which disinboged on the Stard. side about 1½ miles above our encampment of last evening, it is 30 yards wide and contains some water. the bed is gravley and intermixed with some stone, it takes its rise in the mountains which are situated in a Northwardly direction from its entrance, distant about 30 miles.[4] the air is so pure in this open country that mountains and other elivated objects appear much nearer than they really are; these mountains do not appear to be further than 15 m. we sent a man up this creek to explore the country he returned late in the evening and informed that he had proceeded ten miles directly towards these mountains and that he did not think himself by any mean half way these mountains are rockey and covered with some scattering pine. This stream we call *North Mountain creek*. the next stream in order is a creek which falls in on Lard. 2½ miles higher; this is 15 yds. wide no water; a large village of the burrowing or barking squirrels on the Stard. side opposite it's entrance, hence the name *Little dog Ck.*[5] that being the name by which the French Engages call this anamal. at three miles and at 10 ms. from hence still ascending 2 Small creek fall in on the Stard. side, no water. 5½ miles higher a small river falls in on Lard. side this we called South Mountain creek as from it's direction it appeared to take it's rise in a range of Mountains lying in a S. Westerly direction from it's entrance distant 50 or 60 m.; this creek is 40 yards wide and discharges a handsome stream of water.[6] it's bed is rockey with gravel and sand, the banks high and country broken it's bottom narrow and no timber. The country high and broken, a considerable portion of black rock and brown sandy rock appear in the faces of the hills; the tops of the hills covered with scattering pine spruce and dwarf cedar; the soil poor and sterile, sandy near the tops of the hills, the whole producing but little grass; the narrow bottoms of the Missouri producing little else but Hysop or southern wood and the pulpy leafed thorn. Capt. Clark walked on shore this evening and killed a buffaloe cow, we left 2 Canoes and six men to dress the Cow and bring on the meat, they did not overtake us this evening. game is becoming more scarce, particularly beaver, of which we have seen but few for several days the beaver appears to keep pace with the timber as it declines in quantity they also become more scarce.

	mls.	*Courses and distances May 24th 1805*[7]
S. 60° W.	1 ½	To the entrance of N. Mountain Creek in a bend Std. side
S. 20° W.	1	To a point of wood Stard. point opposite to a bluff
S. 75° W.	¼	Along the Stard. point opposite to a bluff
N. 65° W.	1	Along the Stard. side opposite an Island near the Lard side under a bluff in a bend, a creek falls in above this bluff opposite to a Village of burrowing squirrels
N. 45° W.	¼	To a point on the Lard. side, passing bad water—
N. 70° W.	2 ¾	To a grove of trees at the entrance of a Creek in a bend on Stard. passing a stard. point at 1 ½ miles.
S. 48° W.	1	To a point of woodland Lard. side.
S. 50° W.	1 ½	To a point of woodland Stard. side, opposite to a low bluff and high piney hill.
West	2 ½	To the lower point of the timber in a bend on Lard. passing a Stard. point at 1 ½ mes. opposite the lower point of a small Island.
N. 60° W.	2 ¼	To the lower point of the timber in a Stard. bend, passing the Island at ¼ of a mile, a creek falls in on the Stard.— small and no water.—
S. 50° W.	1 ¼	To a bluff in a Lard. bend passing a small Island
S. 80° W.	1 ¼	To a point of wood Stard. passed a bluff Lard.
West	3	To the point of a high bluff in a bend on Lard. just below which S. Mtn. Creek falls in on Lard.
N. 70° W.	½	To a Stard. point of wood.
N. 50° W.	1	To a point of woodland Stard side
West	2	To some high timber on the Stard. side oppst. a bluff
N. 70° W	2	To a point of woodland Lard the trees here have no leaves here we encamped for the night.—
	Miles 24 ¼[8]	

[Clark]   *May 24th Friday 1805*

a Cold night   the water in the Small vestles frosed ⅛ of an inch thick, and the thermometer Stood this morning at the freesing point.   we Set out at an early hour and proceeded on, at 9 oClock we had a Breeze from the S E which Continued all day.   This Breeze afforded us good Sailing, the river rising fast   Current verry rapid.   passed Several Small Islands, two large & two Small Creeks, the 1st of those Creeks or Small rivers 1 ½ m. above our Camp is 30 yards wide and Contains water and appears to take its rise in the North Mountns. which is Situated in a northerley derection about 20 miles distant.   2 ½ m. higher a Creek falls in on the Lard. Side, opposit a large village of Barking Squirels.   3 miles Still higher a Small Creek falls in on the Stard.[9]   13 miles higher up a Small river falls in on the Lard Side which is 40 yards wide and has running water. This Stream appears to take its rise in the South Mountains which is Situated in a Southerly direction 30 or 40 miles distant.   I walked on the high countrey on the Stard. Side found it broken & Dry   Some pine, Spruce & Dwarf Cedar on the hill sides, I Sent one man 10 mile out   he reports a Similarity of Countrey back   I killed a fat buffalow a Short distance below the place we dined   2 Canoes & 6 men we left to get the meat did not join us this evening.   we Camped on the Lard point.[10]   the Cotton wood in this point is beginning to put out a Second bud, the first being killed by the frost

	miles	*Course & Distance May 24th*
S. 60° W.	1 ½	to the mouth of N M. in a bend Stard Side
S. 20° W.	1	to a point of wood Stard Side opsd. a bluff L S.
S. 75° W.	¼	along the Stard point opsd. a bluff L. S.
N. 65° W.	1 ¼	allong the Stard. Side opsd. an Island near the Lard Side under a bluff in a bend. a Creek falls in Lard. opsd. a village of barking Squirels S. S.
N. 45° W.	¼	to a point on the Lard Side, passed bad water
N. 70° W.	2 ¾	to a grove of trees at the mouth of a Creek in a bend to the Stard. passed Sd pt. at 1 ½ m.
S. 48° W.	1	to a point of wood land Lard Side

S. 50° W.	1 ½	to a point of wood land Stard. Side opsd. to a low Bluff & high pine hill
West	2 ½	to the lower point of the timber in a bend on Lard. passing a Stard. point at 1 ½ m. opsd. the lower point of a Small Isld.
N. 60° W.	2 ¼	to the lower point of the timber in a Stard. bend, passing the Isld. at ¼ of a m. a Small Creek falls in on the Stard. Side
S. 50° W.	1 ¼	to a bluff in a Lard. bend passing an Island
S. 80° W.	1 ¼	to a point of wood Stard passd. a bluff Ld.
West	3	to the point of a high bluff in a bend on Lard. a large Stream falls in just below on Lard. Sd.
N. 70° W	½	to a Stard point of wood
N. 50° W.	1	to a point of wood land Stard Side
West	2	to Some high timber on the Std. Side opsd. a bluff
N. 70° W.	2	to a point of wood, trees have no leaves on the Lard Side. Where we Camped
miles	24 ¼	

1. Lewis's astronomy note is found on the flyleaf of Codex E, preceding the daily entry for this day.

2. Here begin the daily entries in Lewis's notebook Codex E.

3. Lewis explains his concept of the "Black Hills," actually including various disconnected small ranges east of the Rockies. This concept, elaborated on Clark's postexpeditionary maps, continued until corrected in the 1850s. Allen (PG), 202, 239, 240.

4. "North Mountain Creek" on *Atlas* maps 39, 51, 59, now Rock Creek, in Phillips County, Montana. It rises in the Little Rocky Mountains. MRC map 70.

5. Today's Sand Creek, in Fergus County, Montana. *Atlas* maps 39, 51, 59; MRC map 70.

6. South Mountain Creek, in Fergus County, later known by that name or as Armells Creek. The mountains are the Judith Mountains (and possibly Moccasin Mountains) in Fergus County. *Atlas* maps 39, 51, 59, 60; MRC map 70; Allen (PG), 265.

7. Also given on *Atlas* map 39, in both captains' hands.

8. The correct total is 25 ¼, but the captains had the total given in both their journals and on *Atlas* map 39. The mistake was perhaps made on the map, where the last two distances were added to an erroneous subtotal of 20 ¼. Lewis oddly did not correct this although he had the correct subtotal in his journal.

9. Later Siparyann Spring Creek, in Phillips County. *Atlas* maps 39, 51, 59, 60; MRC map 70.

10. In either Fergus or Phillips County, some three miles above where U.S. Highway 191 crosses the Missouri. *Atlas* maps 39, 51, 60; MRC map 71.

[Lewis]   *Saturday May 25th 1805.*

The Two canoes which we left behind yesterday to bring on the meat did not arrive this morning untill 8 A M. at which time we set out; the wind being against us we did not proceed with so much ease or expedition as yesterday, we imployed the toe line principally which the banks favored the uce off; the courant strong particularly arround the points against which the courant happened to set, and at the entrances of the little gullies from the hills, those rivulets having brought down considerable quantities of stone and deposited it at their entrances forming partial barriers to the water of the river to the distance of 40 or 50 feet from the shore, arround these the water run with great violence, and compelled us in some instances to double our force in order to get a perorogue or canoe by them. as we ascended the river today I saw several gangs of the big-horned Anamals on the face of the steep bluffs and clifts on the Stard. side and sent drewyer to kill one which he accomplished; Capt. Clark and Bratton who were on shore each killed one of these anamals this evening.[1] The head and horns of the male which Drewyer killed weighed 27 lbs. it was somewhat larger than the male of the common deer, the boddy reather thicker deeper and not so long in proportion to it's hight as the common deer; the head and horns are remakably large compared with the other part of the anamal; the whole form is much more delicate than that of the common goat, and there is a greater disparity in the size of the male and female than between those of either the deer or goat. the eye is large and prominant, the puple of a deep sea green and small, the iris of a silvery colour much like the common sheep; the bone above the eye is remarkably prominant; the head nostrils and division of the upper lip are precisely in form like the sheep. there legs resemble the sheep more than any other animal with which I am acquainted tho' they are more delicately formed, like the sheep they stand forward in the knee and the lower joint of the foreleg is smallest where it joins the knee, the hoof is black & large in proportion, is divided, very open and roundly pointed at the toe, like the sheep; is much hollowed and sharp on the under edge like the Scotch goat, has two small hoofs behind each foot below the ankle as the goat sheep and deer have.   the belley, inside of the legs, and the extremity of the rump and butocks for about two inches arround the but of the tale, are white, as is also the tale excet just at it's extremity on the upper side which is of a dark brown.   the tail is about three inches in length covered with short hair, or at least not longer than that of the boddy; the outher parts of the anamal are of a duskey brown or reather a leadcoloured light brown; the anamal is now sheding it's winter coat which is thick not quite as long as that of the deer and appears to be intermixed with a considerable quantity of a fine fur which lyes next to the skin & conceald by the coarcer hear; the shape of the hair itself is celindric as that of the antelope is but is smaller shorter, and not compressed or flattened as that of the deer's winter coat is, I believe this anamal only sheds it's hair once a year.   it has eight fore teeth in the under jaw and no canine teeth. The horns are lagest at their base, and occupy the crown of the head almost entirely.   they are compressed, bent backwards and lunated; the surface swelling into wavy rings which incircleing the horn continue to succeed each other from the base to the extremity and becoming less elivated and more distant as they recede from the head.   the horn for about two thirds of it's length is filled with a porus bone which is united with the frontal bone. I obtained the bones of the upper part of the head of this animal at the big bone lick.[2]   the horns of the female are small, but are also compress bent backwards and incircled with a succession of wavy rings.   the horn is of a light brown colour; when dressed it is almost white extreemly transparent and very elastic.   this horn is used by the natives in constructing their bows; I have no doubt but it would eligant and ucefull hair combs, and might probably answer as many valuable purposes to civilized man, as it dose to the savages, who form their watercups spoons and platters of it.   the females have already brought forth their young   indeed from the size of the young I suppose that they produce them early in March.   they have from one to two at a birth.   they feed on grass but principally on the arromatic herbs which grow on the clifts and inaccessable hights which they usually frequent.   the places they gerally celect to lodg is the cranies or cevices of the rocks in the faces of inacessable precepices, where the wolf nor bear can reach them and where indeed man himself would in many instancies find a similar deficiency; yet these anamals bound from rock to rock and stand apparently in the most careless manner on the sides of precipices of many hundred feet.   they are very shye and are quick of both sent and sight.—

At the distance of two ¾ miles above our encampment of last evening we passed a Creek 20 yard wide affording no runing water,[3] we also passed 7 Islands in the course of the day. The Country on either hand is high broken and rockey; the rock is either soft brown sand stone covered with a thin strata of limestone, or a hard black rugged grannite, both usually in horizontal stratas and the Sandy rock overlaying the other.—   Salts and quarts still appear, some coal and pumice stone also appear;[4] the river bottoms are narrow and afford scarcely any timber.   the bars of the river are composed principally of gravel, but little pine on the hills. We saw a Pole-cat[5] this evening it is the first we have seen for many days.   buffalow are now scarce and I begin to fear our harvest of white puddings are at an end.

Courses and distances May 25th 1805.[6]

S. 50° W.	2 ¾	to the entrance of a creek 20 yds. wide in a bend on Lard. side passing a small Island in a deep bend on Lard. side—
N. 50° W.	1 ¼	To the Stard. Side of tea Island, which is seperated from the Stard. shore by a narrow channel
N. 35° W.	1 ½	Along the Stard. side passing a sand Island
N. 15° W.	2	To a point of woodland on the Lard. side passing the upper point of Tea Island.
N. 30° W.	2	to a point of woodland Stard. side, opposite to the lower point of an Island.
N. 25° W.	¼	to a bluff bank in a Stard. bend.
N. 65° W	¾	to a bluff point on the Stard. opposite the upper point of the Island
N. 60° W.	4 ½	to a clump of trees in a Stard. bend under a high bluff passing a Lard.[7] point at 2 ½ mes. and a Small Island at 3 ½ mes.
N. 80° W.	1	to the Point of a high plain on the Stard. side passing an Isd. near the Std. side ¾ of a me. in length.

2. Ibex (bighorn sheep, *Ovis canadensis*), May 25, 1805, Voorhis no. 1

S. 80° W.	2	to the lower point of an untimbered Island situated in the middle of the river, passg. a Sd. pt. at 1½ mes.
S. 60° W.	1	to a pt. on the Lard. side, passing the head of the Ild. at ¾
Miles 18		of a mile and incamped on the Lard. Side.[8]

[Clark]   *May 25th Satturday 1805*[9]

The two Canoes left for meat yesterday did not joint us untill 8 oClock this morning at which time we Set out, the morning Cool & pleasent   wind a head all day from the S. W.   we pass a Creek on the Lard. Side about 20 yards wide, which does not run, we also passd 7 Islands, I walked on Shore and killed a female *Ibex* or big horn animal   in my absence Drewyer & Bratten killed two others, this animale is a species peculiar to this upper part of the Missouri, the head and horns of the male which Drewyer killed to day weighed 27 lbs   it was Somewhat larger than the Mail of the Common Deer; ⟨(Female very near the Size of the Male)⟩   The body reather thicker deeper and not So long in proportion to its hight as the common Deer; the head and horns of the male are remarkably large Compared with the other parts of the animal; the whole form is much more delicate than that of the common goat, and there is a greater disparity in the Size of the mail and female than between those of either the deer or goat.   the eye is large and prominant, the puple of a deep Sea green and Small, the iris of a Silvery Colour much like the common Sheep; the bone above the Eye is remarkably prominant; the head nostrils and division of the upper lip are precisely in form like the Sheep. their legs resemble the Sheep more than any other animal with which I am acquainted tho' they are more delicately formed, like the Sheep they stand foward in the Knee and the lower joint of the fore leg is Smallest where it joins the Knee, the hoof is black and large in perpotion, is divided, very open and roundly pointed at the toe; like the Sheep; is much hollowed and Sharp on the under edge like the Scotch goat, has two Small Hoofs behind each foot below the ankle as the goat Sheep and Deer have. the belley, iner Side of the legs, and the extremity of the rump and buttocks for about two inches ½ around the but of the tail, are white, as is also the tail except just at its extremity on the upper Side which is of a dark brown. the tail is about 3 inches in length covered with Short hair, or at least not longer than that of the boddy; the outer part of the animal are of a duskey brown or reather a lead coloured light brown; the animal is now Sheding its winter coat which is thick not quite as long as that of the Deer and appears to be inter mixt with a considerable quantity of fine fur which lies next to the Skin and concealed by the Coarcer hair; the Shape of the hair itself is cylindric as that of the Antilope is, but is Smaller, Shorter and not Compressed or flattened as that of the deers winter Coat is. I believe this animal only Sheds it's hair once a year. it has Eight fore teeth in the underjaw and no canine teeth. The *Horns* are large at their base, and occupy the Crown of the head almost entirely, they are compressed, bent backwards and lunated; the Surface Swelling into wavey rings which incircleing the horn continue to Succeed each other from the base to the extremity and be-comeing less elivated and more distant as they receed from the head. The horn for about two thirds of its length is filled with a porus bone which is united with the frontal bone   (Capt. Lewis obtained the bones of the upper part of the head of this Animal at the *big Bone Lick* in the State of Kentucky which I Saw and find to be the Same in every respect with those of the Missouri and the Rockey Mountains)   the horns of the *female* are Small, but are also compressed and bent backwards and incircled with a Succession of wavy rings. the horn is of a light brown Colour; when

Dressed it is almost white extreamly transparent and very elastic. this horn is used by the nativs in constructing their bows; I have no doubt of it's elegance and usefullness in hair Combs, and might probably answer as maney valuable purpoces to civilized man, as it does to the native indians, who form their water Cups, Spoons and platters of it. the females have already brought forth their young indeed from the Size of the young, I Suppose that they produce them early in March. they have from one to two at a birth. they feed on grass, but principally on the arramatic herbs which grow on the Clifts and inaccessable hights which they frequent most commonly, and the places they generally collect to lodge is the Cranies or Cevices of the rocks in the face of inaccessable precepices, where the wolf nor Bear Can reach them, and where indeed man himself would in maney instances find a Similar deficiency; yet those animals bound from rock to rock and Stand apparently in the most Careless manner on the Side of precipices of maney hundred feet. they are very Shy and quick of both Sent and Sight. The flesh of this animal is dark and I think inferior to the flesh of the Common Deer, and Superior to the antilope of the Missouri and the Columbian Plains—.[10] In my walk of this day I saw mountts. on either side of the river at no great distance, those mountains appeared to be detached, and not ranges as laid down by the *Minetarrees*, I also think I saw a range of high mounts. at a great distance to the S S W. but am not certain as the horozon was not clear enough to view it with Certainty.[11] The country on either side is high broken and rockey a dark brown hard rugid Stone intermixed with a Soft white Sand Stone. the hills contain Coal or cabonated wood as below and Some Scattering pumistone. the Sides of the river is bordered with coars gravel, which in maney places have washed either together or down Small brooks and forms bars at Some distance in the water, around which the current passes with great valocity. the bottoms between hills and river are narrow and Contain Scercely any timber. The appearence of Salts, and bitumun Still Continue. we Saw a polecat to day being the first which we have Seen for Some time past. The Air of this quarter is pure and helthy. the water of the Missouri well tasted not quite So muddy as it is below, not withstanding the last rains has raised the river a little it is less muddy than it was before the rain.

Course and Distance of May 25th 1805

S. 50° W.	2 ¾	Miles to the enterance of a Creek in a bend to the Lard Side 20 yards wide passing a Small island in a deep bend to Lard.
N. 50° W.	1 ¼	to the Stard. Side of tea island which is Seperated from the main Stard. Shore by a narrow chanel.
N. 35° W.	½	on the Stard Side passing a Sand Island.
N. 15° W.	2	to a point of wood land on the Lard. Side passing the upper point of tea Island.
N. 30° W.	2	to a point of wood land on the Stard. Side opposit to the lower point of an island.
N. 25° W.	¼	to a bluff bank in the Stard Bend.
N. 65° W.	¾	to a Bluff point on the Stard. opposit to the upper point of an island.
N. 60° W.	4 ½	to a Clump of trees in a Stard. bend under a high bluff, passing a Lard. point at 2 ½ miles a Small island at 3 ½ miles.
N. 80° W.	1	mile to a high plain on the Stard. Side passing an island near the Stard Side ¾ of a m in length.
S. 80° W.	2	to the lower point of an open island Situated in the middle of the river, passing a Lard pt. at 1 ½ miles on this course.
S. 60° W.	1	to a point on the lard. Side passing the head of the Island at ¾ of a mile and Encamped on the Larboard Side.
	18	

    1. Here they obtained their first specimens of the bighorn sheep, which had already been described in 1804 from a specimen obtained in Canada. See also April 26, 1805. Burroughs, 171. Someone drew a red vertical line through the passages which follow to the end of the paragraph.

    2. Big Bone Lick was a famous fossil deposit southwest of Covington, Kentucky, which Lewis visited during his westbound journey in October 1803, to obtain fossils for Jefferson. Jackson (LLC), 1 : 126–32; Cutright (LCPN), 33. Fossil remains of an extinct Pleistocene race of bighorn have been recovered from Big Bone Lick. Information of Bill Melton, Curator, University of Montana Geological Museum, Missoula, March 5, 1986. It is unknown if the bones that Lewis found here were those of a bighorn.

    3. Two Calf Creek, in Fergus County, Montana, nameless on *Atlas* maps 39, 51, 60. MRC map 71.

4. The broken country (the Missouri Breaks) was formed when the Missouri River cut a new course from Virgelle, Chouteau County, Montana, to Fort Peck Dam, Montana, when its former course (the Milk River valley) was blocked by glacial ice. The sandstone and limestone (actually molluscan shells cemented with lime) and coal are part of the Judith River Formation. The black rock is probably the Claggett Shale which underlies the Judith River Formation. There is no granite near the river here.

5. A skunk, *Mephitis mephitis*.

6. Also given on *Atlas* map 40, in both captains' hands.

7. "Lard" agrees with *Atlas* map 40, but Clark's journal entry apparently has "Stard."

8. In Fergus County, some five or six miles below the present Cow Island Landing Recreation Area and near the present ferry crossing the Missouri, by the Goodrich's Island on *Atlas* maps 40, 52, 60. MRC map 71.

9. Here Clark has made a rough sketch of a bighorn sheep (fig. 2).

10. The reference to the plains of the Columbia indicates that Clark wrote the passage at least several months later. In fact, Clark wrote most of the May 25 entry—starting with his description of the bighorn—and the first part of the entry for May 26 in a neater and smaller hand than the material immediately preceding and following, and the end of the neater passage on May 26 is obviously crowded in. Clark probably left a space here to insert material later. Much of the following writing in this journal is obviously copied from Lewis and may well have been done at Fort Clatsop, or on the return journey in 1806. See the Introduction, vol. 2.

11. The mountains to the north would be the Little Rocky and Bears Paw mountains and to the south, the Judith range. In the distance Clark was probably seeing the Highwood Mountains near the Great Falls. Allen (PG), 265–66.

[Lewis]   *Sunday May 26th 1805.*

Set out at an early hour and proceeded principally by the toe line, using the oars mearly to pass the river in order to take advantage of the shores.   scarcely any bottoms to the river; the hills high and juting in on both sides, to the river in many places.   the stone tumbleing from these clifts and brought down by the rivulets as mentioned yesterday became more troublesome today.   the black rock has given place to a very soft sandstone which appears to be washed away fast by the river, above this and towards the summits of the hills a hard freestone of a brownish yellow colour shews itself in several stratas of unequal thicknesses frequently overlain or incrusted by a very thin strata of limestone which appears to be formed of concreted ⟨cemented⟩ shells.[1]   Capt. Clark walked on shore this morning and ascended to the summit of the river hills   he informed me on his return that he had seen mountains on both sides of the river runing nearly parrallel with it and at no great distance; also an irregular range of mountains on lard. about 50 mes. distant, the extremities of which boar W and N. W. from his station.[2] he also saw in the course of his walk, some Elk, several herds of the Big horn, and the large hare; the latter is common to every part of this open country. scarcely any timber to be seen except the few scattering pine and spruce which crown the high hills, or in some instances grow along their sides. In the after part of the day I also walked out and ascended the river hills which I found sufficiently fortiegueing. on arriving to the summit one of the highest points in the neighbourhood I thought myself well repaid for any labour; as from this point I beheld the Rocky Mountains for the first time, I could only discover a few of the most elivated points above the horizon, the most remarkable of which by my pocket compass I found bore N. 65° W. being a little to the N. of the N. W. extremity of the range of broken mountains seen this morning by Capt. C. these points of the Rocky Mountains were covered with snow and the sun shone on it in such manner as to give me the most plain and satisfactory view. while I viewed these mountains I felt a secret pleasure in finding myself so near the head of the heretofore conceived boundless Missouri; but when I reflected on the difficulties which this snowey barrier would most probably throw in my way to the Pacific, and the sufferings and hardships of myself and party in them, it in some measure counterballanced the joy I had felt in the first moments in which I gazed on them; but as I have always held it a crime to anticipate evils I will believe it a good comfortable road untill I am compelled to beleive differently. saw a few Elk & bighorns at a distance on my return to the river I passed a creek about 20 yds. wide near it's entrance it had a handsome little stream of runing water;[3] in this creek I saw several softshelled Turtles[4] which were the first that have been seen this season; this I believe proceeded reather from the season than from their non existence in the portion of the river from the Mandans hither. on the Stard. shore I killed a fat buffaloe which was very acceptable to us at this moment; the party came up to me late in the evening and encamped for the night on the Lard. side. it was after dark before we finished butchering the buffaloe, and on my return to camp I trod within five inches of a rattle snake but being in motion I passed before he could probably put himself in a striking attitude and fortunately escaped his bite, I struck about at random ⟨lying⟩ with my espontoon being directed in some measure by his nois untill I killed him. Our hunters had killed two of the Bighorned Anamals since I had left them. we also passed another creek a few miles below Turtle Creek on the Stard. 30 yds in width which also had runing water bed rockey.— [*NB: we called it Windsor Cr:*][5] late this evening we passed a very bad rappid which reached quite across the river, [*NB: water deep channel narrow gravel &c. on each side*] the party had considerable difficulty in ascending it altho' they doubled their crews and used both the rope and the pole. while they were passing this rappid a female Elk and it's fawn swam down throught the waves which ran very high, hence the name of Elk rappids which they instantly gave this place,[6] these are the most considerable rappids which we have yet seen on the missouri and in short the only place where there has appeared to be a suddon decent. opposite to these rappids there is a high bluff and a little above on Lard. a small cottonwood bottom in which we found sufficient timber for our fires and encampment.[7] here I rejoined the party after dark. The appearances of coal in the face of the bluffs, also of birnt hills, pumice stone salt and quarts continue as yesterday.[8] This is truly a desert barren country and I feel myself still more convinced of it's being a continuation of the black hills. we have continued every day to pass more or less old stick lodges of the Indians in the timbered points, there are two even in this little bottom where we lye.—

Courses and distances of May 26th 1805.[9]

S 45° W.	1	to the point of a plain on the Stard. side opposite to a bluff on Lard. side.
N. 70° W.	¼	Along the Stard. point opposite to a bluff
N. 45° W.	¼	Along the Stard. point opposite to a bluff
N. 10° W.	¼	Along the Std. do. do. do. do.
N. 70° E.	¼	Along the Stard. point opposite to a high hill
N. 35° E.	2	to a few trees on a Lard. point.
N. 10° W.	¾	to a point in a bend on Stard. side
N. 75° W.	½	to a point of timber on the Stard. side

N. 66° W.	1	to a point of timber on the Lard. side
N. 18° W.	1	to a gravley point on the Stard. side
N. 12° E.	1	to the entrance of a creek [*EC: Windsor's*] 30 yds. wide on Stard. side
West	¾	to some trees on a Lard. point
S. 80 W.	1 ½	to the upper point of some timber in a bend on Lard. Side.
N. 80 W.	1 ½	to an open point on the Lard. side.
West	2	to the entrance of a creek [*EC: Turtle*] in a stard. bend, no timber on either side of the river, pine scattered on the hills.
S. 24 W.	2	to a Clift in a bend on Lard. side
West	2	to a point on the Lard. side no timber
S. 60° W.	½	to a bluff point Lard. opposite to the upper point of a small sand Island.
S. 45° W.	4	to the point of a small plain Lard. side, passing high bluffs on either hand.—
S. 70° W.	1	to the point of a high bluff in a Lard. bend, at which place is a very considerable riffle which we call the Elk rappids.—
N. 80° W.	¼	to the upper point of a small grove of timber on Lard.
Mes. 22 ¾		side where we encamped for the night

[Clark]   *May 26th Sunday 1805*

We Set out early and proceeded as yesterday wind from the S. W.   the river enclosed with very high hills on either Side. I took one man and walked out this morning, and ascended the high countrey to view the mountains which I thought I Saw yesterday, from the first Sumit of the hill [10] I could plainly See the Mountains on either Side which I Saw yesterday and at no great distance from me, those on the Stard Side is an errigular range, the two extremities of which bore West and N. West from me.   those Mountains on the Lard. Side appeared to be Several detached Knobs or mountains riseing from a leven open Countrey, at different distances from me, from South West to South East, on one the most S. Westerly of those Mountains there appeared to be Snow. I crossed a Deep holler and assended a part of the plain elevated much higher than where I first viewed the above mountains; from this point I beheld the Rocky Mountains for the first time with Certainty, I could only discover a fiew of the most elivated points above the horizon.   the most remarkable of which by my pocket Compas I found bore S. 60 W.   those points of the rocky Mountain were Covered with Snow and the Sun Shown on it in Such a manner as to give me a most plain and Satisfactory view.   whilst I viewed those mountains I felt a Secret pleasure in finding myself So near the head of the heretofore Conceived boundless Missouri; but when I reflected on the difficulties which this Snowey barrier would most probably throw in my way to the Pacific Ocean, and the Sufferings and hardships of my Self and party in them, it in Some measure Counter ballanced the joy I had felt in the first moments in which I gazed on them; but as I have always held it little Short of Criminality to anticipate evils I will allow it to be a good Comfortable road untill I am Compelled to believe otherwise—. The high Country in which we are at present and have been passing for Some days I take to be a continuation of what the Indians as well as the French Engages call the Black hills. This tract of Country So Called Consists of a Collection of high broken and irregular hills and Short Chains of Mountains, sometimes 100 miles in width and again becoming much narrower, but always much higher than the Country on either Side; they commence about the head of the Kanzas river and to the west of that river near the Arkansaw river, from whence they take their Cource a little to the west of N. W. approaching the Rocky Mountains obliquely passing the river Platt near the forks, and intersepting the River Rochejhone near the big bend of that river, and passing the Missouri at this place—, and probably Continueing to Swell the Country as far North as the Saskashawan river. tho' they are lower here than they are discribed to the South and may therefore termonate before they reach the Saskashawan.   the Black hills in their Course northerly appear to approach more nearly the Rocky Mountains. I Saw a great number of white brant, also the common brown brant, Geese of the common Size & kind and a Small Species of geese, which differs considerably from the Common or Canadian Goose; their necks, head and backs are considerably thicker, Shorter and larger than the other in propotion to its Size they are also more than a third

Smaller, and their note more like that of the brant or young goose which has not perfectly acquired his note, in all other respect they are the Same in Colour habits and the number of feathers in the tail, they frequently also ascocate with the large Geese when in flocks, but never Saw them pared off with the larger or common goose. The white Brant ascocates in very large flocks, they do not appear to be mated or pared off as if they intended to raise their young in this quarter, I therefore doubt whether they reside here dureing the Summer for that purpose. this bird is larger than the Common brown brant or ⅔ of the common goose. it is not So long by Six inches from point to point of the wings when extended as the other; the back head and neck are also larger and Stronger; their beak, legs and feet are of a redish flesh coloured white. the eye of a moderate Size, the puple of a deep Sea green encircled with a ring of yellowish brown. it has 16 feathers of equal length in the tail their note differs but little from the Common brant. they are of a pure white except the large feathers of the 1st and 2d joint of the wings which are jut black.

The country which borders the river is high broken and rocky, generally imbeded with a Soft Sand Stone higher up the hill the Stone is of a brownish yellow hard and gritty those Stones wash down from the hills into the river and cause the Shore to be rocky &c. which we find troublesom to assend there is Scerce any bottom ⟨to⟩ between the Hills & river and but a fiew trees to be Seen on either Side except Scattering pine on the Sides of the emence hills; we passed 2 Creeks on the Stard Side both of them had running water in one of those Creek Capt Lewis tells me he saw Soft Shell Turtle Capt Lewis in his walk killed a fat Buffalow which we were in want of our hunters killed 2 Mountain rams or big horns in the evening late we passed a rapid which extended quite across the river we assended it by the assistance of a Cord & poles on the Lard. Side the Cliffs jut over, the opposit Side is a Small leavel bottom, we Camped a little above in a Small grove of Cotton trees on the Lard. Side in the rapid we saw a Dow Elk & her faun, which gave rise to the name of Elk & faun Riffle we had a few drops of rain at Dark.— the Salts Coal & Burnt hills & Pumicston Still Continue, game Scerce this Countrey may with propriety I think be termed the Deserts of America, as I do not Conceive any part can ever be Settled, as it is deficent in water, Timber & too

Steep to be tilled. We pass old Indian lodges in the woody points everry day & 2 at our camp &c

	mile	*Course & Distance 26th of May 1805*
S. 45° W.	1	to the point of a plain on the Stard. Side opposit to a Bluff. L. S.
N. 70° W.	¼	allong the Stard. point opsd. a Bluff
N. 45° W.	¼	allong the Stard. point opsd. a Bluff
N. 10° W	¼	allong the Stard. Point opsd. a Bluff
N. 20° E.	¼	allong the Stard point opsd. a high hill
N. 35° E.	2	to a fiew trees on a point to Lard Side
N. 10° W	¾	to a point in a bend to the Stard Side
N. 75° W	½	to a point of timber on the Stard.
N. 66° W.	1	to a point of timber on the Lard. Side
N. 18° W	1	to graveley point on the Stard. Side
N. 12° E	1	to the mouth of a Creek Stard. Side Windsors Creek
West	¾	to Some trees on the Lard point
S. 80° W	1 ½	to the upper point of Some timber in a bend to the Lard. Side
N 80° W	½	to a open point on the Lard Side
West	2	to the mouth of a Creek in a bend to the Stard. Side no timber on either Side of the river, pine Scattered on the hills &c.
S. 24° W.	2	to a Clift in a bend to the Lard. Side
West	2	to a point on the Lard Side (no timber)
S. 60° W.	½	to a Bluff point Lard. opposit the upper point of a Small Sand Island
S 45° W.	4	to the point of a Small plain Lard. passing a high bluff on either Side
S. 70° W	1	to the point of a high bluff in Lard. bend at which place is a verry considerable riffle which we Call Elk & faun rifflee
N. 80° W.	¼	to the upper part of ⟨Some⟩ the timber in a small grove [*ML: on Lard.*] where we encamped
miles	22 ¾	

[Lewis]   May 26, 1805.[11]

One of the party killed a bighorned ⟨antelope⟩, the head and horns of which weighed 27 lbs. a hare was also killed which weighed 8 ½ lbs. the hare are now of a plale lead brown colour— [*EC: ovis montana   Lepus campestris*]

1. Numerous faults cut the late Cretaceous formations south of the Bears Paw Mountains, fracturing the rock. These rock fragments and the oval-shaped concretions of the Judith River Formation are easily displayed by erosion. The faulting in this area exposes the Claggett Shale in a few places, but most of the rock belongs to the Judith River Formation.

2. The ranges Clark saw are identified in the previous entry.

3. Soft Shell Turtle Creek on *Atlas* maps 40, 52, 60, later Snake Creek and then Bullwhacker Creek, in Blaine County, Montana. MRC map 71.

4. The western spiny softshell turtle, *Trionyx spiniferus hartwegi*. Benson (HLCE), 88.

5. After Private Richard Windsor; now Cow Creek, in Blaine County. A mile or so below is Cow Island Crossing, where the Nez Perces crossed in 1877, on their flight from the U.S. Army. *Atlas* maps 40, 52, 60; MRC map 71.

6. "Elk fawn rapid" on *Atlas* maps 40, 52, 60, now Bird Rapids; Clark's route appears as a dotted line on the first and last of these maps. MRC map 72.

7. In Fergus County, Montana, above the rapids and some two miles below the mouth of later Windsor Creek in Blaine County, which is not Lewis and Clark's Windsor's Creek. Coues (HLC), 1 : 327; MRC map 72.

8. The coal is one of several beds in the Judith River Formation. The term "burnt hills" may refer to the color of the sandstone. There is insufficient coal here to produce the appearance noted with the Paleocene formations. The "quartz" is selenite and the salts are derived principally from the Bearpaw Shale which caps some of the hills.

9. Also given on *Atlas* map 40, in both captains' hands.

10. The hill is clearly marked on *Atlas* maps 40, 52, 60; Clark's route appears as a dotted line on the first and last of these maps.

11. Lewis's zoological note from Codex Q; he is commenting on the bighorn sheep and the white-tailed jackrabbit.

[Lewis]   *Monday May 27th 1805.*

The wind blew so hard this morning that we did not sent out untill 10 A. M. we employed the chord most of the day; the river becomes more rappid and is intercepted by shoals and a greater number of rocky points at the mouths of the little gulies than we experienced yesterday. the bluffs are very high steep rugged, containing considerable quantities of stone and border the river closely on both sides; once perhaps in the course of several miles there will be a few acres of tolerably level land in which two or thre impoverished cottonwood trees will be seen.[1] great quantities of stone also lye in the river and garnish it's borders, which appears to have tumbled from the bluffs where the ⟨water⟩ rains had washed away the sand and clay in which they were imbeded. the bluffs are composed of irregular tho' horizontal stratas of yellow and brown or black clay, brown and yellowish white sand, of soft yellowish white sand stone and a hard dark brown free stone, also of large round kidneyformed and irregular seperate masses of a hard black Iron stone, which is imbeded in the Clay and sand. some little pine spruce and dwarf cedar on the hills. some coal or carbonated wood still makes it's appearance in these bluffs, pumicestone and birnt hills it's concommutants also are seen. the salts and quarts are seen but not in such abundance.[2] the country more broken and barren than yesterday if possible. about midday it was very warm to this the high bluffs and narrow channel of the river no doubt contributed greatly. we passed a small untimbered Island this morning on the Lard. side of the river just above our encampment of last evening.[3] saw a few small herds of the Bighorned anamals and two Elk only, of the last we killed one, the river is generally about 200 yds. wide, very rappid and has a perceptable fall or declination through it's whole course.

This evening we encamped, for the benefit of wood, near two dead toped cottonwood trees on the Lard. side; the dead limbs which had fallen from these trees furnished us with a scanty supply only, and more was not to be obtained in the neighbourhood.—[4]

Courses and Distances May 27th 1805.[5]

West	1 ¾	Along the Lard. shore to a point on the Lard. side no timber a bluff close on both sides.
S 80° W.	3 ¼	to a bluff point on the Stard. side, in a Stard. bend
S. 50° W.	1	to a Lard. point.
S. 8° W.	1 ½	to the point of a bluff Lard. in a Lard. bend, the river making a considerable bend to the S. E.
S 60° W.	½	to a point on the Lard. side
S. 26° W.	1 ½	to a single cottonwood tree on the Lard. point.

S. 55° W.	1	to a bluff point on the Lard. side.
S. 45° W.	3 ½ [6]	to a bluff on the Lard. side, passing a Lard. point at 1 m.
Miles 14		& a Stard. point at 2 ½ ms. we encamped on Lard. side 1 ½ ms. on this course.

Point of Observation No. 24.

On the Lard. shore one mile short of the extremity of the second course of this day, observed Merdn. Altd. of ⊙'s L. L. with Octant by the back Observatn. 57° 27′

Latitude deduced from this observation [*blank*]

[Clark]   *May 27th Monday 1805.*

The wind blew hard from the S W. which detained us untill about 10 oClock, at which time we Set out and proceeded on, passed a Small nacked Island on the Lard Side imediately above the timber in which we Camped   The river is verry Shoaley and the bad places are verry numerous, i e at the mouth of every Drean the rocks which is a hard dark gritey Stone[7] is thrown out Some distance in the river which Cause a Considerable riffle on that Side, the hills approach the river verry Close on either Side, river narrow & no timber except Some Scattering pine on the hills & hill Sides, the Salts, Coal, burn hills & Pumice Stone &c. Continue, the hills are Generally Bluffs of various Coloured earth ⟨Genly⟩ most commonly black with different quallities stone intermixed Some Stratums of Soft Sand Stone, Some hard, Some a dark brown & yellow hard grit, those Stones are loosened by the earths washing from them into the river and ultimately role down into the river, which appears to be Crowded with them.[8] This day is verry worm—   we only Saw a fiew Small herds of the big horn animals on the hills, and two Elk one of which We killed, we Camped at 2 dead top trees on the Lard Side. The river is Genly about 200 yards wide and Current very Swift to day and has a verry perceptiable fall in all its Course—   it rises a little.

	miles	*Course & Distance May 27th*
West	1 ¾	allong the Lard Shore to a point on the Lard Sd. (no timber) a Bluff opposit on both Sides

S. 80° W.	3 ¼	a bluff point on the Stard. Side in a Stard. Bend.
S. 50° W.	1	to a Larboard point.
S. 8° W.	1 ½	to the point of a Bluff on Lard. in a Lard. Bend; the river makeing a Considerable bend to the S. E.
S. 60° W.	½	to a open point on the Lard. Side
S. 26° W.	1 ½	to a Single Cotton tree on Stard. point
S 55° W.	1	to a bluff point on the Lard. Side
S. 45° W.	3 ½	to a Bluff on the Lard. Side, passed a Lard point at 1 miles,
miles	14	a Stard. point at 2 ½ miles. we Camped on Lard Sd. 1 ½ on this Course

1. The party was traveling through the Missouri River Breaks, a region which today is still much as it was in Lewis and Clark's time. The Missouri cuts through another pre-glacial stream divide here creating a deep, narrow channel. See also the geology note of May 25, 1805.

2. The stone along the river is derived from the fractured sandstones and from the concretions of the Judith River Formation, which is the only formation exposed along today's route. The Bearpaw Shale, with its salts and selenite, caps some of the river hills. The kidney-form stones are concretions, often up to five feet in diameter; they are dark, reddish brown and cemented with iron compounds. The coal is part of the Judith River Formation but is present in limited quantities and does not produce the extensive baked and fused rocks of the Paleocene coals downstream.

3. The island is misplaced in relation to the campsite on *Atlas* map 60, but is correct on maps 40 and 52; apparently it no longer exists. MRC map 72.

4. In Fergus County, Montana, near later McGarry Bar. *Atlas* maps 40, 52, 60; MRC map 72. The dearth of wood was a problem to later steamboat traffic on the river. Wood hawkers nearly denuded the river banks in the last century.

5. Also given on *Atlas* map 40, in both captains' hands.

6. Given as "3" on *Atlas* map 40, giving a total mileage of 13½.

7. Blocks of sandstone or concreations derived from the Judith River Formation.

8. The Judith River Formation commonly weathers to a light-brown color but many variations occur because of the several types of rock found in this formation. The darker color may be derived from the overlying Bearpaw Shale which also contains most of the salts.

[Lewis]   *Tuesday May 28th 1805.*

This morning we set forward at an early hour; the weather dark and cloudy, the are smokey, had a few drops of rain; we employed the chord generally to which we also gave the assistance of the pole at the riffles and rocky points; these are as numerous and many of them much worse than those we passed yesterday; arround those points the water drives with great force, and we are obliged in many instaces to steer our vessels through the appertures formed by the points of large sharp rocks which reach a few inches above the surface of the water, here sould [*NB: Should*] our chord give way the bough is instantly drivin outwards by the stream and the vessel thrown with her side on the rocks where she must inevitably overset or perhaps be dashed to peices; our ropes are but slender, all of them except one being made of Elk's skin and much woarn, frequently wet and exposed to the heat of the weather are weak and rotten; they have given way several times in the course of the day but happily at such places that the vessel had room to wheel free of the rocks and therefore escaped injury; with every precaution we can take it is with much labour and infinite risk that we are enabled to get around these points. found a new indian lodge pole today which had been brought down by the stream, it was woarn at one end as if draged by dogs or horses; a football also,[1] and several other articles were found, which have been recently brought down by the courant; these are strong evedences of Indians being on the river above us, and probably at no great distance; the football is such as I have seen among the Minetaries and therefore think it most probable that they are a band of the Minetaries of Fort de Prarie.[2] the river country &c continued much as yesterday untill late in the evening when we arrived at the entrance of a large Creek discharges itself on the Stard. side, is 35 Yd. wide and contains runing water; [*ML: this we called Thompson's C.*] [*NB: after one of the party*][3] here the hills recede from the river on both sides, the bottoms extensive particularly on the Stard. side where the hills are comparitively low and open into three large vallies which extend for a considerable distance in a Northwardly direction; here also the river spreads to more than 3 times it's former width and is filled with a number of small and handsome Islands covered with cottonwood some timber also in the bottoms, the land again fertile. These appearances were quite reviving after the drairy country through which we had been passing. Capt. C. walked on shore in the early part of the day and killed a big horned anamal; he saw a great number of them as well as ourselves in the broken country. at 10 A. M. a few drops of rain again fell and were attended with distant thunder which is the first we have heared since we left the Mandans.— This evening we encamped on Stard. opposite to the entrance of a small [EC: Bull] Creek.[4] I beleive the bighorn have their young at a very early season, say early in March for they appear now to be half grown. One of the party saw a very large bear today but being some distance from the river and no timber to conceal him he did not think proper to fire on him.

Courses and distances of May 28th 1805.[5]

South	1[6]	to a point on Stard. side.
S. 35° W.	2	to the point of a bluff on Stard. side.
S. 60° W.	1	to a point on the Stard. side.
N. 70° W.	1	to a point on the Lard. side
S. 65° W.	2	to a point on the Stard. side
N. 65° W.	1	to a solitary cottonwood tree on a Lard. point
West	1 ½	to a do. do. do. on a Stard. point
N. 82° W.	1	to a grove of cottonwood trees on a Lard. point
N. 76° W.	2	to a tree on a Lard. point.
S. 68° W.	2	to a point on the Stard. side, just below the entrance of a large Creek, [EC: Thompson's] here the hills recede from the river which also becomes much wider.—
West	3 ½	to the upper part of a timbered bottom in a bend on the Stard. side passing two small Islnd. and the large creek mentioned in the last course.
S. 20° W.	2 ½	to a bluff point in a bend on Lard. passing two small Islands.
N. 46° W.	1	to the upper part of the timber in a bottom on the Stard. side, at which place we encamped opposite to the entrance of a small Creek ☞ this creek we called Bull Creek

21 ½ Miles [NB: last ⟨cours⟩ day add 1 ½]

[Clark]   *May 28th Tuesday 1805*

a Cloudy morning Some fiew drops of rain and verry Smokey wind from the S. W.   we Set out at an early hour, the Shoaley places are verry

numerous and Some bad to get around   we have to make use of the Cord
& Poles, and our tow ropes are all except one of Elkskin, & Stretch and
Sometimes brake which indanger the Perogues or Canoe, as it imedeately
turns and if any rock Should chance to be below, the rapidity of the current would turn her over, She Should chance to Strike the rock we observe great Caution at those places.

I walked on Shore found the Countrey ruged and as described yesterday, I Saw great numbers of the Big horned animals, one of which I
killed   their fauns are nearly half grown— one of the Party Saw a verry
large bear, picked up on the Shore a pole which had been made use of by
the Nativs for lodge poles, & haul'd by dogs   it is new and is a Certain
Sign of the Indians being on the river above   a foot ball and Several
other articles are also found to Substantiate this oppinion—.   at 1 oClock
we had a few drops of rain and Some thunder whic is the first thunder we
have had Sinc we Set out from Fort Mandan; at 10 miles the ⟨river⟩ the
hills begin to widen & the river Spreds & is crouded with Islands   the
bottoms Contain Some Scattering Cotton wood   the Islands also Contain
timber—   passed a Creek of running water on the Stard Side about 35
yards wide and camped imedeately opposit to a Small Creek on the Lard.
Side   we call Bull Creek from the Circumstance of a Buffalow Bull swiming from the opposit Side and comeing out of the river imedeately across
one of the Perogues without Sinking or injureing any thing in the Perogue, and passing with great violence thro' our Camp in the night makeing 3 angles without hurting a man, altho they lay in every direction, and
it was very dark

The Creek below 35 yards wide I call Thompsons Creek after a valuable member of our party—   this Creek contains a Greater preportion of
running water than Common.

	miles	*Course & Distance May 28th 1805*
South	1	to a point on the Stard Side
S. 35° W.	2	to the point of a Bluff on Stard Side
S. 60° W.	1	to a point on the Stard. Side
N. 70° W.	1	to a point on the Lard. Side

S. 65° W.	2	to a point on the Stard. Side
N. 65° W.	1	to a Single Cotton tree on Lard point
West	1 ½	to a do Cotton tree on the Stard. point
N. 82° W	1	to a grove of Cotton trees on Lard. point
N. 76° W.	2	to a tree on the Lard point
S 68° W.	2	to a point on the Stard. ⟨point⟩ Side, here the Hills Seperate & river widen
West	3 ½	to the upper part of a timbered bottom in a bend to the Stard Side, passed two Small Islands, & a large Creek Std. Side Thompsons Creek
S. 20° W.	2 ½	to a Bluff point in a bend on Lard. passed two Small Islands
N. 64° W.	1	to the upper part of the timber in a bottom on the Stard
	21 ½	Side at which place we Camped opsd. to a Creek L. S.

1. Perhaps a buckskin ball used in a game played by the women of many tribes of the Great Plains. Lowie (IP), 134–35.

2. The Atsinas, a small nomadic tribe of the Algonquian language family, a separated branch of the Arapahoes, at this time closely allied with the Blackfeet. They have no known connection with the Siouan-language Minitaris or Hidatsas; the confusion undoubtedly arises from both groups being called *Gros Ventres,* or Big Bellies, by early traders. The same sign language term, suggesting an expanded abdomen, was sometimes used for both peoples. "Atsina" is from a Blackfeet term said to mean "gut people." Later in the nineteenth century the terms "Gros Ventres of the Prairie" (Atsina) and "Gros Ventres of the Missouri" (Hidatsa) were used to distinguish them. "Fort de Prairie" was one of two North West Company posts on the Saskatchewan, both called Fort des Prairies, at which the Blackfeet and Atsinas traded. Hodge, 1:113, 508, 547–49; Flannery; Clark, 67, 193–99.

3. Named after Private John B. Thompson; present Birch Creek, which meanders across the boundary of present Chouteau and Blaine counties, Montana, and meets the Missouri in Chouteau County. *Atlas* maps 40, 52, 60; MRC map 73. Lewis may have added the interpolation at the time or later; Biddle's words are in red.

4. In Chouteau County near the present Judith Landing Recreation Area, and opposite present Dog (Bull) Creek, in Fergus County. *Atlas* maps 40, 52, 60; MCR map 73.

5. Also given on *Atlas* map 40, in both captains' hands.

6. Given as "½" on *Atlas* map 40.

[Lewis]   *Wednesday May 29th 1905.*

Last night we were all allarmed by a large buffaloe Bull, which swam over from the opposite shore and coming along side of the white perogue, climbed over it to land, he then alarmed ran up the bank in full speed directly towards the fires, and was within 18 inches of the heads of some of the men who lay sleeping before the centinel could allarm him or make him change his course, still more alarmed, he now took his direction immediately towards our lodge, passing between 4 fires and within a few inches of the heads of one range of the men as they yet lay sleeping, when he came near the tent, my dog saved us by causing him to change his course a second time, which he did by turning a little to the right, and was quickly out of sight, leaving us by this time all in an uproar with our guns in or hands, enquiring of each other the case of the alarm, which after a few moments was explained by the centinel; we were happy to find no one hirt. The next morning we found that the buffaloe in passing the perogue had trodden on a rifle, which belonged to Capt. Clark's black man, who had negligently left her in the perogue, the rifle was much bent, he had also broken the spindle, pivit, and shattered the stock of one of the bluntderbushes on board, with this damage I felt well content, happey indeed, that we had sustaned no further injury.   it appears that the white perogue, which contains our most valuable stores, is attended by some evil gennii. This morning we set out at an early hour and proceded as usual by the Chord.   at the distance of 2½ miles passed a handsome river which discharged itself on the Lard. side, I walked on shore and acended this river about a mile and a half in order to examine it. I found this river about 100 yds. wide from bank to bank, the water occupying about 75 yard.   the bed was formed of gravel and mud with some sand; it appeared to contain much more water as [*NB: than*] the Muscle-Shell river, was more rappid but equally navigable; there were no large stone or rocks in it's bed to obstruct the navigation; the banks were low yet appeared seldom to overflow; the water of this River is ⟨Clear⟩ [*NB: clearer much*] than any we have met with   great abundance of the Argalia or [*NB: or*] Bighorned animals in the high country through which this river passes   Cap. C who assended this R. much higher than I did has ⟨thought proper to⟩ call [*NB:*

ed] it *Judieths* River.[1]   The bottoms of this stream as far as I could see were wider and contained more timber than the Missouri; here I saw some box alder intermixed with the Cottonwood willow rose bushes and honeysuckle with some red willow constitute the undergrowth.   on the Missouri just above the entrance of the *Big Horn* [NB: *Judith*] *River*[2] I counted the remains of the fires of 126 Indian lodges which appeared to be of very recent date perhaps 12 or 15 days. Capt. Clark also saw a large encampent just above the entrance of this river on the Stard. side of reather older date, probably they were the same Indians. The Indian woman with us exmined the mockersons which we found at these en-campments and informed us that they were not of her nation the Snake Indians, but she beleived they were some of the Indians who inhabit the country on this side of Rocky Mountains and North of the Missoury and I think it most probable that they were the Minetaries of Fort de Prarie.[3] At the distance of six ½ ms. from our encampment of last night we passed a very bad rappid to which we gave the name of the Ash rappid[4] from a few trees of that wood growing near them; this is the first ash I have seen for a great distance.   at this place the hills again approach the river closely on both sides, and the same seen which we had on the 27th and 28th in the morning again presents itself, and the rocky points and riffles reather more numerous and worse; there was but little timber; salts coal &c still appear.   today we passed on the Stard. side the remains of a vast many mangled carcases of Buffalow which had been driven over a precipice of 120 feet by the Indians and perished; the water appeared to have washed away a part of this immence pile of slaughter and still their remained the fragments of at least a hundred carcases   they created a most horrid stench.   in this manner the Indians of the Missouri distroy vast herds of buffaloe at a stroke; for this purpose one of the most active and fleet young men is scelected and ⟨being⟩ disguised in a robe of buffaloe skin, having also the skin of the buffaloe's head with the years and horns fas-tened on his head in form of a cap, thus caparisoned he places himself at a convenient distance between a herd of buffaloe and a precipice proper for the purpose, which happens in many places on this river for miles together; the other indians now surround the herd on the back and flanks and at a signal agreed on all shew themselves at the same time moving forward towards the buffaloe; the disguised indian or decoy has taken care to place himself sufficiently nigh the buffaloe to be noticed by them when they take to flight and runing before them they follow him in full speede to the precepice, the cattle behind driving those in front over and seeing them go do not look or hesitate about following untill the whole are precipitated down the precepice forming one common mass of dead an mangled carcases; the ⟨Indian⟩ decoy in the mean time has taken care to secure himself in some cranney or crivice of the clift which he had previously prepared for that purpose. the part of the decoy I am informed is extreamly dangerous, if they are not very fleet runers the buffaloe tread them under foot and crush them to death, and sometimes drive them over the precepice also, where they perish in common with the buffaloe.—[5] we saw a great many wolves in the neighbourhood of these mangled carcases they were fat and extreemly gentle, Capt. C. who was on shore killed one of them with his espontoon. just above this place we came too for dinner opposite the entrance of a bold runing river 40 yds. wide which falls in on Lard. side. this stream we called slaughter river.[6] it's bottoms are but narrow and contain scarcely any timber. our situation was a narrow bottom on the Stard. possessing some cottonwood. soon after we landed it began to blow & rain, and as there was no appearance of even wood enough to make our fires for some distance above we determined to remain here untill the next morning, and accordingly fixed our camp and gave each man a small dram. notwithstanding the allowance of sperits we issued did not exceed ½ pn. [X: jill] man several of them were considerably effected by it; such is the effects of abstaining for some time from the uce of sperituous liquors; they were all very merry.— The hunters killed an Elk this evening, and Capt. C. killed two beaver.

Courses and distances of May 29th 1805.[7]

S. 65° W.	2 ½	To a small willow Island, close under a Stard. point, opposite the entrance of *big horn* [NB: *Judith*] river on Lard. passing an Island and 2 sand bars
S. 80° W.	1	to the upper part of some scattering timber at the entrance of a small creek[8] on the Stard. above a large old Indian incampment.

S 50° W.	2	to a tree in a Stard. bend, opposite to a Lard. point of high land, some timber on Stard⁹ side.
South	1	to an Ash tree on a Stard. point, at a rappid [*EC: Ash Rap.*], a high hill on the Lard. side.
S. 18° W.	2 ½	to the upper part of some scattering trees in a bend on the Lard. side
S. 75° W.	2	to a few trees on a Stard. point, passing a bluff on each side of the river.
N. 70° W.	1	to a point of wood on the Lard. side
N. 80° W.	¼	On the Lard. side opposite to a bluff
S. 70° W.	1	to an open point on the Stard. side.
West	1	to a few trees on a Lard. point
S. 72° W.	1 ¼	to a few trees on a Stard. point Passing a riffle
S. 85° W.	1 ½	to a bluff point on the Stard. side, opposite to the entrance of a small river [*EC: Slaughter*] on Lard. side
West	½	Along the Stard. bluff
N. 85° W.	¼	to a point of woodland on the Stard. side where we en-
Miles 17 ¾		camped for the night.—

[Clark]   *May 29th Wednesday 1805*

In the last night we were alarmed by a Buffalow which Swam from the opposit Shore landed opposit the Perogue in which Capt Lewis & my Self were in   he Crossed the perogue, and went with great force up to the fire where Several men were Sleeping and was 18 inches of their heads, when one man Sitting up allarmed him and he turned his course along the range of men as they lay, passing between 4 fires and within a fiew Inches of Some of the mens heads as they lay imediately in a direction to our lodge about which Several men were lying.   our Dog ⟨all⟩ flew out & he changed his course & passed without doeing more damage than bend a rifle & brakeing hir Stock and injureying one of the blunder busts in the perogue as he passed through—   We Set out this morning at the usial hour & proceeded on   at 2½ miles passed the mouth of a river [*blank*] yards wide, discharging a great quantity of water, and Containing more wood in its bottoms than the Missouri—   this river Capt Lewis walked up for a Short distance & he Saw an old encampment of Indians   (I also saw large encampment on the Stard Side at the mouth of a Small Creek of about 100 Lodges which appeared to be 5 or 6 weeks past, the Indian woman examined the mockersons &c. and told us they were the Indians which resided below the rocky mountains & to the North of this river,— that her nation make their mockersons differently[)]   at 6½ miles passed a considerable rapid at which place the hills approach near the river on both Sides, leaving a narrow bottom on the Stard. Side, (ash rapid) and continue Close all day but little timber, I walked on ⟨Shore⟩ the bank in the evening and saw the remains of a number of buffalow, which had been drove down a Clift of rocks   I think from appearances that upwards of 100 of those animals must have perished here, Great numbers of wolves were about this place & verry jentle   I killed one of them with my Spear. The hills above ash rapid Contains more rock and Coal, and the more rapid points.   we Came too for Dinner opposit the enterence of a Small river which falls in on the Lard Side and is about [*blank*] yards wide, has a bold running Stream, Soon after we Came too it began to rain & blow hard, and as we were in a good harbor & Small point of woods on the Stard Side, and no timber for some distance above, induced us to conclude to Stay all night.   we gave the men a dram, altho verry Small it was Sufficent to effect Several men.   one of our hunters killed an elk this evening—   I killed 2 beaver on the Side of the bank   a table Spoon full of water exposed to the air in a Saucer would avaperate in 36 hours when the mercury did not Stand higher than the temperate point[10] in the heat of the day.

	miles	*Course and distance May 29th*
S. 65° W.	2 ½	to a Small willow Island close under the Stard point opposit the enterence of a large river on Lard Side passed an Island & 2 Sand bars or Ids. *Big Horn* river 100 yds. wide water 45 yds.—
S 80° W.	1	to the upper part of a scattering timber at the mouth of a Small Creek on the Stard. Side, above a large Indn. incampment
S. 50° W.	2	to a tree in the Stard bend opposit the Lard point of high land Some timber on S S.

South	1	to a *Ash* tree in the Stard point, at a rapid a high hill on the Lard. Side
S. 18° W.	2 ½	to the upper of Some Scattering trees in a bend to the Lard Side
S 75° W.	2	to a fiew trees on a Stard. point a Bluff each Side
N. 70° W	1	to a point of wood on the Lard Side
N. 80° W.	¼	on the Lard Side opposit to a bluff
S. 70° W.	1	to an open point on the Stard. Side
West	1 ⟨¼⟩ [11]	to a few trees on the Lard point
S. 72° W.	¼	to a fiew trees on the Stard point (pass a riffle[)]
S. 85° W.	1 ½	to a Bluff point on the Stard. opposit to the mouth of a Small river on the L. S.
West	½	allong the Stard Bluff
N. 85° W.	¼	to a point of wood land on Stard Side where we en-
miles	17 ¾	camped for the night

1. Judith River, meeting the Missouri in Fergus County, Montana, still bears the name Clark gave it, after Julia (or Judith) Hancock, of Fincastle, Virginia, whom he married in 1808. Jackson provides evidence that she used both forms of her name. Lewis's writing and then crossing out "thought proper to" suggests he at first had some doubts about the propriety of the name; later he imitated Clark by naming Marias River after a cousin, Maria Wood. Steffen, 12; Jackson (FLCE), 12; *Atlas* maps 49, 52, 60; MRC map 73. It appears that Lewis erased the word Big Horn and substituted Judith, although he did not continue the substitutions. Biddle was apparently the one who interlined Judith over Big Horn in the remaining mentions, but not in his usual red ink. See n. 2 below.

2. Apparently the river Lewis wished to call the Big Horn was the one Clark called the Judith, its present name. This is the first stream on the larboard side of the Missouri above the campsite of May 28, 1805. It has no name on *Atlas* map 40, and is the Big Horn (perhaps written in Lewis's hand) on map 52. The next larboard stream on the latter map is the one they called Slaughter River, present Arrow Creek; the next is nameless on map 52 and the one after that (on map 53) is Crevis Creek. Slaughter River is the stream opposite whose mouth they camped on May 29. However, on Clark's 1810 map (*Atlas* map 125) and the Clark-Maximilian map of 1833 (*Atlas* map 60) the Judith-Big Horn is the Judith and the next three larboard streams are the Big Horn, the Slaughter, and Crevis Creek. From the evidence of the journals and *Atlas* maps 52 and 53 it would appear that Clark made an error on his 1810 map, probably because of the extra stream between Slaughter River and Crevis Creek. In fact, there is only one drainage in the area just above

Arrow Creek, modern Sheep Shed Coulee. The copyist of 1833 may have worked from differing versions and in resolving the discrepancy made the wrong choice. Coues (HLC), 1:333–36 nn. 20, 22; MRC map 73.

3. Sacagawea may have been referring to the Blackfeet Indians, but Clark's wording relates to the Atsina. See entry and notes, May 28, 1805.

4. Later Drowned Man's Rapid, now Deadman Rapids. *Atlas* maps 40, 52, 60; MRC map 73. Lewis's mention of green ash is noteworthy in that this common eastern tree is at its western-most limit in the United States along the Missouri River here in northwestern Fergus County. Little, 130-W.

5. The method of slaughter Lewis describes is one frequently used by the plains tribes especially before they obtained horses, metal arrowheads, and firearms in large quantities. However, the broken country back of this bluff is not really suitable for concentrating and stampeding buffalo; it is likely that the dead animals had in fact drowned in the Missouri, floated downstream, and washed ashore at this location. The site is in Chouteau County, Montana, a little over one mile downstream from the mouth of Arrow Creek (Lewis and Clark's Slaughter River) and about nine miles upstream from the mouth of the Judith. Wood (MMA); Wood (SR); Appleman (LC), 302–3; *Atlas* maps 41, 52, 60; MRC map 73.

6. Present Arrow Creek, the boundary between Chouteau and Fergus counties. The party camped opposite and somewhat above the mouth of Arrow Creek, at the Slaughter River Landing Recreation Area in Chouteau County. *Atlas* maps 41, 53, 60; MRC map 73.

7. Also given on *Atlas* map 40, in both captains' hands.

8. Given as "Valley run" or "Valley Creek" on *Atlas* maps 40, 52, 60; earlier Sage Creek, today's Chip Creek, Chouteau County.

9. Apparently "Lard" on *Atlas* map 40, but Clark's journal entry agrees with Lewis.

10. A standard dictionary would give this temperature as 66° F., but Coues (HLC), 1:336, defines it as 55° F.

11. Not crossed out on *Atlas* map 40, giving a total mileage of 18.

[Lewis]   *Thursday May 30th 1805.*

The rain which commenced last evening continued with little intermission untill 11 this morning when we set out; the high wind which accompanied the rain rendered it impracticable to procede earlyer.   more rain has now fallen than we have experienced since the 15th of September last.   many circumstances indicate our near approach to a country whos climate differs considerably from that in which we have been for many months.   the air of the open country is asstonishingly dry as well as pure. I found by several experiments that a table spoon full of water exposed to the air in a saucer would avaporate in 36 hours when the murcury did not stand higher than the temperate point at the greatest heat of the day; my inkstand so frequently becoming dry put me on this experiment. I also observed the well seasoned case of my sextant shrunk considerably and the joints opened.[1] The water of the river still continues to become clearer and notwithstanding the rain which has fallen it is still much clearer than it was a few days past. this day we proceded with more labour and difficulty than we have yet experienced; in addition to the imbarrasments of the rappid courant, riffles, & rockey point which were as bad if not worse than yesterday, the banks and sides of the bluff were more steep than usual and were now rendered so slippery by the late rain that the men could scarcely walk. the chord is our only dependance for the courant is too rappid to be resisted with the oar and the river too deep in most places for the pole. the earth and stone also falling from these immence high bluffs render it dangerous to pass under them. the wind was also hard and against us. our chords broke several times today but happily without injury to the vessels. we had slight showers of rain through the course of the day, the air was could and rendered more disagreeable by the rain. one of the party ascended the river hills and reported on his return that there was snow intermixed with the rain which fell on the hights; he also informed us that the country was level ⟨and untimbered⟩ a little back from the river on both sides. there is now no timber on the hills, an only a few scattering cottonwood, ash, box Alder and willows to be seen along the river. in the course of the day we passed several old encampment of Indians, from the apparent dates of which we conceived that they were the several encampments of a band of about 100 lodges who were progressing slowly up the river; the most recent appeared to have been evacuated about 5 weeks since. these we supposed to be the Minetares or black foot Indians who inhabit the country watered by the Suskashawan and who resort to the establishment of Fort de Prarie, no part of the Missouri from the Minetaries to this place furnishes a perminent residence for any nation yet there is no part of it but what exhibits appearances of being occasionally visited by some nation on hunting excurtions. The Minnetares of the Missoury we know extend their excurtions on the S. [*NB: south*] side as high as the yellowstone river; the Assinniboins still higher on the N. side most probably as high as about Porcupine river and from thence upwards most probably as far as the mountains by the Minetares of Fort de

Prarie and the Black Foot Indians who inhabit the S. fork of the Sus-kashawan. I say the Missouri to the Rocky mountains for I am convinced that it penetrates those mountains for a considerable distance.— Two buffaloe killed this evening a little above our encampment.[2]

Courses and Distances May 30th 1805.[3]

N. 70° W.	¼	Along the timbered bottom on the Stard. side opposite to a high clift.
N. 50° W.	2	to a few trees on a Lard. point
N. 60° W.	¾	to a broken trunk of a tree on a Stard point opposite to a high black bluff.
N. 70° W.	¼	On the Stard. side to a few willows.
N. 30° W.	1 ¼	On the Stard. side to the entrance of a run in a bend.[4]
S. 55° W.	2 ½	to a grove of trees in a bend, on Lard. side at the entrance
Miles 8		of a run,[5] passing a small Island on the Stard. side at 2 ms., above which we encamped on the Stard. side—

[Clark]   *May 30th Thursday 1805*

The rain conmmenced yesterday eivening, and continued moderately through the course of the night, more rain has now fallin than we have experienced Since the 15th of September last, the rain continued this morning, and the wind too high for us to proceed, untill about 11 oClock at which time we Set out, and proceeded on with great labour, we were obliged to make use of the Tow rope & the banks were So muddey & Slip-ery that the men could Scercely walk not with Standing we proceeded on as well as we could   wind hard from the N W.   in attempting to assend a rapid our toe Cord broke & we turned ⟨on⟩ without injurey, those rapids or Shoaley points are noumerous and dificuelt, one being at the mouth of every drean   Some little rain at times all day   one man assended the high Countrey and it was raining & Snowing on those hills, the day has proved to be raw and Cold. Back from the river is tollerably leavel, no timber of any kind on the hills, and only a fiew Scattering cotton willow & ash near the river, much hard rock; & rich earth, the Small portion of rain which has fallen causes the rich earth as deep as is wet to Slip into the river or bottoms &c.

we discover in Several places old encampments of large bands of Indians, a fiew weeks past and appear to be makeing up the river— Those Indians we believe to be the Blackfoot Inds. or Menetares who inhabit the heads of the Saskashowin & north of this place and trade a little in the *Fort de Prarie* establishments.   we Camped in a grove of Cotton trees on the Stard Side, river rise 1 ½ In.

	mile	*Course & Distance May 30th 1805*
N. 70° W	¼	along the timbered bottom on the Stard point opsd. a high Clift
N. 50° W.	2	to a few trees on a Lard point
N. 60° W.	¾	to a Stump on the Stard. point opposit a high black bluff
N. 70° W.	1 ¼	on the Stard Side to a fiew willows
N. 30° W.	1 ¼	on the Stard Side to the mouth of a run in a bend.
S. 55° W.	2 ½	to a grove of trees in a bend to the Lard Side at the mouth of a run passed a Small Island on the Stard. Side at 2 miles above which we encamped on the Stard Side
miles 8	=	

1. Lewis is testing the relative humidity of the dry air of the High Plains of Montana (cf. Clark's remark in the weather data of September 23, 1804). Large.

2. In Chouteau Country, Montana, a little above Pablo Island and nearly opposite the mouth of Sheep Shed Coulee. *Atlas* maps 41, 52, 53, 60; MRC map 73.

3. Also given on *Atlas* map 41, in Clark's hand.

4. Unnamed on *Atlas* maps 41, 52, 60, and apparently without a modern name.

5. Perhaps Sheep Shed Coulee.

[Lewis]   *Friday May 31st 1805.*

This morning we proceeded at an early hour with the two perogues leaving the canoes and crews to bring on the meat of the two buffaloe that were killed last evening and which had not been brought in as it was late and a little off the river.   soon after we got under way it began to rain and continued untill meridian when it ceased but still remained cloudy through the ballance of the day. The obstructions of rocky points and riffles still continue as yesterday; at those places the men are compelled to be ⟨much⟩ in the water even to their armpits, and the water is yet very could, and so frequent are those point that they are one fourth of their time in the water, added to this the banks and bluffs along which they are obliged to pass are so slippery and the mud so tenacious that they are unable to wear their mockersons, and in that situation draging the heavy burthen of a canoe and walking ocasionally for several hundred yards over the sharp fragments of rocks which tumble from the clifts and garnish the borders of the river; in short their labour is incredibly painfull and great, yet those faithfull fellows bear it without a murmur. The toe rope of the white perogue, the only one indeed of hemp, and that on which we most depended, gave way today at a bad point, the perogue swung and but slightly touched a rock, yet was very near overseting; I fear her evil gennii will play so many pranks with her that she will go to the bottomm some of those days.— Capt. C. walked on shore this morning but found it so excessively bad that he shortly returned. at 12 OCk. we came too for refreshment and gave the men a dram which they received with much cheerfullness, and well deserved.—

The hills and river Clifts which we passed today exhibit a most romantic appearance.[1] The bluffs of the river rise to the hight of from 2 to 300 feet and in most places nearly perpendicular; they are formed of remarkable white sandstone which is sufficiently soft to give way readily to the impression of water; two or thre thin horizontal stratas of white free-stone, on which the rains or water make no impression, lie imbeded in these clifts of soft stone near the upper part of them; the earth on the top of these Clifts is a dark rich loam, which forming a graduly ascending plain extends back from ½ a mile to a mile where the hills commence and rise abruptly to a hight of about 300 feet more. The water in the course of time in decending from those hills and plains on either side of the river has trickled down the soft sand clifts and woarn it into a thousand grotesque figures, which with the help of a little immagination and an oblique view at a distance, are made to represent eligant ranges of lofty freestone buildings, having their parapets well stocked with statuary; columns of various sculpture both grooved and plain, are also seen supporting long galleries in front of those buildings; in other places on a much nearer approach and with the help of less immagination we see the remains or ruins of eligant buildings; some collumns standing and almost entire with their pedestals and capitals; others retaining their pedestals but deprived by time or accident of their capitals, some lying prostrate an broken othes in the form of vast pyramids of connic structure bearing a sereis of other pyramids on their tops becoming less as they ascend and finally terminating in a sharp point.   nitches and alcoves of various forms and sizes are seen at different hights as we pass.   a number of the small martin[2] which build their nests with clay in a globular form attatched to the wall within those nitches, and which were seen hovering about the tops of the ⟨broken⟩ collumns did not the less remind us of some of those large stone buildings in the U' States.   the thin stratas of hard freestone intermixed with the soft sandstone seems to have aided the water in forming this curious scenery. As we passed on it seemed as if those seens of visionary inchantment would never have and end; for here it is too that nature presents to the view of the traveler vast ranges of walls of tolerable workmanship,[3] so perfect indeed are those walls that I should have thought that nature had attempted here to rival the human art of masonry had I not recollected that she had first began her work. These walls rise to the hight in many places of 100 feet, are perpendicular, with two regular faces and are from one to 12 feet thick, each wall retains the same thickness at top which it possesses at bottom. The stone of which these walls are formed is black, dence and dureable, and appears to be composed of a large portion of earth intermixed or cemented with a small quantity of sand and a considerable portion of talk or quarts.   these stones are almost invariably regular parallelepipeds, of unequal sizes in the walls, but equal in their horizontal ranges, at least as to debth.   these are laid regularly in ranges on each other like bricks, each breaking or covering the interstice of the two on which it rests.   thus the purpendicular interstices are broken, and the horizontal ones extend entire throughout the whole extent of the walls. These stones seem to bear some proportion to the thickness of the walls in which they are employed, being larger in the thicker walls; the greatest length of the parallelepiped appears to form the thickness of the thiner walls, while two or more are employed to form that of the thicker walls. These walls pass the river in several places, rising from the water's edge much above the sandstone bluffs, which they seem to penetrate; thence continuing their course on a streight line on either side of the river through the gradually ascending plains, over which they tower to the hight of from ten to seventy feet untill they reach the hills, which they finally enter and conceal themselves. these walls sometimes run parallel to each other, with several ranges near each other, and at other times intersceting each other at right angles, having the appearance of the walls of ancient houses or gardens. I walked on shore this evening and examined these walls minutely and preserved a specimine of the stone. I found the face of many of the river hills formed of Clifts of very excellent free stone of a light yellowish brown colour;[4] on these clifts I met with a species of pine which I had never seen, it differs from the pitchpine in the particular of it's leaf and cone, the first being vastly shorter, and the latter considerably longer and more pointed.[5] I saw near those bluffs the most beautifull fox that I ever beheld, the colours appeared to me to be a fine orrange yellow, white and black, I endevoured to kill this anamal but it discovered me at a considerable distance, and finding that I could get no nearer, I fired on him as he ran, and missed him; he concealed himself under the rocks of the clift; it appeared to me to be about the size of the common red fox of the Atlantic states, or reather smaller than the large fox common to this country; convinced I am that it is a distinct species.[6] The appearance of coal continu[e]s but in small quantities, but litt[l]e appearance of birnt hills or pumice stones the mineral salts have in some measure abated and no quarts.[7] we saw a great number of the Bighorn some mule deer and a few buffaloe and Elk, no antelopes or common deer. Drewyer who was with me and myself killed two bighorned anamals; the sides of the Clifts where these anamals resort much to lodg, have the peculiar smell of the sheepfolds. the party killed in addition to our hunt 2 buffaloe and an Elk. the river today has been from 150 to 250 yds. wide but little timber today on the river.

Courses and distances of May 31st 1805.[8]

N. 45° W.	2	to a few trees in a bend on Stard. side
S. 80° W.	½	to a few trees on a Stard. point
N. 80° W.	¼	On the Stard. point
N. 60° W.	1 ¾	to the lower part of the timber in a Stard. bend
West	¼	to a few trees on the Stard. side.
N. 78° W.	2	to some trees on the Stard. side.

West	2	to a point on the Stard. side.
N. 45° W.	¼	Along the Stard. point.
N. 30° W.	¼	Along the Stard. point passing a high wall of black rock[9] on Lard. rising from the water's edge above the river clifts
North	1 ½	to a tree in a bend on Stard. opposite to a high open bottom.
N. 42 W.	1	to a point on the Stard. side
N. 10 E.	¾	to a point on the Lard. side opposite to a wall of black rock 200 feet high penetrating the bluff
N. 20 W.	2	to four trees in a bend on Lard. side
North	3 ½	to the upper part of a timbered bottom on the Stard. side above the entrance of stone wall [*EC: Stonewall*] creek affording water and 28 yds. wide just above the mouth of which we encamped.[10] at 1 m on this course passed a high stone wall[11] on Std. 12 feet thick and rising 200 feet.
Miles	18	

[Clark] *May 31st Friday 1805.*[12]

A cloudy morning   we dispatched all the Canoes to Collect the meat of 2 Buffalow killed last night a head and a little off the river, and proceeded on with the perogues at an early hour. I attempted to walk on Shore   Soon found it verry laborious as the mud Stuck to my mockersons & was verry Slippery. I return'd on board.   it continued to rain moderately untill about 12 oClock when it ceased, & Continued Cloudy.   the Stone on the edge of the river continue to form verry Considerable rapids, we [which] are troublesom & dificuelt to pass, our toe rope which we are obliged to make use of altogether broke & we were in Some danger of turning over in the perogue in which I was, we landed at 12 and refreshed the men with a dram, our men are obliged to under go great labour and fatigue in assending this part of the Missouri, as they are compelled from the rapidity of the Current in many places to walk in the water & on Slippery hill Sides or the Sides of rocks, on Gravel & thro' a Stiff mud bear footed, as they Cannot keep on Mockersons from the Stiffness of the mud & decline of the Slipy. hills Sides—   The Hills and river Clifts of this day exhibit a most romantick appearance   on each Side of the river is a white Soft Sand Stone bluff which rises to about half the hight of the hills, on the top of this Clift is a black earth on points, in maney places this Sand Stone appears like antient ruins some like elegant buildings at a distance, Some like Towers &c. &c. in maney places of this days march we observe on either Side of the river extraodanary walls of a black Semented Stone which appear to be regularly placed one Stone on the other, Some of those walls run to the hite of 100 feet, they are from about 1 foot to 12 feet thick and are perpendicular, those walls Commence at the waters edge & in Some places meet at right angles— those walls appear to Continue their Course into the Sand Clifts, the Stones which form those walls are of different Sizes all Squar edged, Great numbers has fallen off from the walls near the river which cause the walls to be of uneaquil hite, in the evening the Countrey becomes lower and the bottoms wider, no timber on the uplands, except a few Cedar & pine on the Clifts a few Scattering Cotton trees on the points in the river bottoms, The apparance of Coal Continus Capt Lewis walked on Shore & observed a Species of Pine we had never before Seen, with a Shorter leaf than Common & the bur different, he also Collected Some of the Stone off one of the walls which appears to be a Sement of Isin glass black earth we Camped on the Stard Side in a Small timbered bottom above the mouth of a Creek on the Stard Side our hunters killed, 2 animals with big horns, 2 Buffalow & an Elk, we Saw Great numbers of those big horned animals on the Clifts, but fiew Buffalow or Elk, no antelope, a fiew mule deer, Saw a fox to day. The river rises a little it is from 150 to 250 yds. wide

[Clark]   *May 31st Friday 1805*

Cloudy morning, we proceeded on at an early hour with the two Perogues leaving the Canoes and crews to bring on the meat of two Buffalow that were killed last evening and which had not been brought in as it was late and a little off the river. Soon after we got under way it began to rain and Continued untill 12 oClock when it Seased but Still remained cloudy through the ballance of the day. the obstructions of rocky points and riffles Still continue as yesterday; at those places the men are compelled to be in the water even to their armpits, and the water is yet very cold, and So frequent are those points that they are one fourth of their time in the water. added to this the bank and bluff along which they are obliged to pass are So Slippery and the mud So tenatious that they are unable to bare their mockersons, and in that Situation dragging the heavy burthen of a Canoe and Walking occasionally for Several hundred yards over the Sharp fragments of rocks which tumble from the Clifts; and in Short their labour is incredibly painfull and great, yet those faithfull fellows bear it without a murmer.

The toe rope of the white perogue, the only one indeed of hemp, and that on which we most depended, gave way to day at a bad point, the perogue Swong and but slightly touched a rock, yet was very near oversetting; I fear her evil Ginnie will play So many pranks with her that She will go to the bottom Some of those days.

I attempted to walk on Shore this morning but found it so excessivily bad that I Soon returned on board. at 12 oClock we came too for refreshment and gave the men a dram which they received with much Chearfulness, and well deserved all wet and disagreeable. Capt. Lewis walked on Shore, he informed one that he Saw "the most butifull fox in the world" the Colour appeared to him to be of a fine Orrange yellow, white and black, he fired at this fox running and missed him, he appeared to be about the size of the common red fox of the united States, or rather smaller.

The hills and river clifts which we pass to day exhibit a most romantic appearance. The Bluffs of the river rise to the hight of from 2 to 300 feet and in most places nearly perpendicular; they are formed of remarkable white Sandstone which is Sufficiently Soft to give way readily to the impression of water; two or three thin horizontal Stratas of white free Stone, on which the rains or water make no impression, lie imbeded in those clifts of Soft Stone near the upper part of them; the earth on the top of these clifts is a dark rich loam, which forming a gradual ascending plain extend back from ½ a mile to a mile where the hills commence and rise abruptly to the hight of about 300 feet more. The water in the Course of time acecending from those hills and plains on either Side of the river has trickled down the Soft Sand Clifts and woarn it into a thousand grotesque figures; which with the help of a little imagination and an oblique view at a distance are made to represent elegant ranges of lofty freestone buildings, haveing their parapets well Stocked with Statuary; Colloms of various Sculptures both Grooved and plain, are also Seen Supporting long galleries in part of those buildings; in other places on a much nearer approach and with the with the help of less immagination we See the remains of ruins of eligant buildings; Some Collumns Standing and almost entire with their pedestals and Capitals, others retaining their pedestals but deprived by time or accedint of their capitals, Some lying prostrate and broken, others in the form of vast Pyramids of connic Structure bearing a Serious of other pyramids on their tops becomeing less as they ascend and finally termonateing in a Sharp point. nitches and alcoves of various forms and Sizes are Seen at different hights as we pass. a number of the Small martin which build their nests with Clay of a globular form attached to the wall within those nitches, and which were Seen hovering about the top of the collumns did not the less remind us of Some of those large Stone buildings in the United States. The thin Stratas of hard free Stone intermixed with the Soft Sand Stone Seems to have aided the water in forming this Curious Scenery.

as we passed on it Seemed as if those Seens of Visionary enchantment would never have an end; for here it is too that nature presents to the view of the traveler vast ranges of walls of tolerable workmanship, So perfect indeed are those falls [walls] that I Should have thought that nature had attempted here to rival the human art of Masonry had I not recollected that She had first began her work. These walls rise to the hight in many places of 100 feet, are perpindicular, with two regular faces, and are from one to 12 feet thick, each wall retains the Same thickness to the top which it possesses at bottom. The Stone of which these walls are formed is black, dense and dureable, and appears to be Composed of a large portion of earth intermixed or Cemented with a Small quantity of Sand and a Considerable portion of quarts. these Stones are almost invariably regular parallelepipeds, of unequal Sizes in the wall, but equal in their horizontal ranges, at least as to debth. These are laid regularly in ranges on each other like bricks, each breaking or covering this interstice of the two on which it rests, thus the pirpendicular interstices are broken, and the horizontal ones extend entire throughout the whole extent of the walls. These Stones Seam to bear Some proportion to the thickness of the walls in which they are employd, being larger in the thicker walls; the greatest length of the parallelepiped appear to form the thickness of the thiner walls, while two or more are employed to form that of the thicker walls. Those walls pass the river in Several places rising from the waters edge much above the Sand Stone Bluffs, which they Seam to penetrate; thence Continueing their course on a Streight line on either Side of the river thorough the gradually ascending plains over which they tower to the hight of from ten to 90 feet untill they reach the hills which they finally enter and Conceal themselves. these walls Some-times run parallel to each other, with Several ranges near each other, and at other times intersecting each other at right angles, haveing the appear-ance of the walls of ancient houses or gardins. both Capt Lewis and My self walked on Shore this evening and examined those walls minutely and preserved a Specimine of the Stone.— I found many clifts of very excel-lent free Stone of a light yellowish brown Colour. Capt. Lewis observed a Species of pine which I had never Seen, it differs from the pitch pine in the particular of its leaf and Cone, the first being partly Shorter, and the latter considerably longer and more pointed. The appearance of Coal Continues but in Smaller quantities, but little appearance of burnt hills or pumicestone. the mineral Salt in Some measure have abated and no quarts. we Saw a great number of the Big Horn, Some mule deer, and a few Buffalow and Elk, no antelopes or Common Deer—. Capt. Lewis killed a Big horn animal. the party killed 2 Buffalow one Elk and a Big horn or Ibex to day—. The river has been from 150 to 250 yards wide but little timber on the river to day. river less muddy than it was below.

	miles	*Course & Distance May 31st 1805*
N. 45° W.	2	to a fiew trees in a bend Stard. Side
S. 80° W.	½	to a fiew trees on the Stard. point
N. 80° W.	¼	on the Stard point
N. 60° W.	1 ¾	to the lower part of a timber in a Stard. bend.
West	¼	to a fiew trees on the Stard. Side
N. 78° W	2	to Some trees on the Stard. Side
West	2	to the point on the Stard. Side
N. 45° W	¼	on the Stard. point

N. 30° W	¼	on the Stard. point opsd. a high Steep black rock riseing from the waters edge
North	1 ½	to a tree in a bend to the Stard. Side opsd. a high open bottom
N. 42° W.	1	to the point on the Stard. Side
N. 10° E	¾	to a point on the Lard. Side a high black Conical rock of 200 feet high on the Std. Sd.
N. 20° W.	2	to 4 trees in a bend to the Lard. Side
North	3 ½	to the upper part of a timbered bottom on the Stard. Side
miles	18	above the mouth of Stone wall[13] Creek which Contains water passed a high Stone wall about 200 feet high & 12 feet thick on the Std Side & encamped at the mouth of the Creek S. S. in a thickly timbered bottom of Small Cotton Woods this Creek is a bold Stream of Clear Water

1. They were within the White Cliffs area of the Missouri River Breaks, in Chouteau County, Montana. *Atlas* maps 41, 53, 60, 61; MRC map 74. Subsequent travelers were also impressed with the "romantic appearance" of these cliffs and over the years names have been applied to the more prominent formations. The names are given in notes that follow as Lewis and Clark make reference to the formations. During the glacial period, ice forced the Missouri River to cut a new channel from near Virgelle to Fort Peck Dam, Montana. The channel here has been cut more than three hundred feet deep through late Cretaceous formations of the Claggett Shale, Eagle Sandstone, and Marias River Shale. The most conspicuous of these is the nearly white sandstone of the Virgelle Member of the Eagle Sandstone. Red-brown iron concretions up to eight feet in diameter occur at the top of the Virgelle Member in many places. The concretions are very resistant to erosion and protect the softer, underlying sandstone. Sandstone not protected by concretions erodes away leaving columns and pillars of white sandstone. Various degrees of protection by overlying materials has produced a variety of geometric figures.

2. The cliff swallow, *Hirundo pyrrhonota* [AOU, 612]. Holmgren, 32.

3. Intruded into the Claggett Shale, Eagle Sandstone, and Marias River Shale that flank the river are numerous, near-vertical sheets of igneous rock (shonkinite) called dikes. Their average width is about four feet. The dikes greatly resist erosion and, consequently, stand out from the surrounding sedimentary formations rather like walls. They contain no talc or quartz.

4. The term "freestone" was used to describe any easily cut or quarried limestone or sandstone. The rock described here belongs to the Eagle Sandstone, especially the Virgelle Member. Someone, perhaps Biddle, drew a red vertical line through the passages that begin, "I found the face" to "kill this animal."

5. These are the needles and cones of *Pinus flexilis* James, limber pine. This locality is

a range extension from the nearest present known locality in the Little Belt Mountains, approximately fifty miles to the south. Limber pine is typically found growing in exposed, rocky locations at middle elevations east of the continental divide and reaches outward onto the Great Plains in this area of central Chouteau County. Little, 56-W; Hahn, *Pinus* map.

6. Not a distinct species as Lewis supposed, but a cross fox, a color phase of the red fox, *Vulpes vulpes*. Burroughs, 91, 321 n. 7; Jones et al., 258–61.

7. The upper, unnamed, member of the Eagle Sandstone contains several thin beds of coal. The Eagle Sandstone contains a few salts and no selenite. Some salts are derived from the overlying Claggett Shale.

8. Also given on *Atlas* map 41, in Clark's hand.

9. Later Citadel Rock, in Chouteau County, and marked on *Atlas* maps 41, 53, 60; MRC map 74.

10. Stonewall Creek is present Eagle Creek, in Chouteau County. The camp was above its mouth on the same side. *Atlas* maps 41, 53, 60; MRC map 74.

11. Probably later Grand Natural Wall, in Chouteau County. *Atlas* maps 41, 53, 60; MRC map 74.

12. This entry is found at the end of Clark's notebook journal Voorhis No. 1. His other entry for the day, which is the regular sequence of daily entries in the same journal, is largely copied from Lewis, but it is the only one of the two that has the courses and distances for the day. It is not clear which was composed first.

13. Lewis appears to have interpolated the words "Stone wall."

[Lewis and Clark]   [*Weather, May 1805*][1]

Day of the Month	State of the thermometer at ⊙ rise	Weather	Wind at ⊙ rise	State of the thermometer at 4 P. M.	Weather	Wind at 4 P. M.	State of the river raised or fallen	Feet	Inches & parts
1st	36 a	c	E	46 a	c a f	N. E.	f		1 ½
2cd	28 a	s.	N E	34 a	c a s.	N. W.	f		1
3rd	26 a	f	W.	46 a	c	W.	f		¼
4th	38 a	c	W.	48 a	f a c	W.			
5th	38 a	f	N W	62 a	f a r	S. E.	r		1
6th	48 a	f	E	61 a	c a r	S E	r		2
7th	42 a	c	S.	60 a	f	N. E.	r		1 ½
8th	41 a	c	E.	52 a	c. a. r	E	f		¼
9th	38 a	f	E.	58 a	f	W.	r		¾
10th	38 a	f a c	W N W	62 a	c. a. r	N W	f		¾
11th	44 a	f	N E	60 a	c	S. W.			
12th	52 a	f	S. E.	54 a	c. a. r.	N W	r		2
13th	52 a	c. a. r	N. W.	54 a	f a c	N. W.	f		2 ¼
14th	32 a	f	S. W.	52 a	c	S W	f		1 ¾

15th	48	c a r	S W	54 a	c	N W	f	¾
16th	48	c	S W.	67 a	f	S. W		
17th	60 a	f	N E	68 a	f	S W		
18th	58 a	f	W.	46 a	c a r	N. W.	f	1
19th	38 a	fair	E.	68 a	f. a. c	S. W.		
20th	52 a	f	N. E.	76 a	f	E	f	1
21st	50 a	f	S. W.	76 a	f	N W		
22cd	46 a	c	N W	48 a	c.	N. W.	f	½
23rd	32 a	f	S W	54 a	f	S W	f	½
24th	32 a	f	N. W.	68 a	f	S. E.	r	3 ½
25th	46 a	f	S W	82 a	f	S. W.	r	2
26th	58 a	f	S W	80 a	f	S. W.	r	½
27th	62 a	f	S. W.	82 a	f	S. W.		
28th	62 a	c	S W	72 a	c & r	S W	r	½
29th	62 a	c a r	S. W.	67 a	r	S. W.	r	1
30th	56 a	c a r	S W.	50 a	r	S W	r	5
31st	48 a	c a r	W	53 a	c a r	S W	r	1 ½

[Remarks][2]

1st   wind violent from 12 oC. to 6 P. M.

2cd   snow 1 inch deep   the wind continued so high from 12 oClock yesterday, untill 5 this evening that we were unable to proceed. the snow which fell last night and this morning one inch deep has not yet disappeared.— it forms a singular contrast with the trees which are now in leaf.—

3rd   hard frost last night.   at four P. M. the snow has not yet entirely disappeared.— the new horns of the Elk begin to appear.

4th   the black martin makes it's appearance.   the snow has disappeared.   saw the first grasshoppers today.—[3]   there are great quantities of a small blue beatle feeding on the willows.—

5th   a few drops of rain only

6th   rain very inconsiderable as usual

8th   rain inconsiderable   a mear spinkle   the bald Eagle, of which there are great numbers, now have their young.   the *turtledove*[4] appears.

9th   The choke Cherry is now in blume.

10th   rain but slight   a few drops.

11th   frost this morning

12th   rain but slight.

13th   do. do. do.

14th   white frost this morning

15th   slight shower

17th   the Gees have their young; the Elk begin to produce their young, the Antelope and deer as yet have not.—   the small species of Goatsucker or whiperwill[5] begin to cry—   the blackbirds both small and large have appeared.[6]   we have had scarcely any thunder and lightning.   the clouds are generally white and accompanyed with wind only

18th   a good shower   saw the wild rose in blume.   the brown thrush or mocking bird[7] has appeared.—   had a good shower of rain today, it continued about 2 hours; this is the first shower that deserves the appellation of *rain,* which we have seen since we left Fort Mandan.—   no thunder or lightning

19th   heavy fog this morning on the river

22cd   the wind excessively hard all night—   saw some particles of snow fall today it did not lye in sufficient quantity on the ground to be perceptible.—

23rd   hard frost last night; ice in the eddy water along the shore, and the water friezed on the oars this morning. Strawburies in bloom.[8] saw the first king fisher.

24th   frost last night   ice 1/8 of an inch thick

25th   saw the kingbird, or bee martin;[9] the grouse disappear.   killed three of the bighorned antelopes.

26th   The last night was much the warmest we have experienced, found the covering of one blanket sufficient.   the air is extreemly dry and pure.

27th wind so hard we are unable to proceed in the early part of the day

28th a slight thundershower; the air was turbid in the forenoon and appeared to be filled with smoke; we supposed it to proceed from the burning of the plains, which we are informed are frequently set on fire by the Snake Indians to compell the antelopes to resort to the woody and mountanous country which they inhabit.— saw a small white and black woodpecker with a red head;[10] the same which is common to the Atlantic states.—

29th rained but little, some dew this morning.

30th the rain commenced about 4 Oclock in the evening, and continued moderately through the course of the night; more rain has now fallen than we have experienced since the 15th of September last.

31st but little rain   The Antelope now bring forth their young.   from the size of the young of the bighorned Antelope I suppose they bring forth their young as early at least as the Elk.

1. This weather table follows Lewis's in his Codex Fe, with discrepancies between it and Clark's table in Codex I being noted. The tables are accompanied in each case by remarks in both the margins of the tables and separately.

2. The remarks are found in the margins of the weather tables and in separate sections following the tables of Lewis's Codex Fe and Clark's Codex I. We follow Lewis, with notes to significant differences with Clark's remarks.

3. Perhaps *Eritettix simplex*.

4. The English name for a similar Eurasian species was given to the mourning dove, *Zenaida macroura* [AOU, 316], long before Lewis and Clark's time. Holmgren, 34; Burroughs, 234.

5. The common poorwill, *Phalaenoptilus nuttallii* [AOU, 418], described by Lewis on October 16, 1804.

6. The large blackbird is probably the common grackle, *Quiscalus quiscula* [AOU, 511], while the small blackbird could be the rusty blackbird, *Euphagus carolinus* [AOU, 509], and/or Brewer's blackbird, *E. cyanocephalus* [AOU, 510]. If the latter, then Lewis was its discoverer. Holmgren, 28; Cutright (LCPN), 167–68.

7. Brown thrush and brown mockingbird are old names for the brown thrasher, *Toxostoma rufum* [AOU, 705]. Holmgren, 34.

8. Either *Fragaria virginiana* Duchn. var. *glauca* Wats., wild strawberry, or *F. vesca* L. var.

americana Porter, woodland strawberry, although the former is more common in the area. Barkley, 140–41; Booth & Wright, 112.

9. Perhaps the eastern kingbird, *Tyrannus tyrannus* [AOU, 444]. Holmgren, 28. See also June 10, 1805.

10. The red-headed woodpecker, *Malanerpes erythrocephalus* [AOU, 406]. Holmgren, 34.

[Lewis] *Saturday June 1st 1805*

The moring was cloudy and a few drops of rain. Set out at an early hour and proceeded as usual by the help of our chords.   the river Clifts and bluffs not so high as yesterday and the country becomes more level.   a mountain or a part of the N. Mountain appears to approach the river within 8 or 10 ms. bearing N. from our encampment of the last evening.[1] Capt C. who walked on shore today informed me that the river hills were much lower than usual and that from the tops of those hills he had a delightfull view of rich level and extensive plains on both sides of the river; in those plains, which in many places reach the river clifts, he observed large banks of pure sand which appeared to have been d[r]iven by the S W. winds from the river bluffs and there deposited.[2]   the plains are more fertile at some distance from the river than near the bluffs where the surface of the earth is very generally covered with small smothe pebbles which have the appearance of having been woarn by the agitation of the waters in which they were no doubt once immerced.[3] A range of high Mountains appear to the S. W. at a considerable distance covered with snow, they appear to run Westerly.[4]   no timber appears on the highlands; but much more than yesterday on the river and Islands.   rockey points and shoals less freequent than yesterday but some of them quite as bad when they did occur.   the river from 2 to 400 yards wide, courant more gentle and still becoming clearer.   game is by no means as abundant as below; we killed one male bighorn and a mule deer today; saw buffalow at a distance in the plains particularly near a small Lake on Lard. side about 8 ms. distant.   some few drops of rain again fell this evening.   we passed six Islands and encamped on the 7th;[5] they are all small but contain some timber.   the wind has been against us all day.— I saw the choke cherry the yellow and red courant bushes; the wild rose appears now to be in full bloom as are also the prickley pear which are numerous in these plains.—[6]   We also saw some Indian Lodges of sticks today which did not appear to have been long evacuated.—   some coal appear in the bluffs.

Courses and distances of June 1st 1805.[7]

N. 58° W.	2 ½	to a Point on the Stard. side
N. 45° W.	1 ¼	to a point on the Lard. side
N. 60° W.	1 ¼	to a point on the Stard. side
N. 50° W.	1 ½	to a tree on the Lard. side
N. 25° W.	1 ¼	to a point on the Stard. side
N. 30° W.	¾	Along the Stard. shore to a point of woodland.
N. 20° W.	1	to a point of timber on the Lard. side opst. to a bluff
N. 48° W.	¾	to a point of timbered land Stard.
N. 55° W.	1 ½	to a point of timbered land Lard.
N. 60° W.	1 ¾	to the point of a bluff in a bend on Stard. oppst. to a small Island.
S. 58° W.	1 ½	to a point on the Stard. side
S. 60° W.	1	to the upper point of a small Island on the Std. side passing a Lard. point at ¾ of a mile.
S. 40° W.	¾	to a bluff point in a bend on Lard. side
West	1	to the centre of a Stard. bend.
South	2 ½[8]	to a Stard. point opposite to a high bluff
S. 20° W.	¾	to a bluff on the Stard. side opposite to an Island
N. 65° W.	2	to a small island near a high bluff on Stard., passing two other Islands; the 1st on Lard. and 2cd near the extremity of this course. encamped on the 3rd Island at the termineation of this course.—
Miles 23		

[Clark]   June 1st Satterday 1805

a Cloudy morning   we Set out at an early hour and proseeded on as usial with the toe rope   The Countrey appears to be lower and the Clifts not So high or Common, a mountain or a part of the north Mountain about 8 or 10 miles N. of this place, I walked on Shore to day found the

⟨high⟩ Plains much lower than we have Seen them and on the top we behold an extencive plain on both Sides, in this plain I observed maney [X:
k]noles of fine Sand which appeared to have blown from the river bluffs
and collected at these points[9] Those plains are fertile   near the river a
great no. of Small Stone, I observed at Some distance to the S. W. a high
mountain which appears to bear westerly   The Cole appear as usial, more
Cotton trees Scattered on the Shores & Islands than yesterday—   no timber on the high land, the river from 2 to 400 yards wide & current more
jentle than yesterday but fiew bad rapid points to day—   the wild animals
not So plenty as below   we only killed a ram & mule Deer to day, we Saw
Buffalow at a distance in the plains, particularly near a Lake on the Lard.
Side about 8 miles distant from the river—   We passed Six Islands and
encamped on the 7th   all those Islands are Small but contain Some timber
on them   The river riseing a little   Wind to day from the S. W.   Som fiew
drops of rain in the morning and also in the evening, flying Clouds all day

	miles	Course and Distance June the 1st 1805
N. 58° W.	2 ½	to a point on the Stard Side
N. 45° W.	1 ¼	to a point on the Lard. Side
N. 60° W.	1 ¼	to a point on the Stard. Side
N. 50° W	1 ½	to a tree on the Lard. Side
N. 25° W	1 ¼	to a point on the Stard. Side
N. 30° W.	¾	allong the Stard Shore to a point of woodland
N. 20° W.	1	to a point of timber on the Lard Side opsd. to a bluff on the Stard. Side.
N. 48° W.	¾	to a point of timbered land Stard. Side
N. 55° W	1 ½	to a point of timbered land on the Lard Sd.
N. 60° W	1 ¾	to the point of a bluff in a bend on Stard. opposit to a Small Island
S. 58° W.	1 ½	to a point on the Stard Side
S. 60° W.	1	to the upper point of a Small Island, on the Stard. Side passd. Lard. pt. at ¾ of a m.
S. 40° W.	¾	to a bluff point in a bend to the Lard. Side
West	1	to the Center of a Stard. bend

South	2 ½	to a Stard. point opposit a high bluff
S. 20° W.	¾	to a Bluff on the Stard Side opsd. an Isd.
N 65° W.	2	to a Small Island near a high bluff on the Stard., passing two other Islands first on the Lard. & the 2d near the extremity of the Course and Encamped on the 3rd Island
miles 23		

Saw Several Indian camps made of Sticks & bark Set up on end and do not appear to be long evacuated— The roses are in full bloome, I observe yellow berries, red berry bushes Great numbers of Wild or choke Cheries, prickley pares are in blossom & in great numbers

1. Part of the Bears Paw Mountains.

2. The intensely strong winds that blow from the southwest easily move silt and fine sand from river banks and bars and redeposit them in lee areas.

3. Several extensive deposits of sand and gravel occur here at elevations of as much as one hundred and sixty feet above the river. They were deposited by the Missouri before it entrenched its channel.

4. Probably the Highwood Mountains.

5. In the vicinity of present Boggs Island, in Chouteau County, Montana. Both captains say they camped on an island, as shown on *Atlas* map 41, but *Atlas* maps 53 and 61 show the campsite on the starboard shore. MRC map 74.

6. Someone, perhaps Biddle, drew a red vertical line through this sentence.

7. Also given on *Atlas* map 61, in both captains' hands.

8. On *Atlas* map 41 the whole number appears to be "3," with "2" written over it; use of the first number may account for the map's incorrect mileage total of 24.

9. Lewis appears to have added the words from "appeared to" to here. He may have added other words above in this entry.

[Lewis] *Sunday June 2ed 1805*

The wind blew violently last night and was attended by a slight shower of rain; the morning was fair and we set out at an early hour. imployed the chord as usual the greater part of the day. the courant was strong tho' regular, and the banks afforded us good toeing. the wind was hard and against us yet we proceded with infinitely more ease than the two precedeing days. The river bluffs still continue to get lower and the plains leveler and more extensive; the timber on the river increases in quantity; the country in all other rispects much as discribed yesterday. I think we are now completely above the black hills [*NB: see note of May 29*][1] we had a small shower of rain today but it lasted only a few minutes and was very moderate. Game becomeing more abundant this morning and I thought it best now to loose no time or suffer an opportunity to escape in providing the necessary quantity of Elk's skins to cover my leather boat which I now expect I shall be obliged to use shortly. Accordingly I walked on shore most of the day with some of the hunters for that purpose and killed 6 Elk 2 buffale 2 Mule deer and a bear.   these anamals were all in good order we therefore took as much of the meat as our canoes and perogues could conveniently carry.   the bear was very near catching Drewyer; it also pursued Charbono who fired his gun in the air as he ran but fortunately eluded the vigilence of the bear by secreting himself very securely in the bushes untill Drewyer finally killed it by a shot in the head; the [*NB: only*] shot indeed that will conquer the farocity of those tremendious anamals.—   in the course of the day we passed 9 Islands all of them small and most of them containing some timber.—

we came too on the Lard. side in a handsome bottom of small cottonwood timber opposite to the entrance of a very considerable river;[2] but it being too late to examine these rivers minutely to night we determined to remain here untill the morning, and as the evening was favourable to make some obsevations.—

Courses and distances June 2cd 1805.[3]

N. 85° W.	¾	to a few trees on a Lard. point.
S. 60° W.	¼	Along the Lard. point opposite to a bluff.
S. 40° W.	¼	to some trees in a Stard bend.
S. 20° E.	1	to some willows on the Lard. side
S. 30° E.	1	to a bush on a Stard. point opposite to a low bluff
South	¼	Along the Stard. point.
S 45° W.	½	to a tree in a Lard. bend
West	2	to a point on Lard. side opposite to a bluff
S. 68° W.	¼	Along the Lard. shore oppst. an Island.
S. 35° W.	¼	Along the Lard. shore
S. 25° W.	1	to the point of a timbered bottom on Lard.

South	2 ¾	to a point on Stard. oppst. a dark bluff, passing three Islands; small.—
S. 60° W.	1	Along the Stad. side passing two small Islands on Lard.
N. 80° W.	1 ¾	to a Lard. point opposite to a bluff.
S. 10° W.	1 ½	to the Lower point of an Island near a Stard. point.
S. 65° W.	2	to a point of timber on the Lard. side opposite a bluff the Island and also another small one near the Stard. side.
S. 20° W.	½	to the head of an island
South	½	to a point of timber on the Stard. side.
S. 72° W.	¼ [1]	to a point between two large rivers one of which is 362 Yds. and the 2cd or right hand fork [*EC: Maria's*] is 200 Yd. wide. encamped on the Lard. shore opposite the junction of those rivers.—
Miles 18		

June 2cd

Point of observation No. 25.

On the Lard. side, one mile from the commencement of the 12th course of this day, observed Meridian altd. of ⊙'s L. L. with Octant by the back observation   57° 52′

Latitude deduced from this observation [*blank*]

Point of Observation No. 26.

At our encampment of this evening on the Lard. side of the Missouri. Observed time and distance of ☽'s Western limb from Spica ♍, ★ East, with Sextant.

	Time			*Distance*		
	h	m	s			
P. M.	10	58	53	53°	56′	45″
	11	3	33	″	55	30
	″	5	52	″	54	30
	″	8	15	″	52	30
	″	10	52	″	52	30
	″	13	16	″	50	45
	″	15	6	″	49	15
	″	18	22	″	48	

	Time			Distance		
	h	m	s			
P. M.	11	30	43	53°	42'	45"
	"	33	46	"	41	15
	"	36	2	"	40	15
	"	38	35	"	38	45
	"	41	28	"	36	30
	"	43	16	"	36	15
	"	45	12	"	34	45
	"	47		"	33	

[Clark]   *June 2nd Sunday 1805*

we had a hard wind and a little rain last night, this morning fair   we
Set out at an early hour, wind from the S W.   Some little rain to day wind
hard a head, the Countrey much like that of yesterday as discribed   Capt
Lewis walked on Shore, himself & the hunters killed 6 Elk & a Bear and
2 mule deer, and 2 buffalow which was all in good order   a beaver also
killed to day, passed 9 Islands to day   the Current Swift but regular, we
Camped on the Lard Side at the forks of the river   the Currents & Sizes
of them we Could not examine this evening   a fair night   we took Some
Luner observations of moon & Stears

	miles	*Course Distance 2nd of June 1805*
N 85° W	¾	to a fiew trees on the Lard point
S. 60° W	¼	on the Lard. point opposit a bluff
S. 40° W.	½	to Some trees in the Stard. bend
S. 20° E.	1	to some willows on the Lard. Side
S. 30 E	1	to a bush on the Stard. point opsd. a low bluff.
South	¼	on the Stard. point.—
S. 45° W.	½	to a tree in a bend on Lard. Side
West	2	to a point on the Lard. Side opposd. to a bluff
S. 68° W	¼	on the Lard. Side opsd. an Island
S. 35° W.	¼	on the Lard Side
S. 25° W.	1	to a point of a timbered bottom on the Lard Side

South	2 ¾	to a point on Stard. Side opsd. a dark bluff passed 3 Small Islands
S. 60° W.	1	m. on the Stard. Side passed 2 Isds. on Lard Side
N. 80° W.	1 ¾	to the Lard. point opsd. a bluff
S. 10° W.	1 ½	to the lower point of an Island near the Stard point.
S. 65° W.	2	to a point of timber on the Lard Side opsd. a bluff passed the Isd. and one near Stard. Side
S. 20° W.	½	to the head of an Island
South	½	to a point of timber on the Stard. Side
S. 72° W	¼	to a point between two large rivers one 362 yards & the other ⟨half the width⟩ 200
miles	18	

1. It was probably Biddle who also added parentheses in red around the preceding sentence.

2. They camped on the larboard side in Chouteau County, Montana, opposite the mouth of Marias River, then perhaps a mile or so below the present mouth. Appleman (LC), 306; *Atlas* maps 41, 53, 61; MRC map 75.

3. Also given on *Atlas* map 41, in both captains' hands.

4. This course is "S. 60° W. ¼" on *Atlas* map 41. Clark's course appears to be overwritten to match Lewis's.

June 3rd

[Lewis]   *Point of Observation No. 27.*

On the point formed by the junction of Maria's river and the Missouri, Observed equal altds. of ☉ with Sextant.

	h	m	s		h	m	s	
A. M.	8	57	19	P. M.	5	42	39	Altd. at the time
"		58	55		"	44	14	of observation.
	Lost by Clouds				"	45	48	65° 12′ —″

Observed Meridian Altd. of ☉'s L. L. with Octant by the back observation   56° 6′

Latitude deduced from this observation   47° 24′ 12.8″

Observed time and distance of ☉'s and ☽'s nearest limbs with Sextant ☉ West.

	Time			Distance		
	h	m	s			
P. M.	5	54	49	85°	47′	30″
	″	57	7	″	48	
	″	58	19	″	48	15
	″	59	47	″	48	45
	6	2	8	″	49	45
	″	3	36	″	49	45
	″	5	7	″	50	15
	″	6	4	″	51	

	Time			Distance		
	h	m	s			
P. M.	6	14	30	85°	53′	45″
	″	16	56	″	55	
	″	17	12	″	55	30
	″	18	12	″	55	30
	″	20	46	″	56	45
	″	21	49	″	57	15
	″	22	33	″	55	15
	″	23	11	″	58	15

Monday June 3rd 1805

This morning early we passed over and formed a camp on the point formed by the junction of the two large rivers.[1]   here in the course of the day I continued my observations as are above stated. An interesting question was now to be determined; which of these rivers was the Missouri, or that river which the Minnetares call *Amahte Arz zha*[2] or Missouri, and which they had discribed to us as approaching very near to the Columbia river.   to mistake the stream at this period of the season, two months of the traveling season having now elapsed, and to ascend such stream to the rocky Mountain or perhaps much further before we could inform ourselves whether it did approach the Columbia or not, and then be obliged to return and take the other stream would not only loose us the whole of this season but would probably so dishearten the party that it might defeat the expedition altogether.   convinced we were that the utmost circumspection and caution was necessary in deciding on the stream to be

taken.   to this end an investigation of both streams was the first thing to
be done; to learn their widths, debths, comparitive rappidity of their courants and thence the comparitive bodies of water furnished by each; accordingly we dispatched two light canoes with three men in each up those
streams;[3] we also sent out several small parties by land with instructions
to penetrate the country as far as they conveniently can permiting themselves time to return this evening and indeavour if possible to discover the
distant bearing of those rivers by ascending the rising grounds.   between
the time of my A. M. and meridian Capt. C & myself stroled out to the
top of the hights in the fork of these rivers from whence we had an extensive and most inchanting view; the country in every derection around us
was one vast plain in which innumerable herds of Buffalow were seen attended by their shepperds the wolves; the solatary antelope which now
had their young were distributed over it's face; some herds of Elk were
also seen; the verdure perfectly cloathed the ground, the weather was
pleasent and fair; to the South we saw a range of lofty mountains which
we supposed to be a continuation of the S. Mountains, streching themselves from S. E. to N. W. terminating abbrubtly about S. West from us;
these were partially covered with snow; behind these Mountains and at a
great distance, a second and more lofty range of mountains appeared to
strech across the country in the same direction with the others, reaching
from West, to the N of N. W., where their snowey tops lost themselves
beneath the horizon.   this last range was perfectly covered with snow.[4]
the direction of the rivers could be seen but little way, soon loosing the
break of their channels, to our view, in the common plain.   on our return
to camp we boar a little to the left and discovered a handsome little river[5]
falling into the N. fork on Lard. side about 1 ½ ms. above our camp.   this
little river has as much timber in it's bottoms as either of the larger streams.
there are a great number of prickley pears in these plains; the Choke
cherry grows here in abundance both in the river bottoms and in the
steep ravenes along the river bluffs.   saw the yellow and red courants,
not yet ripe; also the goosberry which begins to ripen; the wild rose which
grows here in great abundance in the bottoms of all these rivers is now in
full bloom, and adds not a little to the beaty of the cenery.[6]   we took the
width of the two rivers, found the left hand or S. fork 372 yards and the

N. fork 200. The noth fork is deeper than the other but it's courant not so swift; it's waters run in the same boiling and roling manner which has uniformly characterized the Missouri throughout it's whole course so far; it's waters are of a whitish brown colour very thick and terbid, also characteristic of the Missouri; while the South fork is perfectly transparent runds very rappid but with a smoth unriffled surface it's bottom composed of round and flat smooth stones like most rivers issuing from a mountainous country.   the bed of the N. fork composed of some gravel but principally mud; in short the air & character of this river is so precisely that of the missouri below that the party with very few exceptions have already pronounced the N. fork to be the Missouri; myself and Capt. C. not quite so precipitate have not yet decided but if we were to give our opinions I believe we should be in the minority, certain it is that the North fork gives the colouring matter and character which is retained from hence to the gulph of Mexico. I am confident that this river rises in and passes a great distance through an open plain country   I expect that it has some of it's souces on the Eastern side of the rocky mountain South of the Saskashawan, but that it dose not penetrate the first range of these Mountains and that much the greater part of it's sources are in a northwardly direction towards the lower and middle parts of the Saskashawan in the open plains.   convinced I am that if it penetrated the Rocky Mountains to any great distance it's waters would be clearer unless it should run an immence distance indeed after leaving those mountains through these level plains in order to acquire it's turbid hue.   what astonishes us a little is that the Indians who appeared to be so well acquainted with the geography of this country should not have mentioned this river on wright hand if it be not the Missouri; *the river that scolds at all others,* as they call it if there is in reallity such an one, ought agreeably to their account, to have fallen in a considerable distance below, and on the other hand if this right-hand or N. fork be the Missouri I am equally astonished at their not mentioning the S. fork which they must have passed in order to get to those large falls which they mention on ⟨that⟩ the Missouri.   thus have our cogitating faculties been busily employed all day.[7]

Those who have remained at camp today have been busily engaged in dressing skins for cloathing, notwithstanding that many of them have their feet so mangled and bruised with the stones and rough ground over which they passed barefoot, that they can scarcely walk or stand; at least it is with great pain they do either.   for some days past they were unable to wear their mockersons; they have fallen off considerably, but notwithstanding the difficulties past, or those which seem now to mennace us, they still remain perfectly cheerfull. In the evening the parties whom we had sent out returned agreeably to instructions. The parties who had been sent up the rivers in canoes informed that they ascended some distance and had then left their canoes and walked up the rivers a considerable distance further barely leaving themselves time to return; the North fork was not so rappid as the other and afforded the easiest navigation of course; Six [*NB: 7*] feet appeared to be the shallowest water of the S. Branch and 5 feet that of the N. Their accounts were by no means satisfactory nor did the information we acquired bring us nigher to the decision of our question or determine us which stream to take. Sergt. Pryor hand [had] ascended the N. fork and had taken the following courses and distances—viz—[8]

S. 60° W.	2	mes. to some timber on the Lard. side
West	2	to a point on the Stard. side, passing the entrance of a river at ½ m. on Lard. side which was 60 yards wide and three feet deep boald. court.
N. 50° W.	3	to a point on Lard. side
S. 80° W.	3	to a point on Lard side.— thence the river bares to the N of West leaving a high hill to the Stard.—

Sergt. Gass ascended the South fork and took the following courses (viz.)

S. 30 W.	1	mes. to a point Lard. passing three Islands.
South	1	to the Lard. point of an Island
S. 60° E.	2	to a tree on the Stard. side
N. 50° E	1	to on object in a bank Lard. side opst. to the lower point of an Island.

S. 70° E	½	to a tree on the Lard. side passing an Island
S. 10° E	1	m. thence the general cource S 30 W. 5 mes. or as far as he could discover the direction of the river.

Joseph and Reubin Fields reported that they had been up the South fork about 7 mes. on a streight course somewhat N of W. and that there the little river which discharges itself into the North fork just above us, was within 100 yards of the S. fork; that they came down this little river and found it a boald runing stream of about 40 yds. wide containg much timber in it's bottom, consisting of the narrow and wide leafed cottonwood with some birch[9] and box alder undrgrowth willows rosebushes currents &c. they saw a great number of Elk on this river and some beaver. Those accounts being by no means satisfactory as to the fundamental point; Capt. C. and myself concluded to set out early the next morning with a small party each, and ascend these rivers untill we could perfectly satisfy ourselves of the one, which it would be most expedient for us to take on our main journey to the Pacific. accordingly it was agreed that I should ascend the right hand fork and he the left. I gave orders to Sergt. Pryor Drewyer, Shields, Windsor, Cruzatte and La Page to hold themselves in readiness to accompany me in the morning. Capt. Clark also selected Reubin & Joseph Fields, Sergt. Gass, Shannon and his black man York, to accompany him. we agreed to go up those rivers one day and a halfs march or further if it should appear necessary to satisfy us more fully of the point in question. the hunters killed 2 Buffaloe, 6 Elk and 4 deer today. the evening proved cloudy. we took a drink of grog this evening and gave the men a dram, and made all matters ready for an early departure in the morning. I had now my sack and blanket happerst[10] in readiness to swing on my back, which is the first time in my life that I had ever prepared a burthen of this kind, and I am fully convinced that it will not be the last. I take my Octant with me also, this I confide La Page.

[Clark]

we formed a Camp on the point in the junction of the two rivers, and dispatched a Canoe & three men up each river to examine and find if possible which is the most probable branch, the left fork which is the largest we are doubtfull of, the Indians do not mention any river falling in on the right in this part of the Missouri, The Scolding river, if there is Such a one Should have fallen in below agreeable to their accts.   we also dispatched men in different dircts. by land, to a mountain Covered with Snow to the South & other up each river—   Capt Lewis and my Self walked out & assended the hill in the point observed a leavel open Countrey to the foot of the mountains which lye South of this, also a River which falls into the Right hand fork about 1 ½ miles above its mouth on the Lard. Side   this little river discharges a great deal of water & contains as much Cotton timber in its bottoms as either of the others   we saw Buffalow & antelopes &c.   wild Cheries, red & yellow burries, Goose berries &c. abound in the river bottoms, prickley pares on the high plains, we had a meridian altitude and the Lattd. produced was $47°\ 24'\ 12''$ N.   the after part of the day proved Cloudy, we measured each river and found the one to Right hand 200 yards wide of water & the Left hand fork 372 yards wide & rapid—   the right hand fork falling the other at a Stand and Clear, the right fork and the river which fall into it is Coloured & a little muddey. Several men Complain of their feet being Sore in walking in the Sand & their being Cut by the Stones   They to be Sure have a bad time of it obliged to walk on Shore & haul the rope and 9/10 of their time bear footed, in the evening late the Canoes returned and the men informed us that they had assended Some miles by water & left their Canoes & walked on land the greater part of the day, their accounts by no means Satisfactory, Serjt. Pryor assended the right hand fork and took the following Courses, &c

S. 60° W.	2	to a timber on the Lard Side
West	2	to a point on the Stard. Side passd. a River L S. 60 yds. wide 3 feet deep
N. 50° W	3	to a point on the Lard Side

S. 80° W   3   to a point on the Larrd. Side   thence the river bears to the N. of west leaveing a Knob to the right—

Serjt. Gass assended the left hand fork and took the following Courses viz.

S. 30° W.   1   m to a pt. L. S. pass 2 Isds.

South   1   mile to a Lard. point of an Island

S. 60° E.   2   m. to a tree on the Starboard Side

N. 50° E   1   m. to an object in the bank Lard. Side opsd. the Lower point of an Island

S. 70° E   1 ½   m: to a tree on the Lard. Side passing an Island   Genl. cours from there S. 30° W for 5 miles

S. 10° E.   1   mile then S. W.—

Joseph & Rubin Fields ⟨assended⟩ went up the left fork 7 miles on a direct line at which place, the Small river which falls into the right hand fork approaches within 100 yards of the South fork, they Came down the Small river which is a bold Stream Covered with Elk & Some beaver, its bottoms Covered with wood, as the Information given by those parties respecting the rivers did not Satisfy us as to the main & principal branch Capt. Lewis & my Self deturmined to go up each of those rivers one Day & a half with a view to Satisfy ourselves which of the two was the principal Stream and best calculated for us to assend—   The hunters Killed 2 buffalow, 6 Elk & Several deer to day   we refreshed our party with a dram &c   Cloudy evining.—

1. The site is probably now on an island below the present mouth of the Marias, southeast of the town of Loma, Chouteau County, Montana. Here the party would remain until June 12, 1805. *Atlas* maps 41, 53, 61; MRC map 75.

2. See linguistic notes for part 1 of chapter 10.

3. Sergeant Pryor went up the Marias and Sergeant Gass up the Missouri; Whitehouse says he was with the latter.

4. The first range was probably the Highwood Mountains, beyond being the Little Belt and Big Belt ranges. Allen (LCDM), 10 n. 20.

5. The Teton River, a tributary of the Marias, which the captains called the Tansey River, after the plant found along its banks (see June 6, 1805, below). *Atlas* maps 41, 42, 53, 61; MRC map 75.

6. Someone, perhaps Biddle, drew a red vertical line to this point, beginning at "a great number."

7. The captains were puzzled that the Hidatsas and Mandans had not told them of a river as large as the Marias. They momentarily considered the possibility that it was the "River Which Scolds at All Others" described by the Indians, but description of that river fit the Milk River much too well, so the idea was discarded. Biddle, in working with the journals, concluded that the Marias was the actual "River Which Scolds" and inserted a note to that effect in Codex D (see above, May 8, 1805). This note misled later historians, but more recent research indicates that Lewis and Clark were right from the first. The Milk is the "River Which Scolds" and the captains never seriously thought otherwise. Saindon, (RSO); Allen (PG), 244 n. 5. The episode at the Marias is ably covered in Allen (LCDM).

8. Also given on *Atlas* map 41, in Clark's hand.

9. *Populus angustifolia* James, narrowleaf cottonwood, then new to science. Lewis provides a detailed description of this tree on June 12. Clark calls it the "cotton willow" in entries of June 17 and July 16. This tree grows in the Rocky Mountains at middle elevations and foothills along streams and out onto the plains. This location at the mouth of the Marias River is important since the species is not found lower on the Missouri River and, like the limber pine, illustrates the presence of Rocky Mountain biota eastward at its limits here on the Missouri. The wide leaf cottonwood is the earlier identified plains cottonwood whose western distributional limit comes sixty to seventy miles farther upstream. Lewis's notice of birch is the first mention of *Betula occidentalis* Hook., water, or river, birch, also new to science, a Rocky Mountain species found growing along river banks and reaching its apparent eastward limit along the Missouri, at the mouth of the Marias River. Booth & Wright, 22, 30; Little, 149-W; Cutright (LCPN), 158, 415.

10. Evidently some form of knapsack, perhaps from "hoppas," an Indian knapsack, derivation uncertain. Criswell, 46, 48; Jackson (LLC), 1: 74–75 and n. 8.

[Lewis]   *Tuesday June 4th 1805*

This morning early Capt. C. departed, and at the same time I passed the wright hand fork opposite to our camp below a small Island; from hence I steered N. 30 W. 4½ to a commanding eminence;[1] here I took the following bearings of the mountains which were in view. The North Mountains[2] appear to change their direction from that of being parallel with the Missouri turning to the North and terminating abruptly; their termineation bearing N. 48° E distant by estimate 30 mes. The South Mountains[3] appear to turn to the S. also terminating abrubtly, their extremity bearing S. 8 W. distant 25 mes. The Barn Mountain,[4] a lofty mountain so called from it's resemblance to the roof of a large Barn, is a seperate

Mountain and appears reather to the wright of and retreating from the extremity of the S. mts.; this boar S. 38 W. distant 35 ms. The North fork which I am now ascending lies to my left and appears to make a considerable bend to the N. W. on it's Western border a range of hills about 10 mes. long appear to lye parallel with the river and from hence bear N. 60° W. to the N. of this range of hills an Elivated point of the river bluff on it's Lard. side boar N. 72° W. distant 12 mes. to this last object I now directed my course through a high level dry open plain. the whole country in fact appears to be one continued plain to the foot of the mountains or as far as the eye can reach; the soil appears dark rich and fertile yet the grass is by no means as high nor dose it look so luxurient as I should have expected, it is short just sufficient to conceal the ground. great abundance of prickly pears which are extreemly troublesome; as the thorns very readily perce the foot through the Mockerson; they are so numerous that it requires one half of the traveler's attention to avoid them In these plains I [NB: we] observed great numbers of the brown Curloos, a small species of curloo or plover of a brown colour about the size of the common snipe and not unlike it in form with a long celindric curved and pointed beak; it's wings are proportionately long and the tail short; in the act of liteing this bird lets itself down by an extention of it's wings without motion holding their points very much together above it's back, in this rispect differing ascentially from any bird I ever observed.[5] a number of sparrows also of three distinct species I observed. also a small bird which in action resembles the lark,[6] it is about the size of a large sparrow of a dark brown colour with some white fathers in the tail; this bird or that which I take to be the male rises into the air about 60 feet and supporting itself in the air with a brisk motion of the wings sings very sweetly, has several shrill soft notes reather of the plaintive order which it frequently repeats and varies, after remaining stationary about a minute in his aireal station he descends obliquely occasionly pausing and accomnying his decension with a note something like *twit twit twit;* on the ground he is silent. thirty or forty of these birds will be stationed in the air at a time in view, these larks as I shall call them add much to the gayety and cheerfullness of the scene. All those birds are now seting and laying their eggs in the plains; their little nests are to be seen in great abundance as we pass. there are meriads of small grasshoppers in these plains which no doubt furnish the principal aliment of this numerous progeny of the feathered creation. after walking about eight miles I grew thisty and there being no water in the plains I changed my direction and boar obliquely in towards the river, on my arrival at which about 3 mes. below the point of observation, we discovered two deer at feed at some distance near the river; I here halted the party and sent Drewyer to kill one of them for breakfast; this excellent hunter so[o]n exceeded his orders by killing of them both; they proved to be two Mule Bucks in fine order; we soon kindled a fire cooked and made a hearty meal. it was not yet twelve when we arrived at the river and I was anxious to take the Meridian Altd. of the sun but the clouds prevented my obtaining the observation. after refreshing ourselves we proceded up the river to the extremity of the first course, from whence the river boar on it's general course N. 15° W. 2 M. to a bluff point on Stard. here Drewyer killed four other deer of the common kind; we skined them and hung up a part of the meat and the skins as we did also of the first, and took as much of the meat as we thought would answer for our suppers and proceeded N. 30 W. 2 m. to the entrance of a large creek on Lard. side[7] the part of the river we have passed is from 40 to 60 yds. wide, is deep, has falling banks, the courant strong, the water terbid and in short has every appearance of the missouri b[e]low except as to size. it's bottoms narrow but well timbered. Salts coal and other mineral appearances as usual; the bluffs principally of dark brown, yellow and some white clay; some freestone also appears in places.[8] The river now boar N. 20° E. 12 mes. to a bluff on Lard. At the commencement of this course we ascended the hills which are about 200 feet high, and passed through the plains about 3 m. but finding the dry ravines so steep and numerous we determined to return to the river and travel through it's bottoms and along the foot and sides of the bluffs, accordingly we again reached the river about 4 miles from the commencement of the last course and encamped a small distanc above on the Stard. side in a bend among the willow bushes which defended us from the wind which blew hard from the N. W. it rained this evening and wet us to the skin; the air was extremely could. just before we encamped Drewyer fired at a large brown bar across the river and wounded him badly but it was too late to pursue him.   killed a braro and a beaver, also at the place of our encampment, a very fine Mule deer.   we saw a great number of Buffaloe, Elk, wolves and foxes today.   the river bottoms form one emence garden of roses, now in full bloe.

[Clark]   *June 4th Tuesday 1805*

Capt. Lewis & my Self each with a Small party of men Set out early— those who accompanied Capt Lewis were G. Drewyer Serjt. Pryor, J Shields, P. Crusat J. B. de Page, R. Winser, went up the N. side of the N. fork.   those who accompanied me were Serjt. Gass Jos: & Ruben Fields G. Shannon & my black man York, and we Set out to examine the South fork, our first Course was S. 25° W. 7 miles to the S. fork at a Spring, at which place the little river which falls into the N. fork is 100 yards distant only Seperated from the ⟨right⟩ South fork by a narrow ridge.[9]   our course from thence S. 20° W. 8 miles to the river at an Island where we dined below a Small river falls in on the S E Side which heads in a mountain to the S. E about 20 miles.[10] North of this place about 4 miles the little river brakes thro' a high ridge into the open Leavel plain thro which we have passd. from the point, this plain is covered with low grass & prickley pear, emence number of Prarie dogs or barking Squirel are thro this plain—   after eating we proceeded on N. 45° W.   Struck the river at 3 miles 5, 9 & 13 miles at which place we encamped in an old Indian lodge made of Stiks and bark[11]   at the river near our camp we Saw two white Bear, one of them was nearly catching Joseph Fields[12] who could not fire, as his gun was wet   the bear was So near that it Struck his foot, and we were not in a Situation to give him assistance, a Clift of rocks Seperated us   the bear got allarmed at our Shot & yells & took the river.—   Some rain all the afternoon   Saw Several Gangues of Buffalow at a distance in the open plains on each Side, Saw Mule deer antilopes & wolves—   The river is rapid & Closely himed on one or the other Side with high bluffs, Crouded with Islands & graveley bars Containing but a Small quantity of timber on its bottoms & none on the high land.

1. Lewis's courses and distances for this day and the next are summarized in Clark's entry of June 8.

2. Probably the Bears Paw Mountains.

3. Probably the Highwood Mountains.

4. Square Butte, east of the Highwood Mountains and south of Geraldine, Chouteau County, Montana. Lewis's "S. 38 W." should read "S. 38 E."; he says that Barn Mountain is "reather to the wright [*east*]" of the Highwoods.

5. The long-billed curlew, although Holmgren believes Lewis describes two birds: "brown Curloos" and a "small species of curloo." The latter she supposes to be the Eskimo curlew, *Numenius borealis* [AOU, 266]. Holmgren, 29.

6. McCown's longspur, *Calcarius mccownii* [AOU, 539], then new to science. Cutright (LCPN), 157. Someone, perhaps Biddle, drew a red vertical line through these passages, beginning with "I observed" to "numerous progeny."

7. Sheep Coulee, some distance above which Lewis camped on the opposite side.

8. Like the Missouri, the Marias River was forced by glacial ice to cut a new channel. The formations exposed in this trench-like channel are the Claggett Shale, Eagle Sandstone, and Marias River Shale. The Claggett Shale is covered by glacial till. The salts are derived from the shale and the till. The coal occurs in the upper member of the Eagle Sandstone.

9. The Teton River is separated from the Missouri by a ridge or high ground which was later called *Cracon du Nez* by French rivermen and may be loosely translated, "bridge of the nose." It is now called Vimy Ridge. Wheeler, 1:302; Coues (HLC), 1:346 n. 29; *Atlas* maps 42, 53, 61; MRC map 75.

10. "Snow River" on *Atlas* maps 42, 53, 61; later Shonkin Creek, in Chouteau County, Montana. MRC map 75.

11. Marked on *Atlas* maps 42 and 54 as "my old camp" and on map 61 as "W. Cs Camp 4 June." The last does not quite agree with the other two, which are probably correct. About a mile and one-half upstream of present Carter Ferry, in Chouteau County. MRC map 76.

12. Apparently Lewis added the man's name a second time here, as "Joseph Field."

[Lewis]   *Wednesday June 5th 1805.*

This morning was cloudy and so could that I was obleged to have recourse to a blanket coat in order to keep myself comfortable altho' walking.   the rain continued during the greater part of last night.   the wind hard from N. W.   we set out at sunrise and proceded up the river eight miles on the course last taken yesterday evening, at the extremity of which a large creek falls in on the Stard. 25 yards. wide at it's entrance, some timber but no water, notwithstanding the rain; it's course upwards is N. E. it is astonishing what a quantity of water it takes to saturate the soil of this country, the earth of the plains are now opened in large crivices in many places and yet looks like a rich loam from the entrance of this Creek (which

I called Lark C.)[1] the river boar N. 50. W. 4 m.   at the entrance of this creek the bluffs were very steep and approached the river so near on the Stard. side that we assended the hills and passed through the plains; at the extremity of this course we returned to the river which then boar North 2 mes. from the same point, I discovered a lofty single mountain which appeard to be at a great distance, perhaps 80 or more miles   it boar N. 52 W.   from it's conic figure I called it tower Mountain.[2]   we now passed through the river bottoms to the extremity of the last course thence with the river S 60° W 1½ m. S 10 W. 3 m N 50 W 1½ at the extremity of which I again ascended the bluffs and took a course to a point of the Lard. bluffs of the river which boar West 10 m. the river making a deep bend to the south that is of at least five miles from the center of the chord line to the center of the bend.   on this course we passed through the plains found the plains as yesterday extreemly leavel and beautifull, great quanties of Buffaloe, some wolves foxes and Antelopes seen.   near the river the plain is cut by deep ravines in this plain and from one to nine miles from the river or any water, we saw the largest collection of the burrowing or barking squirrels that we had ever yet seen;[3] we passed through a skirt of the territory of this community for about 7 miles. I [NB: we] saw [NB: near the hills] a flock of the mountain cock,[4] or a large species of heath hen with a long pointed tail which the Indians informed us were common to the Rockey Mountains, I sent Shields to kill one of them but he was obliged to fire a long distance at them and missed his aim.   as we had not killed or eat anything today we each killed a burrowing squrrel as we passed them in order to make shure of our suppers.   we again [in]tersepted the river at the expiration of the last course or the lard. bluffs, from whence it now boar N 80° W.   2 mes. from this point saw some other lofty mountains to the N. W. of Tower Mtn. which boar N. 65° W. 80 or 100 mes. distant[5]   at the expiration of this course we killed five Elk and a blacktailed or mule deer and encamped on Stard. side of the river in a handsome well timbered bottom[6] where there were several old stick lodges. in the forepart of the day there was but little timber in the river bottoms but the quantity is now greater than usual.   the river is about 80 yds. wide with a strong steady courant and from 6 to 10 feet water. I had the burrowing squirrels roasted by way of experiment and found the flesh well flavored and tender; some of them were very fat.

[Clark]   *June 5th Wednesday 1805*

Some little rain & Snow last night   the mountains to our S E. covered with Snow this morning   air verry Cold & raining a little, we Saw 8 buffalow opposit, the[y] made 2 attempts to Cross, the water being So Swift they Could not, about the time we were Setting out *three* white bear approached our Camp   we killed the three & eatc part of one & Set out & proceeded on N. 20° W 11 miles. Struck the river at maney places in this distance to a ridge on the N. Side from the top of which I could plainly See a mountain to the South & W. covered with Snow at a long distance,[7] The mountains opposit to us to the S. E. is also Covered with Snow this morning.—   a high ridge from those mountains approach the river on the S E Side forming Some Clifts of hard dark Stone.[8]—   From the ridge at which place I Struck the river last, I could [*letters unclear*] discover that the river run west of South a long distance, and has a Strong rapid Current, ⟨a few minets of⟩   as this river Continued its width debth & rapidity and the Course west of South, going up further would be useless, I deturmined to return, I accordingly Set out, thro' the plain on a Course N. 30° E on my return & Struck the little river at 20 miles passing thro a Leavel plain, at the little river we killed 2 buck Elk & dined on their marrow ⟨bones⟩, proceeded on a few miles & Camped, haveing killed 2 deer which was verry fat, Some few drops of rain to day, the evening fair wind hard from the N. E.   I Saw great numbers of Elk & white tale deer, Some beaver, antelope mule deer & wolves & one bear on this little river marked my name in a tree N. Side near the ridge where the little river brakes thro'[9]

1. Later Black Coulee. Coues (HLC), 1 : 349 n. 34.

2. The southern end of the Sweetgrass Hills, on the Montana-Alberta border. Allen (LCDM), 12.

3. Lewis's wording seems to imply this was the already familiar prairie dog (see above, September 7, 1804); Coues believes it to be Richardson's ground squirrel. Since Lewis's

party actually killed some to eat, it would seem he would have noted the difference in size and color. See also April 9, 1805. Coues (HLC), 1 : 349–50 n. 36; Burroughs, 102–6.

4. The sage grouse, *Centrocercus urophasianus* [AOU, 309], then unknown to science. Lewis gave a detailed description on March 2, 1806. Cutright (LCPN), 157; Burroughs, 213–15. It was probably Biddle who drew a red vertical line through the passage about the grouse.

5. The rest of the Sweetgrass Hills.

6. Lewis's farthest point up the Marias in 1805; on July 19, 1806, he described it as being about six miles below where he reached the river in the latter year, and about four miles downstream from the mouth of later Pondera Creek.

7. Probably the Little Belt range, perhaps with the Big Belt range behind.

8. The high ridge is probably part of Shepherd Butte. The dark stone is shale and siltstone of the Blackleaf Formation.

9. Roughly west or west-northwest of present Fort Benton, Chouteau County, Montana. Clark's camp this day was evidently somewhere east of this point on the Teton River. *Atlas* maps 42, 53, 61; MRC map 75.

[Lewis]   *Thursday June 6th 1805.*

I now became well convinced that this branch of the Missouri had it's direction too much to the North for our rout to the Pacific, and therefore determined to return the next day after taking an observation of the ⊙'s Meridian Altitude in order to fix the latitude of the place. The forepart of the last evening was fair but in the latter part of the night clouded up and contnued so with short intervals of sunshine untill a little before noon when the whole horizon was overcast, and I of course disappointed in making the observation which I much wished. I had sent Sergt. Pryor and Windsor early this morning with orders to procede up the river to some commanding eminence and take it's bearing as far as possible. in the mean time the four others and myself were busily engaged in making two rafts on which we purposed descending the river; we had just completed this work when Sergt. Pryor and Windsor returned, it being about noon; they reported that they had proceded from hence S 70 W. 6 m. to the summit of a commanding eminence from whence the river on their left was about 2 ½ miles distant; that a point of it's Lard. bluff, which was visible boar S 80 W. distant about 15 ms.; that the river on their left bent gradually arround to this point, and from thence seemed to run Northwardly. we now took dinner and embarcked with our plunder and five Elk's skins on

the rafts but were soon convinced that this mode of navigation was hazer-
dous particularly with those rafts they being too small and slender.   we
wet a part of our baggage and were near loosing one of our guns; I therefore determined to abandon the rafts and return as we had come, by land.
I regreted much being obliged to leave my Elk's skins, which I wanted to
assist in forming my leather boat; those we had prepared at Fort Mandan
being injured in such manner that they would not answer.   we again
swung our packs and took our way through the open plains for about 12
mes. when we struck the river; the wind blew a storm from N. E. accompanyed by frequent showers of rain; we were wet and very could.   ⟨we⟩
continued our rout down the river only a few miles before the abbruptness
of the clifts and their near approach to the river compelled us take the
plains and once more face the storm; here we boar reather too much to the
North and it was late in the evening before we reached the river, in our way
we killed two buffaloe and took with us as much of the flesh as served us
that night, and a part of the next day.   we encamped a little below the
entrance of the large dry Creek called Lark C. having traveled abut 25 mes.
since noon.   it continues to rain and we have no shelter, an uncomfortable
nights rest is the natural consequence.—

[Clark]   *June 6th Thursday 1805*
   a Cloudy Cold raw day wind hard from the N. E.   we Set out early &
traveled down the little river which was imedeately in our Course   on this
river we killed 7 Deer for their Skins   the bottoms of this little river is in
everry respect except in extent[1] like the large bottoms of the Missouri below the forks containing a great perpotion of a kind of Cotton wood with
a leaf resembling a wild Cherry—. I also observed wind [wild] Tanzey[2] on
this little river in great quantities, we halted at 12 oClock and eate a part
of a fat Buck, after Dinner we assended the Plain at which time it began
to rain and Continued all day, at 5 oClock we arrived at our Camp on the
point, where I expected to meet Capt Lewis—   he did not return this
evening.—   my Self and party much fatigued haveing walked Constantly
as hard as we Could march over a Dry hard plain, dcending & assending
the Steep river hills & gullies, in my absence the party had killed an Elk & 2

buffalow, I Sent out for the meat a part of which was brought in— nothing remarkable had transpired at camp in my absence

1. Lewis may have written the words "except in extent."

2. The identity of the plant is problematic. The possibilities include *Dyssodia papposa* (Vent.) Hitch., fetid marigold or false dog fennel, or more likely *Matricaria matricarioides* (Less.) Porter, pineapple weed, also known as *Chamomilla suaveolens* (Pursh) Rydb. Booth & Wright, 278; Welsh, 237. Clark is comparing this to *Tanacetum vulgare* L., the cultivated common tansy or golden-buttons, introduced to eastern U.S. gardens from Europe, probably in colonial times. Fernald, 1518.

[Lewis]   *Friday June 7th 1805.*

It continued to rain almost without intermission last night and as I expected we had a most disagreable and wrestless night.   our camp possessing no allurements, we left our watery beads at an early hour and continued our rout down the river.   it still continues to rain ⟨and⟩ the wind hard from N. E. and could.   the grownd remarkably slipry, insomuch that we were unable to walk on the sides of the bluffs where we had passed as we ascended the river.   notwithstanding the rain that has now fallen the earth of these bluffs is not wet to a greater debth than 2 inches; in it's present state it is precisely like walking over frozan grownd which is thawed to small debth and slips equally as bad.   this clay not only appears to require more water to saturate it as I before observed than any earth I ever observed but when saturated it appears on the other hand to yeald it's moisture with equal difficulty.[1] In passing along the face of one of these bluffs today I sliped at a narrow pass of about 30 yards in length and but for a quick and fortunate recovery by means of my espontoon I should been precipitated into the river down a craggy pricipice of about ninety feet. I had scarcely reached a place on which I could stand with tolerable safety even with the assistance of my espontoon before I heard a voice behind me cry out god god Capt. what shall I do   on turning about I found it was Windsor who had sliped and fallen abut the center of this narrow pass and was lying prostrate on his belley, with his ⟨one⟩ wright hand arm and leg over the precipice while he was holding on with the left arm and foot as well as he could which appeared to be with much difficulty. I discovered his danger and the trepedation which he was in gave me still further concern for I expected every instant to see him loose his strength and slip off; altho' much allarmed at his situation I disguised my feelings and spoke very calmly to him and assured him that he was in no kind of danger, to take the knife out of his belt behind him with his wright hand and dig a hole with it in the face of the bank to receive his wright foot which he did and then raised himself to his knees; I then directed him to take off his mockersons and to come forward on his hands and knees holding the knife in one hand and the gun in the other   this he happily effected and escaped.   those who were some little distance bhind returned by my orders and waded the river at the foot of the bluff where the water was breast deep.   it was useless we knew to attempt the plains on this part of the river in consequence of the numerous steep ravines which intersected and which were quite as had as the river bluffs.   we therefore continued our rout down the river sometimes in the mud and water of the bottom lands, at others in the river to our breasts and when the water became so deep that we could not wade we cut footsteps in the face of the steep bluffs with our knives and proceded.   we continued our disagreeable march th[r]ough the rain mud and water untill late in the evening having traveled only about 18 miles, and encamped in an old Indian stick lodge which afforded us a dry and comfortable shelter.   during the day we had killed six deer some of them in very good order altho' none of them had yet entirely discarded their winter coats.   we had reserved and brought with us a good supply of the best peices; we roasted and eat a hearty supper of our venison not having taisted a mosel before during the day; I now laid myself down on some willow boughs to a comfortable nights rest, and felt indeed as if I was fully repaid for the toil and pain of the day, so much will a good shelter, a dry bed, and comfortable supper revive the sperits of the waryed, wet and hungry traveler.—

[Clark]   *June 7th Friday 1805*

rained moderately all the last night and Continus this morning, the wind from the S. W, off the mountains, The Themometer Stood at 40° above o, I allow Several men to hunt a Short time to day, the rain Continue moderately all day   the bottom verry muddey   2 buffalow an Elk & Deer killed to day—   Capt. Lewis not returned yet.   river falling

1. The clay is derived from glacial till and Claggett Shale. Clays of this type are commonly called gumbo. Only a small amount of moisture is needed to make it extremely slippery, yet, even a good rainfall rarely penetrates the gumbo more than a fraction of an inch. When the gumbo does become wet, it is very plastic—and very sticky—as well as slippery.

Chapter Fifteen

From the Marias to the Great Falls of the Missouri

June 8–20, 1805

[Lewis]

It continued to rain moderately all last night   this morning was cloudy untill about ten oClock when it cleared off and became a fine day.   we breakfasted and set out about sunrise and continued our rout down the river bottoms through the mud and water as yesterday, tho' the road was somewhat better than yesterday and we were not so often compelled to wade in the river.   we passed some dangerous and difficult bluffs. The river bottoms affording all the timber which is to be seen in the country they are filled with innumerable litle birds that resort thither either for shelter or to build their nests.   when sun began to shine today these birds appeared to be very gay and sung most inchantingly; I observed among them the brown thrush, Robbin, turtle dove, linnit goaldfinch, the large and small blackbird, wren and several other birds of less note.[1]   some of the inhabitants of the praries also take reffuge in these woods at night or from a storm. The whole of my party to a man except myself were fully peswaided that this river was the Missouri, but being fully of opinion that it was neither the main stream or that which it would be advisable for us to take, I determined to give it a name and in honour of Miss Maria W——d. called it Maria's River. it is true that the hue of the waters of this turbulent and troubled stream but illy comport with the pure celestial virtues and amiable qualifications of that lovely fair one; but on the other hand it is a noble river; one destined to become in my opinion an object of contention between the two great powers of America and Great Britin with rispect to the adjustment of the North westwardly boundary of the former; and that it will become one of the most interesting brances of the Missouri in a commercial point of view, I have but little doubt, as it abounds with anamals of the fur kind, and most probably furnishes a safe and direct communication to that productive country of valuable furs exclusively enjoyed at present by the subjects of his Britanic Majesty; in adition to which it passes through a rich fertile and one of the most beatifully picteresque countries that I ever beheld, through the wide expance of which, innumerable herds of living anamals are seen, it's borders garnished with one continued garden of roses, while it's lofty and open forrests, are the habitation of miriads of the feathered tribes who salute the ear of the passing traveler with their wild and simple, yet s[w]eet and cheerfull melody.— I arrived at camp about 5 OClock in the evening much fatiegued, where I found Capt. Clark and the ballance of the party waiting our return with some anxiety for our safety having been absent near two days longer than we had engaged to return. on our way to camp we had killed 4 deer and two Antelopes; the skins of which as well as those we killed while on the rout we brought with us. Maria's river may be stated generally from sixty to a hundred yards wide, with a strong and steady current and possessing 5 feet water in the most sholly parts.—

As the incidents which occurred Capt. C. during his rout will be more fully and satisfactoryley expressed by himself I here insert a copy of his journal during the days we wer seperated.—[2]

I now gave myself this evening to rest from my labours, took a drink of grog and gave the men who had accompanyed me each a dram. Capt. Clark ploted the courses of the two rivers as far as we had ascended them. I now began more than ever to suspect the varacity of Mr. Fidler or the correctness of his instruments. for I see that Arrasmith in his late map of N. America has laid down a remarkable mountain in the chain of the

Rocky mountains called the tooth nearly as far South as Latitude 45°, and this is said to be from the discoveries of Mr. Fidler.[3] we are now within a hundred miles of the Rocky Mountains, and I find from my observation of the 3rd Inst that the latitude of this place is 47° 24′ 12.8″. the river must therefore turn much to the South, between this and the rocky Mountain to have permitted Mr. Fidler to have passed along the Eastern border of these mountains as far S. as nearly 45° without even seeing it. but from hence as far as Capt. C. had ascended the S. fork or Missouri being the distance of 55 [*NB: 45 miles in Straight line*] miles it's course is S. 29° W. and it still appeared to bear considerably to the W. of South as far as he could see it. I think therefore that we shall find that the Missouri enters the rocky mountains to the North of 45°— we did take the liberty of placing his discoveries or at least the Southern extremity of them about a degree further N. in the sketh which we sent on to the government this spring mearly from the Indian information of the bearing from Fort Mandan of the entrance of the Missouri into the Rocky Mountains, and I reather suspect that actual observation will take him at least one other degree further North. The general Course of Maria's river from hence to the extremity of the last course taken by Sergt. pryor is N 69° W. 59 mes.—

[Clark]   *June 8th Saturday 1805*

rained moderately all the last night & Some this morning untill 10 oClock, I am Some what uneasy for Capt. Lewis & party as days has now passed the time he was to have returned, I had all the arms put in order and permited Severall men to hunt, aired and dried our Stores &c. The rivers at this point has fallen 6 Inches Sinc our arrival, at 10 oClock cleared away and became fair— the wind all the morning from the S. W. & hard— The water of the South fork is of a redish brown colour this morning the other river of a whitish colour as usual—The mountains to the South Covered with Snow. Wind Shifted to the N E in the evening, about 5 oClock Capt. Lewis arrived with the party much fatigued, and inform'd me that he had assended the river about 60 miles by Land and that the river had a bold current of about 80 or 100 yards wide the bottoms of Gravel & mud, and may be estimated at 5 feet water in Sholest parts

The courses which Capt. Lewis went to examine the N. fork of the Missouri

the 4th of June 1805

N. 30° W.	4 ½	to a hite on the Stard Side from the top of this hite the N. Mountains appear to turn to the N. & terminiate, they bear N. 48° E about 30 miles, the countrey is a leavel plain— The South mountains bear S, and appear to terminate, bearing S. 80° W. 35 ms The barn mountains S. 38° W. 40, the river on the left appears to be ⟨about⟩ turning to the N. W.
N. 70° W.	12	to the N. E. of a high hill
N. 15° W.	2	to the river bluff
N. 30° W.	2	to the mouth of a large Creek on Lard. Side a chain of high hills which run parrelal to the river on the S. Side cease
N. 20° E	12	to the river Bluffs camped. a Dry creek falls in at the end of the Course on the Stard. Side from the N E.

June 5th

N. 50° W.	4	up the river
North	2	The Tower Mountain bore N. 52 W. about 60 miles a high single Mtn.
S. 60° W.	1 ½	allong the river
S. 10° W.	3	allong the river
N. 50° W.	1 ½	allong the river.
West	10	to the river bluff across a Plain river haveing a considerable bend to the South. Cntr. of bend 5 ms.
N. 80° W.	2	miles on the river
S. 70° W	6	to a high hill on S. S. 2 ½ miles N. from the river in a plain
S. 80° W.	15	m. with the genl. course of the river the Countrey leavele open Plain, near the river Steep reveins the bottoms narrow but well timbered, bluff ¼ to ¾ asunder. The Countrey as far as Could be Seen is a leavel plain
	77 ½	

Some rain in the evening.   the left hand fork rose a little.

1. Lewis's "goaldfinch" is the American goldfinch, *Carduelis tristis* [AOU, 529]. The wren may be the winter wren, *Troglodytes troglodytes* [AOU, 722], or any of several other birds. Holmgren, 34. Burroughs questions Criswell's identification of the linnet as the pine siskin, *Carduelis pinus* [AOU, 533]. Holmgren says the term linnet was used for any small bird with a red crown, especially the common redpoll, *C. flammea* [AOU, 528], the purple finch, *Carpodacus purpureus* [AOU, 517], and the house finch, *C. mexicanus* [AOU, 519]. Burroughs, 259; Criswell, 53; Holmgren, 32. It was probably Biddle who drew a red vertical line through this passage about the birds.

2. Here Lewis copies Clark's entries from Voorhis No. 1 covering the period of separation, June 4–8. Having only slight differences in wording, the material is not repeated. Biddle has some emendations in red on the deleted pages, but they are of little consequence to the narrative.

3. Peter Fidler, surveyor for the Hudson's Bay Company, supplied the first information on the drainage network of the upper Missouri along the eastern front of the Rockies, information that went into the 1802 map of the London cartographer Aaron Arrowsmith, a copy of which Jefferson obtained for Lewis and Clark. Lewis was correct in doubting that Fidler had been as far south as 45° N. Latitude; the surveyor had been no farther south than the Oldman River in southern Alberta, approximately 50° N. Fidler obtained his information in 1801 from a map drawn for him by Ackomokki, a Blackfeet chief. Fidler placed the rivers and mountains too far south because his estimate of distance was based on Indian information, expressed in terms of days' travel, rather than miles. Lewis's impression that Fidler claimed to have seen these landmarks himself was apparently mistaken. MacGregor, 73–75; Moodie & Kaye; Allen (PG), 79–82, 122–23, 276–77; Tooley.

[Lewis]   *Sunday June 9th 1805.*

We determined to deposite at this place the large red perogue all the heavy baggage which we could possibly do without and some provision, salt, tools powder and Lead &c with a view to lighten our vessels and at the same time to strengthen their crews by means of the seven hands who have been heretofore employd. in navigating the red perogue; accordingly we set some hands to diging a hole or cellar for the reception of our stores. these holes in the ground or deposits are called by the engages *cashes* [*NB: cache's*]; on enquiry I found that Cruzatte was well acquainted this business and therefore left the management of it intirely to him. today we examined our maps, and compared the information derived as well from them as from the Indians and fully settled in our minds the propryety of addopting the South fork for the Missouri, as that which it would be most expedient for us to take. The information of Mr. Fidler incorrect as it is strongly argued the necessity of taking the South fork, for if he has been along the Eastern side of the rocky mountains as far as even Latd. 47°, which I think fully as far south as he ever was in that direction, and saw only small rivulets making down from those mountains the presumption is very strong that those little streams do not penetrate the rocky Mountains to such distance as would afford rational grownds for a conjecture that they had their sources near any navigable branch of the Columbia, and if he has seen those rivulets as far south as 47° they are most probably the waters of some Nothern branch of the Missouri or South fork probably the river called by the Indians Medicine River; we therefore cannot hope by going Northwardly of this place being already in Latitiude 47° 24″ to find a stream between this place and the Saskashawan which dose penetrate the Rocky mountains, and which agreeably to the information of the Indians with rispect to the Missouri, dose possess a navigable curent some distance in those mountains. The Indian information also argued strongly in favour of the South fork.   they informed us that the water of the Missouri was nearly transparent at the great falls, this is the case with the water of the South fork; that the falls lay a little to the South of sunset from them; this is also brobable as we are only a few minutes North of Fort Mandan and the South fork bears considerably South from hence to the Mountains; that the falls are below the rocky mountains and near the Nothern termineation of one range of those mountains.   a range of mountains which apear behind the S. Mountains and which appear to terminate S. W. from this place and on this side of the unbroken chain of the Rocky Mountains gives us hope that this part of their information is also correct, and there is sufficient distance between this and the mountains for many and I fear for us much too many falls.   another impression on my mind is that if the Indians had passed any stream as large as the South fork on their way to the Missouri that they would not have omitted mentioning it; and the South fork from it's size and complexion of it's waters must enter the Ry. Mountains and in my opinion penetrates them to a great distance, or els whence such an immence body of water as it discharges; it cannot procede from the dry plains to the N. W. of the Yellow Stone river on the East side of the Rocky Mountains for those numerous large dry channels which we witnessed on that side as we ascended the Missouri forbid such a conjecture; and that it should take it's sourses to the N. W. under those mountains the travels of Mr. Fidler fobid us to beleive. Those ideas as they occurred to me I indevoured to impress on the minds of the party all of whom except Capt. C. being still firm in the beleif that the N. Fork was the Missouri and that which we ought to take; they said very cheerfully that they were ready to follow us any wher we thought proper to direct but that they still thought that the other was the river and that they were affraid that the South fork would soon termineate in the mountains and leave us at a great distance from the Columbia. Cruzatte who had been an old Missouri navigator and who from his integrity knowledge and skill as a waterman had acquired the confidence of every individual of the party declared it as his opinion that the N. fork was the true genuine Missouri and could be no other. finding them so determined in this beleif, and wishing that if we were in an error to be able to detect it and rectify it as soon as possible it was agreed between Capt. C. and myself that one of us should set out with a small party by land up the South fork and continue our rout up it untill we found the falls or reached the snowy Mountains by which means we should be enabled to determine this question prety accurately. this expedition I prefered undertaking as Capt. C best waterman &c. and determined to set out the day after tomorrow; I wished to make some further observations at this place, and as we had determined to leave our blacksmith's bellows and tools here it was necessary to repare some of our arms, and particularly my Airgun the main spring of which was broken, before we left this place. these and some other preperations will necessarily detain us two perhaps three days. I felt myself very unwell this morning and took a portion of salts from which I feel much releif this evening. The cash being completed I walked to it and examined it's construction.[1] it is in a high plain about 40 yards distant from a steep bluff of the South branch on it's nothern side; the situation a dry one which is always necessary. a place being fixed on for a cash, a circle abut 20 inches in diameter is first discribed, the terf or sod of this circle is carefully removed, being taken out as entire as possible in order that it may be replaced in the same situation when the chash is filled and secured. this circular hole is then sunk perpendicularly to the debth of one foot, if the ground be not firm somewhat deeper. they then begin to work it out wider as they proceed downwards untill they get it about six or seven feet deep giving it nearly the shape of the kettle or lower part of a large still. it's bottom is also somewhat sunk in the center. the dementions of the cash is in proportion to the quantity of articles intended to be deposited. as the earth is dug it is handed up in a vessel and carefully laid on a skin or cloth and then carryed to some place where it can be thrown in such manner as to conseal it usually into some runing stream wher it is washed away and leaves no traces which might lead to the discovery of the cash. before the goods are deposited they must be well dryed; a parsel of small dry sticks are then collected and with then [them] a floor is maid of three or four inches thick which is then covered with some dry hay or a raw hide well dryed; on this the articles are deposited, taking care to keep them from touching the walls by putting other dry sticks between as you stoe away the merchandize, when nearly full the goods are covered with a skin and earth thrown in and well ramed untill with the addition of the turf furst removed the whole is on a level with the serface of the ground. in this manner dryed skins or merchandize will keep perfectly sound for several years. the traders of the Missouri, particularly those engaged in the trade with the Siouxs are obliged to have frequent recourse to this method in order to avoyd being robed. most of the men are busily engaged dressing skins for cloathing. In the evening Cruzatte gave us some music on the violin and the men passed the evening in dancing singing &c and were extreemly cheerfull.—

Point of observation No. 27.

June 9th 1805

At our camp on the point of land formed by the junction of the Missouri and Maria's rivers made the following observations.

Magnetic Azimuth of ⊙ with Circumferentr.	Time by Chronometer			Altitude of ⊙'s. U. L. with Sextant		
		h	m	s		
N. 70° E.	A. M. 8	30	44	58°	12′	45″
N. 71° E.	8	37	35	69°	29	45

Took Equal Altitudes of ⊙ with Sextant.

	h	m	s		h	m	s	
A. M	8	42	56	P. M.	5	50	43	Atld. by Sextant at
"		42	32	"		52	15	the tim of observation
"		46	9	"		53	52	62° 18′ 15″

	h	m	s
Chronometer too fast on mean time	1	19	45.7

Observed Magnetic azimuth of the Sun.

Azimuth by Circumferentr.	Time by Chronometer	Altitude by Sextant of ⊙'s. L. L.
	h m s	
S. 77° W.	P. M. 6 12 15	55° 6′ 15″
S. 78° W.	6 17 4	53° 29′ 45

Observed Meridian Altitude of ⊙'s L. L. with Octant by the back observation 54° 54′   ″

Latitude deduced from this observation.   47° 28′ 46.2″

Observed time and distance of ⊙'s Western limb from, α Aquilae ★ East; with Sextant.

Time	*Distance*
h m s	
P. M. 11 9 26	58° 55′ 00″
" 13 33	" 54 15
" 16 00	" 52 30

Time	*Distance*
h m s	
P. M 11 18 30	58° 51′ 15″
" 22 5	" 50 00
" 24 20	" 49 30

☞ The Standing error of the Sextant is 8′ 45″ − or Subs. That of the Octant by the back observation 2° 4° + or addetive by the direct observation with the same instumt. 2° + only.

Observed time and distance of ⊙'s Western limb from Spica ♍ ★ West with Sextant.

	Time			Distance		
	h	m	s			
P. M.	11	29	31	35°	55'	00"
	"	33	56	"	55	30
	"	36	6	"	56	00

	Time			Distance		
	h	m	s			
P. M.	11	39	9	35°	57'	00"
	"	41	4	"	57	45
	"	44	14	"	59	

Observed Magnetic Azimuth of Pole Star.

	h	m	s
Time by Chromometer, Astronomical P. M.	12	58	12

Azimuth by Circumferentor N. 15° W.

[Clark]

June 9th Sunday a fair morning   the wind hard from the S. W.   the river during the night fell 1 Inch, we conclude to burry a few of our heavy articles, Some Powder & Lead provisions & a fiw Tools, in case of accident and leave one perogue at this place, and as Soon as those things are accomplished to assend the South fork, which appears to be more in our Course than the N. fork   the Genl. Course of the South fork for 35 miles is S. 29° W.—   that of the N. fork is N. 69° W. for 59 miles, and as we are North of Fort mandan it is probable the most Southerley fork is the best for us.—   Capt. Lewis a little unwell to day & take Salts &c.   Send out 7 men to make a cache or hole to burry the Stores, air out Cloathes &c. &c.   finish'd the cache or Seller &c.   the men all engaged dressing Skins for their clothes, in the evening the party amused themselves danceing and Singing Songes in the most Social manner.   had a meridian altitude which gave 47° 24' 29"   took some Luner observations which gave for Longitude [*blank*] variation 15½° East

1. The location of the cache is marked on *Atlas* maps 53 and 61.

[Lewis] *Monday June 10th 1805.*

The day being fair and fine we dryed all our baggage and merchandize. Shields renewed the main Spring of my air gun   we have been much indebted to the ingenuity of this man on many occasions; without having served any regular apprenticeship to any trade, he makes his own tools principally and works extreemly well in either wood or metal, and in this way has been extreenely servicable to us, as well as being a good hunter and an excellent waterman.   in order to guard against accedents we thout it well to conceal some ammunicion here and accordingly buryed a tin cannester of 4 lbs. of powder and an adequate quantity of lead near our tent; a cannester of 6 lbs. lead and an ax in a thicket up the S. Fork three hundred yards distant from the point.   we concluded that we still could spare more amunition for this deposit   Capt. Clark was therefore to make a further deposit in the morning, in addition to one Keg of 20 lbs. and an adequate proportion of lead which had been laid by to be buryed in the large Cash.   we now scelected the articles to be deposited in this cash which consisted of 2 best falling axes, one auger, a set of plains, some files, blacksmiths bellowses and hammers Stake tongs &c.   1 Keg of flour, 2 Kegs of parched meal, 2 Kegs of Pork, 1 Keg of salt, some chissels, a cooper's Howel, some tin cups, 2 Musquets, 3 brown bear skins, beaver skins, horns of the bighorned anamal, a part of the men's robes clothing and all their superfluous baggage of every discription, and beaver traps.—   we drew up the red perogue into the middle of a small Island at the entrance of Maria's river, and secured and made her fast to the trees to prevent the high floods from carrying her off   put my brand on several trees standing near her,[1] and covered her with brush to shelter her from the effects of the sun. At 3 P. M. we had a hard wind from the S. W. which continued about an hour attended with thunder and rain.   as soon as the shower had passed over we drew out our canoes, corked, repared and loaded them. I still feel myself somewhat unwell with the disentary, but determined to set out in the morning up the South fork or Missouri leaving Capt. Clark to compleat the deposit and follow me by water with the party; accordingly gave orders to Drewyer, Joseph Fields, Gibson and Goodrich to hold themselves in readiness to accompany me in the morning. *Sâh-câh-gâh, we â,* our Indian woman is very sick this evening; Capt. C. blead her.   the night was cloudy with some rain.—

Observed meridian Altitude of ⊙'s L. L with Octant by the Back observation   54° 32'

Latitude deduced from this observation   47° 22' 52.8"

Mean Latitude of the Entrance of Maria's river as deduced from three observations of ⊙ Altd. 47° 25' 17.2" North.

I saw a small bird today which I do not recollect ever having seen before.[2]   it is about the size of the blue thrush or catbird, and it's contour not unlike that bird.   the beak is convex, moderately curved, black, smoth, and large in proportion to its' size.   the legs were black, it had four toes of the same colour on eah foot, and the nails appeared long and somewhat in form like the tallons of the haulk, the eye black and proportionably large.   a bluish brown colour occupied the head, neck, and back, the belly was white; the tail was reather long in proportion and appeared to be composed of feathers of equal length of which a part of those in the center were white the others black.   the wings were long and were also varigated with white and black.   on each side of the head from the beak back to the neck a small black stripe extended imbrasing the eye.   it appeared to be very busy in catching insects which I presume is it's usual food; I found the nest of this little bird, the female which differed but little in size or plumage from the male was seting on four eggs of a pale blue colour with small black freckles or dots.—   the bee martin or *King-bird*[3] is common to this country tho' there are no bees in this country, nor have we met with a honey bee[4] since we passed the entrance of the ⟨Osage⟩ [*NB: Kanzas*] river.—

[Clark]   *June 10th Monday 1805*

a fine day   dry all our articles arrange our baggage burry Some Powder & lead in the point, Some Lead a canister of Powder & an ax in a thicket in the point at Some distance, buried on this day and in the large cache or whole we buried on the up land near the S. fork 1 mile up S. S.[5]   we drew up our large Perogue into the middle of a Small Island in the North fork and covered her with bushes after makeing her fast to the trees, branded several trees to prevent the Indians injureing her, at 3 oClock we had hard wind from the S. W.   thunder and rain for about an hour after which we repaired & Corked the Canoes & loadded them— *Sah cah gah, we â* our Indian woman verry Sick   I blead her, we deturmined to assend the South fork, and one of us, Capt. Lewis or My self to go by land as far as the Snow mountains S. 20° W. and examine the river & Countrey Course & to be Certain of our assending the proper river, Capt Lewis inclines to go by land on this expedition, according Selects 4 men George Drewyer, Gibson, Jo. Fields & S. Gutrich to accompany him & deturmine to Set out in the morning—   The after noon or night Cloudy Some rain, river riseing a little.

1. Lewis's branding iron bore the legend "U. S. Capt. M. Lewis." Now in the possession of the Oregon Historical Society, it is one of the few authenticated articles associated with the expedition known to have survived. Files of the society are inexact and sources disagree on the item's provenance. It was found in 1892, 1893, or 1894, by Lineaus Winans of Hood River, Oregon, near present The Dalles, Oregon, on or below one of the Memaloose Islands before Columbia River dams inundated the area. See October 5 and 29, 1805. Wheeler, 2:118; Appleman (LC), 179–80, 373 n. 120; Oregon Historical Society files on the branding iron (courtesy of Robert E. Lange, Portland).

2. Cited as the first description of the white-rumped shrike, *Lanius ludovicianus excubitorides*, the western form of the loggerhead shrike; it is no longer considered a separate subspecies of the loggerhead, *L. ludovicianus* [AOU, 622]. Cutright (LCPN), 157. The birds used for comparison are the eastern bluebird, *Sialia sialis* [AOU, 766], and the gray catbird, *Dumetella carolinensis* [AOU, 704]. Holmgren, 29, 33.

3. Either the eastern kingbird or the western kingbird, *Tyrannus verticalis* [AOU, 447]. The latter would be more common in Montana. Cf. Burroughs, 244, and Holmgren, 28. See also weather remarks for May 25, 1805.

4. The honey bee is *Apis mellifera*. Werner et al., 47. Its western limit in 1804 would probably be closer to the Osage River than to the Kansas as Biddle has emended. It was probably Biddle who drew a red vertical line through this passage about the birds and the honey bee.

5. From "and in the large . . ." to here the passage appears to be crossed out.

[Lewis]   Tuesday June 11th 1805

This morning I felt much better, but somewhat w[e]akened by my disorder.   at 8 A. M. I swung my pack, and set forward with my little party.   proceeded to the point where Rose [*NB: Tansey*] River a branch Maria's River approaches the Missouri so nearly.[1]   from this hight we discovered a herd of Elk on the Missouri just above us to which we desended and soon killed four of them. we butchered them and hung up the meat and skins in view of the river in order that the party might get them. I determined to take dinner here, but before the meal was prepared I was taken with such violent pain in the intestens that I was unable to partake of the feast of marrowbones. my pain still increased and towards evening was attended with a high fever; finding myself unable to march, I determined to prepare a camp of some willow boughs and remain all night. having brought no medecine with me I resolved to try an experiment with some simples; and the Choke cherry which grew abundanly in the bottom first struck my attention; I directed a parsel of the small twigs to be geathered striped of their leaves, cut into pieces of about 2 Inches in length and boiled in water untill a strong black decoction of an astringent bitter tast was produced;[2] at sunset I took a point [pint] of this decoction and abut an hour after repeated the dze by 10 in the evening I was entirely releived from pain and in fact every symptom of the disorder forsook me; my fever abated, a gentle perspiration was produced and I had a comfortable and refreshing nights rest. Goodrich who is remarkably fond of fishing caught several douzen fish of two different species— one about 9 inches long of white colour round and in form and fins resembles the white chub common to the Potomac;[3] this fish has a smaller head than the Chubb and the mouth is beset both above and below with a rim of fine sharp teeth; the eye moderately large, the puple dark and the iris which is narrow is of a yellowish brown colour, they bite at meat or grasshoppers. this is a soft fish, not very good, tho' the flesh is of a fine white colour. the other species is precisely the form and about the size of the well known fish called the *Hickory Shad* or *old wife,*[4] with the exception of the teeth, a rim of which garnish the outer edge of both the upper and lower jaw; the tonge and pallet are also beset with long sharp teeth bending inwards, the eye of this fish is very large, and the iris of a silvery colour and wide. of the 1st species we had caught some few before our arrival at the entrance of Maria's river, but of the last we had seen none untill we reached that place and took them in Missouri above it's junction with that river. the latter kind are much the best, and do not inhabit muddy water; the white cat continue as high as the entrance of Maria's R, but those we have caught above Mandans never excede 6 lbs. I beleive that there are but few in this part of the Missouri. saw an abundance of game today even in our short march of 9 miles.—

[Clark]   *June 11th Tuesday* 1805

a fair morning wind from the S W. hard we burry 1 keg in the Cash & 2 Canisters of Powder in ⟨3 places⟩ 2 seperate places all with Lead; & in the Cash 2 axes, auger, Plains, 1 Keg flour, 2 Kegs Pork, 2 Kegs Parchd meal 1 Keg salt, files Chisel, 2 Musquits, Some tin cups, howel, 3 bear Skins, Beaver Skins, Horns, & parts of the mens robes & clothes.— Beaver Traps and blacksmith's tools.[5] Capt. Lewis Set out at 8 oClock we delayed to repare Some guns out of order & complete our deposit, which took us the day the evening fair and fine wind from the N. W. after night it became cold & the wind blew hard, the Indian woman verry Sick, I blead her which appeared to be of great Service to her both rivers riseing fast

1. Lewis made camp for the day southeast of the *Cracon du Nez*, or Vimy Ridge, a few miles northeast of present Fort Benton. *Atlas* maps 42, 53, 61; MRC map 75.

2. The choke cherry was here used as an astringent. Chuinard (OOMD), 287 n. 6.

3. The first description of the sauger, *Stizostedion canadense*. The chub used for comparison is probably the striped bass, *Morone saxatilis*. Cutright (LCPN), 427; Lee et al., 745, 576. It was probably Biddle who drew a red vertical line through this passage about the fishes.

4. The first descripton of the goldeye, *Hiodon alosoides*. The hickory shad mentioned for comparison is the gizzard shad, *Dorosoma cepedianum*. Cutright (LCPN), 425; Lee et al., 74, 69.

5. Lewis may have added the words "and blacksmith's tools" and perhaps other words above in this entry.

[Lewis]   Wednesday June 12th 1805.

This morning I felt myself quite revived, took another portion of my decoction and set out at sunrise. I now boar out from the river in order to avoid the steep ravines of the river which usually make out in the plain to the distance of one or two miles; after gaining the leavel plain my couse was a litte to the West of S. W.— having traveled about 12 miles by 9 in the morning, the sun became warm, and I boar a little to the south in order to gain the river as well to obtain water to allay my thirst as to kill something for breakfast; for the plain through which we had been passing possesses no water and is so level that we cannot approach the buffaloe within shot before they discover us and take to flight. we arrived at the river about 10 A. M. having traveled about 15 m. at this place there is a handsom open bottom with some cottonwood timber, here we met with two large bear, and killed them boath at the first fire, a circumstance which I beleive has never happend with the party in killing the brown bear before. we dressed the bear, breakfasted on a part of one of them and hung the meat and skins on the trees out of the reach of the wolves. I left a note on a stick near the river for Capt. Clark, informing him of my progress &c.— after refreshing ourselves abut 2 hours we again ascended the bluffs and gained the high plain; saw a great number of burrowing squirrels in the plains today. also wolves Antelopes mule deer and immence herds of buffaloe. we passed a ridge of land considerably higher than the adjacent plain on either side, from this hight we had a most beatifull and picturesk view of the Rocky mountains which wer perfectly covered with Snow and reaching from S. E. to the N. of N. W.— they appear to be formed of several ranges each succeeding range rising higher than the preceding one untill the most distant appear to loose their snowey tops in the clouds;[1] this was an august spectacle and still rendered more formidable by the recollection that we had them to pass. we traveled about twelve miles when we agin struck the Missoury at a handsome little bottom of Cottonwood timber and altho' the sun had not yet set I felt myself somewhat w[e]ary being weakened I presume by late disorder; and therfore determined to remain here during the ballance of the day and night, having marched about 27 miles today.[2] on our way in the evening we had killed a buffaloe, an Antelope and three mule deer, and taken a sufficient quantity of the best of the flesh of these anamals for three meals, which we had brought with us. This evening I ate very heartily and after pening the transactions of the day amused myself catching those white fish mentioned yesterday; they are here in great abundance I caught upwards of a douzen in a few minutes; they bit most freely at the melt of a deer[3] which goodrich had brought with him for the purpose of fishing.

The narrow leafed cottonwood grows here in common with the other species of the same tree with a broad leaf or that which has constituted the major part of the timber of the Missouri from it's junction with the Mississippi to this place. The narrow leafed cottonwood differs only from the other in the shape of it's leaf and greater thickness of it's bark. the leaf is a long oval acutely pointed, about 2 ½ or 3 Inches long and from ¾ to an inch in width; it is thick, sometimes slightly grooved or channeled; margin slightly serrate; the upper disk of a common green while the under disk is of a whiteish green; the leaf is smoth.[4] the beaver appear to be extremely fond of this tree and even seem to scelect it from among the other species of Cottonwood, probably from it's affording a deeper and softer bark than the other species.— saw some sign of the Otter as well as beaver near our camp, also a great number of tracks of the brown bear; these fellows leave a formidable impression in the mud or sand I measured one this evening which was eleven inches long exclusive of the tallons and seven and ¼ in width.—

[Clark]   *June 12th 1805 Wednesday*

last night was Clear and Cold, this morning fair we Set out at 8 oClock & proceeded on verry well wind from the S. W. The interpreters wife verry Sick So much So that I move her into the back part of our Covered part of the Perogue which is Cool, her own situation being a verry hot one in the bottom of the ⟨Canoe⟩ Perogue exposed to the Sun— Saw emence No. of Swallows in the 1st bluff on the Lard. Side, water verry Swift, the bluff are blackish Clay & Coal for about 80 feet. the earth above that for 30 or 40 feet is a brownish yellow, a number of bars of corse gravil and Stones of different Shape & Size &c.[5] Saw a number of rattle Snakes to day one of the men cought one by the head in Catch'g hold of a bush on which his head lay reclined three canoes were in great danger to day one diped water, another was near turning over &c. at 2 oClock P M a fiew drops of rain I walked thro' a point and killed a Buck Elk & Deer, and we camped on the Stard Side,[6] the Interpreters woman verry Sick worse than She has been. I give her medison one man have a fellon riseing on his hand one other with the Tooth ake has taken cold in the Jaw &c.

miles   *Course & distance the 12th of June 1805*[7]

S. 30° W.   1   to a point on the Lard Shore passd. 3 Islands

South	1	to a Lard point of an Island
S. 60° E	2	to a tree on the Lard[8] Side, passd. 2 Small Islands
N. 50° E	1	to an object in the Lard bend opsd. an Island
S. 50° E	1 ½	to a tree on the Lard. Side passd. the Isld.
S. 10° W.	1	to a point on the Stard. Side
S. 40° W.	½	to a point of wood on the Stard. Side passd. 2 Islands one Small
S. 80° W	½	to a bluff point on Stard. Side passd. a Isld.
West	½	to the lower point of a Small Island
S 30° E.	1 ½	to a high black bluff in a bend Lard. Side
S. 50° W.	1 ½	to a tree under a hill Lard Side passed four Islands two on each Side
West	3	to the *grog* spring[9] at the Stard. Side at which place the Little river which falls into the North fork is 100 yards distant
N. 45° E	1 ¾	to a low bluff on the Stard Side pass: a point on Std. & one on the Lard Side
East	1	to a Bluff on the Lard Side
West	¼	to a low Bluff at the upper part of a wood on the Stard Side opposit a Island. here we camped at a large Indian encampment about 12 months past
	miles 18	

1. Lewis could have been seeing the Highwood, Little Belt, and Big Belt mountains, the Lewis range, and the main Rockies, marking the Continental Divide.

2. Lewis camped in Chouteau County, Montana, a little upstream from present Black Coulee. MRC map 76.

3. The deer's spleen.

4. This paragraph to here has a red vertical line drawn through it, probably by Biddle.

5. These bluffs are composed of the dark-gray to black Marias River Shale. The upper, brownish-yellow material is glacial till. There is no coal in these bluffs. The gravel bars reflect the proximity of a source of more indurated rock.

6. In Chouteau County, in the vicinity of Evans Bend, about five miles downstream from Fort Benton. *Atlas* maps 53, 61; MRC map 75.

7. Also given on *Atlas* map 42, in Clark's hand.

8. "Stard." on *Atlas* map 42.

9. Not marked on any of Clark's maps, but in the vicinity of the close approach of the Missouri and Teton rivers to each other.

Thursday June 13th 1805.

This morning we set out about sunrise after taking breakfast off our venison and fish. we again ascended the hills of the river and gained the level country. the country through which we passed for the first six miles tho' more roling than that we had passed yesterday might still with propryety be deemed a level country; our course as yesterday was generally S W. the river from the place we left it appeared to make a considerable bend to the South. from the extremity of this roling country I overlooked a most beatifull and level plain of great extent or at least 50 or sixty miles; in this there were infinitely more buffaloe than I had ever before witnessed at a view. nearly in the direction I had been travling or S. W. two curious mountains presented themselves of square figures,[1] the sides rising perpendicularly to the hight of 250 feet and appeared to be formed of yellow clay; their tops appeared to be level plains; these inaccessible hights appeared like the ramparts of immence fortifications; I have no doubt but with very little assistance from art they might be rendered impregnable. fearing that the river boar to the South and that I might pass the falls if they existed between this an the snowey mountains I altered my course nealy to the South leaving those insulated hills to my wright and proceeded through the plain; I sent Feels on my right and Drewyer and Gibson on my left with orders to kill some meat and join me at the river where I should halt for dinner. I had proceded on this course about two miles with Goodrich at some distance behind me whin my ears were saluted with the agreeable sound of a fall of water and advancing a little further I saw the spray arrise above the plain like a collumn of smoke which would frequently dispear again in an instant caused I presume by the wind which blew pretty hard from the S. W. I did not however loose my direction to this point which soon began to make a roaring too tremendious to be mistaken for any cause short of the great falls of the Missouri. here I arrived about 12 OClock having traveled by estimate about 15 Miles. I hurryed down the hill which was about 200 feet high and difficult of access, to gaze on this sublimely grand specticle.[2] I took my position on the top of some rocks about 20 feet high opposite the center of the falls. this chain of rocks appear once to have formed a part of those over which the waters tumbled, but in the course of time has been sepe-

rated from it to the distance of 150 yards lying prarrallel to it and forming a butment against which the water after falling over the precipice
beats with great fury; this barrier extends on the right to the perpendicular clift which forms that board [bound? border?] of the river but to
the distance of 120 yards next to the clift it is but a few feet above the level
of the water, and here the water in very high tides appears to pass in a
channel of 40 yds. next to the higher part of the ledg of rocks; on the left
it extends within 80 or ninty yards of the lard. Clift which is also perpendicular; between this abrupt extremity of the ledge of rocks and the perpendicular bluff the whole body of water passes with incredible swift-
ness.   immediately at the cascade the river is about 300 yds. wide; about
ninty or a hundred yards of this next the Lard. bluff is a smoth even sheet
of water falling over a precipice of at least eighty feet, the remaining part
of about 200 yards on my right formes the grandest sight I ever beheld,
the hight of the fall is the same of the other but the irregular and somewhat projecting rocks below receives the water in it's passage down and
brakes it into a perfect white foam which assumes a thousand forms in a
moment sometimes flying up in jets of sparkling foam to the hight of fifteen or twenty feet and are scarcely formed before large roling bodies of
the same beaten and foaming water is thrown over and conceals them.   in
short the rocks seem to be most happily fixed to present a sheet of the
whitest beaten froath for 200 yards in length and about 80 feet perpendicular.   the water after decending strikes against the butment before
mentioned or that on which I stand and seems to reverberate and being
met by the more impetuous courant they role and swell into half formed
billows of great hight which rise and again disappear in an instant.   this
butment of rock defends a handsom little bottom of about three acres
which is deversified and agreeably shaded with some cottonwood trees; in
the lower extremity of the bottom there is a very thick grove of the same
kind of trees which are small, in this wood there are several Indian lodges
formed of sticks.   a few small cedar grow near the ledge of rocks where I
rest.   below the point of these rocks at a small distance the river is divided by a large rock which rises several feet above the water, and extends
downwards with the stream for about 20 yards.   about a mile before the
water arrives at the pitch it decends very rappidly, and is confined on the

Lard. side by a perpendicular clift of about 100 feet, on Stard. side it is also perpendicular for about three hundred yards above the pitch where it is then broken by the discharge of a small ravine, down which the buffaloe have a large beaten road to the water, [*NB: Qu.*] for it is but in very few places that these anamals can obtain water near this place owing to the steep and inaccessible banks. I see several skelletons of the buffaloe lying in the edge of the water near the Stard. bluff which I presume have been swept down by the current and precipitated over this tremendious fall. about 300 yards below me there is another butment of solid rock with a perpendicular face and abot 60 feet high which projects from the Stard. side at right angles to the distance of 134 yds. and terminates the lower part nearly of the bottom before mentioned; there being a passage arround the end of this butment between it and the river of about 20 yardes; here the river again assumes it's usual width soon spreading to near 300 yards but still continues it's rappidity. from the reflection of the sun on the spray or mist which arrises from these falls there is a beatifull rainbow produced which adds not a little to the beauty of this majestically grand senery. after wrighting this imperfect discription I again viewed the falls and was so much disgusted with the imperfect idea which it conveyed of the scene that I determined to draw my pen across it and begin agin, but then reflected that I could not perhaps succeed better than pening the first impressions of the mind; I wished for the pencil of Salvator Rosa [*EC: a Titian*] or the pen of Thompson,[3] that I might be enabled to give to the enlightened world some just idea of this truly magnificent and sublimely grand object, which has from the commencement of time been concealed from the view of civilized man; but this was fruitless and vain. I most sincerely regreted that I had not brought a crimee obscura[4] with me by the assistance of which even I could have hoped to have done better but alas this was also out of my reach; I therefore with the assistance of my pen only indeavoured to trace[5] some of the stronger features of this seen by the assistance of which and my recollection aided by some able pencil I hope still to give to the world some faint idea of an object which at this moment fills me with such pleasure and astonishment, and which of it's kind I will venture to ascert is second to but one in the known world. I retired to the shade of a tree where I determined to fix my camp[6] for the prèsent and dispatch a man in the morning to inform Capt. C. and the party of my success in finding the falls and settle in their minds all further doubts as to the Missouri. the hunters now arrived loaded with excellent buffaloe meat and informed me that they had killed three very fat cows about ¾ of a mile hence. I directed them after they had refreshed themselves to go back and butcher them and bring another load of meat each to our camp determining to employ those who remained with me in drying meat for the party against their arrival. in about 2 hours or at 4 OClock P. M. they set out on this duty, and I walked down the river about three miles to discover if possible some place to which the canoes might arrive or at which they might be drawn on shore in order to be taken by land above the falls; but returned without effecting either of these objects; the river was one continued sene of rappids and cascades which I readily perceived could not be encountered with our canoes, and the Clifts still retained their perpendicular structure and were from 150 to 200 feet high; in short the river appears here to have woarn a channel in the process of time through a solid rock. on my return I found the party at camp; they had butchered the buffaloe and brought in some more meat as I had directed. Goodrich had caught half a douzen very fine trout[7] and a number of both species of the white fish. these trout [*NB: caught in the falls*] are from sixteen to twenty three inches in length, precisely resemble our mountain or speckled trout in form and the position of their fins, but the specks on these are of a deep black instead of the red or goald colour of those common to the U.' States. these are furnished long sharp teeth on the pallet and tongue and have generally a small dash of red on each side behind the front ventral fins; the flesh is of a pale yellowish red, or when in good order, of a rose red.—

I am induced to believe that the Brown, the white and the Grizly bear of this country are the same species only differing in colour from age or more probably from the same natural cause that many other anamals of the same family differ in colour. one of those which we killed yesterday was of a creemcoloured white while the other in company with it was of the common bey or rdish brown, which seems to be the most usual colour of them. the white one appeared from it's tallons and teath to be the youngest; it was smaller than the other, and although a monstrous beast we supposed that it had not yet attained it's growth and that it was a little upwards of two years old.   the young cubs which we have killed have always been of a brownish white, but none of them as white as that we killed yesterday.   one other that we killed sometime since which I mentioned sunk under some driftwood and was lost, had a white stripe or list of about eleven inches wide entirely arround his body just behind the shoalders, and was much darker than these bear usually are.   the grizly bear we have never yet seen. I have seen their tallons in possession of the Indians and from their form I am perswaded if there is any difference between this species and the brown or white bear it is very inconsiderable. There is no such anamal as a black bear in this open country or of that species generally denominated the black bear

my fare is really sumptuous this evening; buffaloe's humps, tongues and marrowbones, fine trout parched meal pepper and salt, and a good appetite; the last is not considered the least of the luxuries.

[Clark]   *June 13th Thursday 1805*

a fair morning, Some dew this morning   the Indian woman Verry sick   I gave her a doste of Salts. We Set out early, at a mile & ½ passed a Small rapid Stream on the Lard Side which heads in a mountain to the S. E 12 or 15 miles, which at this time covered with Snow, we call this stream Snow river,[8] as it is the conveyance of the melted snow from that mountain at present.   numbers of gees & goslings, the gees cannot fly at this Season—   goose berries are ripe and in great abundance, the yellow Current is also Common, not yet ripe   Killed a buffalow & Campd on the Lard Side near an old Indian fortified camp[9]   one man Sick[10] & 3 with Swellings, the Indian woman verry Sick. Killed a goat & fraser 2 Buffalow

	miles	*Course and distance June 13th 1805*[11]
S. 45° W	1 ½	to the mouth of Snow river on the Lard. Side opsd. an Island passed 2 Islands
S. 60° W.	1 ½	to the lower point of an Island [*overwritten,* "Timber"] on the Stard. Side passed the Island
South	¼	on the Stard. Side to the point opposit a black Slate bluff.
S 45° W.	1 ½	to the upper part of a wood Stard Side

S. 20° W	1 ¼	to a black bluff on the Lard Side
S. 30° W	1	to the lower point of an Island
West	1 ¾	to a Bush on the Side of a bluff in the Stard. bend passed 2 Islds. & a Lard point
S 60° E	¾	to a hollow in the bluff in Lard bend passed 2 Small Islands
South	¼	to a Lodge on a small Island
S. 80° W.	1	to the lower point of an Island
S. 40° W.	¼	to a Stoney bluff Stard. Side, at the head of the Island a rapid across R
South	1 ¼	to a tree on a Small Island in the Lard. bend under a high hill passed 2 Islands
S. 70° W.	<u>1 ½</u> 13	to the Lower point of an Island passed 2 Small Islands— Camped on the Lard Shore

The river verry rapid maney Sholes great nos of large Stones   passed Some bluffs or low cliffts of Slate to day

1. These are probably buttes just south of Black Horse Lake along Highway 87 north of Great Falls, Cascade County, Montana.

2. Lewis had arrived at the Great Falls, first of a series of five falls in Cascade County, northeast of the present city of Great Falls. The spectacle he saw has been considerably reduced by Ryan Dam. Appleman (LC), 309–17; *Atlas* maps 44, 54, 61; MRC map 77. The cliffs surrounding the Falls of the Missouri are composed of the lower Cretaceous Kootenai Formation. It contains light-brown and red-brown sandstone, red-to-purple shale, and green shale. The gorge was cut during the glacial period when ice diverted the Missouri from its former course.

3. Salvator Rosa, seventeenth-century Italian landscape painter, generally painted wild, desolate scenes. James Thomson, eighteenth-century Scottish poet, was a forerunner of the English Romantic movement; his best-known poem was "The Seasons."

4. A camera obscura, basically a box with a lens mounted on one wall; light entering through the lens would project an image on the opposite wall of the dark box, which an artist could then trace, getting an almost photographic image.

5. No drawing of the falls by Lewis has ever been known to exist.

6. Near the Great Falls, on the north side of the river, in Cascade County. The area, but not the campsite, appears on *Atlas* maps 54, 61; MRC map 77.

7. The cutthroat trout, *Salmo clarkii* after William Clark, a species new to science. Cutright (LCPN), 157–58; Lee et al., 105, 114. The fish used for comparison is the brook

trout, *Salvelinus fontinalis*. It was probably Biddle who drew a red vertical line through this passage about the trout and part of the next about the bears.

8. Shonkin Creek; see above, June 4, 1805.

9. In Chouteau County, Montana, perhaps in the vicinity of Bird Coulee. *Atlas* maps 54, 61; MRC map 76.

10. Whitehouse says he was very sick and had "a violent head ack."

11. Also given on *Atlas* map 42, in Clark's hand.

[Lewis]   *Friday June 14th 1805.*

This morning at sunrise I dispatched Joseph Fields with a letter to Capt. Clark and ordered him to keep sufficiently near the river to observe it's situation in order that he might be enabled to give Capt. Clark an idea of the point at which it would be best to halt to make our portage. I set one man about preparing a saffold and collecting wood to dry the meat   Sent the others to bring in the ballance of the buffaloe meat, or at least the part which the wolves had left us, for those fellows are ever at hand and ready to partake with us the moment we kill a buffaloe; and there is no means of puting the meat out of their reach in those plains; the two men shortly after returned with the meat and informed me that the wolves had devoured the greater part of the meat.   about ten OClock this morning while the men were engaged with the meat I took my Gun and espontoon and thought I would walk a few miles and see where the rappids termineated above, and return to dinner.   accordingly I set out and proceeded up the river about S. W.   after passing one continued rappid and three small cascades of abut for or five feet each at the distance of about five miles I arrived at a fall of about 19 feet; the river is here about 400 yds. wide.   this pitch which I called the crooked falls [1] occupys about three fourths of the width of the river, commencing on the South side, extends obliquly upwards about 150 yds. then forming an accute angle extends downwards nearly to the commencement of four small Islands lying near the N. shore; among these Islands and between them and the lower extremity of the perpendicular pitch being a distance of 100 yards or upwards, the water glides down the side of a sloping rock with a volocity almost equal to that of it's perpendicular decent.   just above this rappid the river makes a suddon bend to the right or Northwardly. I should have returned from hence but hearing a tremendious roaring above me I continued my rout across the point of a hill a few hundred yards further and was again presented by one of the most beatifull objects in nature, a cascade of about fifty feet perpendicular streching at rightangles across the river from side to side to the distance of at least a quarter of a mile.[2] here the river pitches over a shelving rock, with an edge as regular and as streight as if formed by art, without a nich or brake in it; the water decends in one even and uninterupted sheet to the bottom wher dashing against the rocky bottom rises into foaming billows of great hight and rappidly glides away, hising flashing and sparkling as it departs the sprey rises from one extremity to the other to 50 f. I now thought that if a skillfull painter had been asked to make a beautifull cascade that he would most probably have pesented the precise immage of this one; nor could I for some time determine on which of those two great cataracts to bestoe the palm, on this or that which I had discovered yesterday; at length I determined between these two great rivals for glory that this was *pleasingly beautifull,* while the other was *sublimely grand.* I had scarcely infixed my eyes from this pleasing object before I discovered another fall above at the distance of half a mile;[3] thus invited I did not once think of returning but hurried thither to amuse myself with this newly discovered object. I found this to be a cascade of about 14 feet possessing a perpendicular pitch of about 6 feet. this was tolerably regular streching across the river from bank to bank where it was about a quarter of a mile wide; in any other neighbourhood but this, such a cascade would probably be extoled for it's beaty and magnifficence, but here I passed it by with but little attention, determining as I had proceded so far to continue my rout to the head of the rappids if it should even detain me all night. at every rappid cateract and cascade I discovered that the bluffs grew lower or that the bed of the river rose nearer to a level with the plains. still pursuing the river with it's course about S. W. passing a continued sene of rappids and small cascades, at the distance of 2½ miles I arrived at another cataract of 26 feet.[4] this is not immediately perpendicular, a rock about ⅓ of it's decent seems to protrude to a small distance and receives the water in it's passage downwards and gives a curve to the water tho' it falls mostly with a regular and smoth sheet. the river is near six hundred yards wide at this place, a beatifull level plain on the S. side only a few feet above the level of the pitch; on the N. side where

I am the country is More broken and immediately behind me near the river a high hill. below this fall at a little distance a beatifull little Island well timbered is situated about the middle of the river. in this Island on a Cottonwood tree an Eagle has placed her nest; a more inaccessable spot I beleive she could not have found; for neither man nor beast dare pass those gulphs which seperate her little domain from the shores. the water is also broken in such manner as it decends over this pitch that the mist or sprey rises to a considerable hight. this fall is certainly much the greatest I ever behald except those two which I have mentioned below. it is incomparably a geater cataract and a more noble interesting object than the celibrated falls of Potomac or Soolkiln[5] &c. just above this is another cascade of about 5 feet, above which the water as far as I could see began to abate of it's valosity, and I therefore determined to ascend the hill behind me which promised a fine prospect of the adjacent country, nor was I disappointed on my arrival at it's summit. from hence I overlooked a most beatifull and extensive plain reaching from the river to the base of the Snowclad mountains to the S. and S. West; I also observed the missoury streching it's meandering course to the South through this plain to a great distance filled to it's even and grassey brim; another large river flowed in on it's Western side about four miles above me and extended itself though a level and fertile valley of 3 miles in width a great distance to the N. W. rendered more conspicuous by the timber which garnished it's borders. in these plains and more particularly in the valley just below me immence herds of buffaloe are feeding. the missouri just above this hill makes a bend to the South where it lies a smoth even and unruffled sheet of water of nearly a mile in width bearing on it's watry bosome vast flocks of geese which feed at pleasure in the delightfull pasture on either border. the young geese are now completely feathered except the wings which both in the young and old are yet deficient. after feasting my eyes on this ravishing prospect and resting myself a few minutes I determined to procede as far as the river which I saw discharge itself on the West side of the Missouri convinced that it was the river which the Indians call *medicine river*[6] and which they informed us fell into the Missouri just above the falls I decended the hills and directed my course to the bend of the Missouri near which there was a herd of at least a thousand buffaloe; here I thought it would be well to kill a buffaloe and leave him untill my return from the river and if I then found that I had not time to get back to camp this evening to remain all night here there being a few sticks of drift wood lying along shore which would answer for my fire, and a few sattering cottonwood trees a few hundred yards below which would afford me at least a semblance of a shelter.   under this impression I scelected a fat buffaloe and shot him very well, through the lungs; while I was gazeing attentively on the poor anamal discharging blood in streams from his mouth and nostrils, expecting him to fall every instant, and having en-tirely forgotton to reload my rifle, a large white, or reather brown bear, had perceived and crept on me within 20 steps before I discovered him; in the first moment I drew up my gun to shoot, but at the same instant recolected that she was not loaded and that he was too near for me to hope to perform this opperation before he reached me, as he was then briskly advancing on me; it was an open level plain, not a bush within miles nor a tree within less than three hundred yards of me; the river bank was sloping and not more than three feet above the level of the water; in short there was no place by means of which I could conceal myself from this monster untill I could charge my rifle; in this situation I thought of retreating in a brisk walk as fast as he was advancing untill I could reach a tree about 300 yards below me, but I had no sooner terned myself about but he pitched at me, open mouthed and full speed, I ran about 80 yards and found he gained on me fast, I then run into the water   the idea struk me to get into the water to such debth that I could stand and he would be obliged to swim, and that I could in that situation defend myself with my espontoon; accordingly I ran haistily into the water about waist deep, and faced about and presented the point of my espontoon, at this instant he arrived at the edge of the water within about 20 feet of me; the moment I put myself in this attitude of defence he sudonly wheeled about as if frightened, declined the combat on such unequal grounds, and retreated with quite as great precipitation as he had just before pursued me.   as soon as I saw him run of[f] in that manner I returned to the shore and charged my gun, which I had still retained in my hand throughout this curious adventure. I saw him run through the level open plain about three miles, till he disappeared in the woods on medecine river; during the whole of this distance he ran at full speed, sometimes appearing to look behind him as if he expected pursuit. I now began to reflect on this novil occurrence and indeavoured to account for this sudden retreat of the bear. I at first thought that perhaps he had not smelt me before he arrived at the waters edge so near me, but I then reflected that he had pursued me for about 80 or 90 yards before I took the water and on examination saw the grownd toarn with his tallons immediately on the impression of my steps; and the cause of his allarm still remains with me misterious and unaccountable.— so it was and I feelt myself not a little gratifyed that he had declined the combat. My gun reloaded I felt confidence once more in my strength; and determined not to be thwarted in my design of visiting medicine river, but determined never again to suffer my peice to be longer empty than the time she necessarily required to charge her. I passed through the plain nearly in the direction which the bear had run to medecine river, found it a handsome stream, about 200 yds. wide with a gentle current, apparently deep, it's waters clear, and banks which were formed principally of darkbrown and blue clay[7] were about the hight of those of the Missouri or from 3 to 5 feet; yet they had not the appearance of ever being overflown, a circumstance, which I did not expect so immediately in the neighbourhood of the mountains, from whence I should have supposed, that sudden and immence torrants would issue at certain seasons of the year; but the reverse is absolutely the case. I am therefore compelled to beleive that the snowey mountains yeald their warters slowly, being partially effected every day by the influence of the sun only, and never suddonly melted down by haisty showers of rain.—

having examined Medecine river I now determined to return, having by my estimate about 12 miles to walk. I looked at my watch and found it was half after six P. M.— in returning through the level bottom of Medecine river and about 200 yards distant from the Missouri, my direction led me directly to an anamal that I at first supposed was a wolf;[8] but on nearer approach or about sixty paces distant I discovered that it was not, it's colour was a brownish yellow; it was standing near it's burrow, and when I approached it thus nearly, it couched itself down like a cat looking immediately at me as if it designed to spring on me. I took aim at it and fired, it instantly disappeared in it's burrow; I loaded my gun and exmined the place which was dusty and saw the track from which I am still further convinced that it was of the tiger kind.   whether I struck it or not I could not determine, but I am almost confident that I did; my gun is true and I had a steady rest by means of my espontoon, which I have found very serviceable to me in this way in the open plains. It now seemed to me that all the beasts of the neighbourhood had made a league to distroy me, or that some fortune was disposed to amuse herself at my expence, for I had not proceded more than three hundred yards from the burrow of this tyger cat, before three bull buffaloe, which wer feeding with a large herd about half a mile from me on my left, ⟨singled⟩ seperated from the herd and ran full speed towards me, I thought at least to give them some amusement and altered my direction to meet them; when they arrived within a hundred yards they mad a halt, took a good view of me and retreated with precipitation. I then continued my rout homewards passed the buffaloe which I had killed, but did not think it prudent to remain all night at this place which really from the succession of curious adventures wore the impression on my mind of inchantment; at sometimes for a moment I thought it might be a dream, but the prickley pears which pierced my feet very severely once in a while, particularly after it grew dark, convinced me that I was really awake, and that it was necessary to make the best of my way to camp.[9]   it was sometime after dark before I returned to the party; I found them extremely uneasy for my safety; they had formed a thousand conjectures, all of which equally forboding my death, which they had so far settled among them, that they had already agreed on the rout which each should take in the morning to surch for me. I felt myself much fortiegued, but eat a hearty supper and took a good night's rest.—   the weather being warm I had left my leather over shirt and had woarn only a yellow flannin one.

[Clark]   *June 14th Friday 1805*

    a fine morning, the Indian woman complaining all night & excessively bad this morning—   her case is Somewhat dangerous—   two men with the Tooth ake 2 with Tumers, & one man with a Tumor & Slight fever passed the Camp Capt. Lewis made the 1st night at which place he had left part of two bear their skins &c three men with Tumers went on shore and Stayed out all night one of them killed 2 buffalow, a part of which we made use of for brackfast, the Current excesevely rapid more So as we assend we find great difficuelty in getting the Perogue & Canoes up in Safety, Canoes take in water frequently, at 4 oClock this evening Jo: Fields returned from Capt. Lewis with a letter for me, Capt Lewis dates his letter from the Great falls of the Missouri, which Fields informs me is about 20 miles in advance & about 10 miles above the place I left the river the time I was up last week Capt. L. informs the [party?] that those falls; in part answer the discription given of them by the Indians, much higher the Eagles nest which they describe is there, from those Signs he is Convinced of this being the river the Indians call the Missouri, he intends examine-ing the river above untill my arrival at a point from which we can make a portage, which he is apprehensive will be at least 5 miles & both above & below there is Several Small pitches, & Swift troubled water we made only 10 miles to day and Camped on the Lard Side,[10] much hard Slate in the Clifts[11] & but a Small quantity of timber.

	miles	*Course & Distance June 14th*[12]
S. 35° W.	2	to a Small Island in the Lard bend passing Sundery bad places
S. 55° W.	1	to a tree on the Lard Side opsd. ⟨an Island⟩ a bluff passed a Island near Std. Side.
N. 70° W.	1	to the Lard point passing an Island
West	1	to a tree in the bend Stard. Side
South	¼	to a clift on the Lard. Side at a rapid
West	1	to the ⟨upper⟩ pt. ⟨of a Small Island in a⟩ on the Lard Side
S. 45° W.	¼	to the upper pt. of a Small Isld. ⟨in a bend⟩ in a Stard. bend opposit a large Island
S. 10° W.	1 ¼	to naked point on the Stard. Side
S. 70° W.	¼	to my old Camp of the 4th inst: on the Stard Side opsd. a large graveley Bar.

South	1 ½	the upper point of an Island [13]
S. 56° W.	½	on the Stard Side to a bluff
S. 60° W.	¼	to a wood on the Lard point & Campd.

miles 10 ¼

1. Crooked Falls still bears that name. *Atlas* maps 44, 54, 61; MRC map 77.

2. Rainbow Falls, Lewis and Clark's "Handsom Falls," now greatly altered by Rainbow Dam. *Atlas* maps 44, 54, 61; MRC map 77.

3. Colter Falls (now submerged), it does not appear on *Atlas* maps 42, 54 and 61. MRC map 77.

4. Black Eagle Falls, just below the present town of Black Eagle, Cascade County, Montana. The eagle's nest on the island below the falls, a distinguishing feature referred to by the Hidatsas in their directions to the captains, was still there in 1860. Wheeler, 1: 322–23; *Atlas* maps 42, 54, 61; MRC map 77.

5. Probably the Schuylkill River in Pennsylvania.

6. Today's Sun River, which meets the Missouri at the present city of Great Falls. *Atlas* maps 54, 61; MRC map 77.

7. The north bank of the Sun River is alluvium derived from dark-gray shales of the Blackleaf Formation. The south bank is composed of clay, silt, and sand deposited in Glacial Lake, Great Falls, during the glacial period.

8. Perhaps a wolverine, *Gulo luscus* (or *G. gulo*). Burroughs, 82–83; Hall, 2:1006–9; Jones et al., 297–98.

9. Evidently the same as the previous night's camp.

10. The campsite, in Chouteau County, Montana, is on the wrong side of the river on *Atlas* map 61. It was near the entrance of Black Coulee. *Atlas* maps 42, 54; MRC map 76; USGS map Fort Benton.

11. The "slate" is dark gray shale and siltstone of the Marias River Shale and Blackleaf Formation.

12. Also given on *Atlas* map 42, in Clark's hand.

13. Perhaps later Black Bluff Island, that has since disappeared. *Atlas* maps 42, 54, 61; MRC map 76.

[Lewis] *Saturday June 15th 1805.*

This morning the men again were sent to bring in some more meat which Drewyer had killed yesterday, and continued the opperation of drying it. I amused myself in fishing, and sleeping away the fortiegues of yesterday. I caught a number of very fine trout which I made Goodrich dry; goodrich also caught about two douzen and several small cat of a yellow colour which would weigh about 4 lbs.[1]   the tails was seperated with a deep angular nitch like that of the white cat of the missouri from which indeed they differed only in colour.   when I awoke from my sleep today I found a large rattlesnake coiled on the leaning trunk of a tree under the shade of which I had been lying at the distance of about ten feet from him. I killed the snake and found that he had 176 scuta on the abdomen and 17 half formed scuta on the tale; it was of the same kinde which I had frequently seen before; they do not differ in their colours from the rattle snake common to the middle attlantic states, but considerably in the form and figures of those colours. This evening after dark Joseph Fields returned and informed me that Capt Clark had arrived with the party at the foot of a rappid about 5 miles below which he did not think proper to ascend and would wait my arrival there.[2] I had discovered from my journey yesterday that a portage on this side of the river will be attended by much difficulty in consequence of several deep ravines which intersect the plains [*NB: Qu*] nearly at right angles with the river to a considerable distance, while the South side appears to be a delighfull smoth unbroken plain; the bearings of the river also make it pobable that the portage will be shorter on that side than on this.—   I directed Fields to return early in the morning to Capt. C. and request him to send up a party of men for the dryed meat which we had made. I finde a very heavy due on the grass about my camp every morning which no doubt procedes from the mist of the falls, as it takes place no where in the plains nor on the ⟨hills⟩ river except here.

[Clark]   *June the 15th Satturday 1805*

a fair morning and worm, we Set out at the usial time and proceeded on with great dificuelty as the river is more rapid   we can hear the falls this morning verry distinctly—   our Indian woman Sick & low Spirited   I gave her the bark & apply it exteranaly to her region which revived her much.   the curt. excessively rapid and dificuelt to assend great numbers of dangerous places, and the fatigue which we have to encounter is incretiatable   the men in the water from morning untill night hauling the Cord & boats walking on Sharp rocks and round Sliperery Stones which alternately cut their feet & throw them down, not with Standing all this dificuelty they go with great chearfulness, aded to those dificuelties the rattle Snakes inumerable & require great caution to prevent being bitten.— we passed a Small river on the Lard Side about 30 yards wide verry rapid which heads in the mountains to the S. E.[3] I Sent up this river 5 miles, it has Some timber in its bottoms and a fall of 15 feet at one place, above this river the bluffs are of red earth mixed with Stratums of black Stone, below this little [river], we pass a white clay which mixes with water like flour in every respect,[4] the Indian woman much wors this evening, She will not take any medison, her husband petetions to return &c., river more rapid   late in the evening we arrived at a rapid which appeared So bad that I did not think it prudent to attempt passing of it this evening as it was now late, we Saw great numbers of Gees Ducks, Crows Blackbirds &c Geese & Ducks with their young.   after Landing I detached Joseph Fields to Capt. Lewis to let him know where I was &c   river rises a little this evening   we could not get a Sufficency of wood for our use

	miles	Course & Distance June 15th[5]
South	1 ½	to a point on the Stard Side
S. 28° W.	2 ¼	to a rock resembling a tour [tower] in the Stard bend
S 10° E.	1 ¾	to the Stard. point passing a rapid
S 60° W.	¾	to a tree in the Std. bend rocks & rapds all the dist
South	¾	to some bushes on a Lard point passed a large Creek at ½ a mile on the Lard. Side which we called Shield's Creek[6]
S. 10° E.	1 ½	to the Stard point
S. 50° W.	1	to a point on the Lard. Side
South	1 ¼	to the Stard point opposit an Island opposit a Bluff.
S. 10° W.	1 ¼	to the point (a few trees) Lard. Side at a rapid, passed red bluffs & Camped on the Stard. Side
miles	12	
S 10 W	¾	to the foot of a rapid at which place we commed the portage, formed a Camp & unloaded on the Lard Side[7]
	12 ¾	

1. Probably the channel catfish, which the party had seen all along the river. It was probably Biddle who drew a red vertical line through the passage.

2. Clark's camp was in Cascade County, Montana, a little below and on the opposite side from the mouth of Belt Creek (the captains' Portage Creek), not far from the Chouteau County line. *Atlas* maps 42, 54, 61; MRC map 76.

3. Present Highwood Creek, in Chouteau County. Clark named it Shields River, suggesting that John Shields was the man sent up to explore it. Gass, Ordway, and Whitehouse call it Strawberry River or Creek. *Atlas* maps 42, 54, 61; MRC map 76.

4. The contact between dark siltstone and shale of the Blackleaf Formation and the reddish-brown sandstone and shale of the Kootenai Formation is just upstream of Highwood Creek. The white clay is probably a bentonite bed of the Blackleaf Formation.

5. Also given on *Atlas* map 42, in Clark's hand.

6. Lewis apparently added the words "which we called Shield's Creek."

7. This last course is not found on *Atlas* map 42. Instead, Clark has on the map five other undated courses, a total of two miles which may represent the foot exploration, after a short canoe trip of ¼ mile, on June 16, when he found the river impassable because of rapids.

[Lewis]   *Sunday June 16th 1805.*

J. Fields set out early on his return to the lower camp, at noon the men arrived and shortly after I set out with them to rejoin the party. we took with us the dryed meat consisting of about 600 lbs. and several douzen of dryed trout. about 2 P. M. I reached the camp found the Indian woman extreemly ill and much reduced by her indisposition.[1] this gave me some concern as well for the poor object herself, then with a young child in her arms, as from the consideration of her being our only dependence for a friendly negociation with the Snake Indians on whom we depend for horses to assist us in our portage from the Missouri to the columbia River. I now informed Capt. C. of my discoveries with rispect to the most proper side for our portage, and of it's great length, which I could not estimate at less than 16 miles. Capt. C. had already sent two men this morning to examine the country on the S. side of the river; he now passed over with the party to that side and fixed a camp about a mile blow the entrance of a Creek[2] where there was a sufficient quantity of wood for fuel, an article which can be obtained but in few places in this neighbourhood. after discharging the loads four of the canoes were sent back to me, which by means of strong ropes we hawled above the rappid and passed over to the south side from whence the water not being rappid we can readily convey them into the creek by means of which we hope to get them on the high plain with more ease. one of the small canoes was left below this rappid in order to pass and repass the river for the purpose of hunting as well as to procure the water of the Sulpher spring,[3] the virtues of which I now resolved to try on the Indian woman. this spring is situated about 200 yards from the Missouri on the N. E. side nearly opposite to the entrance of a large creek; it discharges itself into the Missouri over a precepice of rock about 25 feet, forming a pretty little [*erasure, perhaps "cactaract"*] the water is as transparent as possible strongly impregnated with sulpher, and I suspect Iron also, as the colour of the hills and bluffs in the neighbour- hood indicate the existence of that metal. the water to all appearance is precisely similar to that of Bowyer's Sulpher spring in Virginia.[4] Capt. Clark determined to set out in the morning to examine [*NB: the country*] and survey the portage, and discover the best rout. as the distance was too great to think of transporting the canoes and baggage on the men's shoulders, we scelected six men, and ordered them to look out some tim- ber this evening, and early in the morning to set about making a parsel of truck wheels in order to convey our canoes and baggage over the por- tage. we determined to leave the white perogue at this place, and sub- stitute the Iron boat, and also to make a further deposit of a part of our stores. in the evening the men who had been sent out to examine the country and made a very unfavourable report. they informed us that the creek just above us and two deep ravenes still higher up cut the plain between the river and mountain in such a manner, that in their opinions a portage for the canoes on this side was impracticable. g[o]od or bad we must make the portage. notwithstanding this report I am still convinced from the view I had of the country the day before yesterday that a good portage may be had on this side at least much better than on the other, and much nearer also. I found that two dozes of barks and opium which I had given her since my arrival had produced an alteration in her pulse for the better; they were now much fuller and more regular. I caused her to drink the mineral water altogether. wen I first came down I found that her pulse were scarcely perceptible, very quick frequently irregular and attended with strong nervous symptoms, that of the twitching of the fingers and leaders of the arm; now the pulse had become regular much fuller and a gentle perspiration had taken place; the nervous symptoms have also in a great measure abated, and she feels herself much freeer from pain. she complains principally of the lower region of the abdomen, I therefore continued the cataplasms of barks and laudnumn [5] which had been previously used by my friend Capt Clark. I beleive her disorder originated principally from an obstruction of the mensis in consequence of taking could.— I determined to remain at this camp in order to make some celestial observations, restore the sick woman, and have all matters in a state of readiness to commence the portage immediately on the return of Capt. Clark, who now furnished me with the dayly occurrences which had taken place with himself and party since our seperation which I here enter in his own words.— [6]

[Clark]   *June 16th of Sunday 1805*

Some rain last night   a cloudy morning wind hard from the S. W.   we Set out passed the rapid by double manning the Perogue & Canoes and halted at ¼ of a mile to examine the rapids above, which I found to be an Continued *Cascade* for as far as could be Seen which was about 2 miles, I walked up on the Lard Side as high as a large Creek,[7] which falls in on the Lard. Side one mile above & opposit a large Sulpher Spring which falls over the rocks on the Std. Side   the wind rored from the S. W. hard & Some rain, at about 2 oClock Capt Lewis joined me from the falls 5 miles distant, & infd. that the Lard Side was the best portage   I despatched 2 men this morning on the Lard. Side to examine the portage.—   the Indian woman verry bad, & will take no medisin what ever, untill her husband finding her out of her Senses, easyly provailed on her to take medison, if She dies it will be the fault of her husband as I am now convinced—.   we crossed the river after part of the day and formed a Camp from which we intended to make the first portage, Capt. Lewis stayed on the Std Side to direct the Canoes over the first riffle   4 of them passed this evening the others unloaded & part of the Perogue Loading taken out—   I deturmined to examine & Survey the Portage find a leavel rout if possible—   The 2 men despatched to examine the Portage gave an unfavourable account of the Countrey, reporting that the Creek & 2 deep reveens [8] cut the Prarie in such a manner between the river and mountain as to render a portage in their oppinion for the Canoes impossible—   we

Selected 6 men to make wheels & to draw the Canoes on as the distance was probably too far for to be caried on the mens Sholders

1. Chuinard believes Sacagawea may have suffered from chronic pelvic inflammatory disease, due to gonorrheal infection. Some of her symptoms, such as twitching of the fingers and arms, could have been due to loss of minerals resulting from the captains' bleeding her. Chuinard (OOMD), 287–89 and 289 n. 7; Cutright (LCPN), 160–61.

2. The "Lower Portage Camp" in Chouteau County, Montana, below the mouth of Belt Creek (Lewis and Clark's Portage Creek), the starting point for the month-long portage of the Great Falls. *Atlas* maps 42, 54, 61; MRC map 77.

3. Sulphur, or informally, Sacagawea, Springs is still to be found about three hundred yards from the Missouri, opposite the mouth of Belt Creek, in Cascade County, Montana. Appleman (LC), 317; *Atlas* maps 42, 61.

4. Unidentified, but there were a number of mineral springs in Virginia, operated by their owners as medicinal springs and spas. Jefferson, 34–36.

5. Poultices of Peruvian bark (*cinchona*) and laudanum (tincture of opium). Cutright (LCPN), 24, 63–64; Chuinard (OOMD), 156–57.

6. Here Lewis copies Clark's entries from Voorhis No. 1 covering the period of separation, June 11–16. Having only slight differences in wording, the material is not repeated.

7. Belt Creek, Lewis and Clark's Portage Creek, the boundary between Cascade and Chouteau counties. *Atlas* maps 54, 61; MRC map 77.

8. The second of these, which they called Willow Run, is now Box Elder Creek, in Cascade County. *Atlas* maps 54, 61; MRC map 77.

[Lewis]   *Monday June 17th 1805.*

Capt. Clark set out early this morning with five me[n][1] to examine the country and survey the river and portage as had been concerted last evening. I set six men at work to pepare four sets of truck wheels with couplings, toungs and bodies, that they might either be used without the bodies for transporting our canoes, or with them in transporting our baggage   I found that the Elk skins I had prepared for my boat were insufficient to compleat her, some of them having become dammaged by the weather and being frequently wet; to make up this deficiency I sent out two hunters this morning to hunt Elk; the ballance of the party I employed first in unloading the white perogue, which we intend leaving at this place, and bring the whole of our baggage together and arranging it in proper order near our camp.   this duty being compleated I employed them in taking five of the small canoes up the creek which we now call portage creek about

1¾ miles; here I had them taken out and lyed in the sun to dry. from this place ther is a gradual ascent to the top of the high plain to which we can now take them with ease; the bluffs of this creek below and those of the river above it's entrance are so steep that it would be almost impracticable to have gotten them on the plain. we found much difficulty in geting the canoes up this creek to the distance we were compelled to take them, in consequence of the rappids and rocks which obstruct the channel of the creek. one of the canoes overset and was very near injuring 2 men essencially. just above the canoes the creek has a perpendicular fall of 5 feet and the cliffts again become very steep and high. we were fortunate enough to find one cottonwood tree just below the entrance of portage creek that was large enough to make our carrage wheels about 22 Inches in diameter; fortunate I say because I do not beleive that we could find another of the same size perfectly sound within 20 miles of us. the cottonwood which we are obliged to employ in the other parts of the work is extreemly illy calculated for it being soft and brittle. we have made two axeltrees of the mast of the white peroge, which I hope will answer tolerably well tho' it is reather small. The Indian woman much better to-day, I have still continued the same course of medecine; she is free from pain clear of fever, her pulse regular, and eats as heartily as I am willing to permit her of broiled buffaloe well seasoned with pepper and salt and rich soope of the same meat; I think therefore that there is every rational hope of her recovery. saw a vast number of buffaloe feeding in every direction arround us in the plains, others coming down in large herds to water at the river; the fragments of many carcases of these poor anamals daily pass down the river, thus mangled I pesume in decending those immence cataracts above us. as the buffaloe generally go in large herds to water and the passages to the river about the falls are narrow and steep the hi[n]der part of the herd press those in front out of their debth and the water instally takes them over the cataracts where they are instantly crushed to death without the possibility of escaping. in this manner I have seen ten or a douzen disappear in a few minutes. their mangled carcases ly along the shores below the falls in considerable quantities and afford fine amusement for the bear wolves and birds of prey; this may be one reason and I think not a bad one either that the bear are so tenatious of their right of soil in this neighbourhood.

[Clark]   *June 17th Monday 1805*

a fine morning   wind as usial   Capt. Lewis with the party unloaded the Perogue & he determined to keep the party employed in getting the loading to the Creek about 1 mile over a low hill in my absence on the Portage.

I Set out with 5 men at 8 oClock, and proceeded on up the Creek Some distance to examine that & if possable assend that Suffcently high, that a Streight Cours to the mouth of Medison river would head the 2 ⟨hollo⟩ reveins, the Creek I found Confined rapid and Shallow [g]eneralley[2]

Monday 17th of June   passed through an open roleing Prarie, So as to head the two reveins   after heading two we Stand our Course So as to Strike the river below the great pitch on our Course to the river Crossed a Deep rivein near its mouth with Steep Clifts   this rivein had running water which was very fine, the river at this place is narrow & Confined in perpindicular clifts of 170 feet from the tops of those Clifts the Countrey rises with a Steep assent for about 250 feet more   we proceeded up the river passing a Sucession of rapids & Cascades to the Falls, which we had herd for Several miles makeing a dedly Sound, I beheld those Cateracts with astonishment   the whole of the water of this great river Confined in a Channel of 280 yards and pitching over a rock of 97 feet ¾ of an, from the foot of the falls arrises a Continued mist which is extended for 150 yds. down & to near the top of the Clifts on L Sd.   the river below is Confined a narrow Chanl. of 93 yards haveing a Small bottom of timber on the Stard Side which is definded by a rock, rangeing Cross wise the river a little below the Shoot, a Short distance below this Cataract a large rock divides the Stream, I in assendering the Clifts to take the hith of the fall was near Slipping into the water, at which place I must have been Sucked under in an instant, and with deficuelty and great risque I assended again, and decended the Clift lower down (but few places Can be descended to the river) and took the hight with as much accuricy as possible with a Spirit Leavels &c.   dined at a fine Spring 200 yards below the pitch near which place 4 Cotton willow trees grew.   on one of them I marked my name the date, and hight of the falls,— we then proceeded up on the river passing a Continued Cascade & rapid to a fall of 19 feet at 4 Small Islands, this fall is diaguanally across the river from the Lard Side, forming an angle of ¾ of the width from ⟨to⟩ the Lard. from which Side it pitches for ⅔ of that distance. on the Stard Side is a rapid decline— below this Shoot a Deep revein falls in in [which?] we Camped[3] for the night which was Cold (The mountains in every derection has Snow on Them) The plain to our left is leavel we Saw one Bear & inumerable numbers of Buffalow, I Saw 2 herds of those animals watering immediately above a considerable rapid, they decended by a narrow pass to the bottom Small, the rier forced those forwd into the water Some of which was taken down in an instant, and Seen no more[4] others made Shore with difficuelty, I beheld 40 or 50 of those Swimming at the Same time those animals in this way are lost and accounts for the number of buffalow carcases below the rapids

1. Including Alexander Willard, John Colter, and perhaps Joseph Field.

2. At this point Clark apparently inserted four extra sheets (eight pages) into Voorhis No. 1, on which he wrote a clean copy of the notes of the survey of the Great Falls portage and the falls themselves (six pages), with a two-page map of the area (see fig. 4, chapter 16). Evidently he still had more empty space than he needed and for some reason he carried a portion of his entry of June 20 to this spot. That material was actually copied from Lewis's entries of July 4 and 11, but he also included some reflections on his personal experience with the mysterious noise of which Lewis wrote in the copied passages (see June 20 below). Since the captains were separated from July 10 to 13, he could not have done this copying from Lewis until after the latter date. See Introduction, vol. 2.

3. Clark's camp was below Crooked Falls in Cascade County, Montana, north of present Malmstrom Air Force Base. *Atlas* maps 54, 61; MRC map 77.

4. Before the next sentence, at the top of a page of Voorhis No. 1, Clark has written, "No. 10." The meaning is unknown.

[Lewis]   *Tuesday June 18th 1805.*

This morning I employed all hands in drawing the perogue on shore in a thick bunch of willow bushes some little distance below our camp; fastened her securely, drove out the plugs of the gage holes of her bottom and covered her with bushes and driftwood to shelter her from the sun. I now scelected a place for a cash and set tree men at work to complete it, and employed all others except those about the waggons, in overhawling airing and repacking our indian goods ammunicion, provision and stores of every discription which required inspection. examined the frame of my Iron boat and found all the parts complete except one screw, which the ingenuity of Sheilds can readily replace, a resource which we have very frequent occasion for. about 12 O'Clk. the hunters returned; they had killed 10 deer but no Elk. I begin to fear that we shall have some difficulty in procuring skins for the boat. I wold prefer those of the Elk because I beleive them more durable and strong than those of the Buffaloe, and that they will not shrink so much in drying. we saw a herd of buffaloe come down to water at the sulpher spring this evening, I dispatched some hunters to kill some of them, and a man also for a cask of mineral water. the hunters soon killed two of them in fine order and returned with a good quantity of the flesh, having left the remainder in a situation that it will not spoil provided the wolves do not visit it. The waggons are completed this evening, and appear as if they would answer the purpose very well if the axetrees prove sufficiently strong. the wind blew violently this evening, as they frequently do in this open country where there is not a tree to brake or oppose their force. The Indian woman is recovering fast she set up the greater part of the day and walked out for the fist time since she arrived here; she eats hartily and is free from fever or pain. I continue same course of medecine and regimen except that I added one doze of 15 drops of the oil of vitriol[1] today about noon.

There is a species of goosberry which grows very common about here in open situations among the rocks on the sides of the clifts.[2] they are now ripe of a pale red colour, about the size of a common goosberry, and like it is an ovate pericarp of soft pulp invelloping a number of smal whitish coloured seeds; the pulp is a yelloish slimy muselaginous substance of a sweetish and pinelike tast, not agreeable to me. the surface of the berry is covered with a glutinous adhesive matter, and the frut altho' ripe retains it's withered corollar. this shrub seldom rises more than two feet high and is much branched, the leaves resemble those of the common goosberry only not so large; it has no thorns. the berry is supported by seperate peduncles or footstalks of half an inch in length. immence quantities of small grasshoppers of a brown colour in the plains,[3] they no doubt contribute much to keep the grass as low as we find it which is not generally more than three inches, the grass is a narrow leaf, soft, and affords a fine pasture for the Buffaloe.—[4]

[Clark] *June 18th Tuesday 1805*

we Set out early and arrived at the second great Cataract a[t] about 200 yds above the last of 19 feet pitch— this is one of the grandest views in nature and by far exceeds any thing I ever Saw, the Missouri falling over a Shelveing rock for 47 feet 8 Inches with a Cascade &c of 14 feet 7 Inches above the Shoot for a ¼ mile I decended the Clift below this Cateract with ease measured the hight of the purpendicular fall of 47 feet 8 Inches at which place the river is 473 yards wide as also the hight of the Cascade &c. a continuel mist quite across this fall* after which we proceeded on up the river a little more than a mile to the largest fountain or Spring I ever Saw,[5] and doubt if it is not the largest in America Known, this water boils up from under th rocks near the edge of the river and falls imediately into the river 8 feet and keeps its Colour for ½ a mile which is emencely Clear and of a bluish Cast, proceeded on up the river passed a Succession of rapids to the next great fall of 26 Ft. 5 I. river 580 yards wide this fall is not intirely perpdincular a Short bench gives a Curve to the water as it falls a butifull Small Island at the foot of this fall near the Center of the Channel Covered with trees, the Missouri at this fall is 36 yards wide, a Considerable mist rises at this fall ocasionally, from this pitch to the head of the rapids is one mile & has a fall of 20 feet, this is also a handsome Scenery a fall in an open leavel plain, after takeing the hight & measureing the river proceeded on, Saw a gange of Buffalow Swiming the river above the falls, Several of which was drawn in to the rapids and with dificuelty mad Shore half drowned, we killed one of those Cows & took a[s] much meat as we wished. emence herds of those animals in every direction, passed 2 groves in the Point just above the rapids & dined in one opposit the mouth of Medison River, which fails in on the Stard. Side and is 137 yards wide at its mouth the Missouri ⟨nearly one mile⟩ above is 800 yards wide, as the river [Missouri] appears to bear S Easterley I assended about 4 miles high to a Creek which appeared to head in South mountains[6] passed a Island of[7] [*blank*] and a little timber in an Easterly bend at 1 mile, passed Some timber in a point at 2 mile at or near the lower point of a large Island on which we Shot at a large white *bear*. passed a Small Island in the middle and one close on the Lard Shore at 3 miles behind the head of which we Camped.[8] those 3 Islands are all opposit, Soon after we Camped two ganges of Buffalow crossed one above & the other below we killed 7 of them & a calf and Saved as much of the best of the meat as we could this evening, one man A Willard going for a load of meat at 170 yards distance on an Island was attact by a white bear and verry near being Caught, prosued within 40 yards of Camp where I was with one man I collected 3 others of the party and prosued the bear (who had prosued my track from a buffalow I had killed on the Island at about 300 yards distance and chance to meet Willard) for fear of his attacking one man Colter at the lower point of the Island, before we had got down the bear had allarmed the man and prosued him into the water, at our approach he retreated, and we relieved the man in the water, I Saw the bear but the bushes was So thick that I could not Shoot him and it was nearly dark, the wind from the S W & Cool killed a beaver & an elk for their Skins this evening

1. Sulphuric acid, used as a tonic and astringent. Chuinard (OOMD), 291–92.

2. *Ribes cereum* Dougl. var. *inebrians* (Lindl.) C. L. Hitchc., squaw, or western red, currant. It is interesting that Lewis refers to this currant as a gooseberry. Gooseberries are commonly distinguished from currants by the presence of spines or prickles on the stem. See also July 25, 1805. Booth & Wright, 107; Barkley, 134. It was probably Biddle who drew a red vertical line through this passage about the "gooseberry" to nearly the end of the entry.

3. Lewis is probably seeing several varieties of grasshoppers which are in their nymphal stage, most likely *Ageneotetix deorum*.

4. The grass is probably blue grama, *Bouteloua gracilis* (HBK.) Lag., or possibly buffalograss, *Buchloe dactyloides* (Nutt.) Engelm. Fernald, 182, 184.

5. Giant Springs is now located in a park northeast of the city of Great Falls, in Cascade County, Montana. *Atlas* maps 42, 54, 61; MRC map 77. It has been said to discharge 388,800,000 gallons of water every twenty-four hours, but more recent measurements indicate 174–213,000,000 gallons a day. Appleman (LC), 316–17; *Montana Guide*, 156–57; information of Robert N. Bergantino, July 18, 1986. The asterisk in the preceding sentence cannot be explained.

6. Flattery Run on *Atlas* maps 54, 62; later Sand Coulee Creek. MRC map 77.

7. After this word, at the bottom of a page of Voorhis No. 1, Clark has written the words "No. 10." The meaning is unknown.

8. The "Upper Portage Camp," occupied until July 12, is about three-quarters of a mile north of Sand Coulee Creek. The "White Bear Islands" themselves have virtually disappeared, merging with the banks of the Missouri in Cascade County. Appleman (LC), 314; *Atlas* maps 42, 54, 61; MRC map 77.

[Lewis]   *Wednesday June 19th 1805.*

This morning I sent over several men for the meat which was killed yesterday, a few hours after they returned with it, the wolves had not discovered it. I also dispatched George Drewyer Reubin Fields and George Shannon on the North side of the Missouri with orders to proceed to the entrance of Medecine river and indeavour to kill some Elk in that neighbourhood.   as there is more timber on that river than the Missouri I expect that the Elk are more plenty. The cash completed today. The wind blew violently the greater part of the day.   the Indian woman was much better this morning   she walked out and gathered a considerable quantity of the white apples of which she eat so heartily in their raw state, together with a considerable quantity of dryed fish without my knowledge that she complained very much and her fever again returned. I rebuked Sharbono severely for suffering her to indulge herself with such food he being privy to it and having been previously told what she must only eat. I now gave her broken dozes of diluted nitre[1] untill it produced perspiration and at 10 P. M. 30 drops of laudnum which gave her a tolerable nights rest. I amused myself in fishing several hours today and caught a number of both species of the white fish,[2] but no trout nor Cat. I employed the men in making up our baggage in proper packages for transportation; and waxed the stoppers of my powder canesters anew.   had the frame of my Iron boat clensed of rust and well greased.   in the evening the men mended their mockersons and prepared themselves for the portage. After dark my dog barked very much and seemed extreemly uneasy which was unusual with him; I ordered the sergt. of the guard to reconniter with two men, thinking it possible that some Indians might be about to pay us a visit, or perhaps a white bear; he returned soon after & reported that he believed the dog had been baying a buffaloe bull which had attempted to swim the river just above our camp but had been beten down by the stream landed a little below our camp on the same side & run off.

Observed Meridian Altitude of ☉'s L. L. with Octant by the back observation   53° 15′ —″

Latitude deduced from this observation   47° 8′ 59.5″

[Clark]   *June 19th Wednesday 1805*

We went on the Island to hunt the White bear this morning but Could not find him, after plotting my Courses &c. I deturmined to dry the meat we killed and leave here, and proceed up the river as far as it bent to the S. E. and examine a Small Creek above our Camp, I Set out and found the Creek only Contained back water for 1 mile up, assend near the Missouri 3 miles to the bend, from which place it turnd. Westerly, from this bend I with 2 men went forward towards the Camp of the party to examine the best ground for the portage, the little Creek has verry extencive bottoms which Spread out into a varriety of leavl rich bottoms quite to the mountains to the East, between those bottoms is hills low and Stoney on this declivity where it is Steep. I returned to Camp late and deturmined that the best nearest and most eassy rout would be from the lower part of the 3rd or white bear Island, the wind all this day blew violently hard from the S W. off the Snowey mountains, Cool, in my last rout I lost a part of my notes which could not be found as the wind must have blown them to a great distance. Summer duck Setting[3]   great numbers of buffalow all about our Camp

1. Saltpetre, here used for fever. Chuinard (OOMD), 156.
2. See identifications at entry of June 11, 1805.
3. The wood duck, *Aix sponsa* [AOU, 144].

[Clark]   *[June 17–19, 1805]*[1]

Course from the Perogue & Distances &c

S. 9° E   286   poles to the mouth of the Creek   passed the first rapid at 80 poles of 4 feet fall one of 3 feet fall above the Creek   the Creek is 55 yards wide at its mouth.

S 35° E.	270	poles to a high hill in Prarie
S 29° W	48	poles to a pile of Stones on a Dividing ridge in a Direction the 1st rivein
S. 37° E	180	poles to a high part of the plain
S. 22° E	194	poles to 3 piles of Stones in the leavel plain leaving the Course of the Creek
S 31° W.	112	poles to a rock & pile in a leavele Pln.
S. 15° W	400	poles to a pile of Stones, passing the head of a rivein at 280 poles
S. 36° W.	80	poles to a pile of buffalow Dung passed the head of the 2d holl. at 2 poles

(To the river)

N. 70° W	700	poles to the river, at which place the river only 90 yards wide confined in Clifts, passed a Deep revein at 420 and one near its mouth of deep bluff banks at 644 poles— at the mouth of this last revein a rapid of 3 feet up the river
N 82° W.	340	poles to the Grand falls or Shoot at which place the Missouri is Confined within 280 yards and Pitches 87 feet ¾ of an inch a cascade for 200 yards above which has a fall of about 18 feet below 93 yds. a rapid of 6 feet fall
S 24° W.	90	poles, passed a rappid 2 feet fall
S. 19° W.	80	poles, passed a revein. Cascade
S. 11° W.	80	poles to a 2nd riffle of 4 feet fall
S. 31° W	520	poles opposit a rapid of 3 ½ feet fall and a Cascade of ½ a mile of 4 ½ feet
S. 52° W.	178	poles, through a hand Some Plain river bends to the right 2 feet Dist.
S. 40° W	970	poles to a fall & pitch of 19 feet passed a Deep revein near its mouth at which a rapid of 5 feet fall, & 10 feet
N. 84 W	102	poles to the 2d great falls or Pitch of *47 feet 8* Inches, a Small rock attached to a bench of 5 feet fall on the Stard Side at this fall Re: th 479 yards wide river as far Can be Seen down 1 ½ miles N. 40 E. Passed a desent of 7f the
N 86° W.	135	poles passed a fall & Cascade of 14 : ½ the fall about 6 feet pitch

S 49° W.	58	poles rapid water desent of 2 feet
S 78° W.	156	poles to a very large & fine fontain of water at a rapid, boils up and throws out an emense Current & quantity of water decline 3 feet.
S 25° W.	124	poles on the river. Several riffles in the *river dest. 4 feet*
S. 35° W.	240	poles passed a rock & 3 trees on bank the fall from the last rappid to this place must be 8 feet
S 58° W.	88	poles up the river dcint 1 foot 6 In
S. 40° W	80	poles to the upper Pitch of 26 Feet 5 In. and Cascade & one Pitch of 5 feet to the head of the rapid is 23 feet about 26.5 ⟨Inches⟩ in all 49 feet 5 Inches fall from the last fall of 14.9 Inc feet to this a Continued rapid & cascade of about 19 feet fall river 580 yds wide
S 81° W.	320	poles to the head of the rapids.
S 55° W	130	poles along the river
S 36° W	278	poles to a tree on the edge of the water. passed a grove at 120 poles. river ⟨about a mile⟩ 1440 yds wide wide
S 6° W.	140	poles to a Small grove at a rapid on the Lard. Side
S. 64° E	78	poles to the lower part a timber in a Deep bend
S. 14° E	90	poles to a tree in the bend opposite to Some low timber
S. 17 W.	160	poles to opposit the mouth of Medison river on the Std. Side this river is 137 yards wide
S. 1° W.	88	poles opsd. the lower point of a Sand Island
S. 45° E	170	poles to Some low timber near Som old lodges
S. 13° E.	381	poles to the lower point of an Island
N, 88° E	70	poles to opsd. a 2d Island
N. 71° E,	120	poles to a pt. opposed a 3rd Island, narrow Chnl.
S. 25° E	664	poles to the river at the ⟨most eastern S Easterly⟩
Deduct	490	bend passed our Camp in Some woods opsd. the heads of the 3 Islands at 174 poles and a Small Creck at 284 poles, this Creck has back water wh it about ¾ of a mile and has a wide butifull valey to the S. Mountain
	5239	
	1320	add to the Distance below the Portg River—
	320⎮6559	[or] Miles 20½

☞ the total descent of the water from the head of the rappids to the entrance of portage Creck is 352 feet 2¾ Inches²

$$\frac{8 \qquad\qquad 2\,¾}{360 \quad 2\,¾}$$

S 70 E 160 poles to the top of a high hill expirt near the most extreem S Esterly bend of the river.

From the top of this hill the Missouri bears S 85° W. about 10 ms.   the gap of the Mountains is S. 25° W. The highest part of the South Mountains is N 84 E

from the mouth of Portage Creek up the Missouri is S 10 W 280 poles & has a fall over repeeted rapids of about 10 feet

Then S 10° E ½ a mile & a fall of 6 feet

South ¾ miles & has a fall of 18 feet

S. 81° W. 1¼ miles   passed a run   the fall of about 13 feet in repeeted rapids.

S. 15° W. ½ a mile repeeted rapids of about 5 feet fall.

S 75° W ¼ of a mile to a mouth of the Deep Ravein [*X: 1 foot fall*] from the Commincement of this Course to the Great fall is 8 feet   the river is narrow Confined with high Bluffs.

Courses of the Missouri from the commencement of the portage below Portage River to the Most South Eastwardly bend above the Medicine River, noting the particular Cataracts Cascades and the hight they fall as Measured, together with an estimate of the decline of the water in rapids &c. &c. Sept. [June] 17 & 18th 1805.   (S E. Side)³

			feet
S 9° E	286	poles to the enterence of portage river 55 yds. wide at 80 poles a rapid of 4 feet, the Computed decent of the water above is 4 feet together makes—	8
S 10° W.	280	Po: from the enterances of portage River up the Lard. Side of the Missouri. the Computed distance the water in this distance is about 10 feet	10

S 10° E	160	Po. do do do do do Decent of	6
South	240	Po. do do do do Computed decent of	18
S. 81° W.	400	Po. do do do do Computed decent of passing a deep Small rivene in this Course	13
S. 15° W.	160	Poles the decent of the water within which distance is about five feet river inclosed in rocks	5
S 75° W.	80	Poles to the enterance of a Steep rivene at which there is a fall of 3 feet which aded to the probably decent of the water in that distance 2 feet makes	5
N. 82° W.	340	Poles to the Grand Cataract of *87 feet ¾ of an inch*. Computed decent of water in the distance 6 feet. The river at this Cataract 280 yards wide and just below 93 yards wide total	93 ¾
S 24° W.	90	Poles passing a fall of 2 feet purpindicular which added to the estimated decent of 13 feet within the first 200 yds. next above the Cataract makes a decent in this distance rather more than	15
S 19° W.	80	Poles passing a rivene and Cascade decent about	3
S 11° W.	80	Poles passing a Cascade of 4 feet, which together with the probable decent of the water 2 feet is	6
S 31° W	320	Poles opposit a rapid of 3 feet 6 inch fall which added to the probably decent of the water within this distance of 5 feet 6 inches is river inclosed in rocks of a dark colour	9
S 52° W.	178	Poles through a handsom leavil plain the river makeing a bend to the right decent of the water probably about three feet	3
S 40° W.	970	Poles to a fall of 19 feet, below which there is a deep rivene at the enterance of with a fall of 5 feet which added to the probable decent in this distance of 10 feet makes	34

N 84° W.	102	Poles to the 2nd. Great Cataract of *47 feet 8 inches* the river at this Cataract is *473* yards wide and confined Clifts of rocks	47.8
N. 86° W.	135	Poles passing a fall of 6 feet 7 inches which added to the probable decent of the water above the pitch of 47 feet 8 inches makes a fall of	14.7
S 49° W.	58	Poles along the river water verry rapid a probable decline of 2 feet	2
S 78° W.	156	Poles to a large fountain near the river. probable decent of the water in this distance may be 3 feet	3
S 25° W.	124	Poles on the river passing Several Small rapids and Swift water the probable decent is this distans four feet	4
S. 35° W	240	Poles passing a rock in the river on three trees on the Lard. Bank the fall of the water within this distance at least 8 feet	8
S 58° W.	88	Poles up the river, the probable decent in this distance Eighteen inches	1.6
S 40°	80	Poles to the upper pitch of *26 feet 5 inches* river is here *580* yards wide. to this fall add the probable decent in this distance of *2 feet,* also [o]ne pitch above of *5 feet* and the decent from the head of the rapids of *18 feet* exclusive of the 5 feet pitch makeing in all *38 feet 5 inches* fall	51.5

4747 poles = 14 miles ¾ and 27 poles   Total Falls 360.2 ¾

S 81° W.	320	Poles to the head of the rapids; passed a rivene
S. 55° W.	130	Poles along the river. low banks.
S 36 W.	278	Poles to a tree on the edge of the water passd. a grove at 120 poles opposit to which the river is 1400 yards wide—
S 6° W.	140	Poles to a Small grove at a rapid on Ld Side.
S 64° E.	78	Poles to the lower point of a timber in a deep bend.—

S 14° E.	90	Poles to a tree in the bend opposit to Some low timber.—
S 17° W.	160	Poles to the river opposit to the enterance of Medicine River which is 137 yards wide, and the Missouri just above it is 300 yards wide—
S 1° W.	88	Poles opposit to the lower point of a Small Island.—
S. 45° E	170	Poles to Some low timber near Some old Lodges.—
S. 13° E.	380	Poles to the river opposit the lower poiont of *white Bear Island*.—
N. 88° E.	70	Poles opposit to the lower point of a Second Island which is Small.—
N. 71° E	120	Poles to a rockey hill Side opposit to a third Island which is Seperated from the Lard. Shore by a very narrow Chanel.
S 25° E	664	Poles to a bend of the river. passing the upper points of the 1st & 3rd Island (at our Camp) at 144 Poles, and flattery run at 284 further river wide Still low banks.—
S 70° E.	160	Poles to the top of a high hill near the moste extreme S Easterly bend of the river— from this point the Missouri bears S 85° W. for about 10 miles. the gap of the Mtn. where the Missouri enters bears S. 25° W. [*blank*] miles and the Penical of the South Mtn. bears N 84° E—

☞ from the Survey and estimate it results, that the Missouri experiences a decent of *360 feet 2 inches and ¾* in the distance of [*blank*] *Miles and* [*blank*] *Poles*—[4]

Portage No. 1[5]

The course from the White Bear Islands above the portage N. 42° E 4 miles leaveing the riveens of flattery run to the right.   thence a course to the South Extremity of a ridge North of the South mountains for 8 miles & a half passing three riveens, the 2d is willow run. 11 miles from the Islands. Thence a course to the highest pinical of the North Mountain, leaveing the riveens of Portage or red Creek to the right, & the riveens of the river to the left to the mouth of Portage Creek 4 miles & a half, to the perogue which is on the river North Side & nearly opposit the place we buried Sundery articles is 1 mile down the river, The Swivel we hid under the rocks in a clift near the river a little above our lower camp

Course & Distance from White Bear Islands to the mouth of Portage Creek

N 42° E	4	miles to a ellevated part of the Plain
N 66° E	3	miles passed the head of a Drean
N 45° E	4	miles passed the head of a Drean
N. 18 E.	4	miles passed the head of a Drean
N. 10° W.	2	miles to the mouth of Portage Creek
N. 9 W.	¾ & 46 P.	to the perogue on South side of the R.[6]
	17 ¾ & 46 P.	Portage through an open butifull plain

1. Here Clark has two sets of survey notes for the Great Falls. They differ sufficiently to justify printing both here under the date given for the first set, July 17–19, 1805. Someone has crossed through the first and rougher set of notes. Because the clearer set of notes and other material is placed in the midst of this first set, they have been slightly rearranged to preserve the integrity of each.

2. This paragraph appears to be in Lewis's hand.

3. Clark wrote this set of notes on four sheets (eight pages) he inserted in Voorhis No. 1 in the midst of the set of survey notes mentioned in the note above. This second set is much neater than the first and differs considerably from it, so both are printed.

4. This paragraph is at the top of the map of the Great Falls area (see fig. 4, chapter 16) together with an astronomical observation dated June 20, 1805, which is placed by date.

5. This note on the Great Falls portage appears at the end of Voorhis No. 1, and is here placed with other portage survey material.

6. This entire line and the total figures below appear to be in Lewis's hand.

[Lewis]   *Thursday June 20th 1805.*

This morning we had but little to do; waiting the return of Capt. Clark; I am apprehensive from his stay that the portage is longer than we had calculated on. I sent out 4 hunters this morning on the opposite side of the river to kill buffaloe; the country being more broken on that side and cut with ravenes they can get within shoot of the buffaloe with more ease and certainty than on this side of the river. my object is if possible while we have now but little to do, to lay in a large stock of dryed meat at this end of the portage to subsist the party while engaged in the transportation of our baggage &c, to the end, that they may not be taken from this duty when once commenced in order to surch for the necessary subsistence. The Indian woman is qute free from pain and fever this morning and appears to be in a fair way for recovery, she has been walking about and fishing. In the evening 2 of the hunters returned and informed me that they had killed eleven buffaloe eight of which were in very fine order, I sent off all hands immediately to bring in the meat   they soon returned with about half of the best meat leaving three men to remain all night in order to secure the ballance.   the buffaloe are in immence numbers, they have been constantly coming down in large herds to water opposite to us for some hours sometimes two or three herds wartering at the same instant and scarcely disappear before others supply their places.   they appear to make great use of the mineral water, whether this be owing to it's being more convenient to them than the river or that they actually prefer it I am at a loss to determine for they do not use it invaryably, but sometimes pass at no great distance from it and water at the river.   brackish water or that of a dark colour impregnated with mineral salts such as I have frequently mentioned on the Missouri is found in small quantities in some of the steep ravenes on the N. side of the river opposite to us and the falls. Capt. Clark and party returned late this evening when he gave me the following relation of his rout and the occurrences which had taken place with them since their departure.[1]

Capt. Clark now furnished me with the field notes of the survey which he had made of the Missouri and it's Cataracts cascades &c. from the entrance of portage Creek to the South Eastwardly bend of the Missouri above the White bear Islands, which are as follow.[2]

June 20th 1805   At our camp below the entrance of portage creek observed Meridian Altd. of ☉'s L. L. with Octant by the back Observtn. 53° 10′

Latitude deduced from this observation   47° 7′ 10.3″

[Clark]   *June 20th Thursday 1805*

a Cloudy morning, a hard wind all night and this morning, I direct Stakes to be Cut to Stick up in the prarie to Show the way for the party to transport the baggage &c. &c.   we Set out early on the portage, Soon after we Set out it began to rain and continued a Short time   we proceeded on thro' a tolerable leavel plain, and found the hollow of a Deep rivein to obstruct our rout as it Could not be passed with Canos & baggage for Some distance above the place we Struck it   I examined it for Some time and finding it late deturmined to Strike the river & take its Course & distance to Camp which I accordingly did   the wind hard from the S. W.   a fair after noon, the river on both Sides Cut with raveins Some of which is passes thro Steep Clifts into the river, the Countrey above the falls & up the Medison river is leavel, with low banks, a chain of mountains to the west Some part of which particuler those to the N W. & S W are Covered with Snow and appear verry high— I Saw a rattle Snake in an open plain 2 miles from any Creek or wood. When I arrived at Camp found all well with great quantites of meet, the Canoes Capt. Lewis had Carried up the Creek 1¾ ⟨of an⟩ mile to a good place to assend the band & taken up. Not haveing Seen[3] the Snake Indians or knowing in fact whither to Calculate on their friendship or hostillity, we have Conceived our party Sufficiently Small, and therefore have Concluded not to dispatch a Canoe with a part of our men to St. Louis as we have intended early in the Spring.   we fear also that Such a measure might also discourage those who would in Such Case remain, and migh possibly hazard the fate of the expedition.   we have never hinted to any one of the party that we had Such a Scheem in contemplation, and all appear perfectly to have made up their minds, to Succeed in the expedition or perish in the attempt.   we all believe that we are about to enter on the most perilous and dificuelt part of our Voyage, yet I See no one repineing; all appear ready to meet those dificuelties which await us with resolution and becomeing fortitude.

We had a heavy dew this morning.   the Clouds near those mountains rise Suddonly and discharge their Contents partially on the neighbouring Plains; the Same Cloud discharge hail alone in one part, hail and rain in another and rain only in a third all within the Space of a fiew Miles; and on the Mountains to the South & S. E. of us Sometimes Snow.   at present there is no Snow on those mountains; that which covered them a fiew days ago has all disappeared.   the Mountains to the N. W. and West of us are Still entirely Covered are white and glitter with the reflection of the Sun.

I do not believe that the Clouds that pervale at this Season of the year reach the Summits of those lofty mountains; and if they do the probability is that they deposit Snow only for there has been no proceptable diminution of the Snow which they Contain Since we first Saw them. I have thought it probable that these mountains might have derived their appellation of *Shineing Mountains,* from their glittering appearance when the Sun Shines in certain directions on the Snow which Cover them.

Dureing the time of my being on the Plains and above the falls I as also all my party repeatedly heard a nois which proceeded from a Direction a little to the N. of West, as loud and resembling precisely the discharge of a piece of ordinance of 6 pounds at the distance of 5 or six miles.[4] I was informed of it Several times by the men J. Fields particularly before I paid any attention to it, thinking it was thunder most probably which they had mistaken. at length walking in the plains yesterday near the most extreem S. E. bend of the River above the falls I heard this *nois* very distinctly, it was perfectly calm clear and not a Cloud to be Seen, I halted and listened attentively about two hour dureing which time I heard two other discharges, and took the direction of the Sound with my pocket Compass which was as nearly West from me as l could estimate from the Sound. I have no doubt but if I had leasure I could find from whence it issued. I have thought it probable that it might be caused by running water in Some of the caverns of those emence mountains, on the principal of the blowing caverns;[5] but in Such case the Sounds would be periodical and regular, which is not the Case with this, being Sometimes heard once only and at other times Several discharges in quick Succession. it is heard also at different times of the day and night. I am at a great loss to account for this Phenomenon. I well recollect hereing the Minitarees Say that those Rocky Mountains make a great noise, but they could not tell me the Cause, neither Could they inform me of any remarkable substance or situation in these mountains which would autherise a conjecture of a probable cause of this noise—. it is probable that the large river just above those Great falls which heads in the derection of the noise has taken it's name *Medicine River* from this unaccountable rumbling Sound, which like all unacountable thing with the Indians of the Missouri is Called Medicine.

The Ricaras inform us of the black mountains making a Simalar noise &c. &c. and maney other wonderfull tales of those Rocky mountains and those great falls.

June 20th[6]

at our Camp below the enterance of Portage River observed Meridian altitude of ⊙s L. L. with Octant by the back observation   53° 10′ 0″
Latitude deduced from the observation 47° 7′ 10″ ³⁄₁₀

1. Lewis gives Clark's narrative of his survey. It is not repeated here being a copy of the material from Voorhis No. 1.

2. Lewis repeats Clark's survey as found in Voorhis No. 1 with only slight variations; it is not included here.

3. Here Clark writes "Continues 10 pages back," a reference to the material written in the midst of the entry of June 17, 1805. The material is dated June 20 but is copied in fact from Lewis's entries of July 4 and 11. See further explanation at June 17.

4. This description largely follows that of Lewis for July 4, 1805. Apparently the captains never did find an explanation for the phenomenon, which is still heard today in the region. Biddle later suggested to Clark that the sound was that of an avalanche. A "piece of ordinance of 6 pounds" would be a cannon firing six-pound iron balls. Clark to Biddle, December 20, 1810, Jackson (LLC), 2:565; Wheeler, 1:337–38; Willard, 13.

5. The Blowing Cave, in Bath County, Virginia, constantly emitted a strong current of air. Jefferson, 24; *Virginia Guide*, 512.

6. This observation appears with Clark's Great Falls survey notes dated June 17–19, 1805. It is placed by its own date.

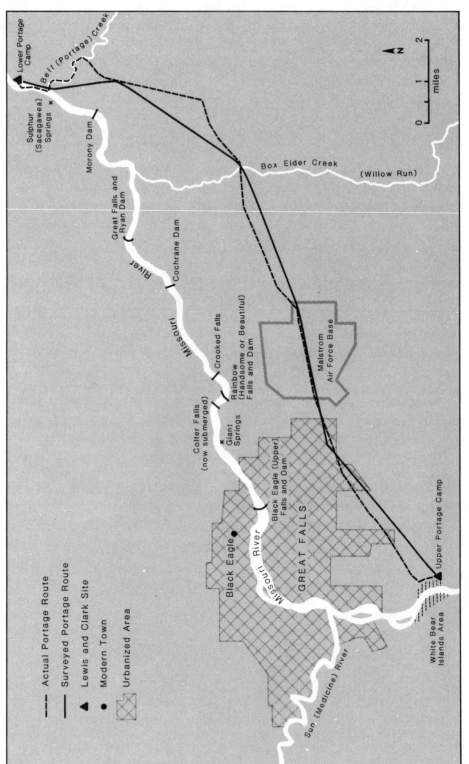

3. Portage and Falls of the Missouri River

Chapter Sixteen

Portaging the Great Falls

June 21–July 14, 1805

[Lewis]   *Friday June 21st 1805.*

This morning I employed the greater part of the men in transporting a part of the bagage over portage creek to the top of the high plain about three miles in advance on the portage. I also had one canoe carryed on truck wheles to the same place and put the baggage in it, in order to make an early start in the morning, as the rout of our portage is not yet entirely settled, and it would be inconvenient to remain in the open plain all night at a distance from water, which would probably be the case if we did not set out early as the latter part of the rout is destitute of water for about 8 miles— having determined to go to the upper part of the portage tomorrow; in order to prepare my boat[1] and receive and take care of the stores as they were transported, I caused the Iron frame of the boat and the necessary tools my private baggage and Instruments to be taken as a part of this load, also the baggage of Joseph Fields, Sergt. Gass and John sheilds, whom I had scelected to assist me in constructing the leather boat. Th[r]ee men were employed today in shaving the Elk skins which had ben collected for the boat. the ballance of the party were employed in cuting the meat we had killed yesterday into thin fletches and drying it, and in bring in the ballance of what had been left over the river with three men last evening. I readily preceive several difficulties in preparing the leather boat which are the want of convenient and proper timber; bark, skins, and above all that of pitch to pay her seams, a deficiency that I really know not how to surmount unless it be by means of tallow and pounded charcoal which mixture has answered a very good purpose on our wooden canoes heretofore. I have seen for the first time on the Missouri at these falls, a species of fishing ducks[2] with white wings, brown and white body and the head and part of the neck adjoining of a brick red, and the beak narrow; which I take to be the same common to James river, the Potomac and Susquehanna.   immence numbers of buffaloe comeing to water at the river as usual.   the men who remained over the river last night killed several mule deer, and Willard who was with me killed a young Elk. The wind blew violently all day. The growth of the neighbourhood what little there is consists of the broad and narrow leafed cottonwood, box alder, the large or sweet willow, the narrow and broad leafed willow.[3]   the sweet willow has not been common to the Missouri below this or the entrance of Maria's river; here attains to the same size and in appearance much the same as in the Atlantic States.   the undergrowth consists of rosebushes, goosberry and current bushes, honeysuckle small, and the red wood, the inner bark of which the engages are fond of smoking mixed with tobacco.—

[Clark]   *June 21st Friday 1805*

a fine morning wind from the S W. off the mountains and hard, Capt Lewis with the men except a few take a part of the baggage & a Canoe up the Hill 3 mile in advance, Several men employed in Shaveing & Graneing Elk hides for the Iron boat as it is called—   3 men were Sent up the Medison river yesterday to kill Elk for the Skins for the boat, I fear that we Shall be put to Some dificuelty in precureing Elk Skins Sufficent—, Cloudy afternoon, we dry meat for the men to eat on their return from the upper part of the portage   Capt Lewis determine to proceed to the upper part of the Portage tomorrow & with 3 men proced to fix the Iron boat with Skins &c. &c.

1. Lewis's iron-frame boat; see below, July 9, 1805.
2. Either the female red-breasted merganser, *Mergus serrator* [AOU, 130], or the female

common merganser, *M. merganser* [AOU, 129]. Holmgren, 29; Burroughs, 189. It was probably Biddle who drew a red vertical line through this passage about the fishing ducks.

3. Lewis notices three different willow species here. The peach-leaved willow is the only large (or Lewis's "sweet") willow known from the area. Lewis's notation of size and habitat from the Atlantic states indicates that he may have been confusing this western tree willow with the eastern black willow, *Salix nigra* Marsh., which extends westward only to eastern Nebraska, along the Missouri River. The broad-leaved willow frequently referred to along the lower and upper Missouri, may be *Salix rigida* Muhl. var. *rigida*, yellow, or diamond, willow. The narrow-leaved willow is the sandbar, or coyote, willow. Booth & Wright 25–28; Barkley 102–5; Little, 189-W, 190-E. It was probably Biddle who drew a red vertical line through the last part of this passage, beginning with "to the Missouri."

[Lewis]   *Saturday June 22cd 1805.*

This morning early Capt Clark and myself with all the party except Sergt. Ordway Sharbono, Goodrich, york and the Indian woman, set out to pass the portage with the canoe and baggage to the Whitebear Islands, where we intend that this portage shall end. Capt. Clarke piloted us through the plains. about noon we reached a little stream about 8 miles on the portage where we halted and dined;[1] we were obliged here to renew both axeltrees and the tongues and howns[2] of one set of wheels which took us no more than 2 hours. these parts of our carriage had been made of cottonwood and one axetree of an old mast, all of which proved deficient and had broken down several times before we reached this place we have now renewed them with the sweet willow and hope that they will answer better. after dark we had reached within half a mile of our intended camp when the tongues gave way and we were obliged to leave the canoe, each man took as much of the baggage as he could carry on his back and proceeded to the river where we formed our encampment much fortiegued. the prickly pears were extreemly troublesome to us sticking our feet through our mockersons. Saw a great number of buffaloe in the plains, also immence quantities of little birds and the large brown curloo;[3] the latter is now seting; it lays it's eggs, which are of a p[a]le blue with black specks, on the ground without any preperation of a nest. there is a kind of larke here that much resembles the bird called the oldfield lark with a yellow brest and a black spot on the croop;[4] tho' this differs from ours in the form of the tail which is pointed being formed of feathers of unequal length; the beak is somewhat longer and more curved and the note differs considerably; however in size, action, and colours there is no perceptable difference; or at least none that strikes my eye.   after reaching our camp[5] we kindled our fires and examined the meat which Capt. Clark had left, but found only a small proportion of it, the wolves had taken the greater part.   we eat our suppers and soon retired to rest.

[Clark]   *June 22nd Satturday 1805*

a fine morning, Capt Lewis my Self and all the party except a Sergeant Ordway Guterich and the Interpreter and his wife *Sar car gah we â* (who are left at Camp to take Care of the baggage left) across the portage with one Canoe on truck wheels and loaded with a part of our Baggage   I piloted thro the plains to the Camp I [made] at which place I intended the portage to end which is 3 miles above the Medesin River   we had great dificuelty in getting on as the axeltree broke Several times, and the Cuppling tongus of the wheels which was of Cotton & willow, the only wood except Boxelder & [*blank*] that grow in this quarter, we got within half a mile of our intended Camp much fatigued at dark, our tongus broke & we took a load to the river on the mens back, where we found a number of wolves which had distroyed a great part of our meat which I had left at that place when I was up day before yesterday   we Soon went to Sleep & Slept Sound   wind from the [*blank*]   we deturmine to employ every man Cooks & all on the portage after to day

1. Box Elder Creek.

2. Hounds, wooden bars connecting the fore-carriage with the splinter-bar or shaft. Criswell, 49.

3. The long-billed curlew (see above, April 17, 1805), but the eggs are either those of another bird or are poorly described. Burroughs, 226.

4. The western meadowlark, then unknown to science; the "oldfield lark" is the eastern meadowlark, *Sturnella magna* [AOU, 501], with which Lewis was already familiar. Holmgren, 31; Cutright (LCPN), 166–67.

5. The upper portage camp.

[Lewis]   *Sunday June 23rd 1805.*

This morning early I scelected a place for the purpose of constructing my boat near the water under some shady willows. Capt Clark had the

Canoe and baggage brought up, after which we breakfasted and nearly consumed the meat which he had left her[e]. he now set out on his return with the party. I employed the three men with me in the forenoon clearing away the brush and forming our camp, and puting the frame of the boat together. this being done I sent Shields and Gass to look out for the necessary timber, and with J. Fields decended the river in the canoe to the mouth of Medicine river in surch of the hunters whom I had dispatched thither on the 19th inst. and from whom we had not heard a sentence. I entered the mouth of medicine river and ascended it about half a mile when we landed and walked up the Stard. side. frequently hooping as we went on in order to find the hunters; at length after ascending the river about five miles we found Shannon who had passed the Medecine river & fixed his camp on the Lard. side, where he had killed seven deer and several buffaloe and dryed about 600 lbs. of buffaloe meat; but had killed no Elk. Shannon could give me no further account of R. Fields and Drewyer than that he had left them about noon on the 19th at the great falls and had come on the mouth of Medicine river to hunt Elk as he had been directed, and never had seen them since. the evening being now far spent I thought it better to pass the Medicine river and remain all night at Shannon's camp; I passed the river on a raft which we soon constructed for the purpose. the river is here about 80 yds. wide, is deep and but a moderate current. the banks low as those of the Missouri above the falls yet never appear to overflow. as it will give a better view of the transactions of the party, I shall on each day give the occurrences of both camps during our seperation as I afterwards learnt those of the lower camp from Capt. Clark. on his return today he cut of several angles of the rout by which we came yesterday, shortened the portage considerably, measured it and set up stakes throughout as guides to marke the rout. he returned this evening to the lower camp in sufficient time to take up two of the canoes from portage creek to the top of the plain about a mile in advance. this evening the men repaired their mockersons, and put on double souls to protect their feet from the prickley pears. during the late rains the buffaloe have troden up the praire very much, which having now become dry the sharp points of earth as hard as frozen ground stand up in such abundance that there is no avoiding them. this is particulary severe on the feet of the men who have not only their own wight to bear in treading on those hacklelike points but have also the addition of the burthen which they draw and which in fact is as much as they can possibly move with. they are obliged to halt and rest frequently for a few minutes, at every halt these poor fellows tumble down and are so much fortiegued that many of them are asleep in an instant; in short their fatiegues are incredible; some are limping from the soreness of their feet, others faint and unable to stand for a few minutes, with heat and fatiegue, yet no one complains, all go with cheerfullness. in evening Reubin Fields returned to the lower camp and informed Capt. Clark of the absence of Shannon, with rispect to whome they were extreemly uneasy. Fields and Drewyer had killed several buffaloe at the bend of the missouri above the falls and had dryed a considerable quantity of meat; they had also killed several deer but no Elk.—

[Clark]   *June 23rd Sunday 1805*

a Cloudy morning wind from the S. E, after getting the Canoe to Camp & the articles left in the plains we eate brackfast of the remaining meat found in Camp & I with the party the truck wheels & poles to Stick up in the prarie as a guide, Set out on our return, we proceeded on, & measured the Way which I Streightened considerably from that I went on yesterday, and arrived at our lower camp in Suffcent time to take up 2 Canoes on the top of the hill from the Creek, found all Safe at Camp the men mended their mockersons with double Soles to Save their feet from the prickley pear, (which abounds in the Praries,) and the hard ground which in Some & maney places So hard as to hurt the feet verry much, the emence number of Buffalow after the last rain has trod the flat places in Such a manner as to leave it uneaven, and that has tried and is wors than frozen ground, added to those obstructions, the men has to haul with all their Strength wate & art, maney times every man ⟨an⟩ all catching the grass & knobes & Stones with their hands to give them more force in drawing on the Canoes & Loads, and notwithstanding the Coolness of the air in high presperation and every halt, those not employed in reparing the Couse; are asleep in a moment, maney limping from the Soreness of their feet Some become fant for a fiew moments, but no man Complains all go Chearfully on— to State the fatigues of this party would take up more of the journal than other notes which I find Scercely time to Set down. I had the best rout Staked out and measured which is 17 miles ¾ to the river & ½ a mile up i. 'e 18¼ miles portage— from the lower rapid to the 1st Creek is 286 poles, to a Deep run of water, Called *Willow Run* is 6 miles thence to the river 3 miles above Medison Riv at 3 Island Called *White Bear* Islands is 11 miles all prarie without wood or water except at the Creek & run which afford a plenty of fine water and a little wood the plain is tolerably leavel except at the river ⟨the Creek⟩ a Small assent & passing a low hill from the Creek a rough & Steep assent for about ¼ of a mile and Several Gullies & a gradual hill for 1½ miles the heads of Several gullies which have Short assents & the willow run of a Steep hill on this run grows Purple & red Currents. the red is now ripe the Purple full grown, an emence number of Prarie birds now Setting of two kinds one larger than a Sparrow dark yellow the Center feathers of its tail yellow & the out Sides black Some Streeks about its neck, the other about the Same Size White tail[1]

1. Neither of these birds can be identified with any certainty. The second one may be the lark bunting, *Calamospiza melanocorys* [AOU, 605], then new to science. Burroughs, 258. See also Weather Remarks for June 5, 1805.

[Lewis]   *Monday June 24th 1805.*

Supposing that Drewyer and R. Fields might possibly be still higher up medicine river, I dispatched J. Fields up the river with orders to proceede about four miles and then return whether he found them or not and join Shannon at this camp. I set out early and walked down the South West side of the river and sent Shannon down the opposite side to bring the canoe over to me and put me across the Missouri; having landed on the Lard. side of the Missouri I sent Shannon back with the canoe to ascend the Medicine river as far as his camp to meet J. Fields and bring the dryed meat at that place to the camp at the white bear Islands which accomplished and arrived with Fields this evening. the party also arrived this evening with two canoes from the lower camp. they were wet and fatiegued, gave them a dram. R. Fields came with them and gave me an account of his & Drewyer's hunt, and informed me that Drewyer was still at their camp with the meat they had dryed. the iron frame of my boat is 36 feet long 4½ F. in the beam and 26 Inches in the hole.

This morning early Capt. Clark had the remaining canoe drawn out of the water; and divided the remainder of our baggage into three parcels, one of which he sent today by the party with two canoes. The Indian woman is now perfectly recovered. Capt. C. came a few miles this morning to see the party under way and returned. on my arrival at the upper camp this morning, I found that Sergt. Gass and Shields had made but slow progress in collecting timber for the boat; they complained of great difficulty in geting streight or even tolerably streight sticks of 4½ feet long. we were obliged to make use of the willow and box alder, the cottonwood being too soft and brittle. I kept one of them collecting timber while the other shaved and fitted them. I have found some pine logs among the drift wood near this place, from which, I hope to obtain as much pitch as will answer to pay the seams of the boat. I directed Fraizer to remain in order to sew the hides together, and form the covering for the boat.

[Clark]   *June 24th Monday 1805*

a Cloudy morning I rose early had, the remaining Canoe hauled out of the water to dry and divided the baggage into 3 parcels, one of which the party took on their backs & one waggon with truk wheels to the Canoes 3 miles in advance   (Those Canoes or 5 of our Canoes were Carried up the Creek 1¾ of a mile taken out on the bank and left to dry from which place they are taken up a point and intersects this rout from the mouth of the Creek at 3 miles from the foot of the rapids)   after getting up their loads they divided men & load & proceeded on with 2 canoes on truck wheels as before, I accompaned them 4 miles and returned, my feet being verry Sore from the walk over ruts Stones & hills & thro the leavel plain for 6 days proceeding Carrying my pack and gun. Some few drops of rain in the fore part of the day, at 6 oClock a black Cloud arose to the N West, the wind shifted from the S to that point and in a short time the earth was entirely Covered with hail, Some rain Succeeded, which Continud for about an hour very moderately on this Side of the river, without the earths being wet ½ an inch, the riveins on the opposit or N W Side discharged emence torrents of water into the river, & Showed evidently that the rain was much heavyer on that Side, Some rain at different times in the night which was worm— Thunder without lightning accompanied the hail Cloud

[Lewis]   *Tuesday June 25th 1805.*

This morning early I sent the party back to the lower camp; dispatched Frazier down with the canoe for Drewyer and the meat he had collected, and Joseph Fields up the Missouri to hunt Elk. at eight OClk. sent Gass and Sheilds over to the large Island for bark and timber. about noon Fields returned and informed me that he had seen two white bear near the river a few miles above and in attempting to get a shoot them had stumbled uppon a third which immediately made at him being only a few steps distant; that in runing in order to escape from the bear he had leaped down a steep bank of the river on a stony bar where he fell cut his hand bruised his knees and bent his gun. that fortunately for him the bank hid him from the bear when he fell and that by that means he had escaped. this man has been truly unfortunate with these bear, this is the second time that he has narrowly escaped from them. about 2 P. M Shields and Gass returned with but a small quantity of both bark and timber and informed me that it was all they could find on the Island; they had killed two Elk the skins of which and a part of the flesh they brought with them. in the evening Drewyer and Frazier arrivd with about 800 lbs. of excellent dryed meat and about 100 lbs of tallow. The river is about 800 yds. wide opposite to us above these islands, and has a very gentle current the bottoms are hadsome [*NB: Qu*] level and extensive on both sides; the bank on this side is not more than 2 feet above the level of the water; it is a pretty little grove in which our camp is situated. there is a species of wild rye[1] which is now heading it rises to the hight of 18 or 20 inches, the beard is remarkably fine and soft it is a very handsome grass the culm is jointed and is in every rispect the wild rye in minuture. great quantities of mint also are here[2] it resemble the pepper mint very much in taste and appearance. the young blackbirds which are almost innumerable in these islands just begin to fly. see a number of water tarripens.[3] I have made an unsuccessfull attempt to catch fish,

and do not think there are any in this part of the river. The party that returned this evening to the lower camp reached it in time to take one
canoe on the plain and prepare their baggage for an early start in the
morning after which such as were able to shake a foot amused themselves
in dancing on the green to the music of the violin which Cruzatte plays
extreemly well.

Capt. C. somewhat unwell today.   he made Charbono kook for the
party against their return.   it is worthy of remark that the winds are sometimes so strong in these plains that the men informed me that they hoisted
a sail in the canoe and it had driven her along on the truck wheels.   this is
really sailing on dry land.

[Clark]   *June 25th Tuesday 1805*

a fair worm morning, Clouded & a few drops of rain at 5 oClock A. M.
fair   I feel my Self a little unwell with a looseness &c. &c.   put out the
Stores to dry & Set Chabonah &c to Cook for the party against their return—he being the only man left on this Side with me   I had a little Cof-
fee for brackfast which was to me a riarity as I had not tasted any Since
last winter. The wind from the N. W. & worm. This Countrey has a romantick appearance river inclosed between high and Steep hills Cut to
pieces by revines but little timber and that Confined to the Rivers & Creek,
the Missourie has but a fiew Scattering trees on its borders, and only one
Solitary Cotton tree in sight of my Camp   the wood which we burn is
drift wood which is broken to pieces in passing the falls, not one large
tree longer than about 8 or 10 feet to be found drifted below the falls   the
plains are inferior in point of Soil to those below, more Stone on the sides
of the hill, grass but a few inches high and but few flowers in the Plains,
great quantites of Choke Cheries, Goose burres, red & yellow berries, &
red & Purple Currents on the edges of water Courses in bottoms & damp
places, about my Camp the Cliffs or bluffs are a hard red or redish brown
earth Containing Iron.[4]   we Catch great quantities of Trout, and a kind
of mustel, flat backs[5] & a Soft fish resembling a Shad and a few Cat.   at
5 oClock the party returned, fatigued as usial, and proceeded to mend
their mockersons &c. and G Shannon & R, Fds. to of the men who ware

Sent up the medison river to hunt Elk, they killed no Elk, Several Buffalow & Deer, and reports that the river is 120 yds wide and about 8 feet deep Some timber on its borders— a powerfull rain fell on the party on their rout yesterday Wet Some fiew articles, and Caused the rout to be So bad wet & Deep thay Could with dificuelty proceed, Capt. Lewis & the men with him much employd with the Iron Boat in fitting it for the water, dispatched one man to George Drewyers Camp below medison river for meat &c. a fair after noon— great numbers of buffalow water opposit to my Camp everry day— it may be here worthy of remark that the Sales were hoised in the Canoes as the men were drawing them and the wind was great relief to them being Sufficently Strong to move the Canoes on the Trucks, this is Saleing on Dry land in every Sence of the word, Serjeant N Pryor Sick, the party amused themselves with danceing untill 10 oClock all Chearfullness and good humer, they all tied up their loads to make an early Start in the morning.

1. *Hordeum jubatum* L., foxtail barley, or possibly *Sitanion hystrix* (Nutt.) J. G. Smith, squirrel tail. Hahn, *Hordeum* and *Sitanion* maps. It was probably Biddle who drew a red vertical line through this passage and those about the mint and turtle.

2. *Mentha arvensis* L., field mint. Booth & Wright, 211.

3. Probably *Chrysemys picta,* painted turtle. Benson (HLCE), 88.

4. This is the lower Cretaceous Kootenai Formation. The reddish color comes from oxidized iron compounds.

5. The mussels could be either *Margaritanidae* or *Unionidae*. Pennak, 704–10. Clark's mention of "flat backs" is unclear. Perhaps it is a regionalism for suckers (family *Catostomidae*). See August 16, 1804.

[Lewis]   *Wednesday June 26th 1805.*

The Musquetoes are extreemly troublesome to us. This morning early I dispatched J. Fields and Drewyer in one of the canoes up the river to hunt Elk. set Frazier at work to sew the skins together for the covering of the boat. Sheilds and Gas I sent over the river to surch a small timbered bottom on that side opposite to the Islands for timber and bark; and to myself I assign the duty of cook as well for those present as for the party which I expect again to arrive this evening from the lower camp. I collected my wood and water, boiled a large quantity of excellent dryed buffaloe meat and made each man a large suet dumpling by way of a treat. about 4 P. M. Shields and Gass returned with a better supply of timber than they had yet collected tho' not by any means enough. they brought some bark principally of the Cottonwood which I found was too brittle and soft for the purpose; for this article I find my only dependence is the sweet willow which has a tough & strong bark. Shields and Gass had killed seven buffaloe in their absence the skins of which and a part of the best of the meat they brought with them. if I cannot procure a sufficient quantity of Elk's skins I shall substitute those of the buffaloe. late in the evening the party arrived with two more canoes and another portion of the baggage. Whitehouse one of them much heated and fortiegued on his arrivall dank a very hearty draught of water and was taken almost instanly extreemly ill. his pulse were very full and I therefore bled him plentifully from which he felt great relief. I had no other instrument with which to perform this opperation but my pen knife, however it answered very well. the wind being from S. E today and favourable the men made considerable progress by means of their sails.

At the lower Camp. The party set out very early from this place, and took with them two canoes and a second alotment of baggage consisting of Parched meal, Pork, powder lead axes, tools, bisquit, portable soupe, some merchandize and cloathing. Capt. C. gave Sergt. Pryor a doze of salts this morning and employed Sharbono in rendering the buffaloe tallow which had been collected there, he obtained a sufficient quantity to fill three empty kegs. Capt. C. also scelected the articles to be deposited in the cash consisting of my desk which I had left for that purpose and in which I had left some books, my specimens of plants minerals &c. collected from fort Mandan to that place.[1] also 2 Kegs of Pork, ½ a Keg of flour 2 blunderbushes, ½ a keg of fixed ammunition and some other small articles belonging to the party which could be dispenced with. deposited the swivel and carriage under the rocks a little above the camp near the river. great numbers of buffaloe still continue to water daily opposite the camp. The antelopes still continue scattered and seperate in the plains. the females with their young only of which they generally have two, and the males alone. Capt. Clarke measured the rout from the Camp at the Whitebear Islands to the lower camp which is as follows.—

N. 42° E.	4	miles to an elivated point of the plain. the rout is a little to the left of this course first down the river and then turning gradually to the right up a long and gentle ascent to the high plain.
N. 66° E.	3	m. passing the head of a drane which falls into the Missouri at the 19 feet or crooked fall.
N. 45° E.	4	m. to willow run, which always has a plenfull supply of good water. and some timber.
N. 18 E.	4	m. passing the head of a drane which falls into the missouri below the great falls.
N. 10° W.	2	m. to the entrance of Portage creek. the rout for the canoes is to the right of this course and strikes the creek about 1 ¾ miles from it's entrance, by that means avoiding a very steep hill which lies above Portage creek.
N. 9° W.	¾	M. to our camp opposite the last considerable rappid.—
Miles 17 ¾		

[Clark]   *June 26th Wednesday 1805*

Some rain last night   this morning verry Cloudy   the party Set out this morning verry early with their loads to the Canoe Consisting of Parched meal Pork Powder Lead axes, Tools Bisquit, P. Soup & Some Merchendize & Clothes &c. &c. I gave Serjt. Pryor a dost of Salts, & Set Chabonah to trying up the Buffalow tallow & put into the empty Kegs &c. I assort our articles for to be left at this place buried, [*blank*] Kegs of Pork, ½ a Keg of flour, 2 blunderbuts, [*blank*] Caterrages a few Small lumbersom articles Capt Lewiss Desk and Some books & Small articles in it

The wind from the N. W. verry worm   flying Clouds   in the evening the wind Shifted round to the East & blew hard, which is a fair wind for the two Canoes to Sail on the Plains across the portage, I had three Kegs of Buffalow Grease tried up. Great numbers of Buffalow opposite to our Camp watering to day.

1. In fact, these specimens were deposited in the cache made at the upper camp, rather than here at the lower camp. Most of them were lost to water damage. See below, July 13, 1806.

[Lewis]   *Thursday June 27th 1805.*

The party returned early this morning for the remaining canoe and baggage; Whitehouse was not quite well this morning I therefore detained him and about 10 A. M. set him at work with Frazier sewing the skins together for the boat; Shields and Gass continued the operation of shaving and fiting the horizontall bars of wood in the sections of the boat; the timber is so crooked and indifferent that they make but little progress, for myself I continued to act the part of cook in order to keep all hands employed.   some Elk came near our camp and we killed 2 of them   at 1 P. M. a cloud arrose to the S. W. and shortly after came on attended with violent Thunder Lightning and hail &c.   (see notes on diary of the weather for June).   soon after this storm was over Drewyer and J. Fields returned. they were about 4 miles above us during the storm, the hail was of no uncommon size where they were. They had killed 9 Elk and three bear during their absence; one of the bear was the largest by far that we have yet seen; the skin appear to me to be as large as a common ox.   while hunting they saw a thick brushey bottom on the bank of the river where from the tracks along shore they suspected that there were bare concealed; they therefore landed without making any nois and climbed a leaning tree and placed themselves on it's branches about 20 feet above the ground, when thus securely fixed they gave a hoop and this large bear instantly rushed forward to the place from whence he had heard the human voice issue, when he arrived at the tree he made a short paus and Drewyer shot him in the head.   it is worthy of remark that these bear never climb.   the fore feet of this bear measured nine inches across and the hind feet eleven and ¾ in length & exclusive of the tallons and seven inches in width.   a bear came within thirty yards of our camp last night and eat up about thirty weight of buffaloe suit which was hanging on a pole.   my dog seems to be in a constant state of alarm with these bear and keeps barking all night.   soon after the storm this evening the water on this side of the river became of a deep crimson colour which I pesume proceeded from some stream above and on this side.   there is a kind of soft red stone in the bluffs and bottoms of the gullies in this neighbourhood which forms this colouring matter.—[1] *At the lower camp.* Capt. Clark completed a draught of the river with the couses and distances from the entrance of the Missouri to Ft. Mandan, which we intend depositing here in order to guard against accedents.[2] Sergt. Pryor is somewhat better this morning.   at 4 P. M. the party returned from the upper camp; Capt. C. gave them a drink of grog; they prepared for the labour of the next day. soon after the party returned it began to rain accompanyed by some hail and continued a short time; a second shower fell late in the evening accompanyed by a high wind from N. W.—   the mangled carcases of several buffaloe pass down the river today which had no doubt perished in the falls.—

[Clark]   *June 27th Thursday 1805*

a fair warm morning wind from the S, E, and moderate. Serjt. Pryor Something better this morning, I proceed to finish a rough draugh of the river & Distances to leave at this place, the wormest day we have had this year, at 4 oClock the Party returned from the head of the portage   Soon after it began to hail and rain hard and continued for a fiew minits & Ceased for an hour ⟨when⟩ and began to rain again with a heavy wind from the N W. I refresh the men with a drink of grog   The river beginning to rise a little the water is Coloured a redish brown, the Small Streams, discharges in great torrents, and partake of the Choler of the earth over which it passes—a great part of which is light & of a redish brown. Several Buffalow pass drowned & ⟨dashed to pices⟩ in passing over the falls Cloudy all night, Cold

1. The soft red stone is shale within the Kootenai Formation.

2. It is not clear whether this was a single map or a series like the twenty-nine sheets covering the same territory—the mouth of the Missouri to Fort Mandan—sent to Jefferson from the latter place. See the Introduction to the *Atlas*. This map is apparently lost.

[Lewis]   *Friday June 28th 1805.*

Set Drewyer to shaving the Elk skins, Fields to make the cross stays for the boat, Frazier and Whitehouse continue their operation with the skins, Shields and Gass finish the horizontal bars of the sections; after which I sent them in surch of willow bark, a sufficient supply of which they now obtained to bind the boat.   expecting the party this evening I prepared a supper for them but they did not arrive.   not having quite Elk skins enough I employed three buffaloe hides to cover one section.   not being able to shave these skins I had them singed pretty closely with a blazeing torch; I think they will answer tolerable well. The White bear have become so troublesome to us that I do not think it prudent to send one man alone on an errand of any kind, particularly where he has to pass through the brush.   we have seen two of them on the large Island opposite to us today but are so much engaged that we could not spare the time to hunt them but will make a frolick of it when the party return and drive them from these islands.   they come close arround our camp every night but have never yet ventured to attack us and our dog gives us timely notice of their visits, he keeps constantly padroling all night. I have made the men sleep with their arms by them as usual for fear of accedents.   the river is now about nine inches higher than it was on my arrival.   *lower Camp.* early this morning Capt. C. dispatched the remaining canoe with some baggage to the top of the plain above Portage creek three miles in advance; some others he employed in carrying the articles to the cash and depositing them and others to mend the carriages which wer somewhat out of repair.   this being accomplished he loaded the two carriages with the remaining baggage and set out with all the party and proceeded on with much difficulty to the canoe in the plain.   portage creek had arisen considerably and the water was of crimson colour and illy tasted.   on his arrival at the canoe he found there was more baggage than he could possibly take at one load on the two sets of trucks and therefore left some barrels of pork & flour and a few heavy boxes of amunition which could not well be injured, and proceeded with the canoe & one set of trucks loaded with baggage to willow run where he encamped for the night, and killed two buffaloe to subsist the party.   soon after his arrival at willow run he experienced a hard shower of rain which was succeeded by a violent wind from the S. W. off the snowy mountains,[1] accompanyed with rain; the party being cold and wet, he administered the consolation of a dram to each.

[Clark]   *June 28th Friday 1805*

a fair morning   wind from the South   I dispatch the remaining Canoe with baggage in her to the top of the Hill three miles, imploy Some hands in Carrying those things we intend to deposit to the *Carsh* or hole, Some to repareing one of the trucks &c. &c.   the water is riseing and of a redish brown Cholour   after Covering the *Carshe* & loading the two Carrges with the remaining part of our Baggage we all Set out passed the Creek which had rose a little and the water nearly red, and bad tasted, we assended the hill to the place the Canoe lay with great labour, at the Canoe at which place we left Some boxes & Kegs of Pork & flour for another Load, and proceeded on with the Canoe & what baggage we could draw on the wheels to willow run 6 miles where we Camped, this run mearly Some water remaining in holes &c. Soon after we halted we had a Shower, and at dark we expereinced a most dredfull wind from off the Snow Mountains to the S. W. accompd. with rain which continued at intervales all night men wet. I refreshed them with a dram. Killed 2 Buffalow. Great nos. about

1. Perhaps the Lewis range of the Rockies, along the Continental Divide.

[Lewis]   *Saturday June 29th 1805.*

   This morning we experienced a heavy shower of rain for about an hour after which it became fair.   not having seen the large fountain of which Capt. Clark spoke I determined to visit it today as I could better spare this day from my attention to the boat than probably any other when the work would be further advanced; accordingly after seting the hands at their several employments I took Drewyer and seet out for the fountain and passed through a level beautiful plain for about Six miles when I reached the brake of the river hills   here we were overtaken by a violent gust of wind and rain from the S. W. attended with thunder and Litning. I expected a hail storm probably from this cloud and therefore took refuge in a little gully wher there were some broad stones with which I purposed protecting my head if we should have a repetition of the seene of the 27th but fortunately we had but little hail and that not large; I sat very composedly for about an hour without sheter and took a copious drenching of rain; after the shower was over I continued my rout to the fountain which I found much as Capt. C; had discribed & think it may well be retained on the list of prodegies of this neighbourhood towards which, nature seems to have dealt with a liberal hand, for I have scarcely experienced a day since my first arrival in this quarter without experiencing some novel occurrence among the party or witnessing the appearance of some uncommon object. I think this fountain the largest I ever beheld, and the hadsome cascade which it affords over some steep and irregular rocks in it's passage to the river adds not a little to it's beauty.   it is about 25 yds. from the river, situated in a pretty little level plain, and has a suddon decent of about 6 feet in one part of it's course.   the water of this fountain is extreemly tranparent and cold; nor is it impregnated with lime or any other extranious matter which I can discover, but is very pure and pleasent.   it's waters marke their passage as Capt. Clark observes for a considerable distance down the Missouri notwithstanding it's rapidity and force.   the water of the fountain boil up with such force near it's center that it's surface in that part seems even higher than the surrounding earth which is a firm handsom terf of fine green grass.   after amusing myself about 20 minutes in examining the fountain I found myself so chilled with my wet cloaths that I determined to return and accordingly set out; on our way to camp we found a buffaloe dead which we had shot as we came out and took a parsel of the meat to camp   it was in very good order; the hump and tongue of a fat buffaloe I esteem great delicasies.   on my arrival at camp I was astonished not to find the party yet arrived, but then concluded that probably the state of the praries had detained them, as in the wet state in which they are at present the mud sticks to the wheels is such manner that they are obliged to halt frequently and clense them. *Transaction and occurrencies which took place with Capt. Clark and party today.*

Shortly after the rain which fell early this morning he found it imposseble from the state of the plains for the party to reach the upper extremity of the portage with their present load, and therefore sent back almost all of the party to bring the baggage which had been left behind yesterday.   he determined himself to pass by the way of the river to camp in order to supply the deficiency of some notes and remarks which he had made as he first ascended the river but which he had unfortunately lost.   accordingly he left one man at Willow run to guard the baggage and took with him his black man York, Sharbono and his indian woman also accompanyed Capt. C.   on his arrival at the falls he perceived a very black cloud rising in the West which threatened immediate rain; he looked about for a shelter but could find none without being in great danger of being blown into the river should the wind prove as violent as it sometimes is on those occasions in these plains; at length about a ¼ of a mile above the falls he discovered a deep rivene where there were some shelving rocks under which he took shelter near the river with Sharbono and the Indian woman; laying their guns compass &c. under a shelving rock on the upper side of the rivene where they were perfectly secure from the rain.   the first shower was moderate accompanyed by a violent rain the effects of which they did but little feel; soon after a most violent torrent of rain decended accompanyed with hail; the rain appeared to decend in a body and instantly collected in the rivene and came down in a roling torrent with irrisistable force driving rocks mud and everything before it which opposed it's passage, Capt. C. fortunately discovered it a moment before it reached them and seizing his gun and shot pouch with his left hand with the right he assisted himself up the steep bluff shoving occasionaly the Indian woman before him who had her child in her arms; Sharbono had the woman by the hand indeavouring to pull her up the hill but was so much frightened that he remained frequently motionless and but for Capt. C. both himself and his [wo]man and child must have perished.   so suddon was the rise of the water that before Capt C could reach his gun and begin to ascend the bank it was up to his waist and wet his watch; and he could scarcely ascend faster than it arrose till it had obtained the debth of 15 feet with a current tremendious to behold.   one moment longer & it would have swept them into the river just above the great cataract of 87 feet where they must have inevitably perished. Sarbono lost his gun shot pouch, horn, tomahawk, and my wiping rod; Capt. Clark his Umbrella and compas or circumferenter.   they fortunately arrived on the plain safe, where they found the black man, York, in surch of them; york had seperated from them a little while before the storm, in pursuit of some buffaloe and had not seen them enter the rivene; when this gust came on he returned in surch of them & not being able to find them for some time was much allarmed.   the bier[1] in which the woman carrys her child and all it's cloaths wer swept away as they lay at her feet she having time only to grasp her child; the infant was therefore very cold and the woman also who had just recovered from a severe indisposition was also wet and cold, Capt C. therefore relinquished his intended rout and returned to the camp at willow run in order also to obtain dry cloathes for himself and directed them to follow him.   on Capt. Clark's arrival at camp he found that the party dispatched for the baggage had returned in great confusion and consternation leaving their loads in the plains; the men who were all nearly naked and [no] covering on the head were sorely mawled with the hail which was so large and driven with such force by the wind that it nocked many of them down and one particulary as many as three times   most of them were bleeding freely and complained of being much bruised.   willow run raised about 6 feet with this rain and the plains were so wet they could do nothing more this evening.   Capt. C. gave the party a dram to console them in some measure for their general defeat.

[Clark]   *June 29th Satturday 1805*

a little rain verry early this morning after Clear, finding that the Prarie was So wet as to render it impossible to pass on to the end of the portage, deturmined to Send back to the top of the hill at the Creek for the remaining part of the baggage left at that place yesterday, leaveing one man to take care of the baggage at this place. I deturmined my Self to proceed on to the falls and take the river, according we all Set out, I took my Servent & one man Chabono our Interpreter & his Squar accompanied, Soon after I arrived at the falls, I perceived a Cloud which appeared black and threaten imediate rain, I looked out for a Shelter but Could See no place without being in great danger of being blown into the river if the wind Should prove as turbelant as it is at Some times   about ¼ of a mile above the falls I obsd a Deep rivein in which was Shelveing rocks under which we took Shelter near the river and placed our guns the Compass &c. &c. under a Shelveing rock on the upper Side of the Creek, in a place which was verry Secure from rain, the first Shower was moderate accompanied with a violent wind, the effects of which we did not feel, Soon after a torrent of rain and hail fell more violent than ever I Saw before, the rain fell like one voley of water falling from the heavens and gave us time only to get out of the way of a torrent of water which was Poreing down the hill in the rivin with emence force tareing every thing before it takeing with it large rocks & mud, I took my gun & Shot pouch in my left hand, and with the right Scrambled up the hill pushing the Interpreters wife (who had her Child in her arms) before me, the Interpreter himself makeing attempts to pull up his wife by the hand much Scared and nearly without motion— we at length retched the top of the hill Safe where I found my Servent in Serch of us greatly agitated, for our wellfar—. before I got out of the bottom of the revein which was a flat dry rock when I entered it, the water was up to my waste & wet my watch, I Scrcely got out before it raised 10 feet deep with a torrent which turrouble to behold, and by the time I reached the top of the hill, at least 15 feet water, I directed the party to return to the Camp at the run as fast as possible to get to our lode where Clothes Could be got to Cover the Child whose Clothes were all lost, and the woman who was but just recovering from a Severe indispostion, and was wet and Cold, I was fearfull of a relaps I caused her as also the others of the party to take a little Spirits, which my Servent had in a Canteen, which revived verry much. on arrival at the Camp on the willow run—met the party who had returned in great Confusion to the run leaveing their loads in the Plain, the hail & wind being So large and violent in the plains, and them naked, they were much brused, and Some nearly killed one knocked down three times, and others without hats or any thing on their heads bloodey & Complained verry much; I refreshed them with a little grog— Soon after the run began to rise and rose 6 feet in a few minits—. I lost at the river in the torrent the large *Compas,* an eligant fusee, Tomahawk *Humbrallo,* Shot pouh, & horn wih powder & Ball, mockersons, & the woman lost her Childs Bear & Clothes bedding &c.— [*X: Sah car gah we â*] The Compass is a Serious loss; as we have no other large one. The plains are So wet that we Can do nothing this evining particilarly as two deep reveins are between ourselves & Load

1. The cradleboard in which Sacagawea carried her child on her back.

[Lewis]   *Sunday June 30th 1805.*

We had a heavy dew this morning which is a remarkable event. Fraizer and Whitehouse still continue their opperation of sewing the skins together. I set Shields and gass to shaving bark and Fields continued to make the cross brases. Drewyer and myself rendered a considerable quantity of tallow and cooked. I begin to be extremely impatient to be off as the season is now waisting a pace   nearly three months have now elapsed since we left Fort Mandan and not yet reached the Rocky Mountains   I am therefore fully preswaded that we shall not reach Fort Mandan again this season if we even return from the ocean to the Snake Indians.   wherever we find timber there is also beaver; Drewyer killed two today. There are a number of large bat or goatsucker here   I killed one of them and found that there was no difference between them and those common to the U' States; I have not seen the leather winged bat for some time nor is there any of the small goatsuckers in this quarter of the country.[1]   we have not the whip-poor-will either.   this last is by many persons in the U' States confounded with the large goat-sucker or night-hawk as it is called in the Eastern States, and are taken for the same bird.[2]   it is true that there is a great resemblance but they are distinct species of the goatsucker.   here the one exists without the other.   the large goat sucker lays it's eggs in these open plains without the preperation of a nest   we have found their eggs in several instances   they lay only two before they set nor do I beleive that they raise more than one brood in a season; they have now just hatched their young.—   This evening the bark was shaved and the leather covering for the sections were also completed and I had them put into the water, in order to toughen the bark, and prepare the leather for sewing on the sections in the morning.   it has taken 28 Elk skins and 4 Buffaloe skins to complete her.   the cross bars are also finished this evening; we have therefore only the way strips[3] now to obtain in order to complete the wood work, and this I fear will be a difficult task. The party have not returned from the lower camp   I am therefore fearfull that some uncommon accedent has happened.

Occurrences with Capt. Clark and Party

This morning Capt. Clark dispatched two men to kill some buffaloe, two others to the falls to surch for the articles lost yesterday, one he retained to cook and sent the others for the baggage left in the plains yesterday.   the hunters soon returned loaded with meat   those sent for the baggage brought it up in a few hours, he then set four men at work to make axeltrees and repare the carrages; the others he employed in conveying the baggage over the run on their sholders it having now fallent to about 3 feet water.   the men complained much today of the bruises and wounds which they had received yesterday from the hail.   the two men sent to the falls returned with the compas which they found covered in the mud and sand near the mouth of the rivene   the other articles were irrecoverably lost.   they found that part of rivene in; which Capt. C. had been seting yesterday, filled with huge rocks.   at 11 A. M. Capt. Clark dispatched the party with a load of the baggage as far as the 6 miles stake, with orders to deposit it there and return with the carriages which they did accordingly.   they experienced a heavy gust of wind this evening from the S. W. after which it was a fair afternoon.   more buffaloe than usual were seen about their camp; Capt. C assured me that he beleives he saw at least ten thousand at one view.—

June 30th 1805

Point of Observation No. 29

At our camp on the Lard. side of the Missouri opposite to the White bear Islands observed Equal Altitudes of the Sun with Sextant.

Equal Altitudes of ☉'s L. L.

	h	m	s			h	m	s
A. M.	8	50	19		P. M.	5	51	54

☞ I have made several attempts to obtain Equal altitudes since my arrival here but have been uniformly defeated untill now by the flying clouds and storms in the evening.—

[Clark]   *June 30th Sunday 1805.*

a fair morning, I dispatch the party except 5 for the remaining baggage Scattered in the plains, two to hunt for meat, two to the falls, and one to Cook   at 10 oClock the hunters Came in loaded with fat meat, & those were dispatched for the baggage returned with it. I Set 4 men to make new axeltrees & repare the Carrages, others to take the load across the run which had fallen & is about 3 feet water, men Complain of being Swore this day dull and lolling about, The two men dispatched in Serch of the articls lost yesterday returned and brought the Compass which they found in the mud & Stones near the mouth of the revein, no other articles found, the place I Sheltered under filled up with hugh Rocks, I Set the party out at 11 oClock to take a load to the 6 mile Stake & return this evening, and I intend to take on the ballance to the river tomorrow if the prarie will permit.   at 3 oClock a Storm of wind from the S. W. after which we had a clear evening. Great numbers of Buffalow in every direction, I think 10,000 may be Seen in a view.

1. The large goatsucker is probably the common nighthawk, *Chordeiles minor* [AOU, 420]; to Burroughs and Coues it was a subspecies, the Pacific nighthawk, *C. m. hesperis*, but the most recent opinion seems to agree with Lewis that there was no significant difference from the Eastern variety. The bird was then colloquially called a "bat," and the mammal was distinguished by Lewis as the "leather-winged bat," which could be any of a number of species. The "small goatsucker" would probably be the common poorwill as identified previously. Coues (HLC), 2:398 and 398 n. 16; Burroughs, 235–36; Holmgren, 28, 34. It was probably Biddle who drew a red vertical line through this passage about the "leather winged bat" down through "toughen the bark."

2. Lewis distinguishes the whip-poor-will, *Caprimulgus vociferus* [AOU, 417], from the common nighthawk.

3. Perhaps what Lewis elsewhere (see below, February 18, 1806) calls "waytape," after a Chippewa word, referring to white spruce roots or bark strips used to fasten together birch-bark canoes. Possibly the reference is to strips of wood with which to launch the boat. Criswell, 90–91.

[Lewis and Clark]   [*Weather, June 1805*][1]

Day of the Month	State of the ther-mometer at ☉ rise	Weather	Wind at ☉ rise	State of the ther-mometer at 4 OC. P. M.	Weather	Wind at 4 OC. P. M.	State of the river raised or fallen	Feet	Inches or parts
1st	50 a	c	S. W.	62 a	c				1 ½
2nd	56 a	c a r	S. W.	68 a	f	S W			
3rd	46 a	f	S W	60 a	f	S W			
4th	48 a	f a c	N E	61 a	f	S W	f		¾
5th	40 a	r	S. W	42 a	c a r	N. E.	f		¾
6th	35 a	c a r	N. E.	42 a	r a r	N E.	f		1 ½
7th	40 a	c a r	S. W.	43 a	r a r	S W	f		1 ½
8th	41	r a r	S. W.	48 a	f a r	S W	f		1 ¼
9th	50	f	S W.	62[2]	f	S W	f		1
10th	52 a	f	S. W	68 a	f a r	S. W.	r		2
11th	54 a	f	S. W	66 a	f	S W.			

12th[3]	54 a	f	S W	64	f a r	S. W.		
13th	52 a	f	S. W.	72	f	S. W.	r	¾
14th	60 a	f	S W	74	f	S. W	f	¾
15th	60 a	f	S. W.	76	f	S W	f	½
16th	64	c a r	S W	58	f	S W	r	½
17th	50 a	c	S W	57	c	S. W	f	½
18th	48 a	c	S. W.	64 a	f a c	S. W.	f	½
19th	52 a	f	S W	70 a	f	S. W	f	½
20th	49 a	c	S W	74 a	f a r	S. W	f	¼
21st	49 a	f	S. W	70 a	c	S. W.	f	¼
22cd	45 a	c	S W	54 a	f	S W	f	½
23d	48 a	f	S. E.	65 a	c	S. E	f	¼
24th	49 a	c a r	S. E.	74 a	f a c	S W	f	
25th	47 a	c a r	S. W.	72 a	f	S. W.		
26th	49 a	f	S. W.	78 a	f	S W	r	½
27th	49 a	f	S. W.	77	f a r & H. T L[4]	S W	r	1 ¼
28th	46 a	f	S. W.	75	c a f	S W	r	2
29th	47 a	r. T & L	S. W.	77	f	S. W.	r	4 ½
30th	49 a	f	S. W.	76	f	S. W.	r	2 ¼

[Remarks][5]

2cd   rained a few drops only

3rd   Cought the 1st White Chub, and a fish resembling the Hickory Shad in the Clear Stream[6]

5th   rained considerably   some Snow fell on the mounts.   great numbers of the sparrows larks, Curloos and other small birds common to praries are now laying their eggs and seting, their nests are in great abundance.   the large batt, or night hawk appears.[7]   the Turkey buzzard appears.—[8]   first saw the mountain cock near the entrance of Maria's river.—

6th   rained hard the greater part of the day—

7th   rained moderately all day

8th   cleared off at 10 A M.

11th   Capt. Lewis & 4 men Set out up the S. fork[9]

13th   Some dew this morng.

14th   Capt. Lewis Discover the falls & Send back Joe Fields to inform me

15th   The deer now begin to bring forth their young   the young Magpies begin to fly. The Brown or grizzly bear begin to coppolate.

16th   Some rain last night

17th   the thermometer placed in the shade of a tree at the foot of the rappids. Capt Clark sets out to survey the river & portage

19th   wind violent all day

20th   wind still violent rain slight   Capt. Clark returns.[10]

22cd   wind not so violent. Thermometer removed to the head of the rappid and placed in the shade of a tree.[11]

24th   slight rain last night & a heavy shower this evening.

27th   at 1 P M a black cloud which arose in the S W. came on accompanyed with a high wind and violent Thunder and Lightning; a great quantity of hail also fell during this storm which lasted about 2½ hours   the hail which was generally about the size of a pigion's egg and not unlike them in form covered the ground to the debth of 1½ inches.—   for about 20 minutes during this storm hail fell of an innomus size driven with violence almost incredible, when they struck the ground they would bound to the hight of ten to 12 feet and pass 20 or thirty before they touched again.[12]   after the rain I measured and weighed many of these hail stones and found several weighing 3 ozs. and measuring 7 Inches in cirumference; they were generally round and perfectly sollid. I am convinced if one of those had struck a man on the neaked head it would have knocked him down, if not fractured his skull.—   Young blackbirds which are abundant in these Islands are now beginning to fly

28th   Cat fish no higher[13]

29th   heavy gust of rain the morning and evening

1. Lewis's tabled observations appear in Codex Fe and Clark's in Codex I. A few discrepancies and other points are noted below. The headings follow Lewis.

2. Clark has "52 a."

3. The dates for June 12–15 appear to be in Clark's hand in Codex Fe.

4. Clark has only "f a r H."

5. The captains have remarks both in the margin of their tabled observations and separately. These are combined for the fullest coverage without duplication or noting minor discrepancies of wording. Significant differences are noted below. Lewis's separate remarks are in Codex D (see Appendix C, vol. 2) and Clark's in Codex I.

6. This remark is found only in Clark's Codex I.

7. The sparrows could be any of a number of small brown birds. The larks are similarly unidentifiable, as are the "Curloos" which could be any shorebird with a long bill. Holmgren, 29, 33. The "large batt, or night hawk" is again the common nighthawk.

8. The turkey vulture, *Cathartes aura* [AOU, 325], already known to science. Holmgren, 28; Burroughs, 203–4.

9. This remark in Codex Fe is in Clark's hand, as are those for June 14.

10. In Codex I Clark has the marginal remark "returned from above the portage make it 18 miles."

11. Lewis dates this latter remark June 22 in Codex D and a slightly different version June 23 in Codex Fe.

12. At this point in his remarks in Codex I Clark adds "during this emence Storm I was with the gereater part of the men on the portage   the men Saved themselves, Some by getting under a Canoe others by putting Sundery articles on their heads   two was kocked down & Seven with their legs & thighs much brused." In his marginal remarks he has only "Falls of Missouri."

13. This is Clark's marginal note in Codex I; the extent of the channel catfish at that time corresponds to distribution maps by present authorities. Lee et al., 446.

[Lewis]   *Monday July 1st 1805.*

This morning I set Frazier and Whitehouse to sewing the leather on the sides of the sections of the boat; Shields and J. Fields to collect and split light wood and prepare a pit to make tar. Gas I set at work to make the way strips out of some willow limbs which tho' indifferent were the best which could be obtained. Drewyer and myself completed the opperation of rendering the tallow; we obtained about 100 lbs.   by evening the skins were all attatched to their sections and I returned them again to the water.   all matters were now in readiness to commence the opperation of puting the parts of the boat together in the morning.   the way strips are not yet ready but will be done in time as I have obtained the necessary timber.   the difficulty in obtaining the necessary materials has retarded my operations in forming this boat extreemly tedious and troublesome; and as it was a novel peice of machinism to all who were employed my constant attention was necessary to every part of the work; this together with the duties of cheif cook has kept me pretty well employed.   at 3 P. M. Capt. Clark arrived with the party all very much fortiegued.   he brought with him all the baggage except what he had deposited yesterday at the six mile stake, for which the party were too much fortiegued to return this evening.   we gave them a dram and suffered them to rest from their labours this evening. I directed Bratton to assist in making the tar tomorrow, and scelected several others to assist in puting the boat together.   the day has been warm and the Musquetoes troublesome of course   the bear were about our camp all last night, we have therefore determined to beat up their quarters tomorrow, and kill them or drive them from their haunts about this place.

[Clark][1]

White Bear Islands above the Falls of the Missouri July 1st Monday 1805

I arrived at this place to day at 3 oClock P. M. with the party from the lower part of the portage much fatigued &c.

[Clark]   *July 1st Monday 1805.*

We Set out early this morning with the remaining load, and proceeded on verry well to Capt Lewis's Camp where we arrived at 3 oClock, the Day worm and party much fatigued, found Capt. Lewis and party all buisey employd in fitting up the Iron boat, the wind hard from the S, W,— one man verry unwell, his legs & theis broke out and Swelled   the hail which fell at Capt. Lewis Camp 27 Ins[2] was 7 Inches in circumfrance & waied 3 ounces, fortunately for us it was not So large in the plains, if it had we Should most certainly fallen victims to its rage as the men were mostly naked, and but few with hats or any covering on their heads, The hunters killed 3 white bear one large, the fore feet of which measured 9 Inchs across, the hind feet 11 Inchs ¾ long & 7 Inch's wide   a bear nearly Catching Joseph Fields Chased him into the water, bear about the Camp every night & Seen on an Isld. in the day

1. Clark's Codex G (July 1–October 10, 1805) has brief entries for July 1, 2, and 3, 1805, overlapping the longer ones for those dates in his Voorhis No. 1. It is likely that the Codex G entries were the first ones, as they are placed here.

2. "Twenty-seventh instant," referring to June 27, 1805; "ultimo," rather than "instant," would be the correct form for referring to the previous month.

[Lewis] *Tuesday July 2cd 1805.*

A shower of rain fell very early this morning after which we dispatched the men for the remaining baggage at the 6 mile stake. Shields and Bratton seting their tarkiln, Sergts. Pryor and Gass at work on the waystrips and myself and all other hands engaged in puting the boat together which we accomplished in about 3 hours and I then set four men at work sewing the leather over the cross bars of Iron on the inner side of the boat, which form the ends of the sections. about 2 P. M. the party returned with the baggage, all well pleased that they had completed the laborious task of the portage. The Musquetoes uncommonly troublesome   the wind hard from the S. W. all day   I think it possible that these almost perpetual S. W. winds proceede from the agency of the Snowey Mountains and the wide level and untimbered plains which streach themselves along their bases for an immence distance (i e) that the air comeing in contact with the snow is suddonly chilled and condenced, thus becoming heaver than the air beneath in the plains, it glides down the sides of these mountains & decends to the plains, where by the constant action of the sun on the face of an untimbered country there is a partial vacuum formed for it's reception.[1] I have observed that the winds from this quarter are always the coldest and most violent which we experience, yet I am far from giving full credit to my own hypothesis on this subject; if hoever I find on the opposite side of these mountains that the winds take a contrary direction I shall then have more faith.[1] After I had completed my observation of Equal Altitudes today Capt. Clark Myself and 12 men passed over to the large Island to hunt bear.   the brush in that part of it where the bear frequent is an almost impenitrable thicket of the broad leafed willow; this brush we entered in small parties of 3 or four together and surched in every part.   we found one only which made at Drewyer and he shot him in the brest at the distance of about 20 feet, the ball fortunately passed through his heart, the stroke knocked the bear down and gave Drewyer time to get out of his sight; the bear changed his course we pursued him about a hundred yards by the blood and found him dead; we surched the thicket in every part but found no other, and therefore returned. this was a young male and would weigh about 400 lbs. the water of the Missouri here is in most places about 10 feet deep. after our return, in moving some of the baggage we caught a large rat.[2] [*NB: Copy for Dr Barton*] it was somewhat larger than the common European rat, of lighter colour; the body and outer part of the legs and head of a light lead colour, the belly and inner side of the legs white as were also the feet and years. the toes were longer and the ears much larger than the common rat; the ears uncovered with hair. the eyes were black and prominent the whiskers very long and full. the tail was reather longer than the body and covered with fine fur or poil of the same length and colour of the back. the fur was very silkey close and short. I have frequently seen the nests of these rats in clifts of rocks and hollow trees but never before saw one of them. they feed very much on the fruit and seed of the prickly pear; or at least I have seen large quantities of the hulls of that fruit lying about their holes and in their nests.

July 2cd 1805

Observed Equal altitudes of ☉ with Sextant—

	h	m	s		h	m	s	
A. M.	8	7	22	P. M.	lost by clouds			
	"	8	55		6	18	4⎫	Altd. at time of
	"	10	33		"	19	4⎭	observation 52° 5′ 30″

	h	m	s

Chronometer too [*blank*] on Mean Time [*blank*]

[Clark]   *July 2nd Tuesday 1805*

Some rain at day light this morning. dispatched the party for the remaining baggage left at the 6 mile Stake, they returned in the evening and we Crossed to a large Island nearly opposit to us to kill *bear* which has been Seen frequently in the Island, we killed one bear & returned at Sun Set. The Roreing of the falls for maney miles above us

4. Falls and Portage of the Missouri River, ca. July 2, 1805, Voorhis no. 1

[Clark]   *July 2nd Tuesday 1805*

Some rain at day light this morn'g after which a fair morning, dispatched the men for the Kegs &c. left at the Six mile Stake, others to get timber for the boat &c. Musquetors verry troublesom to day, day worm, after the return of the men with the articles left at the 6 mile Stake Capt. Lewis my Self & 12 men Crossed to an Island on which we Saw a bear the evening before, & Several had been Seen by the party at this place, we killed one of the bear and returned. The river at this place is [*blank*] yards wide and about 10 feet water   Cought a rat in our Stores, which had done some mischief, this rat was about the Sise of a Comn. large rat, larger ears, long whiskers & toes, with a tail long & hairey like a ground Squirel, verry fine fur and lighter than the Common rat. Wind to day as usial from the S. W. and hard all the after part of the day, those winds are also [air?] Cool and generally verry hard.

1. Modern theories would explain the winds as either chinook, mountain-valley drainage, or synoptic scale winds.

2. The first scientific description of the pack rat, or bushy-tailed woodrat, *Neotoma cinerea*. Cutright (LCPN), 166. It was probably Biddle who drew a red vertical line through this passage.

[Lewis]   *Wednesday July 3rd 1805.*

This morning early we employed all hands; some were making tar or attempting to make it, others were attatching the skins on the boat, other cuting and fiting the bark for lining puting in the woodworke &c   some hunters[1] were sent out to kill buffaloe in order to make pemecon to take with us and also for their skins which we now wa[n]t to cover our baggage in the boat and canoes when we depart from hence.   the Indians have informed us that we should shortly leave the buffaloe country after passing the falls; this I much regret for I know when we leave the buffaloe that we shal sometimes be under the necessity of fasting occasionally.   and at all events the white puddings will be irretreivably lost and Sharbono out of imployment.   our tar-kiln which ought to have began to run this morning has yealded no tar as yet and I am much affraid will not yeald any, if so I fear the whole opperation of my boat will be useless. I fear I have committed another blunder also in sewing the skins with a nedle which has sharp edges these have cut the skin and as it drys I discover

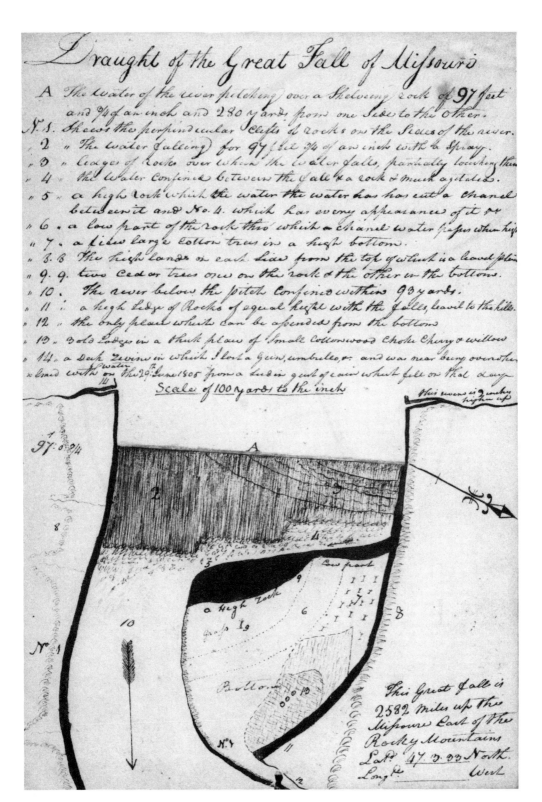

Draught of the Great Fall of Missouri

A The water of the river pitching over a Shelveing rock of **97** feet and ¾ of an inch and 280 yards from one side to the other.

N. 1. Sheews the perpindicular Cliffs of rocks on the sides of the river.

„ 2 „ The water falling for 97 feet ¾ of an inch with a spray.

„ 3 „ ledges of rocks over which the water falls, partially touching them

„ 4 „ the water confined between the fall & a rock & much agitated.

„ 5 „ a high rock which the water the water has has cut a chanel betweeen it and No. 4. which has every appearance of it or

„ 6 „ a low part of the rock thro which a chanel water passes when high

„ 7 „ a few large cotton trees in a high bottom.

„ 8. 8 the high lands on each side from the top of which is a leavel plain

„ 9. 9. two cedar trees one on the rock & the other in the bottoms.

„ 10. The river below the pitch confined within 93 yards.

„ 11 : a high ledge of Rocks of equal hghte with the falls, leavel to the hills.

„ 12 „ the only place which can be apended from the bottom

„ 13. 3 old lodges in a thick place of small cottonwood choke cherry & willow

„ 14. a Deep revine in which I lost a Gun, umbrella, &c. and was near being over other ice lined with water on the 29th. June 1805 from a sudden gust of rain which fell on that day

Scale of 100 yards to the inch

97. 0. 2¼

a high rock

Low part

Bottom

This Great Fall is 2582 miles up the Missouri East of the Rocky Mountains Lat.d 47. 3. 33 North Long.de ___ West

this river is 2 inches higher up

Nº 1

10

5. Great Falls of the Missouri River, ca. July 3, 1805, Voorhis no. 1

355

that the throng dose not fill the holes as I expected tho' I made them sew with a large throng for that purpose. at 10 OCk A. M. we had a slight shower which scarcely wet the grass. One buffaloe only and 2 Antelopes killed today six beaver and 2 otter have been killed within the last three days. The current of the river looks so gentle and inviting that the men all seem anxious to be moving upward as well as ourselves. we have got the boat prety well forward today and think we shall be able to complete her tomorrow except paying her,[2] to do which will require some little time to make her first perfectly dry. she has assumed her shape and looks ex-treemly well. She will be very light, more so than any vessel of her size that I ever saw.

At our camp near the White bear Islands.

July 3rd 1805.[3]

Observed Equal altitudes of the ☉ with Sextant.

	h	m	s		h	m	s	
A. M.	8	16	22	P. M.	6	6	48	Altitude at the
"		17	45	"		3	55	time of observation
"		19	17	"		5	30	54° 49' 45"

h m s

Chronometer too slow on Mean Time [*blank*]

[Clark]   *July 3rd Wednesday 1805*

all of party employd in Sowing the Skins to the boat, burning Tare, pre-paring timber, hunting buffalow for their meat & Skins, drying & repack-ing the Stores, Goods &c. &c. at 1 oClock began to rain. in the evening the hunters killed two antilopes & a Buffalow.

[Clark]   *July 3rd Wednesday 1805*[4]

A fine morning wind from the S. W all the party employd, Some about the boat, attaching the Skins & Sowing them to the Sections, others prepareing timber, Some, burning tar of the drift pine, Some airring and repacking the Stores & Goods, & others hunting for Meet to make pemiti-gon & for the use of their Skins to Cover the Canoes & boat,—. a Small

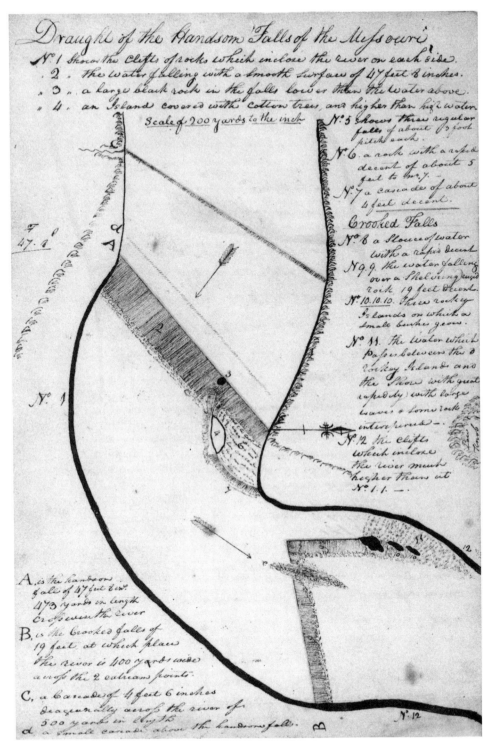

Draught of the Handsom Falls of the Missouri

N° 1 shows the cliffs of rocks which inclose the river on each side.
" 2 " the water falling with a smooth surface of 47 feet 8 inches.
" 3 " a large black rock in the falls lower then the water above.
" 4 " an Island covered with cotton trees, and higher than high water

Scale of 200 yards to the inch

N° 5 shows three regular falls of about 13 foot pitch each.
N° 6 a rock with a rapid decent of about 5 feet to N° 7.
N° 7 a cascade of about 4 feet decent.

Crooked Falls

N° 8 a slower of water with a rapid decent
N° 9 the water falling over a shelving rock 19 feet decent.
N° 10.10.10. Three rocky Islands on which a small bushes grows.
N° 11 the water which pass between the 3 rocky Islands and the shore with great rapidity with large waves & some rock interspersed —
N° 12 the cliffs which inclose the river much higher than at N° 1.1. —

A. is the handson falls of 47 feet 8 in. 473 yards in length cross over the river
B. is the crooked falls of 19 feet at which place the river is 400 yards wide across the 2 outward points.
C. a cascade of 4 feet 6 inches diagonally across the river of 500 yards in length
d a small cascade above the handsom falls.

6. "Handsom Falls" (present Rainbow Falls) of the Missouri River,
ca. July 3, 1805, Voorhis no. 1

357

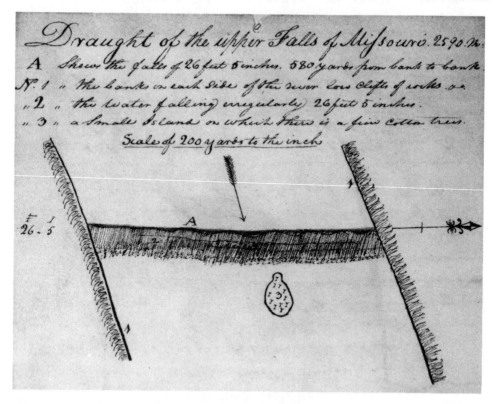

7. "Upper Falls" (present Black Eagle Falls) of the Missouri River,
ca. July 3, 1805, Voorhis no. 1

Shower at 1 oClock which did Scercely wet the grass—. one buffalow
and two Antilopes Killed this evening. Six beaver & 2 orters has been
Killed at this camp within a fiew days   we discover no fish above the falls
as yet—   the only timber in this part of the Countrey is willow, a fiew
Cotton trees which is neither large nor tall, Boxalders and red wood.
(*Bois roche* arrow wood)

   The water tolerably clear and Soft in the river, Current jentle and
bottoms riseing from the water; no appearance of the river riseing more
than a few feet above the falls, as high up as we have yet explored.   but
few trees on the Std Side the grass is high and fine near the river.   the
winds has blown for Several days from the S. W. I think it possible that
those almost perpetial S W. winds, proceed from the agency of the Snowey
mountains and the wide leavel and untimbered plains which Streach themselves along their borders for an emence distance, that the air comeing in

358

Contact with the Snow is Suddenly chilled and condensed, thus become-ing heavyer than the air beneath in the plains   it glides down the Sides of those mountains and decends to the plains, where by the constant action of the Sun on the face of the untimbered country there is a partial vacuom formed for it's reception   I have observed that the winds from this quarter is always the Coaldest and most violent which we experience, yet I am far from giveing full credit to this hypothesis on this Subject; if I find how-ever on the opposit Side of these mountains that the winds take a con-trary direction I Shall then have full faith. (The winds take a contrary direction in the morning or from the mountains on the west Side)[5]

1. Including Drouillard, according to Whitehouse and Ordway.

2. Smearing the boat with pitch or tar to make it waterproof.

3. This observation follows the entry of July 9, 1805, in Lewis's Codex E, and is here placed under the correct date.

4. This is the last daily entry in Voorhis No. 1.

5. At this point in Voorhis No. 1 are three pages of sketch maps of the falls of the Mis-souri (figs. 5, 6, 7), followed by an entry for May 31, 1805, which has been placed accord-ing to date, and a brief description of part of the Great Falls portage, placed at the end of the special entry of June 17–19, 1805.

[Lewis]   *Thursday July 4th 1805.*

Yesterday we permitted Sergt. Gass McNeal and several others who had not yet seen the falls to visit them.   no appearance of tar yet and I am now confident that we shall not be able to obtain any; a serious misfor-tune. I employed a number of hands on the boat today and by 4 P. M. in the evening completed her except the most difficult part of the work that of making her seams secure. I had her turned up and some small fires kindled underneath to dry her. Capt. C. completed a draught of the river from Fort Mandan to this place which we intend depositing at this place in order to guard against accedents.   not having seen the Snake Indians or knowing in fact whether to calculate on their friendship or hostility or friendship we have conceived our party sufficiently small and therefore have concluded not to dispatch a canoe with a part of our men to St. Louis as we had intended early in the spring.   we fear also that such a measure might possibly discourage those who would in such case remain, and might

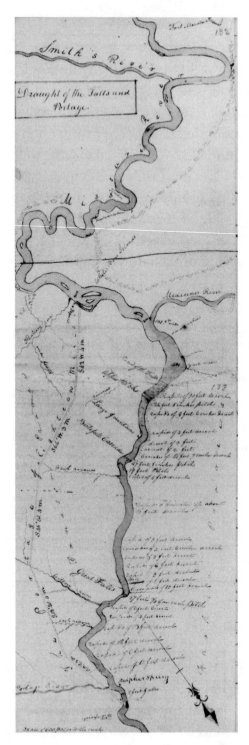

8. Falls and Portage of the Missouri River,
ca. July 4, 1805, Codex E, pp. 132–33

possibly hazzard the fate of the expedition.   we have never once hinted
to any one of the party that we had such a scheme in contemplation, and
all appear perfectly to have made up their minds to suceed in the expedition or purish in the attempt.   we all beleive that we are now about to
enter on the most perilous and difficult part of our voyage, yet I see no
one repining; all appear ready to met those difficulties which wait us with
resolution and becoming fortitude.   we had a heavy dew this morning.
the clouds near these mountains rise suddonly and discharge their[1] contents partially on the neighbouring plains; the same cloud will discharge
hail alone in one part hail and rain in another and rain only in a third all
within the space of a few miles; and on the Mountains to the S. E. of us
sometimes snow.   at present there is no snow on those mountains; that
which covered them when we first saw them and which has fallen on them
several times since has all disappeared.   the Mountains to the N. W. & W.
of us are still entirely covered are white and glitter with the reflection of
the sun. I do not beleive that the clouds which prevail at this season of the
year reach the summits of those lofty mountains; and if they do the probability is that they deposit snow only for there has been no perceptible
deminution of the snow which they contain since we first saw them. I have
thought it probable that these mountains might have derived their appellation of *shining Mountains,* from their glittering appearance when the
sun shines in certain directions on the snow which covers them.   since
our arrival at the falls we have repeatedly witnessed a nois which pro-
ceeds from a direction a little to the N. of West as loud and resembling
precisely the discharge of a piece of ordinance of 6 pounds at the distance
of three miles. I was informed of it by the men several times before I paid
any attention to it, thinking it was thunder most probably which they had
mistaken   at length walking in the plains the other day I heard this noise
very distictly, it was perfectly calm clear and not a cloud to be seen, I halted
and listened attentively about an hour during which time I heard two other
discharges and tok the direction of the sound with my pocket compass. I
have no doubt but if I had leasure I could find from whence it issued.
I have thout it probable that it might be caused by runing water in some
of the caverns of those immence mountains, on the principal of the blow-

ing caverns; but in such case the sounds would be periodical & regular, which is not the case with this, being sometimes heard once only and at other times, six or seven discharges in quick succession. it is heard also at different seasons of the day and night. I am at a loss to account for this phenomenon. our work being at an end this evening, we gave the men a drink of sperits, it being the last of our stock, and some of them appeared a little sensible of it's effects the fiddle was plyed and they danced very merrily untill 9 in the evening when a heavy shower of rain put an end to that part of the amusement tho' they continued their mirth with songs and festive jokes and were extreemly merry untill late at night. we had a very comfortable dinner, of bacon, beans, suit dumplings & buffaloe beaf &c. in short we had no just cause to covet the sumptuous feasts of our countrymen on this day.— one Elk and a beaver were all that was killed by the hunters today; the buffaloe seem to have withdrawn themselves from this neighbourhood; tho the men inform us that they are still abundant about the falls.—

[Clark]   *July the 4th Thursday 1805*

A fine morning, a heavy dew last night, all hands employed in Completeing the leather boat, gave the Party a dram which made Several verry lively, a black Cloud came up from the S. W, and rained a fiew drops   I employ my Self drawing a Copy of the river to be left at this place for fear of Some accident in advance, I have left buried below the falls a Map of the Countrey below Fort Mandan with Sundery private papers   the party amused themselves danceing untill late when a Shower of rain broke up the amusement, all lively and Chearfull, one Elk and a beaver kill'd to day.   our Tar kill like to turn out nothing from the following cause.

The climate about the falls of Missouri appears to be Singular Cloudy every day (Since our arrival near them) which rise from defferent directions and discharge themselves partially in the plains & mountains, in Some places rain others rain & hail, hail alone, and on the mountains in Some parts Snow.   a rumbling like Cannon at a great distance is heard to the west if us; the Cause we Can't account

1. At this point in Codex E is the sketch "Draught of the Falls and Portage" (fig. 8).

[Lewis]

This morning I had the boat removed to an open situation, scaffold her off the ground, turned her keel to the sun and kindled fires under her to dry her more expediciously. I then set a couple of men to pounding of charcoal to form a composition with some beeswax which we have and buffaloe tallow now my only hope and resource for paying my boat; I sincerely hope it may answer yet I fear it will not. the boat in every other rispect completely answers my most sanguine expectation; she is not yet dry and eight men can carry her with the greatest ease; she is strong and will carry at least 8,000 lbs. with her suit of hands; her form is as complete as I could wish it. the stitches begin to gape very much since she has began to dry; I am now convinced this would not have been the case had the skins been sewed with a sharp point only and the leather not cut by the edges of a sharp nedle. about 8 A M. a large herd of buffaloe came near our camp and Capt. Clark with a party of the hunters indeavoured to get a shoot at them but the wind proved unfavourable and they ran off; the hunters pursued and killed three of them; we had most of the meat brought in and set a party to drying it. their skins were all brought in and streached to dry for the purpose of covering the baggage. 2 Wolves and three Antelopes also killed today. we permitted three other men to visit the falls today; these were the last of the party who had not as yet indulged themselves with this grand and interesting seen. the buffaloe again appear in great numbers about our camp and seem to be moving down the river. it is somewhat remarkable that altho' you may see ten or a douzen herds of buffaloe distinctly scattered and many miles distant yet if they are undisturbed by pursuit, they will all be traveling in one direction. the men who were permitted to visit the falls today returned in the evening and reported that the buffaloe were very numerous in that quarter; and as the country is more broken near the river in that quarter we conclude to dispatch a couple of canoes tomorrow with some hunters to kill as many as will answer our purposes.—

The plains in this part of the country are not so fertile as below the entrance [*NB: Qu*] of the Cockkle or missel shell river and from thence down the Missouri there is also much more stone on the sides of the hills and on the broken lands than below.—

[Clark] *July 5th Friday 1805*

A fine morning and but little wind, worm and Sultrey at 8 oClock— I Saw a large gangue of Buffalow and prosued them with Several men the wind was unfavourable and we Could not get near them, the party Scattered & Killed 3 buffalow and brought into [camp] their Skins and Some meat, Killed 2 wolves & 3 Antilopes for their Skins, Capt. Lewis much engaged in Completeing the Leather boat. Three men went to See the Falls, Saw great numbers of Buffalow on both Sides of the river. great numbers of young black birds

[Lewis] *Saturday July 6th 1805*

In the couse of last night had several showers of hail and rain attended with thunder and lightning. about day a heavy storm came on from the S W attended with hail rain and a continued roar of thunder and some lightning. the hail was as large as musket balls and covered the ground perfectly. we hand some of it collected which kept very well through the day and served to cool our water. These showers and gusts keep my boat wet in dispite of my exertions. she is not yet ready for the grease and coal. after the hail and rain was over this morning we dispatched 4 hunters and two canoes to the head of the rappids as we had determined last evening. the red and yellow courants[1] are now ripe and abundant, they are reather ascid as yet. There is a remarkable small fox which ascociate in large communities and burrow in the praries something like the small wolf but we have not as yet been able to obtain one of them;[2] they are extreemly watchfull and take reffuge in their burrows which are very deep; we have seen them no where except near these falls.

[Clark] *July 6th Satturday 1805*

a heavy wind from the S W and Some rain about mid night last, at day light this morning a verry black Cloud from the S W, with a Contined rore of thunder & Some lightining and rained and hailed tremendiously for about ½ an hour, the hail was the Size of a musket ball and Covered the ground. this hail & rain was accompand. by a hard wind which lasted for a fiew minits. Cloudy all the forepart of the day, after Part Clear. dispatched 4 men in 2 Canoes to the falls, to kill Buffalow, for their Skins

& Meat   others employd about the boat, I cought Some Small fish this evening.

1. Probably the squaw currant which Lewis called a gooseberry on June 18, 1805. It is commonly found on dry slopes and ridges.

2. The swift fox (sometimes called the kit fox), then unknown to science. Cf. Cutright (LCPN), 166; Burroughs, 90–91; Jones et al., 256–58; Hall, 2:939–41. It was probably Biddle who drew a red vertical line through this passage about the fox.

[Lewis]   *Sunday July 7th 1805.*

The weather warm and cloudy therefore unfavourable for many operations; I keep small fires under the boat; the blowing flies are innumerable about it; the moisture retained by the bark prevents it from drying as fast as it otherwise would.   we dispatched two other hunters to kill Elk or buffaloe for their skins to cover our baggage.   we have no tents; the men are therefore obliged to have recourse to the sails for shelter from the weather and we have not more skins than are sufficient to cover our baggage when stoed away in bulk on land.   many of the men are engaged in dressing leather to cloath themselves.   their leather cloathes soon become rotton as they are much exposed to the water and frequently wet. Capt. Clarks black man York is very unwell today and he gave him a doze of tartar emettic[1] which operated very well and he was much better in the evening.   this is a discription of medecine that I nevr have recourse to in my practice except in cases of the intermittent fever.   this evening the hunters returned with the canoes and brought thre buffaloe skins only and two Antelope 4 deer and three wolf skins; they reported that the buffaloe had gone further down the river.   the two hunters whom we sent out from hence returned also without having killed anything except one Elk. I set one of the party at work to make me some sacks of the wolf skins, to transport my Instruments when occasion requirs their being carried any distance by land.—   we had a light shower of rain about 4 P. M. attended with some thunder and lightning.   one beaver caught this morning.   the musquetoes are excessively troublesome to us. I have prepared my composition which I should have put on this evening but the rain prevented me.

[Clark]   *July 7th Sunday 1805*

A Warm day wind from the S. W Cloudy as usial, the four men hunters
did not return last night.   dispatched 2 men to kill Elk for the use of
their Skin for the boat.   my man York Sick, I give him a dosh of Tarter.
Some rain in the after part of the day   in the evining the hunters returned with three buffalow Skins two goat Skins, four Deer Skins, two
deer, & 3 wolve Skins, to be used in Covering the boat Canoes & to make
mockersons, one Elk also killed to day

1. Tartar emetic is a white salt compound of potassium, antimony, oxygen, carbon, and
hydrogen, soluble in water and used to induce vomiting. Chuinard (OOMD), 297 n. 15.

[Lewis]   *Monday July 8th 1805.*

Capt. Clark Determined to make a second effort to replace the notes
which he had made with rispect to the river and falls   accordingly he set
out after an early breakfast and took with him the greater part of the men [1]
with a view also to kill buffaloe should there be any in that quarter.   after
geting some distance in the plains he divided the party and sent them in
different directions and himself and two others struck the Missouri at the
entrance of medicine river and continued down it to the great Cataract,
from whence he returned through the plains to camp where he arrived
late in the evening.   the hunters also returned having killed 3 buffaloe
2 Antelopes and a deer.   he informed me that the immence herds of buffaloe which we had seen for some time past in this neighbourhood have
almost entirely disappeared and he beleives are gone down the river.—
The day being warm and fair about 12 OCk. the boat was sufficiently dry
to receive a coat of the composition which I accordingly applyed.   this
adds very much to her appearance whether it will be effectual or not.   it
gives her hull the appearance of being formed of one solid piece.   after
the first coat had cooled I gave her a second which I think has made it
sufficiently thick. The mountains which ly before us from the South, to
the N. W. still continue covered with snow.   one hunter also passed the
river to hunt this morning   in the evening he returned having killed a
Buck and a male Antelope. The party who were down with Capt. Clark
also killed a small fox which they brought with them.   it was a female

appeared to give suck, otherwise it is so much like the comm small fox of this country commonly called the kit fox that I should have taken it for a young one of that species; however on closer examination it did apear to differ somewhat; it's colour was of a lighter brown, it's years proportionably larger, and the tale not so large or the hair not so long which formed it. they are very delicately formed, exceedingly fleet, and not as large as the common domestic cat. their tallons appear longer than any species of fox I ever saw and seem therefore prepared more amply by nature for the purpose of burrowing. there is sufficient difference for discrimination between it and the kit fox, and to satisfy me perfectly that it is a distinct species.[2] the men also brought me a living ground squirrel[3] which is something larger than those of the U' States or those of that kind which are also common here. this is a much hadsomer anamal. like the other it's principal colour is a redish brown but is marked longitudinally with a much greater number of black or dark bron stripes; the spaces between which is marked by ranges of pure white circular spots, about the size of a brister blue shot.[4] these colours imbrace the head neck back and sides; the tail is flat, or the long hair projecting horizontally from two sides of it only gives it that appearance. the belly and breast are of much lighter brown or nearly white. this is an inhabitant of the open plain altogether, wher it burrows and resides; nor is it like the other found among clifts of rocks or in the woodlands. their burrows sometimes like those of the mole run horizontally near the surface of the ground for a considerable distance, but those in which they reside or take refuge strike much deeper in the earth.— Slight rain this afternoon. musquetoes troublesome as usual.—

[Clark]   July 8th Monday 1805

A worm morning flying Clouds   I deturmin take the width of the river at the falls & the Medison river and to take the greater part of the men which Can be Speared to Kill Buffalow for their Skins as well as meat, devided the party & Sent them in different directions to hunt & proceeded my Self to the mouth of Medison river   measured it and found it to be 137 yards wide, in the narrowest part of the Missouri imediately above Medison river the Missouri is 300 yards wide, below and a little above the falls 1440 yards wide with the direction of the upper great fall 580 yards wide, at the great Spring 270 yards wide, at the handsom falls of 47 ft. 8 I. the river is 473 yards wide, at the lower great falls the river is confined within 280 yards, below the falls the water occupies 93 yards only— after takeing the wedth of the river at those Sundery placies I returned thro' the plains in a direct line to Camp. Some rain this evening after a verry hot day.— the mountains which are in view to the South & N W. are Covered with Snow. those nearer us and form a ¾ Circle around us is not Covered with Snow at this time. The hunters killed 3 buffalow, two antelopes, & a Deer to day— the emence herds of buffalow which was near us a fiew days ago, has proceeded on down the river, we Can See but a fiew Bulls in the plains

1. Ordway notes that he was included; he may have been one of the two who accompanied Clark the whole day, although his entry is not clear on this point.

2. Apparently the swift fox, in spite of Lewis's doubts. His use of the common name kit fox, an alternate name for the swift fox, indicates that the animal was popularly known, perhaps in the fur trade, although unknown to science. See note for July 6, 1805. It was probably Biddle who drew a red vertical line through the material beginning with "The party who" to the end of the entry.

3. The first scientific description of the thirteen-lined ground squirrel, *Spermophilus tridecemlineatus*. Cutright (LCPN), 166; Jones et al., 143–45. See also Coues (HLC), 2 : 405–6 n. 23.

4. Apparently Bristol Blue shot, the size still referred to as BB. Pendergast, 40.

[Lewis]   *Tuesday July 9th 1805.*

The morning was fair and pleant. the Islands seem crouded with blackbirds; the young brude is now completely feathered and flying in common with the others. we corked the canoes and put them in the water and also launched the boat, she lay like a perfect cork on the water. five men would carry her with the greatest ease. I now directed seats to be fixed in her and oars to be fitted. the men loaded the canoes in readiness to depart. just at this moment a violent wind commenced and blew so hard that we were obliged to unload the canoes again; a part of the baggage in several of them got wet before it could be taken out. the wind continued violent untill late in the evening, by which time we discovered that a greater part of the composition had seperated from the skins and left the seams of the boat exposed to the water and she leaked in such manner that she would not answer. I need not add that this circumstance mortifyed me not a little; and to prevent her leaking without pich was impossible with us, and to obtain this article was equally impossible, therefore the evil was irraparable   I now found that the section formed of the buffaloe hides on which some hair had been left, answered much the best purpose; this leaked but little and the parts which were well covered with hair about ⅛th of an inch in length retained the composition perfectly and remained sound and dry.   from these circumstances I am preswaided, that had I formed her with buffaloe skins singed not quite as close as I had done those I employed, that she would have answered even with this composition.   but to make any further experiments in our present situation seemed to me madness; the buffaloe had principally dserted us, and the season was now advancing fast. I therefore relinquished all further hope of my favorite boat and ordered her to be sunk in the water, that the skins might become soft in order the better to take her in peices tomorrow and deposite the iron fraim at this place as it could probably be of no further service to us.   had I only singed my Elk skins in stead of shaving them I beleive the composition would have remained and the boat have answered; at least untill we could have reached the pine country which must be in advance of us from the pine which is brought down by the water and which is probably at no great distance where we might have supplyed ourselves with the necessary pich or gum.   but it was now too late to introduce a remidy and I bid a dieu to my boat, and her expected services.—[1]   The next difficulty which presented itself was how we should convey the stores and baggage which we had purposed carrying in the boat.   both Capt. [*NB: Capt*] Clark and myself recollected having heard the hunters [*NB: Capt Clark had previously sent them in quest of timber for the purpose*] mention that the bottoms of the river some few miles above us were much better timbered than below and that some of the trees were large.   the idea therefore suggested itself of building two other canoes sufficiently large to carry the surplus baggage.   on enquiry of the hunters it seemed to be the general opinion that trees sufficiently a large for this purpose might be obtained in a bottom on the opposite side about

8 miles distant by land and reather more than double that distance by water; accordingly Capt. Clark determined to set out early in the morning with ten of the best workmen and proceede by land to that place while the others would in the mean time be employed by myself in taking the Boat in peices and depositing her, toge[the]r with the articles which we had previously determined to deposit at this place, and also in trasporting all the baggage up the river to that point in the six small canoes. this plan being settled between us orders were accordingly given to the party, and the ten men who were to accompany Capt. Clark had ground and prepared their axes and adds this evening in order to prepare for an early departure in the morning. we have on this as well as on many former occasions found a small grindstone which I brought with me from Harper's ferry[2] extreemly convenient to us. if we find trees at the place mentioned sufficiently large for our purposes it will be extreemly fortunate; for we have not seen one for many miles below the entrance of musselshell River to this place, which would have answered.—

July 9th 1805.

Observed Magnetic Azimuth of the ☉

Azimuth by Circumferenter	time by the Chronometer			Altd. of ☉'s U. L. by Sextant.	
		h	m	s	
N. 73° E.	A. M.	8	40	7	62° 38′ 15″ ⎫ Variation of the
N. 74° E.		8	44	47	63° 10 00 ⎭ Magnetic nedle.
					° ″ E

Equal Altitudes of the ☉ with Sextant.

	h	m	s			
A. M.	8	48	15 ⎫	P. M.	lost by the ⎫	Altitude at the time
	″	49	48 ⎬		interferce. ⎬	of observation
	″	51	25 ⎭		of Clouds ⎭	65° 22′ 15″

Observed Meridian Altd. of ☉'s L. L. with octant back Obsn. 55° 4′ —″
Latitude deduced from this observation   N. 47° 3′ 56. ¹⁄₁₀″

[Clark] *July 9th Tuesday 1805*

a clear worm morning wind from the S W. Lanced the Leather boat, and found that it leaked a little; Corked Lanced & loaded the Canoes, burried our truk wheels, & made a Carsh for a Skin & a fiew papers I intend to leave here

on trial found the leather boat would not answer without the addition of Tar which we had none of, haveing Substituted *Cole & Tallow* in its place to Stop the Seams &c. which would not answer as it Seperated from the Skins when exposed to the water and left the Skins naked & Seams exposed to the water   this falire of our favourate boat was a great disapointment to us, we haveing more baggage than our Canoes would Carry. Concluded to build Canoes for to Carry them; no timber near our Camp. I deturmined to proceed on up the river to a bottom in which our hunters reported was large Trees &c.

1. Apparently the boat was abandoned for good; there is no record of its recovery on the return trip in 1806. Rose.

2. The federal armory at Harpers Ferry, Virginia (now West Virginia), where Lewis obtained weapons, the iron boat frame, and various other equipment for the expedition.

[Lewis] *Wednesday July 10th 1805.*

Capt. Clark set out with his party early this morning and passed over to the opposite side.   after which I dispatched Sergt. Ordway with 4 Canoes and 8 men[1] to take up a load of baggage as far as Capt. Clark's camp and return for the remainder of our plunder.   with six others[2] I now set to work on my boat, which had been previously drawn out of the water before the men departed, and in two hours had her fraim in readiness to be deposited.   had a cash dug and deposited the Fraim of the boat, some papers and a few other trivial articles of but little importance.   the wind blew very hard the greater part of the day. I also had the truck wheels buried in the pit which had been made to hold the tar.   having nothing further to do I amused myself in fishing and caught a few small fish; they were of the species of white chub mentioned below the falls, tho' they are small and few in number. I had thought on my first arrival here that there were no fish in this part of the river. Capt. Clark proceeded up the river 8 miles by land (distance by water 23 ¼)³ and found 2 trees of Cottonwood and cut them down; one proved to be hollow and split in falling at the upper part and was somewhat windshaken at bottom; the other proved to be much windshaken.   he surched the bottom for better but could not find any he therefore determined to make canoes of those which he had fallen; and to contract their length in such manner as to clear the craks and the worst of the windsken parts making up the deficiency by allowing them to be as wide as the trees would permit.   they were much at a loss for wood to make axhandles.   the Chokecherry is the best we can procure for this purpose and of that wood they made and broke thir 13 handles in the course of this part of a day.   had the eyes of our axes been round they would have answered this country much better.   the musquetoes were very troublesome to them as well as ourselves today. Sergt. Ordway proceeded up the river about 5 miles when the wind became so violent that he was obliged to ly by untill late in the evening when he again set out with the canoes and arrived within 3 miles of Capt. Clark's Camp where he halted for the night.   about five miles above whitebear camp there are two Islands [*NB: Qu*] in the river covered with Cottonwood box alder and some sweet willow also the undergrowth like that of the islands at this place.—

Observed Equal Altitudes of the ☉ with Sextant;

	h	m	s		h	m	s	
A M.	8	16	9	P. M.	6	2	20	Altitude given at the
"		17	45		"	3	55	times of observation
"		19	17		"	5	30	54° 49′ 45″

h   m   s

Chronometer too slow on Mean Time   [*blank*]

Observed Meridian Altd. of ☉'s L L with Octant by the back observation 55° 27′   ″

Latitude deduced from this observation   N. 47° 3′ 10″

Observed time and distance of ☽'s western limb from α Antares; ★ West; with Sextant.

	Time			*Distance*
	h	m	s	
P. M.	10	47	21	34° 12′ 45″

"	50	8	"	14	
"	52	38	"	14	30
"	54	49	"	15	30"

	Time			*Distance*		
	h	m	s			
P. M.	10	57	73	34°	16'	15"
	"	59	31	"	17	
	"	2	11	"	18	30
	"	4	24	"	19	15

Observed time and distance of ☽'s Western limb from Pegassi; ★ East, with Sextant.

	Time			*Distance*		
	h	m	s			
P. M.	11	47	35	73	11'	15"
	"	51	39	"	15	
	"	54	8	"	13	45

from the distance of this star I am doubtfull that it is not Pegassi therefore observed another.

	Time			*Distance*		
			s			
Astro.	12	11	46	71°	3'	45"
	"	14	25	"	5	30

This I think is most probably Pegassi; but the star appeared very small.

[Clark]   *July 10th Wednesday 1805*

a fair windey day wind hard the most of the day from the S. W.—rained modderately all last night (by Showers) we dispatched Serjt. Ordway with 4 Canoes loaded & 8 men by water to assend as high as I Should have found timber for Canoes & formed a Camp;—. I Set out with Sergt. Pryor four Choppers two Involids[4] & one man to hunt, Crossed to the Std. Side and proceeded on up the river 8 miles by land (distance by water 23¼ ms.) and found two Trees which I thought would make Canoes, had them fallen, one of them proved to be hollow & Split at one End & verry much win Shaken at the other, the other much win Shaken, we Serched the bottoms for better trees and made a trial of Several which proved to be more indifferent. I deturmined to make Canoes out of the two first trees we had fallen, to Contract thir length so as to clear the hollow & winshakes, & ad to the width as much as the tree would allow. The Musquitors emencely noumerous & troublesom, Killed two deer & a goat. The Canoes did not arrive as I expected, owing to the hard wind which blew a head in maney places.   we ar much at a loss for wood to make ax hilthes,[5] 13 hath been made & broken in this piece of a day by the four Choppers, no other wood but Cotton Box elder Choke Cherry and red arrow wood.   we Substitute the Cherry in place of Hickory for ax hilthes ram rods, &c. &c.

1. Whitehouse says he was with this group.

2. Gass says he was one of those with Lewis.

3. This camp, where Clark remained until July 15 making canoes, is in Cascade County, Montana, on the north side of the Missouri, just southeast of Antelope Butte and a few miles east of the present town of Ulm. It is misplaced on *Atlas* map 61. Clark's route by land is shown by a dotted line on the *Atlas* maps. *Atlas* map 54; MRC 78.

4. William Bratton, who was with this group, may have counted as an invalid because of his infected finger.

5. Helves, that is, axe handles.

[Lewis]   *Thursday July 11th 1805.*

We had now nothing to do but wait for the canoes; as they had not returned I sent out some of the small party with me to hunt; in the evening they returned with a good quantity of the flesh of a fat buffaloe which they had killed.   the canoes not arrived this evening. I saw several very large grey Eagles today they are a half as large again as the common bald Eagle of this country. I do not think the bald Eagle here qute so large as those of the U' States; the grey Eagle is infinitely larger and is no doubt a distinct species.[1]   this evening a little before the sun set I heared two other discharges of this unaccounable artillery of the Rocky Mountains proceeding from the same quarter that I had before heard it. I now recollected the Minnetares making mention of the nois which they had frequently heard in the Rocky Mountains like thunder; and which they said the mountains made; but I paid no attention to the information supposing it either false or the fantom of a supersticious immagination. I have also been informed by the engages that the Panis and Ricaras give the same account of the Black mountains which lye West of them. this phenomenon the philosophy of the engages readily accounts for; they state it to be the bursting of the rich mines of silver which these mountains contain.

This morning Capt. Clark dispatched Bratton to meet the canoes which were detained by the wind to get a couple of axes. he obtained the axes and returned in about two hours. this man has been unable to work for several days in consequence of a whitlow on one of his fingers;[2] a complaint which has been very common among the men. one of the canoes arrived at Capt. Clarks camp about 10 A. M. this he had unloaded and set a few miles up the river for a buffaloe which had been killed, the party sent killed another in thir rout and brought in the flesh and skins of both they were in good order; his hunters had also killed two deer and an Antelope yesterday. the three other canoes did not arrive untill late in the evening in consequence of the wind and the fear of weting their loads which consisted of articles much more liable to be injured by moisture than those which composed the load of that which arrived in the morning. Capt. C. had the canoes unloaded and ordered them to float down in the course of the night to my camp, but the wind proved so high after night that they were obliged to put too about 8 miles above and remain untill morning. Capt. C. kept the party with him busily engaged at the canoes. his hunters killed and brought in three very fat deer this evening.—

[Clark]   *July 11th Thursday 1805*

a fair windey morning wind S. W. I dispatch W Bratten (who cannot work he haveing a tumer rising on his finger) to meat the Canoes & bring from them two axes, which is necessary for the work at the perogues or Canoes, and is indespenceable he returned in about two hours & informed that one Canoe was within three miles, about 1 oClock the Canoe which Bratten left arrived haveing killed a Buffalow on the river above our Camp, at which place the bend of the river below & that above is about 1 mile apart, I dispatched Serjt. Pryor with 3 men in the Canoe to get the meat   they killed another buffalow near the one killed and brought the meat of both down.   at Sunset the 3 remaining Canoes arrived unloaded & returned imeadeately with orders to flote down to Camp at the portage to night for the purpose of takeing up the remaining baggage. Musquitors verry troublesom, and in addition to their torments we have a Small Knat, which is as disagreeable, our hunter killed 3 Deer to day one of them verry fat.   all the men with me engaged about the Canoes hunting &c. &.

1. Lewis's gray eagle may be the golden eagle; on the average they are smaller than the bald eagle. Burroughs, 207, 325 nn. 5, 6, 7, suggests that Lewis may have compared a female golden eagle to a male bald eagle. See also Coues (HLC), 2 : 409 n. 25. Holmgren considers this bird to be an immature bald eagle. It was probably Biddle who drew a red vertical line through the passage about the "grey Eagles."

2. A whitlow is an infection, often extremely painful, under and around the nail and sometimes deep into the bone. Chuinard (OOMD), 297–98 n. 16.

[Lewis]   *Friday July 12th 1805.*

The canoes not having arrived and the wind still high I dispatched Sergt. Gass with three men to join Capt. Clark and assist in completing the canoes retaining only a few who in addition to those in the canoes that I expect every moment, will be sufficient to man the six canoes and take up all the baggage we have here at one load. I feel excessively anxious to be moving on.   the canoes were detained by the wind untill 2 P. M. when they set out and arrived at this place so late that I thought it best to detain them untill morning. Bratton came down today for a cople of axes which I sent by him; he returned immediately. Sergt. Gass and party joined Capt. Clark at 10 A. M. Capt. C. kept all the men with him busily engaged some in drying meat, others in hunting, and as ma[n]y as could be employed about the canoes. Segt. Pryor got his sholder dislocated yesterday, it was replaced immediately and is likely to do him but little injury; it is painfull to him today.   the hunters with Capt. C. killed three deer and two otter today.   the otter are now plenty since the water has become sufficiently clear for them to take fish.   the blue crested fisher, or as they are some-times called the *Kingfisher,*[1] is an inhabitant of this part of the country; this bird is very rare on the Missouri; I have not seen more than three or four of those birds during my voyage from the entrance of the Missouri to the mouth of Maria's river and those few were reather the inhabitants of streams of clerer water which discharged themselves into the Missouri than of that river, as they were seen about the entrances of such streams. Musquetoes extreemly troublesome to me today nor is a large black knat[2] less troublesome, which dose not sting, but attacks the eye in swarms and compells us to brush them off or have our eyes filled with them. I made the men dry the ballance of the freshe meet which we had abot the camp amounting to about 200 lbs.—

Observed Equal Altitudes of the ☉ with Sextant.

A M.	10	8	31	P. M.	4	8	6⎫	altitude given at the
"	10	11		"	9	77	⎬	time of observation
"	12	52		"	11	27	⎭	92° 13′ 15

h   m   s

Chronometer too [*blank*] on mean Mean T.   [*blank*]

[Clark]   *July 12th Friday 1805*

a fair windey morning wind from the S. W.   all hands at work at Day light Some at the Canoes, & others drying meat for our voyage— Dispatched W. Brattin to the lower Camp[3] for two axes which are necessary to carry on our work at this place &. Serjt. Pryors Sholder was put out of place yesterday Carrying Meat and is painfull to day.   wind hard all day   dispatched 2 hunters, they returnd in the evening with three Deer & 2 orters.   four men arrived from the lower Camp by land to assist at this place in building the Canoes &c.   musquitors & knats verry troublesom all day.   a fiew wild pigions[4] about our Camp.

1. The belted kingfisher. It was probably Biddle who drew a red vertical line through the passage about the kingfisher and gnats.

2. Apparently correctly identified by Coues (HLC), 2:409, as the buffalo gnat, *Simulium* sp. Criswell, xcv, 42.

3. The White Bear Islands camp, not the now-abandoned lower portage camp.

4. The passenger pigeon, *Ectopistes migratorius* [AOU, 315]. Burroughs, 233–34.

[Lewis]   *Saturday July 13th 1805.*

This morning being calm and Clear I had the remainder of our baggage embarked in the six small canoes and maned them with two men each.[1] I now bid a cheerfull adue to my camp and passed over to the opposite shore. Baptiest La Page one of the men whom I had reserved to man the canoes being sick I sent Charbono in his stead by water and the sick man and Indian woman accompanyed me by land.   from the head of the white bear Islands I passed in a S. W. direction and struck the Missouri at 3 miles and continued up it to Capt. Clark's camp where I arrived about 9 A. M. and found them busily engaged with their canoes Meat &c.   in my way I passed a very extraordinary Indian lodge, or at least the fraim of one; it was formed of sixteen large cottonwood poles each about fifty feet long and at their larger end which rested on the ground as thick as a man's body; these were arranged in a circular manner at bottom and equally distributed except the omission of one on the East side which I suppose was the entrance to the lodge; the upper part of the poles are united in a common point above and secured with large wyths of willow brush.   in the center of this fabric there was the remains of a large fire; and about the place the marks of about 80 leather lodges. I know not what was the intention or design of such a lodge but certain I am that it was not designed for a dwelling of any one family.   it was 216 feet in circumpherence at the base.   it was most probably designed for some great feast, or a council house on some great national concern. I never saw a similar one nor do the nations lower down the Missouri construct such.[2] The canoes and party with Sergt. Ordway poceeded up the river about 5 miles when the wind became so violent that two of the canoes shiped a considerable quanty of water and they were compelled to put too take out the baggage to dry and clense the canoes of the water.   about 5 P. M. the wi[n]d abated and they came on about 8 miles further and encamped. I saw a number of turtledoves and some pigeons today.   of the latter I shot one; they are the same common to the United States, or the wild pigeon as they are called.   nothing remarkable in the appearance of the country; the timber entirely confined to the river and the country back on either side as far as the eye can reach entirely destitute of trees or brush.   the timber is larger and more abundant in the bottom in which we now are than I have seen it on the Missouri for many hundred miles. the current of the river is still extreemly gentle. The hunters killed three buffaloe today which were in good order. the flesh was brought in dryed the skins wer also streached for covering our baggage. we eat an emensity of meat; it requires 4 deer, an Elk and a deer, or one buffaloe, to supply us plentifully 24 hours. meat now forms our food prinsipally as we reserve our flour parched meal and corn as much as possible for the rocky mountains which we are shortly to enter, and where from the indian account game is not very abundant. I preserved specemines of several small plants to day which I have never before seen. The Musquetoes and knats are more troublesome here if possible than they were at the White bear Islands. I sent a man to the canoes for my musquetoe bier which I had neglected to bring with me, as it is impossible to sleep a moment without being defended against the attacks of these most tormenting of all insects; the man returned with it a little after dark.—

[Clark]   *July 13th Saturday 1805.*

a fair Calm Morning, verry Cool before day— we were visited by a Buffalow Bull who came within a fiew Steps of one of the Canoes ⟨as⟩ the men were at work. Capt. Lewis one man &c. arrived over Land at 9 oClock, the wind rose and blew hard from the S. E. the greater part of the day both Canoes finished all to Corking & fixing ores &c. &c. The Hunters killed 3 Buffalow the most of all the meat I had dried for to make Pemitigon. The Musquetors & Knats verry troublesom all day & night

1. Ordway notes that he was again in charge of the canoes, and Whitehouse says he was in one of them.

2. The description sounds much like the medicine lodge in which the Blackfeet sun dance was held, except that Lewis does not mention the center pole which was characteristic of this structure. The region they were now in was Blackfeet (specifically Piegan) territory. Ewers (BRNP), 174–84.

[Lewis]   *Sunday July 14th 1805.*

This morning was calm fair and warm; the Musquetoes of course troublesome. all hands that could work were employed about the canoes. which we completed and launched this evening. the one was 25 feet and the other 33 feet in length and about 3 feet wide.   we have now the seats and oars to make and fit &c. I walked out today and ascended the bluffs which are high rockey and steep; I continued my rout about 3½ when I gained a conspicuous eminence about 2 mes. distant from the river a little below the entrance of Fort Mountain Creek.[1]   from this place I had a commanding view of the country and took the bearings of the following places. (viz)[2]

		miles
To the point at which the Missouri first enters the Rocky Mountains	S. 28° W.	25
To the termineation of the 1st Chain of Rocky Mountains; northwardly, being that through which the Missouri first passes	N. 73° W	80
To the extremity or tirmineation of 2cd Chain of the Rocky Mountains	N. 65 W.	150
To the most distant point of a third and continued chain of the same mts.	N. 50° W.	200
The direction of the 1st Chain of Rocky Mouts. from S. 20 E. to N 20 W.		
The direction of the 2cd Do. from S 45 E. to N. 45. W.—		
To Fort mountain	S. 75° W.	8

The country in most parts very level and in others swelling with gentle rises and decents, or in other wirds what I have heretofore designated a wavy country destitute of timber except along the water-courses. On my return to camp found Sergt. Ordway had arrived with all the canoes about noon and had unloaded them   every preperation except the entire completion of the oars poles &c is made for our departure tomorrow.   the grass and weeds in this bottom are about 2 feet high; which is a much greater hight than we have seen them elsewhere this season.   here I found the sand rush and nittles in small quantities.[3]   the grass in the plains is not more than 3 inches high.   grasshoppers innumerable in the plains and the small birds before noticed together with the brown Curlooe[4] still continue nomerous in every part of the plains.—

had a slight shower at 4 P. M. this evening.

[Clark]   *July 14th Sunday 1805*

a fine morning Calm and worm   musquetors & Knats verry troublesom. The Canoes arrive at 12 oClock & unloade to Dry &c.   finished &
Lanced the 2 Canoes, Some rain this afternoon.   all prepareing to Set
out on tomorrow.

1. Lewis's eminence is not known, but it probably is not Antelope Butte which is too
close to the camp. Fort Mountain Creek is not named on *Atlas* maps 54 or 55, but may be a
nameless stream above Smith River, which enters the Missouri at the town of Ulm, Cascade County, Montana.

2. In the left margin of the page by this table, at right angles to the rest, Lewis has
added a pointing hand symbol and has written, "the Southern extremites of these ranges
not visible and believe they continue probably to mexico." He probably imagined "Mexico"—New Mexico—to be closer than it was, but he was expanding his idea of the extent
of the Rockies. In essence he was correct, for the only real gap in the ranges was in the area
of South Pass, in Wyoming. From his position Lewis was looking south toward the Gates
of the Mountains (see July 19, 1805) and northwest along various divisions of the Lewis
range (the Continental Divide) north to present Glacier National Park.

3. The sand rush could be any of several species of *Equisetum,* horsetail or scouring
rush, in the area; the "nittles" are *Urtica dioica* L., stinging nettle. Hitchcock & Cronquist,
43; Booth & Wright, 32. It was probably Biddle who drew a red vertical line through the
passages about the grass and bird.

4. Probably the same bird described in more detail on July 22, 1805; see the possible
species there.

Chapter Seventeen

From the Great Falls to Three Forks

July 15–27, 1805

[Lewis] *Monday July 15th 1805.*

    We arrose very early this morning, assigned the canoes their loads and had it put on board.   we now found our vessels eight in number all heavily laden, notwithstanding our several deposits; tho' it is true we have now a considerable stock of dryed meat and grease.   we find it extreemly diffi-cult to keep the baggage of many of our men within reasonable bounds; they will be adding bulky articles of but little use or value to them. At 10 A. M. we once more saw ourselves fairly under way much to my joy and I beleive that of every individual who compose the party. I walked on shore and killed 2 Elk near one of which the party halted and dined.   we took the skins marrow bones and a part of the flesh of these Elk.   in order to lighten the burthen of the canoes I continued my walk all the evening and took our only invalledes Potts an LaPage with me.   we passed the river near where we dined and just above the entrance of a beautifull river 80 yards wide which falls in on the Lard. side which in honour of Mr. Robert Smith the Secretary of the Navy we called Smith's River.[1]   this stream meanders through a most lovely valley to the S. E. for about 25 miles when it enters the Rocky mountains and is concealed from our view.   many herds of buffaloe were feeding in this valley.   we again crossed the river to the Stard. side and passed through a plain and struck the river at a Northwardly bend where there was timber   here we waited untill the canoes arrived by which time it was so late that we concluded to encamp for the night.[2]   here Drewyer wouded a deer which ran into the river   my dog pursued caught it drowned it and brought it to shore at our camp.   we have now passed Fort Mountain on our right it appears to be about ten miles distant.   this mountain has a singular appearance   it is situated in a level plain, it's sides stand nearly at right angles with each other and are each about a mile in extent.   these are formed of a yellow clay only without the mixture of rock or stone of any size and rise perpendicularly to the hight of 300 feet.   the top appears to be a level plain and from the eminence on which I was yesterday I could see that it was covered with a similar cost of grass with the plain on which it stands.   the surface appears also to possess a tolerable fertile mole [mold] of 2 feet thick. and is to all appearance inaccessible.   from it's figure we gave it the name of fort mountain.[3]   those mounds before mentioned near the falls have much the same appearance but are none of them as large as this one.   the prickly pear is now in full blume and forms one of the beauties as well as the greatest pests of the plains.   the sunflower is also in blume and is abundant.[4]   this plant is common to every part of the Missouri from it's entrance to this place.   the lambsquarter, wild coucumber, sand rush and narrow dock are also common here.[5] Drewyer killed another deer and an Otter today.   we find it inconvenient to take all the short meanders of the river which has now become cooked and much narrower than below, we therefore take it's general course and lay down the small bends by the eye on our daily traverse or chart.   the river is from 100 to 150 yds. wide.   more timber on the river than below the falls for a great distance.   on the banks of the river there are many large banks of sand much elivated above the plains on which they ly and appear as if they had been collected in the course of time from the river by the almost incessant S. W. winds; they always appear on the sides of the river opposite to those winds.—

The couses and distances from the White bear islands to the camp at which we made the canoes as taken by Sergt. Ordway.—

S. 10° E.   1 ½   to a point of low trees on the Lard. side passing a willow island on Lard. side

S. 36° E.	1	to a point of wood on the Stard. side
South	1	to a clift of rocks in a bend on Lard. side
S. 45° W.	1 ½	to some trees in a bend, passing a timbered islad on the Stard. side.
South	1 ¼	to a point of low timber on Stard. side
S. 24 W.	1	to a bunch of bushes on the Lard. side
West	2	to a grove of trees in a Lard. bend
N. 26° W.	2	to a point of wood on the Lard. side
North	1	Along the Lard. point
N. 20° W.	1 ½	to a small Creek Lard. side
S. 45° W.	¾	to the lower point of a timbered Isd. S. S.
S. 10° E.	1 ½	opposite the island on the Lard. side
S. 16° W.	¾	to a point above the Island Lar. side.
South	1 ½	to a point of low timber on the Stard. side opposite to a bluff on Lard. side
West	½	to a tree in a Lard. bend.
North	½	to a point of timbered land on Lard. side
N. 12° W.	1	to a point on Lard. side
West	1 ½	to a point on the Stard. side.
N. 16° W.	½	to a point of timber on Lard. side
N. 60° W.	½	along the lard. point, passing a large sand bar on Lard. side.
S. 54° W.	½	to a point of woodland Stard. side where we built two canoes.—
Miles 23 ¼		

Courses and distances July 15th 1805.

S. 45° W.	¼	to the upper part of the timber Stard. side
S. 60° E.	¾	to a bend on the Lard. side
S. 20° W.	½	along the lard. side in the bend
N. 70° W.	1 ½	to a point on the Stard. side passing an Isid.
South	¾	to a lard. bend passing the entrance of Fort Mountain creek at the commencement of this course no water at present 10 yds.

S. 30° W.	2 ¼	to a bend on the Stard. side oposit an Island passing a Stard. and Lard. point.
West	1 ½	to the lower point of the woodland at the entrance of Smith's river, which is 80 yds. wide and falls in on Lard. in a bend
N. 45° W.	1 ¾	to a Stard bend.
South	3	to the head of an Island in the Lard. bend passing over the Lard. point.
N. 45° W.	1 ¼	to a stard. bend.
West	½	in the stard. bend.
South	¾	in the Stard. bend.
S. 45° E.	¾	in the Stard. bend.
East	1	in the Stard. bend passing an island Lard. side
S. 45° E	¾	on the Lard. side.
West	2 ½	to a wood in the Stard. bend, where we encamped for the
Miles 19 ¾		evening.—

[Clark] *July 15th Monday 1805*

rained all the last night I was wet all ⟨day⟩ night   this morning wind hard from the S. W.   we Set out at 10 oClock and proceeded on verry well   passed a river on the Lard Side about 80 yards wide which we Call after the Secy of the Navey Smiths River   the river verry Crooked bottoms extensive rich and Passes thro' a butifull vally between 2 mts. Conts. high grass, our Canoes being So Small ⟨we⟩ Several of the men Capt. Lewis & my Self Compelled to walked on Shore & Cross the bends to keep up with the Canoes—   a round mountain on our ⟨left⟩ right abt. 10 miles appears inaxcessable we Call fort mountain. The Prickley pear in bloom but fiew other flowers. Sun flowr are common, also lambs quarter & Nettles. Capt Lew Killed 2 Elk & the hunters killed 2 Deer & a Ortter, we Camped on the Stard Side at which place I Saw many beaver, the timber on the edge of the river more Common than below the falls—   as I am compelled to walk on Shore find it verry dificuelt to take the Courses of the river, as it is verry Crooked more So than below

1. Smith River meets the Missouri in Cascade County, Montana, near the present town of Ulm. Robert Smith was secretary of the navy during Jefferson's entire administration, and was also attorney general for a few months in 1805. *Atlas* maps 54, 62; MRC map 78.

2. In Cascade County, a few miles southwest of Ulm. *Atlas* map 54; MRC map 78.

3. Fort Mountain, which appears prominently on *Atlas* map 54, is now Square Butte, south of the town of Fort Shaw, Cascade County. *Montana Guide*, 267, 284. The lower two-thirds of Square Butte is formed of the late Cretaceous Virgelle Member of the Eagle Sandstone and the Telegraph Creek Formation. The upper third is composed of a basaltic sill. It acts like a caprock to protect the softer sediments below it. The summit of Square Butte is about one thousand feet above the adjacent plains.

4. *Helianthus annuus* L., common sunflower. Booth & Wright, 274; Cutright (LCPN), 188. It was probably Biddle who drew a red vertical line through the passage about the prickly pear, sunflower, and other plants.

5. These plants may be identified as *Chenopodium album* L., lambsquarter; *Echinocystis lobata* (Michx.) T. & G., mock-cucumber; and *Rumex salicifolius* Wienm. (also called *R. mexicanus* Meisn.), Mexican dock. Fernald, 568; Barkley, 83; Booth & Wright, 46, 237, 41.

[Lewis]   *Tuesday July 16th 1805.*

We had a heavy dew last night   sen one man back this morning for an ax that he had carelessly left last evening some miles below,[1] and set out at an early hour.   early this morning we passed about 40 little booths formed of willow bushes to shelter them from the sun; they appeared to have been deserted about 10 days; we supposed that they were snake Indians.   they appeared to have a number of horses with them—.   this appearance gives me much hope of meeting with these people shortly. Drewyer killed a buffaloe this morning near the river and we halted and breakfasted on it.   here for the first time I ate of the small guts of the buffaloe cooked [*NB: Qu:*] over a blazing fire in the Indian stile without any preperation of washing or other clensing and found them very good.—   After breakfast I determined to leave Capt. C. and party, and go on to the point where the river enters the Rocky Mountains and make the necessary observations against their arrival; accordingly I set out with the two invalleds Potts and LaPage and Drewyer; I passed through a very handsome level plain on the Stard. side of the river, the country equally level and beautifull on the opposite side; at the distance of 8 mes. passed a small stream on which I observed a considerable quantity of aspin.[2]   a little before 12 I halted on the river at a Stard. bend and well timbered bottom about 4½ miles below the mountains and made the following observation.

Observed Meridian Altd. of ⊙'s. L. L. with Octant by the back Observation. 56° 38′ —″

Latitude deduced from this observation. N. 46 46 50.2

after this observation we pursued our rout through a high roling plain to a rappid immediately at the foot of the mountain where the Missouri first enters them.[3] the current of the missouri below these rappids is strong for several miles, tho' just above there is scarcely any current, the river very narrow and deep abot 70 yds. wide only and seems to be closely hemned in by the mountains on both sides, the bottoms only a few yards in width. an Indian road enters the mountain at the same place with the river on the Stard side and continues along it's border under the steep clifts these mountains appear to be only about 800 feet above the river and are formed almost entirely of a hard black grannite.[4] with a few dwarf pine and cedar scattered on them. at this place there is a large rock of 400 feet high wich stands immediately in the gap which the missouri makes on it's passage from the mountains; it is insulated from the neighbouring mountains by a handsome little plain which surrounds it base on 3 sides and the Missouri washes it's base on the other, leaving it on the Lard. as it decends. this rock I called the tower.[5] it may be ascended with some difficulty nearly to it's summit, and from it there is a most pleasing view of the country we are now about to leave. from it I saw this evening immence herds of buffaloe in the plains below. near this place we killed a fat elk on which we both dined and suped. the Musquetoes are extreemly troublesome this evening and I ⟨have⟩ had left my bier, of course suffered considerably, and promised in my wrath that I never will be guily of a similar peice of negligence while on this voyage.—

[Clark]   *July 16th Tuesday 1805*

a fair morning after a verry cold night, heavy dew, dispatched one man back for an ax left a fiew miles below, and Set out early Killed a Buffalow on which we Brackfast Capt Lewis & 3 men went on to the mountain to take a meridian altitude, passed about 40 Small Camps, which appeared to be abandoned about 10 or 12 days, Suppose they were Snake Indians, a fiew miles above I Saw the poles Standing in thir position of a verry large lodge of 60 feet Diamater, & the appearance of a number of Leather Lodges about, this Sign was old & appeared to have been last fall   great number of buffalow   the river is not So wide as below from 100 to 150 yards wide & Deep Crouded with Islands & Crooked   Some Scattering timber on its edge Such as Cotton wood Cotton willow, willow and box elder, the Srubs are arrow wod, red wood, Choke Cherry, red berries, Goose beries, Sarvis burey, red & yellow Currents a Spcie of Shomake[6] &c.

I camped on the head of a Small Island near the Stard. Shore at the Rockey Mountains[7]   this Range of mountains appears to run N W & S E and is about 800 feet higher than the Water in the river faced with a hard black rock   the current of the River from the Medison river to the mountain is gentle bottoms low and extensive, and its General Course is S. 10° W. about 30 miles on a direct line

Course Distances &c. from White bear Island Camp to the mountains
July 13th 14th 15th & 16 1805[8]

	miles	
S 10° E	1 ½	to a point of low trees on the Lard Side passed a Willow Island L.
S 36° E	1	to a point of wood on the Stard Side
South	1	to a Clift of rocks in a bend on the L. S.
S W	1 ½	to Some trees in a bend passed a timbered Island on the Std. Side
South	1 ¼	to a point of low wood Std. Side
S. 24° W	1	to a bunch of bushes on the L. S.
West	2	to a grove of trees in a bend L. S.
N. 26° W.	2	to a point of wood on the L. S
North	1	allong the Lard point ⟨psd a Creek⟩
	12 ¼	

⟨16⟩ 14

N. 20° W	1 ½	to a Creek on the ⟨Stard⟩ Lard. Side
S. W.	¾	to the lower point of an Island. S. S.
S. 10° E	1 ½	opposit the Island on the L. S.

S. 16° W.	¾	to a point above the Island L. Side.
South	1 ½	to point of low timber on the Stard. Side a Bluff & rocks on L. S
West	½	to a tree in a bend on the L. Side
North	½	to a point of wood on the L. Side
N. 12° W.	1	to a point on the Lard Side
West	1 ½	to a point on the Stard. Side
N. 16° W	½	to a point of wood on L. Side
N. 60° W.	½	along Said point, passing 2 large Sand bar L. S
S. 54° W.	½	to a point of wood Stard Side at which place I built 2 Canoes.
	23 ¼	

⟨17⟩ 15

S W	¼	to the upper part of a wood St Side
S. 60° E	¾	to a bend on the Lard. Side
S. 20° W.	½	on the Lard Side in the bend
N. 70° W.	1 ½	to a point on the Stard. Side passed an Island
South	¾	to the Lard Bend
S. 30° W.	2 ¼	to a bend on the Stard. Side opsd. an Isld. passed a Stard. & Lard point
West	1 ½	to the lower point of a wood at the mouth of ⟨a⟩ *Smiths* river in the Lard bend 80 yards wide
N. 45° W	1 ¾	to the Stard bend
South	3	to the head of an Island in the Lard bend passing over the Lard point
N. 45° W	1 ¼	to the Stard. bend
West	½	in the Stard. bend
South	¾	in the Stard. bend
S 45° E	¾	in the Stard. bend
East	1	in the Stard. bend passd. an Isld. L. S.
S E	¾	on the Lard Side
West	2 ½	to a wood in the Std bend
	43	

⟨18th⟩ 16th

S 30 E	1 ½	to trees in the Lard bend
West	1 ½	to the Stard. bend passing over a Sd. pt.
S. 10° E	¾	to the mouth of a run Lard bend
S W	1 ½	to a bend on the Stard Side
S 15° E	½	to a bend on the Lard. Side
S W.	2	to the mouth of a run on Std. Side
S E.	1	to a bend Lard Side (opsd. a big Lodge)
South	1	on the Lard Side in a bend opposit an Island
S. 70° W	1	in the Lard bend
	53 ¾	
S. 30° W	1	in the bend to the Lard. Side
South	¾	in the bend to the Lard Side
N. 30° W	1 ¼	to a bend on the Stard. Side passed a Small Island
South	4	to the Lower point of a timber on the Stard Side passed 6 Islands
S. 60° E	½	to the bend on the Lard. Side
S. 50° W	1 ½	to the upper point of an Island
S 18° E	1	to the lower point of an Island
S W	2	to a Bayou on the S. S. passed an Isld.
South	¼	to the Lard. bend encamped on the upper point of the island

⟨17th⟩

West	1 ½	to a Spur of the rocky mountain in a bend to the Stard. Side
S. 10° E	1 ¼	to a Spur of the do. on the L. Side
S. 60° W.	2	to a Small Island in the bend to the Stard Side
South	¼	to a pine tree on the lower point of an Island above ⟨at⟩ a
miles 71		rapid, at the mountains. high rocks on each side

1. Although the captains did not mention his name, Ordway admits to being the guilty man.

2. Probably one of the several creeks near the town of Cascade, Cascade County, Montana, nameless on *Atlas* map 62; MRC map 78. The "aspin" is quaking aspen.

3. Probably the later Half-Breed, or Lone Pine, Rapids, in Cascade County, the Pine Island Rapid of *Atlas* map 62. In this vicinity Lewis made his camp for the day. Coues (HLC), 2:416; MRC map 79.

4. The mountains are composed of the Adel Mountains volcanics of Paleocene age. Near the river the rocks are principally pyroclastic in origin. There is no granite here. The rocks are usually described as pale, red, reddish-purple, brown, and gray in color.

5. Perhaps the "Big Rock" of MRC map 79, now Eagle Rock, but this would appear to be too far upstream. "The Tower" does not appear on *Atlas* map 62.

6. Probably *Rhus trilobata* (Nutt.) Gray, skunkbush sumac, which is common in the area, but also possibly *R. glabra* L., smooth sumac, which is more common in the east and probably familiar to Clark. Booth & Wright, 149; Kartesz & Kartesz, 30.

7. Near what was later called Blackbird Ripple, now Tintinger Slough, Cascade County. *Atlas* map 62; MRC map 79; USGS map South Great Falls.

8. Here Clark begins a practice he often followed subsequently, of placing several days' courses and distances together. He originally misdated these courses July 15, 16, 17, and 18, then corrected by writing over. Part of the courses for July 17 are included, although that date is not in the heading as corrected. There is a gap of most of a page between the end of the July 16 entry and the start of these courses. Clark may have written the courses of these four days first and left space to insert the narrative entries later. The July 17 entry follows immediately after the partial courses and distances for that day.

[Lewis] Wednesday July 17th 1805.[1]

The sunflower is in bloom [*NB: Copy for Dr Barton*] and abundant in the river bottoms. The Indians of the Missouri particularly those who do not cultivate maze make great uce of the seed of this plant for bread, or use it in thickening their soope. they most commonly first parch the seed and then pound them between two smooth stones untill they reduce it to a fine meal. to this they sometimes mearly add a portion of water and drink it in that state, or add a sufficient quantity of marrow grease to reduce it to the consistency of common dough and eate it in that manner. the last composition I think much best and have eat it in that state heartily and think it a pallateable dish. there is but little of the broad leafed cottonwood above the falls, much the greater portion being of the narrow leafed kind.[2] there are a great abundance of red yellow perple & black currants, and service berries now ripe and in great perfection. I find these fruits very pleasent particularly the yellow currant[3] which I think vastly preferable to those of our gardens. the shrub which produces this fruit rises to the hight of 6 or 8 feet; the stem simple branching and erect. they grow closly ascociated in cops either in the oppen or timbered lands near the watercouses. the leaf is petiolate of a pale green and resembles in it's form that of the red currant common to our gardens.[4] the perianth of the fructification is one leaved, five cleft, abreviated and tubular, the corolla is monopetallous funnel-shaped; very long, superior, ⟨permanent tho'⟩ withering and of a fine orrange colour. five stamens and one pistillum; of the first, the fillaments are capillare, inserted into the corolla, equal, and converging; the anther ovate, biffid and incumbent. with rispect to the second the germ is roundish, smoth, inferior pedicelled and small; the style, long, and thicker than the stamens, simple, cylindrical, smooth, and erect, withering and remains with the corolla untill the fruit is ripe. stigma simple obtuse and withering.— the fruit is a berry about the size and much the shape of the red currant of our gardins, like them growing in clusters supported by a compound footstalk, but the peduncles which support the several berries are longer in this species and the berries are more scattered. it is quite as transparent as the red current of our gardens, not so ascid, & more agreeably flavored. the other species differ not at all in appearance from the yellow except in the colour and flavor of their berries. I am not confident as to the colour of the corolla, but all those which I observed while in blume as we came up the Missouri were yellow but they might possibly have been all of the yellow kind and that the perple red and black currants here may have corollas of different tints from that of the yellow currant.— The survice berry differs somewhat from that of the U' States[5] the bushes are small sometimes not more than 2 feet high and scarcely ever exceed 8 and are proportionably small in their stems, growing very thickly ascosiated in clumps. the fruit is the same form but for the most part larger more lucious and of so deep a perple that on first sight you would think them black.— there are two species of goosbirris[6] here allso but neither of them yet ripe. the choke cherries also abundant and not yet ripe. there is Box alder, red willow and a species of sumac here also. there is a large pine tree situated on a small island at the head of these rappids above our cam[p]; it being the first we have seen for a long distance near the river I called the island *pine island*.[7] This range of the rocky mountains runs from S E to N. W.— at 8

A. M. this morning Capt. Clark arrived with the party.   we took breakfast here, after which I had the box which contained my instruments taken by land arround tower rock to the river above the rappid; the canoes ascended with some difficulty but without loss or injury, with their loads.

Point of observation No. 31.

At my camp on the Stard. side of the Missouri below the rappids where the river fist enters the Rocky Mountain

Observed time and distance of ⊙'s and ☽'s nearest limbs with Sextant, ⊙ East.—

		Time			Distance	
	h	′	″			
A. M.	8	14	43	115°	0′	0″
	″	17	32	115	0	0
	″	19	14	114	57	45
	″	21	29	″	57	0
	″	22	39	″	57	0
	″	23	38	″	56	45
	″	26	18	″	55	15
	″	27	35	″	54	45

		Time			Distance	
	h	m	s			
A. M.	8	34	51	114°	52′	00″
	″	35	43	″	51	15
	″	38	10	″	50	30
	″	39	47	″	49	45
	″	41	30	″	48	45
	″	42	34	″	48	30
	″	43	52	″	48	30
	″	44	16	″	48	00

Point of Observation No. 33.[8]

On the Stard. side of the Missouri one mile above the point of observation of this morning.

Observed Meridian Altitude of ⊙'s L. L. with Octant by the back observation   56° 50′

Latitude deduced from this observation   46° 42′ 14.7″

After making those observations we proceed, and as the canoes were still heavy loaded all persons not employed in navigating the canoes walled on shore. the river clifts were so steep and frequently projecting into the river with their perpendicular points in such manner that we could not pass them by land, we wer therefore compelled to pass and repass the river very frequently in the couse of the evening. the bottoms are narrow the river also narrow deep and but little current. river from 70 to 100 yds. wide. but little timber on the river aspin constitutes a part of that little. see more pine than usual on the mountains tho' still but thinly scattered. we saw some mountain rams or bighorned anamals this evening, and no other game whatever and indeed there is but little appearance of any. in some places both banks of the river are formed for a short distance of nearly perpendicular rocks of a dark black grannite of great hight;[9] the river has the appearance of having cut it's passage in the course of time through this solid rock. we ascended about 6 miles this evening from the entrance of the mountain and encamped on the Stard. side where we found as much wood as made our fires.[10] musquetoes still troublesome knats not as much so.— Capt. C. now informed me that after I left him yesterday, he saw the poles of a large lodge in praire on the Stard. side of the river which was 60 feet in diameter and appeared to have been built last fall; there were the remains of about 80 leather lodges near the place of the same apparent date. This large lodge was of the same construction of that mentioned above the white bear Islands. the party came on very well and encamped on the lower point of an island near the Stard. shore on that evening. this morning they had set out early and proceeded without obstruction untill they reached the rappid where I was encamped.

Courses and Distances of the 16th July 1805.[11]

S. 30° E.	1 ½	to some trees in a Lard. bend.
West	1 ½	to a Stard. bend passing over a Stard. point.
S. 10° E.	¾	to the mouth of a run in a Lard. bend
S. 45° W.	1 ½	to a bend on Stard. side.
S. 15° E.	½	to a bend on the Lard. side

S. 45° W.	2	to the mouth of a run on Stard. side
S. 45° E.	1	to a bend on Lard. side opposite a large lodge
South	1	along the Lard. side in a bend opposite an island
S. 70° W.	1	in a Lard. bend.
S. 30° W.	1	in a bend on the Lard. side.
South	¾	in the Lard. bend
N 30° W.	1 ¼	to a bend on Stard. passing a small island
South	4	to the lower point of some timber on Stard. side passing 6 islands.
S. 60° E.	½	to a bend on Lard. side
S. 50° W.	1 ½	to the upper point of an island.
S. 18° E.	1	to the lower point of an island
S. 45° W.	2	to a bayou on Stard. passing an island
South	¼	to a lard. bend, encamped on the upper point of the Island near Stard. shore
Miles 23		

Couses and distances July 17th 1805

West	1 ½	to a spur of the rocky Mountains in a bend Std.
S. 10° E.	1 ¼	to a spur of do. do. on the Lard. side
S. 60° W.	2	to a small Island in a bend on Stard. side
South	¼	to a large pine tree on the lower point of pine Island above the rappids where the river enters the rocky Mountains.
S. 20° W.	¾	to a high clift of the mountain on Lard. side passing pine island at ¼ m. a small run on Lard. just above the island, and a Lard. & stard. point.
West	¼	to a bend on the Stard. side, high clifts on either side
South	¼	to a bend on Lard. side Do. do.
N. 60° E.	½	to a bend on the Stard. side do. do. passd. an Isld.
S. 20° W.	½	to a bend on the Lard. side do. do.
West	½	to a bend on the Stard. side do. do.
S. 30° E.	1	to a bend on the Lard. side do. do. passing an Isd.
West	1 ¼	to a bend on the Stard. side—bottoms reather wider

395

S. 5° W.	½	to a point of rocks in a Lard. bend.
N. 75° W.	¾	to a bend on the Stard. side, opposite a very high clift where we encamped for the evening.
Miles	11 ¼	

[Clark]   *July 17th Wednesday 1805*

Set out early this morning and Crossed the rapid at the Island Cald pine rapid with Some dificuelty, at this rapid I came up with Capt Lewis & party   took a Medn. altitude & we took Some Luner Observations &c. and proceeded on, the emence high Precipies oblige all the party to pass & repass the river from one point to another   the river confined in maney places in a verry narrow Chanel from 70 to 120 yards wide bottoms narrow without timber and maney places the mountain approach on both Sides, we observe great deel of Scattering pine on the mountains, Some aspin, Spruce[12] & *fur* trees   took a meridian altd. which gave for Lattitude *46° 42' 14" 7/10 N*   we proceeded on verry well about 8 miles & Camped on the Stard Side   The river crooked bottoms narrow, Clifts high and Steep, I assended a Spur of the Mountain which I found to be highe & dificuelt of axcess, Containig Pitch Pine & Covered with grass   Scercely any game to be Seen   The yellow Current now ripe also the fussey red Choke Cheries[13] getting ripe   Purple Current are also ripe. Saw Several Ibex or mountain rams to day

1. Here begins Lewis's notebook journal Codex F, running to August 22, 1805. It was probably Biddle who drew a red vertical line through almost this entire entry, stopping at "*pine island.*"

2. As they approach the Rocky Mountains beyond the Great Falls, the expedition is reaching the western limit of the eastern cottonwood species *Populus deltoides,* which is being replaced by the western, montane, narrowleaf cottonwood, *P. angustifolia,* as accurately noted. Little, 149-W.

3. Lewis's yellow currant is the golden currant. The fruit color of this currant is highly variable between plants and varies from black to sometimes red or yellow. See also April 30, 1805. Booth & Wright, 107; Pursh, 104; Cutright (LCPN), 172 n. 1.

4. The common red currant is *Ribes sativum* Syme, garden, or red, currant. Fernald, 751.

5. The eastern serviceberry with which Lewis was probably familiar is *Amelanchier arborea* (Michx. f.) Fern., juneberry, a larger shrub or small tree occurring on the Missouri River to eastern Nebraska. The western serviceberry which occurs along the Missouri

River from Montana to South Dakota is noted on April 20, 1805. Booth & Wright, 110; Barkley, 137–38.

6. The two gooseberry species here are probably bristly, or redshoot, gooseberry and swamp currant, *Ribes lacustre* (Pers.) Poir, based on ecology and distribution. Lewis seems occasionally to have used the term gooseberry to describe currants. See June 18 and July 25, 1805. However, on July 20 he distinguishes between the two. Booth & Wright, 107.

7. Probably later Half-Breed Island. *Atlas* map 62; MRC map 79.

8. Should be numbered 32; observation no. 33 comes under July 18, 1805.

9. The rocks are composed of the Adel Mountains volcanics. Near here they are primarily lava breccias and ashfall tuffs but contain no granite. Their colors are dark red, purplish-red, dark grayish-green, and dark gray.

10. In Lewis and Clark County, Montana, a few miles downstream from the Dearborn River, near where Interstate Highway 15 crosses the Missouri. *Atlas* map 62; MRC map 79.

11. Evidently Lewis copied Clark's courses for July 16 and 17 after their reunion on the latter date—a possible indication that he was keeping Codex F day by day at this time.

12. Clark notices *Picea engelmannii* (Parry) Engelm., Engelmann spruce. Little, 37-W.

13. The use of "fuzzy" and "red" to describe choke cherries is problematic, since the fruits of choke cherry, even when young, are neither. This may be the buffaloberry which was noted earlier in the area and which has silver scurfy or "fuzzy" leaves, and may have ripening red fruits at this time. Booth & Wright, 160.

[Lewis]   *Thursday July 18th 1805.*

Set out early this morning. previous to our departure saw a large herd of the Bighorned anamals on the immencely high and nearly perpendicular clift opposite to us;[1] on the fase of this clift they walked about and bounded from rock to rock with apparent unconcern where it appared to me that no quadruped could have stood, and from which had they made one false step the[y] must have been precipitated at least a 500 feet. this anamal appears to frequent such precepices and clifts where in fact they are perfectly secure from the pursuit of the wolf, bear, or even man himself.— at the distance of 2½ miles we passed the entrance of a considerable river on the Stard. side; about 80 yds. wide being nearly as wide as the Missouri at that place. it's current is rapid and water extreamly transparent; the bed is formed of small smooth stones of flat rounded or other figures. it's bottoms are narrow but possess as much timber as the Missouri. the country is mountainous and broken through which it passes. it appears as if it might be navigated but to what extent must be conjectural. this handsome bold and clear stream we named in honour

of the Secretary of war calling it Dearborn's river.—[2] as we were anxious
now to meet with the Sosonees[3] or snake Indians as soon as possible in
order to obtain information relative to the geography of the country and
also if necessary, some horses we thought it better for one of us either
Capt. C. or myself to take a small party & proceed on up the river, some
distance before the canoes, in order to discover them, should they be on
the river before the daily discharge of our guns, which was necessary in
procuring subsistence for the party, should allarm and cause them to retreat to the mountains and conceal themselves, supposing us to be their
enemies who visit them usually by the way of this river.   accordingly
Capt. Clark set out this morning after breakfast with Joseph Fields, Pots
and his servant York.   we proceeded on tolerably well; the current stonger
than yesterday we employ the cord and oars principally tho' sometimes
the setting pole.   in the evening we passed a large creek about 30 yds.
wide which disembogues on the Stard. side; it discharges a bold current
of water it's banks low and bed frromed of stones altogether; this stream
we called Ordway's creek after Sergt. John Ordway.[4] I have observed for
several days a species of flax[5] growing in the river bottoms the leaf stem
and pericarp of which resembles the common flax cultivated in the U'
States.   the stem rises to the hight of about 2½ or 3 feet high; as many as
8 or ten of which proceede from the same root.   the root appears to be
perennial.   the bark of the stem is thick strong and appears as if it would
make excellent flax.   the seed are not yet ripe but I hope to have an opportunity of collecting some of them after they are so   if it should on
experiment prove to yeald good flax and at the same time admit of being
cut without injuring the perennial root it will be a most valuable plant,
and I think there is the greatest probability that it will do so, for notwithstanding the seed have not yet arrived at maturity it is puting up suckers
or young shoots from the same root and would seem therefore that those
which are fully grown and which are in the proper stage of vegitation to
produce the best fax are not longer essencial to the preservation or support of the root.   the river somewhat wider than yesterday and the mountains more distant from the river and not so high; the bottoms are but
narrow and little or no timber near the river.   some pine on the moun-

tains which seems principally confined to their uper region.   we killed one Elk this morning and found part of the flesh and the skin of a deer this evening which had been kiled and left by Capt. Clark.   we saw several herds of the Bighorn but they were all out of our reach on inacessable clifts.—   we encamped on the Lard. side in a small grove of narrow leafed cottonwood.[6]   there is not any of the broad leafed cottonwood on the river since it has entered the mountains. Capt Clark ascended the river on the Stard. side.[7]   in the early part of the day after he left me the hills were so steep that he gained but little off us; in the evening he passed over a mountain by which means he cut off many miles of the river's circuitous rout; the Indian road which he pursued over this mountain is wide and appears as if it had been cut down or dug in many places; he passed two streams of water, the branches of Ordway's creek, on which he saw a number of beaver dams succeeding each other in close order and extending as far up those streams as he could discover them in their couse towards the mountains.   he also saw many bighorn anamals on the clifts of the mountains.   not far beyond the mountain which he passed in the evening he encamped on a small stream of runing water.   having travelled about 20 m.   the water of those rivulets which make down from these mountains is extreemly cold pure and fine.   the soil near the river is of a good quality and produces a luxuriant growth of grass and weeds; among the last the sunflower holds a distinguished place.   the aspin is small but grows very commonly on the river and small streams which make down from the Mouts.

Courses and distances of July 18th 1805.

S. 15° W.	1 ¼	to a Lard. bend a high clift of the mountain on Ld. sd.
West	1 ¼	to the entrance of Dearborn's river on Stard.
S. 45° W.	2 ½	to a Stard. bend
S. 8° E.	6 ½	to the center of a bend on Lard. side, passing several small bends, a small creek at one mile on Lard.[8] and an island on Stard. near the extretry of course
S. 80° W.	½	to a tree in the center of a Stard. bend.
S. 20° W.	1 ½	to the center of a Stard. bend passing an Island.

S. 70° E.	¼	to a bluff in a Stard. bend.
S. 75° W.	1 ½	to the center of a Stard. bend, passing a small creek at ½ m. on Stard. side.
S. 5° W.	½	to the entrance of Ordway's Creek on the Stard. side in a Stard. bend 30 yds. wide.
S. 30° E.	2 ½	to the center of a Lard. bend. the vally widens
S. 40° W.	¾	to the center of a Stard. bend.
S. 85° E.	2	to the center of a Lard. bend, passing 3 short bends, where we encamped for the evening.—
Miles	21	

Point of obsevation No. 33.

On the Lard. shore two miles above the entrance of Dearborn's River observed time and distance ⊙'s and moon's nearest limbs with Sextant; ⊙ East.

		Time			Distance		
		h	m	s			
A. M.		7	55	50	102°	57′	30″
		″	58	33	″	57	
		8	00	14	″	56	30
		″	2	20	″	54	45
		″	5	50	″	53	45

		Time			Distance		
		h	m	s			
A. M.		8	7	12	102	53	
		″	8	52	″	52	30
		″	10	21	″	51	30
		″	12	47	″	51	15
		″	13	35	″	51	15

I also observed another species [*NB: Copy for Dr Barton*] of flax today which is not so large as the first, sildome obtaining a greater hight than 9 Inches or a foot the stem and leaf resemble the other species but the stem is rarely branched, bearing a single monopetallous bellshaped blue flower which is suspended with it's limb downwards,[9]

[Clark]   *July 18th Tursday 1805*

a fine morning   passed a Considerable river which falls in on the Stard
Side and nearly as wide as the Missouri   we call Dearbournes river after
the Sety. of war.   we thought it prudent for a partey to go a head for fear
our fireing Should allarm the Indians and cause them to leave the river
and take to the mountains for Safty from their enemes who visit them
thro this rout. I deturmined to go a head with a Small partey a few days
and find the Snake Indians if possible   after brackfast I took J. Fields
Potts & my Servent proceeded on.   the Country So Hilley that we gained
but little of the Canoes untill in the evening I passed over a mountain on
an Indian rode by which rout I cut off Several miles of the Meanderings
of the River, the roade which passes this mountain is wide and appears to
have been dug in maney places, we Camped on a Small run of Clear Cold
water, musquitors verry troublesom the forepart of the evening   I Saw
great maney Ibex.   we Crossed two Streams of running water [10] on those
Streams I saw Several Beaver dams.   ordway ⟨river⟩ Creek   the Countrey
is Mountanious & rockey except the valey &c. which is Covered with earth
of a good quallity without timber, The timber which is principally pitch
pine is Confined to the mountains, the Small runs & Creeks which have
water running in them Contain Cotton-Willow, Willow, & aspin.   trees all
Small   I Saw maney fine Springs & Streams of running water which Sink
& rise alternately in the Valies   the water of those Streams are fine, those
Streams which run off into the river are damed up by the beaver from
near ther mouthes up as high as I could See up them

1. Later called Big Rock, now Eagle Rock. *Atlas* map 62; MRC map 79; USGS map
South Great Falls.

2. Dearborn River forms the boundary between Cascade and Lewis and Clark counties, Montana, for a short distance above its mouth. Henry Dearborn, a Revolutionary
War veteran, was secretary of war during Jefferson's entire presidency, and a notably unsuccessful general in the War of 1812. *Atlas* map 62; MRC map 79.

3. Lewis's first use of this word, a variant of "Shoshone," and apparently the only one
before meeting these people in August. It is not clear whether he wrote the entry after the
August meeting or learned the word earlier. It was not the Shoshone name for themselves.

4. Later Little Prickly Pear Creek, in Lewis and Clark County. *Atlas* map 62; MRC map
79.

5. *Linum perenne* L. var. *lewisii* (Pursh) Eat. & Wright, blue flax. This variety of wild flax was named by Pursh in honor of Lewis from the expedition's botanical collections which he examined. The annual cultivated flax is *L. usitatissimum* L., common flax, linseed. Pursh, 210; Hitchcock & Cronquist, 282; Cutright (LCPN), 173. It may have been Biddle who drew a vertical line through this passage about the flax.

6. In Lewis and Clark County, above the present Holter Dam. *Atlas* map 62; MRC map 80.

7. Clark's route is marked by a dotted line on *Atlas* maps 62 and 63. He appears not to have kept separate course tables during this period of separation. MRC maps 79, 80. Robert N. Bergantino suggests the following for his route and camp of this day. Clark probably left the Missouri River near Holter Dam and continued south-southeast to Falls Gulch. He then followed that gulch to Towhead Gulch and down that to Hilger Valley. Clark's camp appears to be south of the summit of the pass on Towhead Gulch about two miles west of Beartooth Mountain. A jeep trail and power line now follow this route. Information of Bergantino, July 18, 1986.

8. Later Stickney Creek, in Lewis and Clark County. *Atlas* map 62; MRC map 79.

9. *Campanula rotundifolia* L., roundleaf harebell. The flower color and leaves are superficially similar to the flax. Booth & Wright, 237. It was probably Biddle who drew a red vertical line through this paragraph.

10. Perhaps later Rock Creek and Little Prickly Pear Creek. *Atlas* map 62; MRC maps 79, 80.

[Lewis] *Friday July 19th 1805*

The Musquetoes are very troublesome to us as usual. this morning we set out early and proceeded on very well tho' the water appears to encrease in volocity as we advance. the current has been strong all day and obstructed with some rapids, tho' these are but little broken by rocks and are perfectly safe. the river deep and from 100 to 150 yds. wide. I walked along shore today and killed an Antelope. whever we get a view of the lofty summits of the mountains the snow presents itself, altho' we are almost suffocated in this confined vally with heat. the pine cedar and balsum fir[1] grow on the mountains in irregular assemleages or spots mostly high up on their sides and summits. this evening we entered much the most remarkable clifts that we have yet seen. these clifts rise from the waters edge on either side perpendicularly to the hight of [*NB: about*] 1200 feet. every object here wears a dark and gloomy aspect. the tow[er]ing and projecting rocks in many places seem ready to tumble on us. the river appears to have forced it's way through this immence body of solid rock for the distance of 5¾ miles and where it makes it's exit below has thown on either side vast collumns of rocks mountains high. the river appears to have woarn a passage just the width of it's channel or 150 yds. it is deep from side to side nor is ther in the 1st 3 miles of this distance a spot except one of a few yards in extent on which a man could rest the soal of his foot. several fine springs burst out at the waters edge from the interstices of the rocks. it happens fortunately that altho' the current is strong it is not so much so but what it may be overcome with the oars for there is hear no possibility of using either the cord or Setting pole. it was late in the evening before I entered this place and was obliged to continue my rout untill sometime after dark before I found a place sufficiently large to encamp my small party; at length such an one occurred on the lard. side where we found plenty of lightwood[2] and pichpine. this rock is a black grannite below and appears to be of a much lighter colour above and from the fragments I take it to be flint of a yelloish brown and light creemcolourd yellow.—[3] from the singular appearance of this place I called it the *gates of the rocky mountains.*[4] the mountains higher today than yesterday, saw some Bighorns and a few Antelopes also beaver and Otter; the latter are now very plenty one of the men killed one of them today with a setting pole. musquetoes less troublesome than usual. we had a thundershower today about 1 P. M. which continued about an hour and was attended with som hail. we have seen no buffaloe since we entered the mounts. this morning early Capt. Clark pursued his rout, saw early in the day the remains of several Indians camps formed of willow brush which appeared to have been inhabited some time this spring. saw where the natives had pealed the bark off the pine trees about this same season. this the indian woman with us informs that they do to obtain the sap and soft part of the wood [*NB: wood*] and bark for food. at 11 A. M. Capt. C. feell in with a gang of Elk of which he killed 2. and not being able to obtain as much wood as would make a fire substituted the dung of the buffaloe and cooked a part of their meat on which they breakfasted and again pursueed their rout, which lay along an old indian road. this evening they passed a hansome valley watered by a large creek[5] which extends itself with it's valley into the mountain to a considerable distance.   the latter part of the evening their rout lay over a hilly and mountanous country covered with the sharp fragments of flint which cut and bruised their feet excessively; nor wer the prickly pear of the leveler part of the rout much less painfull; they have now become so abundant in the open uplands that it is impossible to avoid them and their thorns are so keen and stif that they pearce a double thickness of dressed deers skin with ease. Capt. C. informed me that he extracted 17 of these bryers from his feet this evening after he encamped by the light of the fire. I have guarded or reather fortifyed my feet against them by soaling my mockersons with the hide of the buffaloe in parchment.   he encamped on the river[6] much fortiegud having passed two mountains in the course of the day and travelled about 30 miles.—

Courses and distances of the 19th July 1805.

South	¼	to a pine tree on the Stard. side in a bend
S. 85 E.	2	to the center of a Lard. bend
S. 38 W.	1	to a pine in the Stard. bend
South	1 ½	to the center of a stard bend
N. 10° W.	2 ½	to the center of a Lard. bend
S. 30° E.	1 ¼	to the center of a Stard. bend
S. 25° E.	4 ½	to the center of a Lard. bend
S. 28° W.	1	to the center of a Stard bend passing 2 small islands near the commencement of this course
S. 60° E.	1 ¼	to the center of a stard. bend
N. 70° E.	1 ½	to the entrance of a small creek[7] in a Lard. bend, passing an island near the Stard. side.
S. 25° E.	1 ½	to a point of rocks in a bend on the stard. side; those rocks put in close to the river on both sides, are perpendicular and about 1200 feet high, this place has so singular an appearance that I call it the gates of the rocky mountains. the water appears to have forced it's way through this immence body of solid rock, and thrown on either side below collumns of rock mountains high.
S. 55 E.	¼	to the center of a lard bend in the gates.

S. 10 W.   3 ½   to a bend on Lard. side passing a small island in the middle

Miles 22   of the river at 1 ½ miles.   a little short of the extremity of

this course we encamped on the Lard. side.

[Clark]   *July 19th Fryday 1805*

a find morning   I proceeded on in an Indian path river verry crooked passed over two mountains   Saw Several Indian Camps which they have left this Spring. Saw trees Peeled & found poles &c.   at 11 oC I Saw a gange of Elk as we had no provision Concluded to kill Some   Killd two and dined being oblige to Substitute dry buffalow dung in place of wood, this evening passed over a Cream Coloured flint which roled down from the Clifts into the bottoms, the Clifts Contain flint a dark grey Stone & a redish brown intermixed and no one Clift is Solid rock, all the rocks of everry description is in Small pices appears to have been broken by Some Convulsion—[8]   passed a butifull *Creek* on the *Std. Side* this eveng which meanders thro' a butifull Vallie of great extent, I call after Sgt Pryor[9]   the countrey on the Lard Side a high mountain   Saw Several Small rapids to day   the river Keep its width and appear to be deep, my feet is verry much brused & cut walking over the flint, & constantly Stuck full Prickley pear thorns, I puled out 17 by the light of the fire to ⟨day⟩ night   We camped on the river Same (Lard) Side[10]   Musqutors verry troublesom.

1. The "balsum fir" is actually Douglas fir.

2. Again Lewis uses his familarity with pitch-pine (and a colloquial term for it) for the area's ponderosa pine.

3. The gates are formed of light-to-medium gray, Mississippian-age, Mission Canyon Limestone. Near the upper end of the gates, Mississippian Lodgepole Limestone occurs on the southeast side of the river. These limestones weather to a light gray or yellow-buff color. There is no granite or flint here. There are some dark gray chert nodules in the limestone. The illusion of the black color no doubt comes from the shadows then present on the lower cliffs and the yellow color from sunlight on the upper cliffs.

4. Now called simply "Gates of the Mountains," a stretch of about five and three-quarter miles, roughly midway between Holter and Hauser dams in Lewis and Clark County, Montana. The campsite was apparently at a point where a small drainage enters the river making room for a suitable camp; a short distance downstream from Upper Holter Lake. Appleman (LC), 306–9; *Atlas* map 62; MRC map 80; USGS map Canyon Ferry Dam.

5. Clark and his party returned to the river and continued for some distance until they

discovered an Indian road, perhaps going up Foster Gulch, which they followed. The party then entered Helena Valley and crossed Prickley Pear Creek (Clark's large creek), today joining Hauser Lake to Lake Helena, in Lewis and Clark County. *Atlas* map· 62; MRC map 80; USGS map Canyon Ferry Dam; information of Bergantino, July 18, 1986.

6. Clark apparently continued along the river after crossing Prickley Pear Creek and then probably journeyed overland to his camp. His camp of the evening is not shown on *Atlas* map 62 and is problematic. Bergantino suggests it is about a mile below the mouth of present Spokane Creek near the Guillot Springs, in Lewis and Clark County. *Atlas* map 62; MRC map 80; USGS map Canyon Ferry Dam; information of Bergantino, July 18, 1986. This area is very difficult to plot due to confusion between Lewis's and Clark's journals and the *Atlas* maps. See notes for July 20, 1805.

7. Later Willow Creek, in Lewis and Clark County. *Atlas* map 62; MRC map 80.

8. The rock described as cream-colored flint is probably the light-gray and yellow-buff weathering limestone of the Madison Group (Mission Canyon or Lodgepole limestones). The other rocks probably belong to the Precambrian Greyson Shale. A thrust fault has brought these different-age rocks together and badly shattered them in the process.

9. Prickley Pear Creek (see n. 5, above). It is not shown on *Atlas* map 62 and a "Pryors Valley R or C" is clearly misplaced on map 63. The separation of the captains, Clark's illness, and the difficulty of Clark's not having seen portions of the route explain the discrepancies between journals and maps. See the notes for July 20, 1805, for further clarification.

10. This reads "Lard" quite clearly, but Clark was certainly on the starboard (west) side of the Missouri. *Atlas* map 62; MRC map 80.

[Lewis] *Saturday 20th 1805.*

Set out early this morning as usual, currant strong, we therefore employ the toe rope when ever the banks permit the use of it; the water is reather deep for the seting pole in most places.   at 6 A. M. the hills retreated from the river and the valley became wider than we have seen it since we entered the mountains.   some scattering timber on the river and in the valley.   consisting of the narrowleafed Cottonwood aspin & pine.   vas numbers of the several species of currants goosberries and service berries; of each of these I preserved some seeds. I [*NB: we*] found a black currant which I thought preferable in flavor to the yellow.   this currant is really a charming fruit and I am confident would be prefered at our markets to any currant now cultivated in the U' States.[1]   we killed an Elk this morning which was very acceptable to us.   through the valley which we entered early in the morning a large creek flows from the mountains and discharges itself into the river behind an island on Stard. side about 15 yds. wide   this we called ⟨Smoke Creek in consequence of the Smoke we saw about⟩ Potts's Creek after John Potts one of our party.[2] about 10 A. M. we saw the smoke arrose as if the country had been set on fire up the valley of this creek about 7 ms. distant   we were at a loss to determine whether it had been set on fire by the natives as a signall among themselves on discovering us, as is their custom or whether it had been set on fire by Capt. C. and party accedentally.   the first however proved to be the fact, they had unperceived by us discovered Capt. Clark's party or mine, and had set the plain on fire to allarm the more distant natives [*NB: heard a gun from Capt C's party & fled quite over the mountain thinking it their enemies Blackfoots*] and fled themselves further into the interior of the mountains.[3]   this evening we found the skin of an Elk and part of the flesh of the anamal which Capt. C. had left near the river at the upper side of the valley where he assended the mountain with a note inform- ing me of his transactions [*NB: progressions*] and that he should pass the mounts which lay just above us and wate our arrival at some convenient place on the river.   the other elk which Capt. C. had killed we could not find.   about 2 in the evening we had passed through a range of low moun- tains and the country bacame more open again,[4] tho' still broken and un- timbered and the bottoms not very extensive.   we encamped on the Lard. side near a spring on a high bank[5]   the prickly pears are so abundant that we could scarcely find room to lye.   just above our camp the river is again closed in by the Mouts. on both sides. I saw a black woodpecker[6] [*NB: or Crow*] today about the size of the lark woodpecker as black as a crow. I indevoured to get a shoot at it but could not.   it is a distinct species of woodpecker; it has a long tail and flys a good deel like the jay bird.—

This morning Capt. Clark set out early and proceeded on through a valley leaving the river about six miles to his left; he fell in with an old Indian road which he pursued untill it struck the river about 18 miles from his camp of the last evening just above the entrance of a large creek which we call white paint Creek.[7]   the party were so much fortiegued with their march and their feet cut with the flint and perced with the prickly pears untill they had become so painfull that he proceeded but little further before he determined to encamp on the river and wait my arrival.— Capt. C. saw a smoke today up the valley of Pryor's creek which was no doubt caused by the natives likewise.   he left signals or signs on his rout in order to inform the indians should they pursue his trale that we were not their enemies, but *white men* and their friends.—   [*NB: clothes paper tape ⟨cloth &c⟩ linen,*]

The Courses and distances July 20th 1805.

S. 40° W.	½	to a high rock in a Lard. bend in the gates. here the high and perpendicular rocks cease and the Valley widens sud-only to more than it's usual extent since we have entered the Mountains.
S. 55° W.	1	to the center of a Stard. bend at which place a large creek falls in behind some islands on the Stard. side. the Indians set the plains on fire up this Creek. call it Potts's Creek.
S. 64° E.	2 ½	to the center of a Lard. bend, passing two islands
S. 15° E.	¼	to the center of a Stard. bend. saw a number of the read head ducks; also several sand hill Crains.
East	1 ½	to the center of a Lard. bend, passing 2 small islands on Lard. side.
S. 12° E.	1 ½	to the center of a Stard. bend passing a small Creek[8] on Lard. side at ¾ of a mile.
S. 50° E.	1 ¼	to the center of a Lard. bend
S. 20° E.	2 ½	to the center of a Stard. bend.
S. 65° E.	2	to a point in a Stard. bend passing 3 small islands near Lard. Side at 1 mile.
N. 75° E.	2	to the center of a Lard. bend passing an island near the extremity of the course and encamped on Lard. side at a spring.—
Miles	15	

Point of Observati No. [34]

On the Stard. shore at the extremity of the third course of this day, observed time and distance of ☉'s and ☽'s nearest limbs with Sextant ☉ East.

	Time			Distance		
	h	m	s			
A. M	10	22	16	76°	38′	—″
	″	24	38	″	36	45

	Time			Distance		
	h	m	s			
A. M.	10	35	38	76°	26′	30″
	″	37	3	″	25	45

	Time			Distance		
	h	m	s			
A. M.	10	38	13	76°	25′	—″
	″	39	34	″	24	45

Having lost my post Meridian Observation for Eql. Altitudes in consequence of a cloud which obscured the sun for several minutes about that time, I had recourse to two altitudes of the sun with Sextant.

Point of observation No. 35.

On Stard. shore five miles short of the encampment of this evening observed 2 Altds. of ☉'s L. L.

	Time			Altitudes		
	h	m	s			
P. M.	3	10	39	98°	48′	15″
	4	49	34	66	17	45

[Clark] *July 20th Satturday 1805*

a fine morning   we proceded on thro' a valley leaveing the river about 6 miles to our left and fell into an Indian roade which took us to the river above the mo. of a Creek 18 miles   The Misquetors verry troublesom   my man York nearly tired out, the bottoms of my feet blistered. I observe a Smoke rise to our right up the Valley of the last Creek about 12 miles distant, The Cause of this Smoke I can't account for certainly tho' think it probable that the Indians have heard the Shooting of the Partey below and Set the Praries or Valey on fire to allarm their Camps; Supposeing our party to be a war party comeing against them, I left Signs to Shew the Indians if they Should come on our trail that we were not their enemeys. Camped on the river, the feet of the men with me So Stuck with Prickley pear & cut with the Stones that they were Scerseley able to march at a Slow gate this after noon

1. Lewis notices the golden currant. His palate is confirmed by a botanist who finds the black-fruited individuals superior in taste to yellow or orange fruits of the same species. Personal communication of A. T. Harrison, January 22, 1986. It was probably Biddle who drew a red vertical line to this point, beginning with "narrowleafed Cottonwood."

2. Lewis has made an error in both his journal text and his course and distance table regarding the location of Potts Creek. Clark, endeavoring to reconcile the error with his own limited observations (see notes for July 19, 1805), then compounded Lewis's error on the *Atlas* maps, making modern identifications of this and other streams in the area especially difficult. Potts Creek of Lewis's journal and table is probably Towhead Gulch (Spring Creek of MRC map 80), beyond which he took his observation no. 34. Lewis probably errs in thinking that he saw smoke up this creek. Gass, Ordway, and Whitehouse seem to agree that they did not see smoke until the party had passed today's Beaver Creek (see n. 8, below) in the afternoon, so the fire would have been up present Prickley Pear Creek (not shown on *Atlas* map 62). Notice that below Lewis says that Clark saw the smoke up the valley of "Pryor's creek." Clark in attempting to set map and journals in agreement placed the word "fire" at the head of the stream he called "Pryors Vally R or C" (actually the party's White Earth Creek, today's Beaver Creek, in Broadwater County). Evidently Clark mapped present Towhead Gulch as Prickley Pear Creek but left it unnamed, did not include Prickley Pear Creek, and then placed the name Potts Valley Creek on the next major stream to the south which came in from the west, today's Spokane Creek. *Atlas* map 62; MRC map 80; USGS map Canyon Ferry Dam; information of Bergantino, July 18, 1986.

3. This could be information given by the Shoshones after the meeting in August, suggesting this entry was written later, from notes now lost. Or it could mean only that Lewis learned that Clark's party had not set the fire when the two reunited on July 22. The interlined information must have come from the Indians, probably told by Clark to Biddle. See the Introduction, vol. 2.

4. An interlineation here, apparently by Lewis, has been erased and is illegible.

5. In Lewis and Clark County, on the point of a bend between present Soup and Trout Creeks (unnamed on *Atlas* map 62). MRC map 80; USGS map Canyon Ferry Dam.

6. The first description of Lewis's woodpecker, *Melanerpes lewis* [AOU, 408], more fully described on May 27, 1806. Perhaps the only remaining zoological specimen of the expedition is the skin of a Lewis's woodpecker, now in the Museum of Comparative Zoology, Harvard University. Burroughs, 239–40; Cutright (LCPN), 173, 453.

7. Clark's route, marked by a dotted line on *Atlas* maps 62 and 63, left the Missouri in the vicinity of present Spokane Creek (Potts Valley Creek on *Atlas* map 62) and he proba-

bly camped above today's Beaver Creek, Broadwater County ("Pryors Valley R or C" on *Atlas* map 63).

8. Beaver Creek (unnamed on *Atlas* map 62), Lewis and Clark County, not to be confused with Beaver Creek in Broadwater County. *Atlas* map 62; MRC map 80.

[Lewis]   *Sunday July 21st 1805.*

Set out early this morning and passed a bad rappid[1] where the river enters the mountain about 1 m. from our camp of last evening the Clifts high and covered with fragments of broken rocks.   the current strong; we employed the toe rope principally, and also the pole as the river is not now so deep but reather wider and much more rapid   our progress was therefore slow and laborious.   we saw three swans this morning, which like the geese have not yet recovered the feathers of the wing and could not fly[2]   we killed two of them   the third escaped by diving and passed down with the current; they had no young ones with them therefore presume they do not breed in this country   these are the first we have seen on the river for a great distance.   we daily see great numbers of gees with their young which are perfectly feathered ⟨but⟩ except the wings which are deficient in both young and old.   my dog caught several today, as he frequently dose.   the young ones are very fine, but the old gees are poor and unfit for uce.   saw several of the large brown or sandhill Crain today with their young.[3]   the young Crain is as large as a turkey and cannot fly   they are of a bright red bey colour or that of the common deer at this season.   this bird feeds on grass prinsipally and is found in the river bottoms.   the grass near the river is lofty and green that of the hill sides and high open grounds is perfectly dry and appears to be scorched by the heat of the sun.   the country was rough mountainous & much as that of yesterday untill towards evening when the river entered a beautifull and extensive plain country of about 10 or 12 miles wide which extended upwards further that the eye could reach   this valley is bounded by two nearly parallel ranges of high mountains which have their summits partially covered with snow.   below the snowey region pine succeeds and reaches down their sides in some parts to the plain but much the greater portion of their surfaces is uncovered with timber and expose either a barren sterile soil covered with dry parched grass or black and rugged rocks. the river immediately on entering this valley assumes a different aspect and character, it spreads to a mile and upwards in width crouded with Islands, some of them large, is shallow enough for the use of the seting pole in almost every part and still more rappid than before; it's bottom is smooth stones and some large rocks as it has been since we have entered the mountains. the grass in these extensive bottoms is green and fine, about 18 inches or 2 feet high. the land is a black rich loam and appears very fertile. we encamped in this beatiful valley on the Lard. side[4] the party complain of being much fatiegued with this days travel. we killed one deer today.— This morning we passed a bold creek 28 yds. wide which falls in on Stard. side. it has a handsome and an extensive valley. this we called Pryor's Creek after Sergt. ⟨John⟩ Pryor one of our party.[5] I also saw two fesants today of a dark brown colour much larger than the phesant of the U' States.[6]

this morning Capt. Clark having determined to hunt and wait my arrival somewhere about his preset station was fearfull that some indians might still be on the river above him sufficiently near to hear the report of his guns and therefore proceeded up the river about three miles and [not] finding any indians nor discovering any fresh appearance of them returned about four miles below and fixed his camp near the river;[7] after refreshing themselves with a few hours rest they set out in different directions to hunt. Capt C. killed a buck and Fields a buck and doe. he caught a young curlooe which was nearly feathered. the musquetoes were equally as troublesome to them as to ourselves this evening; tho' some hours after dark the air becomes so cold that these insects disappear. the men are all fortunately supplyed with musquetoe biers [*NB: made of duck or gauze, like a trunk—to get under*] otherwise it would be impossible for them to exist under the fatiegues which they daily encounter without their natural rest which they could not obtain for those tormenting insects if divested of their biers. timber still extreemly scant on the river but there is more in this valley than we have seen since we entered the mountains; the creeks which fall into the river are better supplyed with this article than the river itself.—

Courses and distances July 21st 1805.

S. 5° W.	½	to a Lard. point opposite an Island
S. 30° E.	1	to the center of a Lard. bend, the hills now become low and the country opens on either side
S. 25° W.	3	to the center of a Stard. bend passing a large island on Lard. side at one mile.—
S. 80° E.	3 ½	to a point in the Stard. bend passing a large creek 28 yds. wide on stard. side at 2 ½ miles *Pryor's Creek.* 15 yds. wide.—
N. 40° E.	1	to the center of a Lard. bend.
S. 65° E.	3	to the center of a Stard. bend
S. 60° E.	3 ½	to the center of a Stard. bend. throughout this course the river is divided by a number of islands near the Stard. side, on the Lard. wide bottoms. encamped on Lard. in the bottom.

Miles 15 ½

Point of *Observation No. 36.*

On the Lard. side of the Missouri ½ a mile above the extremity of the 2cd course of this day observed time and distance of ⊙'s and ☽'s nearcst limbs with Sextant ⊙ East.

		Time			Distance		
		h	m	s			
A. M.	8	35	31		63°	54′	30″
	″	36	44		″	54	
	″	38	20		″	52	30
	″	40	24		″	51	15

		Time			Distance		
		h	m	s			
A. M.	8	41	36		63	50	15
	″	43	31		″	50	
	″	44	49		″	49	45
	″	46	10		″	49	15

Also Observed Equal altitudes of ⊙ with Sextant.

	h	m	s			h	m	s	
A. M.	8	50	44	P. M.	4	21	1		Altitude at the time
"		52	17	"		22	18		of observation.
"		53	52	"		24	7		75° 29′ 3″

Point of Observation No. 37.

On the Lard. side of the river at the extremity of the fourth course of this day; observed Meridian Altitude of ☉'s L. L. with Octant by the back observation   57° 14′   ″

Latitude deduced from this observation.   46° 10′ 32.9″

we saw a number of trout today since the river has become more shallow; also caught a fish of a white colour on the belly and sides and of a bluish cast on the back which had been accedentally wounded by a setting pole. it had a long pointed mouth which opened somewhat like the shad.[8]

[Clark]   July 21st Sunday 1805

a fine morning   our feet So brused and Cut that I deturmined to delay for the Canoes, & if possible kill Some meat by the time they arrived, all the Creeks which fall into the Missouri on the Std. Side Since entering the Mountains have extencive Valies of open Plain.   the river bottoms Contain nothing larger than a Srub untill above the last Creek   the Creeks & runs have timber on them generally, the hills or mountains are in Some places thickly covered with pine & Cedar &c. &c. I proceeded on about 3 miles this morning   finding no fresh Indian Sign returned down the river four miles and Camped, turned out to hunt for Some meat, which if we are Suckessfull will be a Seasonable Supply for the partey assending. emence quantities of Sarvice buries, yellow, red, Purple & black Currents ripe and Superior to any I ever tasted particularly the yellow & purple kind. Choke Cheries are Plenty; Some Goose buries—   The wild rose Continue   the Willow more abundant no Cotton wood of the Common kind   Small birds are plenty, Some Deer, Elk, Goats, and Ibex; no buffalow in the Mountains.

Those mountains are high and a great perportion of them rocky: Vallies fertile   I observe on the highest pinicals of Some of the mountains to the West Snow lying in Spots Some Still further North are covered with Snow and cant be Seen from this point

The Winds in those mountains are not Settled generally with the river, to day the wind blow hard from the West at the Camp. The Missouri Continus its width the Current Strong and Crouded with little Islands and Cose graveley bars; but little fine Sand   the Chanel generally a Corse gravel or Soft mud. Musquetors & Knats verry troublesom. I killed a Buck, and J. Fields killed a Buck and Doe this evening. Cought a young Curlough [curlew].

1. Probably later Flume Ripple. *Atlas* map 62; MRC map 80.

2. These swans and geese were familiar to Lewis and Clark and are respectively, the trumpeter swan and the Canada goose. Holmgren, 33; Burroughs, 193–95, 199. It was probably Biddle who drew a red vertical line through the passages about the swans and geese and the sandhill crane.

3. The sandhill crane, *Grus canadensis* [AOU, 206], already known to science. Burroughs, 185–86. Holmgren considers the "brown" as an immature or smaller subspecies of the sandhill crane. Holmgren, 29.

4. In Lewis and Clark County, Montana, a few miles east of Helena, about five miles above present Canyon Ferry Dam, near the Lewis and Clark/Broadwater County line. Canyon Ferry Lake probably covers the site today. *Atlas* map 63; MRC map 81.

5. Pryor's first name was Nathaniel; to Lewis he was probably just "Sergeant Pryor," although he used Nathaniel in a deleted portion of the next day's entry. "John" was crossed out in red ink in this entry, probably by Biddle, but "Nathaniel" was not added, and it is "John" in Biddle's *History*. The stream is Spokane Creek, labeled "Potts Vally Creek" on *Atlas* map 62. See notes for July 20, 1805. MRC map 81.

6. Perhaps the blue grouse, *Dendragapus obscurus* [AOU, 297], then unknown to science. Lewis gives more detail about what may be the same bird on August 1, 1805. Burroughs, 215–16; Holmgren, 30, 32. Biddle corrected Lewis's spelling by overwriting "fesants" to make it "Phesant."

7. Apparently Clark returned to a point about a mile below his previous night's camp, in the vicinity of the mouth of later Beaver Creek, Broadwater County, incorrectly given as "Pryors Vally R or C" on *Atlas* map 63. MRC map 81.

8. The wounded fish may be any of *Salmonidae* sp., whitefish or cisco. Lee et al., 76–120. It was probably Biddle who drew a red vertical line through this paragraph.

[Lewis]   *Monday July 22cd 1805.*

We set out early as usual. The river being divided into such a number of channels by both large and small Island that I found it impossible to lay it down correctly following one channel only in a canoe and therefore walked on shore took the general courses of the river and from the rising grounds took a view of the Islands and it's different channels which I laid don in conformity thereto on my chart. there being but little timber to obstruct my view I could see it's various meanders very satisfactorily. I passed though a large Island which I found a beautifull level and fertile plain about 10 feet above the surface of the water and never overflown. on this Island I [*NB: We*] met with great quantities of a smal onion[1] about the size of a musquit ball and some even larger; they were white crisp and well flavored I geathered about half a bushel of them before the canoes arrived. I halted the party for breakfast and the men also geathered considerable quantities of those onions. it's seed had just arrived to maturity and I gathered a good quantity of it. This appears to be a valuable plant inasmuch as it produces a large quantity to the squar foot and bears with ease the rigor of this climate, and withall I think it as pleasantly flavored as any species of that root I ever tasted. I called this beatifull and fertile island after this plant Onion Island. here I passed over to the stard. shore where the country was higher and ascended the river to the entrance of a large creek which discharges itself into the Missouri on the Stard. side. it is composed of three pretty considerable creeks which unite in a beautifull and extensive vally a few miles before it discharges itself into the river.[2] while wateing for the canoes to arrive I killed an otter which sunk to the bottom on being shot, a circumstance unusual with that anamal. the water was about 8 feet deep yet so clear that I could see it at the bottom; I swam in and obtained it by diving. I halted the party here for dinner; the canoes had taken different channels through these islands and it was sometime before they all came up. I placed my thermometer in a good shade as was my custom about 4 P. M. and after dinner set out without it and had proceeded near a mile before I recollected it I sent Sergt. Ordway back for it, he found it and brought it on. the murcury stood at 80 a. o this is the warmest day except one which we have experienced this summer. The Indian woman recognizes the country and assures us that this is the river on which her relations live, and that the three forks are at no great distance. this peice of information has cheered the sperits of the party who now begin to console themselves with the anticipation of shortly seeing the head of the missouri yet un-

known to the civilized world.   the large creek which we passed on Stard.
15 yds. we call white Earth Creek ⟨in honour of Sergt. Nathaniel pryor
who is a steady valuable and usefull member of our party⟩ from the circumstance of the natives procuring a white paint on this crek.—[3]   Saw
many gees, crains, and small birds common to the plains, also a few phes-
ants and a species of small curlooe or plover[4] of a brown colour which I
first met with near the entrance of Smith's river but they are so shy and
watchfull there is no possibility of geting a shoot at them   it is a different
kind from any heretofore discribed and is about the size of the yellow
leged plover or jack Curlooe.   both species of the willow that of the broad
leaf and narrow leaf still continue, the sweet willow is very scarce.   the
rose bush, small honesuckle, the pulpy leafed thorn, southernwood, sage[5]
Box alder narrow leafed cottonwood, red wod, a species of sumac are all
found in abundance as well as the red and black goosberries, service
berries, choke cherries and the currants of four distinct colours of black,
yellow, red and perple.[6]   the cherries are not yet ripe.   the bear appear
to feed much on the currants.   late this evening we arrived at Capt. Carks
camp on the stard. side of the river; we took them on board with the meat
they had collected and proceeded a short distance and encamped on an
Island[7]   Capt. Clark's party had killed a deer and an Elk today and ourselves one deer and an Antelope only.   altho' Capt C. was much fatiegued
his feet yet blistered and soar he insisted [*NB: deturmined*] on pursuing his
rout in the morning nor weould he consent willingly to my releiving him
at that time by taking a tour of the same kind.   finding him anxious I
readily consented to remain with the canoes; he ordered Frazier and Jo.
& Reubin Filds to hold themselves in readiness to accompany him in the
morning. Sharbono was anxious to accompany him and was accordingly
permitted.   the musquetoes and knats more than usually troublesome to
us this evening.—

Couses and distances of July 22cd 1805

N. 75° E.	2 ¼	to a Lard. bend 1 m. above a large Island
S. 34° E.	3	to the center of a Stard. bend at the upper point of Onion Island.
S. 80° E.	1 ½	to a Stard. bend passing several Islands.

N. 45° E.	1	to a Lard. bend passing several Islands
S. 25° E.	6	passing four long circular bends and several large islands to a point of the bluff on Stard. side; a large creek well timbered falls in on Stard. side ¾ of a mile below the extremity of this course. whiteearth C.
S. 12° E.	6	to a bluff point on the Stard. side; this course and distance
Miles 19 ¾		forms the cord line to a general circular bend of the river, which is formed of 4 other bends, and from the center of which, a line drawn N. 70° E. 3 miles will intersect the center of the general bend of the river—4—miles short of the extremity of this course by water we encamped on an Isld.

[Clark]   *July 22ct Monday 1805*

a fine morning wind from the S. E.   the last night verry cold, my blanket being Small I lay on the grass & Covered with it. I opened the bruses & blisters of my feet which caused them to be painfull   dispatched all the men to hunt in the bottom for Deer, deturmined my Self to lay by & *nurs* my feet.   haveing nothing to eat but venison and Currents, I find my Self much weaker than when I left the Canoes and more inclined to rest & repose to day. These men were not Suckcessfull in hunting killed only one Deer   Capt Lewis & the Party arvd. at 4 oClock & we all proceeded on a Short distance and Camped on an Island   the Musquitors verry troublesom this evening   G Drewyer not knowing the place we Camped Continued on up the river. I deturmined to proceed on in pursute of the Snake Indians on tomorrow and directed Jo Rubin Fields Frasure to get ready to accompany me. Shabono, our interpreter requested to go, which was granted &c. In my absence the hunters had killed Some Deer & a Elk, one fusee found &c. &c.

1. Possibly *Allium cernuum* Roth, nodding onion, or *A. geyeri* S. Wats., Geyer's onion. Hahn, *Allium* maps; Cutright (LCPN), 401: Dorn, 161. It was probably Biddle who drew a red vertical line through this passage about the onion. "Onion Isd." appears on *Atlas* map 63.

2. Beaver Creek, Broadwater County, Montana (see above, July 20, 1805). The streams are present Antelope, Staubach, and Beaver creeks. *Atlas* map 63; MRC map 81.

3. Beaver Creek, Broadwater County. The crossed out portion concerning the name is undoubtedly related in some way to Clark's mislabeling this stream "Pryors Vally R or C" on *Atlas* map 63. The words "white Earth" preceding the deletion were written over an erasure.

4. Probably the same bird mentioned briefly on July 14, 1805. It may be either the mountain plover, *Charadrius montanus* [AOU, 281], or the upland sandpiper (also called upland plover or Bartram's sandpiper), *Bartramia longicauda* [AOU, 261]. Burroughs, 226, 228; Holmgren, 33. The "jack Curlooe" mentioned for comparison may be the greater yellowlegs. Cf. May 9, 1805. It was probably Biddle who drew a red vertical line through the passages about natural history here, to the words "the currants."

5. It is unclear whether two different species of *Artemisia* are being identified here or just the big sagebrush, *A. tridentata,* named earlier as hyssop sage, or wild hyssop. If two species then the southernwood may be *A. cana,* silver sagebrush. See Lewis's earlier description of April 14, 1805.

6. Lewis is probably seeing three currants: *Ribes americanum* (black), *R. cereum* (red), and *R. aureum* (yellow and purple). See entries of April 30 and June 18, 1805.

7. *Atlas* map 63 appears to place this camp on the larboard side of the river, near an island. In any case the site was in Broadwater County, Montana, a few miles upstream from Beaver (White Earth) Creek, and is now under Canyon Ferry Lake. MRC map 81.

[Lewis]   *Tuesday July 23rd 1805.*

Set out early as usual; Capt. Clark left us with his little party of 4 men and continued his rout on the Stard. side of the river. about 10 OCk. A M. we came up with Drewyer who had seperated from us yesterday evening and lay out all night not being able to find where we had encamped. he had killed 5 deer which we took on board and continued our rout. the river is still divided by a great number of islands, it channels sometimes seperating to the distance of 3 miles; the current very rapid with a number of riffles; the bed gravel and smooth stones; the banks low and of rich loam in the bottoms; some low bluffs of yellow and red clay with a hard red slate stone intermixed.[1] the bottoms are wide and but scantily timbered; the underbrush very thick consisting of the narrow & broad leafed willow rose and Currant bushes principally. high plains succeeds the river bottoms and extend back on either side to the base of the mountains which are from 8 to 12 miles assunder, high, rocky, some small pine and Cedar on them and ly parallel with the river. passed a large creek on Lard. side 20 yds. wide which after meandering through a beautifull and extensive bottom for several miles nearly parallel with the river discharges itself opposite to a large cluster of islands which from their number I called the 10 islands and the creek Whitehous's Creek,[2] after Josph. Whitehouse one of the party.   saw a great abundance of the common thistles;[3] also a number of the wild onions of which we collected a further supply.   there is a species of garlic[4] also which grows on the high lands with a flat leaf now green and in bloe but is strong tough and disagreeable.   found some seed of the wild flax ripe which I preserved; this plant grows in great abundance in these bottoms. I halted rearther early for dinner today than usual in order to dry some articles which had gotten wet in several of the canoes. I ordered the canoes to hoist their small flags in order that should the indians see us they might discover that we were not Indians, nor their enemies.   we made great uce of our seting poles and cords the uce of both which the river and banks favored.   most of our small sockets were lost, and the stones were so smooth that the points of their poles sliped in such manner that it increased the labour of navigating the canoes very considerably, I recollected a parsel of giggs which I had brought on, and made the men each atatch one of these to the lower ends of their poles with strong wire, which answered the desired purpose.   we saw Antelopes Crain gees ducks beaver and Otter.   we took up four deer which Capt. Clark & party had killed and left near the river.   he pursued his rout untill late in the evening and encamped on the bank of the river 25 ms. above our encampment of the last evening;[5] he followed an old indian road which lyes along the river on the stard side Capt. saw a number of Antelopes, and one herd of Elk.   also much sign of the indians but all of ancient date. I saw the bull rush and Cattail flag today.—[6]

Courses and distances of July 23rd 1805

S. 20° E.	2	to a point of the Stard. bluff passing several islds.
N. 60° E.	1 ½	to a lad. bend passing a large island on stard.
S. 30° E.	1 ½	to a stard. bend passing the upper point of the island at ½ a mile and two other small ones on it's lower end. a large creek falls in on Lard. behind 20 yds. wide call it Whitehouse's Creek.

S. 70° E.	1 ¾	to a Lard. bend passing several outlets to the river on Stard. and through an assemblage of islands
S. 5° E.	1 ½	to the lower point of an island. the river 300 yds. wide at this place.
S. 20° E.	2	to the center of a Lard. bend passing the upper pt. of the island on Stard. at 1 ¼ m. and a small isld. on Lard. near the extremity of this course.
S. 10° W.	1 ½	to the center of a Stard. bend
S. 80° E.	1	to a point in the Stard. bend.
N. 85° E.	3	to a tree in a Lard. bend passing two small islds
S. 20° W.	3	to a Stard. bend passing over a large island; called it *broad Island*.
N. 70° E.	1 ½	to a point of high timber on stard. side.
S. 20° W.	2	to some dead timber in the center of a Stard. bend just above which we encamped on an island on Lard. opposite to a large isld. on Stard.[7]
Miles 22 ¼		

I saw a black snake today about two feet long the Belly of which was as black as any other part or as jet itself.[8] it had 128 scuta on the belley 63 on the tail.

[Clark] *July 23rd Tuesday 1805*

a fair morning wind from the South. I Set out by land[9] at 6 miles overtook G Drewyer who had killed a Deer. we killed in the Same bottom 4 deer & a antelope & left them on the river bank for the Canoes proceeded on an Indian roade through a wider Vallie which the Missouri Passes about 25 miles & Camped on the bank of the river, High mountains on either Side of the Vallie Containing Scattering Pine & Cedar Some Small Cotton willow willow &c. on the Islands & bank of the river I Saw no fresh Sign of Indians to day Great number of antelopes Some Deer & a large Gangue of Elk

1. The valley through here is underlain by relatively soft sediments of middle to late Tertiary age. The red slate is actually shale, formerly a lateritic soil horizon. The gravel and stones indicate the proximity of a source of consolidated rock.

2. Later Duck, or Gurnett, Creek, in Broadwater County, Montana. On *Atlas* map 63 it was first labeled "Ordway's Creek" and then corrected to the name Lewis gave it. MRC map 81.

3. Probably *Cirsium foliosum* (Hook.) DC., elk thistle. Booth & Wright, 261.

4. Possibly *Allium brevistylum* A. Wats. Dorn, 161; Hahn, *Allium* map. It was probably Biddle who drew a red vertical line through the passages about garlic and flax.

5. Clark's camp was in Broadwater County, about four miles downstream from Toston. *Atlas* map 63; MRC map 82.

6. Probably *Scirpus acutus* Muhl. ex Bigel., western bulrush, and *Typha latifolia* L., common cat-tail. Hahn, *Scirpus* and *Typha* maps; Dorn, 25.

7. In Broadwater County, near the south end of present Canyon Ferry Lake, near present Townsend. *Atlas* map 63; MRC map 82.

8. The western hog-nosed snake, *Heterodon nasicus*, then new to science. Burroughs, 276–77; Cutright (LCPN), 427–28.

9. On *Atlas* map 63 the dotted line indicating Clark's route does not go through the July 22 campsite, his actual starting point on the twenty-third.

[Lewis]   *Wednesday July 24th 1805.*

Set out at sunrise; the current very strong; passed a remarkable bluff of a crimson coloured earth on Stard. intermixed with Stratas of black and brick red slate.[1] the valley through which the river passed today is much as that of yesterday nor is there any difference in the appearance of the mountains, they still continue high and seem to rise in some places like an amphatheater one rang above another as they receede from the river untill the most distant and lofty have their tops clad with snow. the adjacent mountains commonly rise so high as to conceal the more distant and lofty mountains from our view. I fear every day that we shall meet with some considerable falls or obstruction in the river notwithstanding the information of the Indian woman to the contrary who assures us that the river continues much as we see it. I can scarcely form an idea of a river runing to great extent through such a rough mountainous country without having it's stream intersepted by some difficult and gangerous rappids or falls. we daily pass a great number of small rappids or riffles which decend one to or 3 feet in 150 yards but they are rarely incommoded with fixed or standing rocks and altho' strong rapid water are nevertheless quite practicable & by no means dangerous. we saw many beaver and some otter today; the former dam up the small channels of the river between the islands and compell the river in these parts to make other channels; which as soon as it has effected that which was stoped by the beaver becomes dry and is filled up with mud sand gravel and drift wood. the beaver is then compelled to seek another spot for his habitation wher he again erects his dam. thus the river in many places among the clusters of islands is constantly changing the direction of such sluices as the beaver are capable of stoping or of 20 yds. in width. this anamal in that way I beleive to be very instrumental in adding to the number of islands with which we find the river crouded. we killed one deer today and found a goat or Antelope which had been left by Capt. Clark. we saw a large bear but could not get a shoot at him. we also saw a great number of Crains & Antelopes, some gees and a few red-headed ducks[2] the small bird of the plains and curloos still abundant. we observed a great number of snakes about the water of a brown uniform colour, some black, and others speckled on the abdomen and striped with black and brownish yellow on the back and sides. the first of these is the largest being about 4 feet long, the second is of that kind mentioned yesterday, and the last is much like the garter snake of our country and about it's size.[3] none of these species are poisonous I examined their teeth and fund them innosent. they all appear to be fond of the water, to which they fly for shelter immediately on being pursued.— we saw much sign of Elk but met with none of them. from the appearance of bones and excrement of old date the buffaloe sometimes straggle into this valley; but there is no fresh sighn of them and I begin think that our harrvest of white puddings is at an end, at least untill our return to the buffaloe country. our trio of pests still invade and obstruct us on all occasions, these are the Musquetoes eye knats and prickley pears, equal to any three curses that ever poor Egypt laiboured under,[4] except the *Mahometant yoke.* the men complain of being much fortiegued, their labour is excessively great. I occasionly encourage them by assisting in the labour of navigating the canoes, and have learned to *push a tolerable good pole* in their fraize. This morning Capt. Clark [*NB: had*] set out early and pursued the Indian road whih took him up a creek some miles abot 10 A. M. he discovered a horse about six miles distant on his left, he changed his rout towards the horse, on approaching him he found the horse in fine order but so wild he could not get within less than several hundred paces of him. he still saw much indian sign but none of recent date. from this horse he directed his course obliquely to the river where on his arrival he killed a deer and dined. in this wide valley where he met with the horse he passed five handsome streams, one of which only had timber another some willows and much stoped by the beaver. after dinner he continued his rout along the river upwards and encamped having traveled about 30 mes.[5]

Courses and distances of the 24th July 1805.

S. 40° E.	1	to a Lard. bend. passing between two large islands
S. 50° W.	½	to the center of a Stard. bend opposite to an Island
S. 15° E.	1 ½	to a point of high timber in a Lard bend opposite to an island.
S. 40° W.	1 ¼	to the center of a Stard. bend low bluffs touching the river at this point, a small run just below.
South	3 ½	to a bluff point in a Stard. bend passing a small island on Stard. and a bluff of crimson earth & slate.
S. 85° E.	½	to a Lard. bend opposite to a large Island
S. 30° E.	1	to a bluff point in a Stard bend passing an Isld.
East	¾	to a point in a Lard. bend passing a small Isld
S. 30° E.	3	to the lower point of a large island.
S. 85° E.	1 ½	to a tree in a lard. bend passing an assemblage of Islds.
South	½	to a tree on the Stard. shore opposite to the upper point of an island.
S. 80° E.	1	to the center of a Lard. bend passing the upper point of an Island on Lard.
S. 10° W.	1 ½	to the center of a Stard. bend passing an Isld. at ¾ of a mile
East	2	to the center of a Lard. bend passing 2 small islands; en-
Miles 19 ½		camped on Stard. a little short of this course.[6]

Point of Observation No. 38.

On the Stard. side of the Missouri at the extremity of the 8th course of this day observed Equal Altitudes of the ☉ with Sextant.

	h	m	s			h	m	s	
A. M.	9	1	37	P. M.		4	6	20	Altitude at the
"		3	10		"	7	53	time of Observation
"		4	45		"	9	30	79° 8′ 15″

[Clark]   *July 24th Wednesday 1805*

a fine day wind from the N W. I proceeded on up a Creek[7] on the direction of the Indian road   at 10 oClock discovered a horse 6 miles to my left towards the river   as I approached the horse found him fat and verry wild   we could not get near him, we changed our Direction to the river for water haveing previously Crossed 5 handsom Streams in one Vallie[8]   one only had any timber on it one other Willows only & a number of beaver Dams.   when I Struck the river turned down to kill a Deer which we dined on & proceeded on up the river a fiew miles an Campd. on the river.   the river much like it was yesterday.   the mountains on either Side appear like the hills had fallen half down & turned Side upwards[9] the bottoms narrow and no timber a fiew bushes only.[10]

1. The rocks exposed in this bluff belong to the upper part of the Pre-Cambrian Greyson Shale near its contact with the Spokane Shale.

2. Perhaps the same as the "red-headed fishing duck" noted on June 21, 1805, that is, either the red-breasted or common merganser.

3. The brown snake may be the bullsnake, *Pituophis melanoleucus sayi*. The striped snake is the wandering garter snake, *Thamnophis elegans vagrans*, which will enter water when frightened. Burroughs, 277; Benson (HLCE), 89–90.

4. One of the few Biblical references in the journals; see Exodus, 7–12.

5. Clark camped somewhere short of the Three Forks of the Missouri, north of the present village of Trident, in Broadwater County, Montana. *Atlas* map 64; MRC map 83.

6. The camp of the main party was in Broadwater County, about seven miles north of present Toston, Broadwater County, near the mouth of Dry Creek. *Atlas* map 63; MRC map 82.

7. Probably Crow Creek, which mouths a few miles below present Toston. On *Atlas* map 64 it is Gass's Creek, and Clark's route is shown by a dotted line. MRC map 82.

8. Apparently upper branches of Crow (Gass's) Creek. *Atlas* map 64.

9. The Lombard thrust fault crosses through here. The rocks have been intensely deformed and steeply tilted by this fault.

10. At this point Clark enters course and distance material for July 17–20, 1805, which he labels: "Course of the Missouri through the 1st Rock Mountain and distance estimated." This covers the route of the main party from which he was separated. As it is largely a copy of Lewis's daily course log, we do not repeat it.

[Lewis]   *Thursday July 25th 1805.*

Set out at an early hour and proceeded on tolerably well the water still strong and some riffles as yesterday.   the country continues much the same as the two preceeding days.   in the forenoon we saw a large brown bear on an island but he retreated immediately to the main shore and ran off before we could get in reach of him.   they appear to be more shy here than on the Missouri below the mountains.   we saw some antelopes of which we killed one.   these anamals appear now to have collected again is small herds several females with their young and one or two males compose the herd usually.   some males are yet soletary or two perhaps together scattered over the plains which they seen invariably to prefer to the woodlands.   if they happen accedentaly in the woodlands and are allarmed they run immediately to the plains, seeming to plaise a just confidence in their superior fleetness and bottom.   we killed a couple of young gees which are very abundant and fine; but as they are but small game to subsist a party on of our strength I have forbid the men shooting at them as it waists a considerable quantity of amunition and delays our progress.   we passed Capt. Clark's encampment of the 23rd inst.   the face of the country & anamal and vegatable productions were the same as yesterday, untill late in the evening, when the valley appeared to termineate and the river was again hemned in on both sides with high caiggy and rocky clifts.[1]   soon after entering these hills or low mountains we passed a number of fine bold springs which burst out underneath the Lard. clifts near the edge of the water; they wer very cold and freestone water.   we passed a large Crk. today in the plain country, 25 yds. wide, which discharges itself on the Stard. side; it is composed of five streams which unite in the plain at no great distance from the river and have their souces in the Mts.   this stream we called Gass's Creek.[2]   after Sergt. Patric Gass one of our party.—   two rapids near the large spring we passed this evening were the worst we have seen since that we passed on entering the rocky Mountain; they were obstructed with sharp pointed rocks, ranges of which extended quite across the river.   the clifts are formed of a lighter coloured stone than those below   I obseve some limestone also in the bed of the river which seem to have been brought down by the current as they are generally small and woarn smooth.—[3]   This morning Capt. Clark set out early and at the distance of a few miles arrived at the three forks of the Missouri,[4] here he found the plains recently birnt on the stard. side, and the track of a horse which appeared to have passed only about four or five days. after taking breakfast of some meat which they had brought with them, examined the rivers, and written me a note informing me of his intended rout, he continued on up the North fork, which though not larger than the middle fork, boar more to the West, and of course more in the direction we were anxious to pursue. he ascended this stream about 25 miles on Stard. side, and encamped,[5] much fatiegued, his feet blistered and wounded with the prickley pear thorns. Charbono gave out, one of his ankles failed him and he was unable to proceede any further.— I observed that the rocks which form the clifts on this part of the river appear as if they had been undermined by the river and by their weight had seperated from the parent hill and tumbled on their sides, the stratas of rock of which they are composed lying with their edges up; others not seperated seem obliquely depressed on the side next the river as if they had sunk down to fill the cavity which had been formed by the washing and wearing of the river. I have observed a red as well as a yellow species of goosberry[6] which grows on the rocky Clifts in open places of a swetish pine like flavor, first observed in the neighbourhood of the falls; at least the yellow species was first observed there. the red differs from it in no particular except it's colour and size being somewhat larger; it is a very indifferent fruit, but as they form a variety of the native fruits of this country I preserved some of their seeds. musquetoes and knats troublesome as usual.

Courses and distances of July 25th 1805.

S. 25° W.	1	to the center of a Stard. bend
S. 10° W.	1 ¼	to a point in a Stard. bend passing a small Isid. Lard. S.
S. 5° W.	3 ½	to a point in a Stard. bend.
S. 40° E.	1 ¼	to a tree in the Stard. bend passing a Lard. pot. at ½ m
N. 80° E.	2 ½	to the center of a Stard. bend, passing a small island at ½ m. on Stard. opposite or behid which a large Creek discharges itself on Stard. 25 yds. wide which we called Gass's Creek.

South	3	to the center of a Stard. bend
S. 75° E.	1 ½	to a bluff point on Stard. here the river again enters the mountains I beleive it to be a second grand chain of the rocky Mots.
S. 55° E.	1	to a point in a Lard. bend at some large springs.
S. 30° E.	½	to a point in the Lard. bend, high clifts.
South	½	to a Clift of rocks in a Lard. bend; opst. to which we en-
Miles 16		camped for the night under a high bluff[7]

[Clark]   *July 25th Thursday 1805*

a fine morning   we proceeded on a fiew miles to the three forks of the Missouri   those three forks are nearly of a Size, the North fork appears to have the most water and must be Considered as the one best calculated for us to assend   middle fork is quit as large about 90 yds. wide. The South fork is about 70 yds wide & falls in about 400 yards below the midle fork.   those forks appear to be verry rapid & Contain Some timber in their bottoms which is verry extincive,—   on the North Side the Indians have latterly Set the Praries on fire, the Cause I can't account for. I Saw one horse track going up the river about four or 5 days past.   after Brack-fast (which we made on the ribs of a Buck killed yesterday), I wrote a note informing Capt Lewis the rout I intended to take, and proeeded on up the main North fork thro' a vallie, the day verry hot   about 6 or 8 miles up the North fork a Small rapid river falls in on the Lard Side which affords a great Deel of water and appears to head in the Snow mountains to the S W.[8]   this little river falls into the Missouri by three mouthes, haveing Seperated after it arrives in the river Bottoms, and Contains as also all the water courses in this quarter emence number of Beaver & orter   maney thousand enhabit the river & Creeks near the 3 forks (Pho-losiphie's River)—   We Campd on the Same Side we assended Starboard 20 miles on a direct line up the N. fork. Shabono our intrepreter nearly tired one of his ankles falling him—   The bottoms are extencive and toler-able land Covered with tall grass & prickley pears   The hills & mountains are high Steep & rockey. The river verry much divided by Islands   Some Elk Bear & Deer and Some Small timber on the Islands. Great quantities of Currents, red, black, yellow, Purple, also Mountain Currents which grow on the Sides of Clifts; inferior in taste to the others haveing Sweet pineish flaver and are red & yellow, Choke Cheries, Boin roche,[9] and the red buries also abound— musquitors verry trouble Som untill the mountain breeze Sprung up which was a little after night.

1. On *Atlas* map 64, Clark labeled them "Little Gate," and elsewhere "Little Gate of the Mountain." The place is in Broadwater County, Montana, between present Toston and Lombard.

2. Now Crow Creek, Broadwater County, correctly named "Gass's Creek" on *Atlas* map 64. MRC map 82.

3. The Lombard thrust fault cuts through here. Steeply dipping rocks, ranging in age from Precambrian through Cretaceous, are exposed within less than a mile. The Mission Canyon and Lodgepole limestones of the Madison Group occur upstream.

4. The three forks meet near the Broadwater-Gallatin county line, Montana, about four miles northeast of the present town of Three Forks. Part of the area is within the Missouri Headwaters State Monument. Appleman (LC), 328–32; *Atlas* maps 64, 65; MRC map 83.

5. Clark's route appears as a dotted line on *Atlas* map 65, but his campsite does not. It was on the north side of the Jefferson River, in Jefferson County, Montana, above the mouth of Willow Creek (Lewis and Clark's Philosophy River) and the town of Willow Creek, and about three miles downstream from the present crossing of U.S. Highway 287.

6. Lewis's "gooseberry" is probably Clark's "Mountain Currents" of this day and their words illustrate the confusion of the two terms. From Lewis's ecological and morphological descriptions it is clear that both are the single plant, squaw, or western red, currant. The captains may be viewing color variations or perhaps the yellowish fruited individuals were simply immature. As Lewis points out, it is the same shrub encountered on June 18. It was probably Biddle who drew a red vertical line through this passage about the gooseberry; other lines were also drawn through passages about the antelopes and geese above.

7. This camp is misdated July 24 on *Atlas* map 64. It is in Broadwater County, immediately above Toston Dam. MRC map 83.

8. "Pholosophy [Philosophy] River" on *Atlas* map 65; now Willow Creek, in Gallatin County. The mountains are the Tobacco Root range, in Madison County.

9. Probably meaning *bois rouge*, the previously noted red osier dogwood.

[Lewis]   *Friday July 26th 1805.*

Set out early this morning as usual current strong with frequent riffles; employ the cord and seting poles. the oars scarcely ever being used except to pass the river in order to take advantage of the shore and current. at the distance of 3¾ m. passed the entrance of a large Creek 15 yds. wide which discharges itself on Lard. near the center of a Lard. bend it is a bold runing stream   this we called Howard's Creek after Thomas P. Howard one of our party.[1]   at the distance of one mile further we passed the entrance of a small run which falls in just above a rocky clift on Lard.[2] here the hills or reather mountains again recede from the river and the valley again widens to the extent of several miles with wide and fertile bottom lands.   covered with grass and in many places a fine terf of green-sword.   the high lands are thin meagre soil covered with dry low sedge and a species of grass[3] also dry the seeds of which are armed with a long twisted hard beard at the upper extremity while the lower point is a sharp subulate firm point beset at it's base with little stiff bristles standing with their points in a contrary direction to the subulate point to which they answer as a barb and serve also to pres it forward when onece entered a small distance.   these barbed seed penetrate our mockersons and leather legings and give us great pain untill they are removed.   my poor dog suffers with them excessively, he is constantly binting and scratching himself as if in a rack of pain.   the prickly pear also grow here as abundantly as usual.   there is another species of the prickly pear of a globular form,[4] composed of an assemblage of little conic leaves springing from a common root to which their small points are attached as a common center and the base of the cone forms the apex of the leaf which is garnished with a circular range of sharp thorns quite as stif and more keen than the more common species with the flat leaf, like the Cockeneal plant.   on entering this open valley I saw the snowclad tops of distant mountains before us.   the timber and mountains much as heretofore.   saw a number of beaver today and some otter, killed one of the former, also 4 deer; found a deer's skin which had been left by Capt. C. with a note informing me of his having met with a horse but had seen no fresh appearance of the Indians.   the river in the valley is from 2 to 250 yds. wide and crouded with Islands, in some places it is ¾ of a mile wide including islands.   were it passed the hills it was from 150 to 200 yds. the banks are still low but never overflow.   one of the men brought me an indian bow which he found, it was made of cedar and about 2 F. 9 Inh. in length.   it had nothing remarkable in it's form being much such as is used by the Mandans Minetares &c. This morning Capt. Clark left Sharbono and Joseph Fields at the camp of last evening and proceeded up the river about 12 miles to the top of a mountain from whence he had an extensive view of the valley of the river upwards and of a large creek which flowed into it on Std. side.[5]   not meeting with any fresh appearance of Indians he determined to return and examine the middle fork of the missouri and meet me by the time he expected me to arrive at the forks.   he returned down the mountain by the way of an old Indian road which led through a deep hollow of the mountain facing the south   the day being warm and the road unshaded by timber [*X: in the deep valley*] he suffered excessively with heat and the want of water, at length he arrived at a very cold spring, at which he took the precaution of weting his feet head and hands before drank but notwithstanding this precaution he soon felt the effects of the water.   he felt himself very unwell shortly after but continued his march rejoined Sharbono and Fields where the party eat of a fawn which Jo. Fields had killed in their absence   Capt. C. was so unwell that he had no inclination to eat.   after a short respite he resumed his march pass the North fork at a large island; here Charbono was very near being swept away by the current and cannot swim, Capt. C however risqued him and saved his life. Capt. C. continued his march to a small river which falls into the North fork some miles above the junction of the 3 forks it being the distance of about four miles from his camp of last evening   here finding himself still more unwell he determined to encamp.[6]   they killed two brown or Grisley bear this evening on the island where they passed the N. fork of the Missouri.   this stream is much divided by islands and it's current rapid and much as that of the missouri [*NB: Qu*] where we are and is navigable.—   [*X: emence qty of Beaver*]

Courses and distances of July 26th 1805

N. 45° W.	¼	to an object in a Stard. bend
S. 60° W.	1	to a point in a Lard. bend passing 9 small Islds.
S. 55° W.	½	to the center of a Stard. bend passing one Ild. and opt. a 2cd
S. 65° E.	1	to a clift of rocks in a Stard. bend passing 2 Islands.
N. 65° E.	1	to the entrance of a creek 15 yds. wide on Lard. in a Lard. bend we call *Howards Creek.* pag. 1 Ild.

S. 15° E.	1	to the entrance of a small run in a Lard. bend the mouts. here recedes from the river. this run Capt. C. has laid down in mistake for Howard's Creek.
S. 55° W.	1 ½	to the center of a Stard. bend
S. 12° W.	2 ½	to a point in a Stard. bend
S. 15° E.	3 ½	to a point of high timber on the Lard. passing 3 Ilds. on Lard.
S. 25° W.	1	to the center of a Stard. bend
East	1 ¼	to the center of a Lard. bend passing 3 Islds. on Lard. side
S. 20° E.	2 ½	to the center of a Lard. bend passing 4 Islds. on Lard. Sd.
S. 48° W.	1 ½	to a rock in the center of a Lard. bend opposite to 2 Islds. where we encamped for the night on Lard. shore.[7]

Miles 16 ½ [*NB: 18*]

[Clark]   *July 26th Friday 1805*

I deturmined to leave Shabono & one man who had Sore feet to rest & proceed on with the other two[8] to the top of a mountain 12 miles distant west and from thence view the river & vallies a head, we with great dificuelty & much fatigue reached the top at 11 oClock   from the top of this mountain I could see the Course of the North fork about 10 miles meandering through a Vallie but Could discover no Indians or Sign which was fresh. I could also See Some distance up the Small River below, and also the middle fork   after Satisfying my Self returned to the two me[n] by an old Indian parth, on this parth & in the Mountain we Came to a Spring of excessive Cold water, which we drank reather freely of as we were almost famished; not with Standing the precautions of wetting my face, hands, & feet, I Soon felt the effects of the water. We Contind. thro a Deep Vallie without a Tree to Shade us Scorching with heat to the men who had killed a pore Deer, I was fatigued my feet with Several blisters & Stuck with prickley pears. I eate but verry little deturmined to Cross to the middle fork and examine that.   we Crossed the Missouri which was divided by a verry large Island, the first Part was knee deep, the other waste deep & verry rapid—   I felt my Self verry unwell[9] & took up Camp on the little river 3 miles above its mouth & near the place it falls into the bottom   a fiew Drops of rain this evening

we killed 2 bear which was imediately in our way.   both pore   emence number of Beaver and orter in this little river which forks in the bottom

1. Sixteenmile Creek, on the Broadwater-Gallatin county line, Montana, at its mouth. *Atlas* map 64; MRC map 83.

2. Present Garden Gulch, in Gallatin County, mislabeled "Howard's Creek" on *Atlas* map 64. MRC map 83.

3. *Stipa comata* Trin. & Rupr., needle and thread grass. Hahn, *Stipa* map; Cutright (LCPN), 172, 420. It was probably Biddle who drew a red vertical line through several passages, beginning with "covered with" to "Cocheneal plant."

4. *Coryphantha missouriensis* (Sweet) Britton & Rose, yellow pincushion cactus. Booth & Wright, 159; Benson (CUSC), 856–60. The "Cockeneal" used for comparison is *Nopalea cochinillifera* Salm-Dyck, cochineal cactus, which Lewis would have known as an ornamental in the East. Bailey, 702–3.

5. "R. Fields Vally Creek" on *Atlas* map 65, now Boulder River, entering the Jefferson near Cardwell, Jefferson County, Montana. Clark's route is indicated by a dotted line on *Atlas* maps 64, 65; it becomes confused, however, with another dotted line showing Lewis's route of a few days later.

6. On Willow Creek (Philosophy River), in Gallatin County, above the present town of Willow Creek. *Atlas* map 65.

7. The main party camp is misdated July 25 on *Atlas* map 64. It is in Gallatin County, at the landmark of Eagle Rock. MRC map 83.

8. Frazer and Reubin Field, Joseph Field having remained with Charbonneau.

9. Clark's illness may be attributed mostly to fatigue from his great physical output; the illness persisted for several days. See Chuinard (OOMD), 302–4.

[Lewis]   *Saturday July 27th 1805.*

We set out at an early hour and proceeded on but slowly   the current still so rapid that the men are in a continual state of their utmost exertion to get on, and they begin to weaken fast from this continual state of violent exertion.   at the distance of 1¾ miles the river was again closely hemned in by high Clifts of a solid limestone rock which appear to have tumbled or sunk in the same manner of those discribed yesterday.   the limestone appears to be of an excellent quality of deep blue colour when fractured and of a light led colour where exposed to the weather.   it appears to be of a very fine gr[a]in the fracture like that of marble.[1]   we saw

a great number of the bighorn on those Clifts.   at the distance of 3¾ ms.
further we arrived at 9 A. M. at the junction of the S. E. fork of the Missouri and the country opens suddonly to extensive and beatifull plains
and meadows which appear to be surrounded in every direction with distant and lofty mountains; supposing this to be the three forks of the Missouri I halted the party on the Lard. shore for breakfast and walked up
the S. E. fork about ½ a mile and ascended the point of a high limestone
clift from whence I commanded a most perfect view of the neighbouring
country. From this point I could see the S. E. fork about 7 miles.   it is
rapid and about 70 yards wide.   throughout the distance I saw it, it passes
through a smoth extensive green meadow of fine grass in it's course meandering in several streams the largest of which passes near the Lard. hills,
of which, the one I stand on is the extremity in this direction.   a high
wide and extensive plain succeeds the meadow and extends back several
miles from the river on the Stard. sade and with the range of mountains
up the Lard. side of the middle fork.   a large spring arrises in this meadow
about ¼ of a mile from the S. E. fork into which it discharges itself on the
Stard. side about 400 paces above me.   from E to S. between the S. E.
and middle forks a distant range of lofty mountains rose their snow-clad
tops [2] above the irregular and broken mountains which lie adjacent to this
beautifull spot.   the extreme point to which I could see the S. E. fork
boar S. 65° E. distant 7 ms. as before observed.   between the middle and
S. E. forks near their junctions with the S. W. fork there is a handsom site
for a fortification   it consists of a limestone rock of an oblong form; it's
sides perpendicular and about 25 ft high except at the extremity towards
the middle fork where it ascends gradually and like the top is covered
with a fine terf of greenswoard.   the top is level and contains about 2
Acres.   the rock [r]ises from the level plain as if it had been designed for
some such purpose.[3]   the extream point to which I can see the bottom
and meandering of the Middle fork bears S. 15 E distant about 14 miles.
here it turns to the right around a point of a high plain and disappears to
my view.   it's bottoms are several miles in width and like that of the S. E.
fork form one smoth and beautifull green meadow.   it is also divided
into several streams.   betwen this and the S. W. fork there is an extensive
plain which appears to extend up both those rivers many miles and back

to the mountains.   the extreme point to which I can see the S. W. fork bears S. 30 W. distant about 12 miles.   this stream passes through a similar country with the other two and is more divided and serpentine in it's course than either of the others; it a[l]so possesses abundanly more timber in it's bottoms.   the timber here consists of the narrowleafed cottonwood almost entirely.   but little box alder or sweet willow the underbrush thick and as heretofore discribed in the quarter of the missouri.   a range of high mountains at a considerable distance appear to reach from South to West and are partially covered with snow   the country to the right of the S. W. fork like that to the left of the S. E. fork is high broken and mountainous as is that also down the missouri behind us, through which, these three rivers after assembling their united force at this point seem to have forced a passage   these bottom lands tho' not more than 8 or 9 feet above the water seem never to overflow.   after making a draught of the connection and meanders of these streams[4] I decended the hill and returned to the party, took breakfast and ascended the S. W. fork 1¾ miles and encamped at a Lard. bend in a handsome level smooth plain just below a bayou, having passed the entrance of the middle fork at ½ a mile. here I encamped to wait the return of Capt. Clark and to give the men a little rest which seemed absolutely necessary to them.[5]   at the junction of the S. W. and Middle forks I found a note which had been left by Capt. Clark informing me of his intended rout, and that he would rejoin me at this place provided he did not fall in with any fresh sighn of Indians, in which case he intended to pursue untill he over took them calculating on my taking the S. W. fork, which I most certainly prefer as it's direction is much more promising than any other.   beleiving this to be an essential point in the geography of this western part of the Continent I determined to remain at all events untill I obtained the necessary data for fixing it's latitude Longitude &c.   after fixing my camp I had the canoes all unloaded and the baggage stoed away and securely covered on shore, and then permitted several men to hunt. I walked down to the middle fork and examined and compared it with the S. W. fork but could not satisfy myself which was the largest stream of the two, in fact they appeared as if they had been cast in the same mould there being no difference in character or size, therefore to call either of these streams the Missouri would be giving it a preference wich it's size dose not warrant as it is not larger then the other.   they are each 90 yds. wide.   in these meadows I saw a number of the duckanmallad[6] with their young which are now nearly grown. Currants of every species as well as goosberries are found her[e] in great abundance and perfection.   a large black goosberry[7] which grows to the hight of five or six feet is also found here.   this is the growth of the bottom lands and is found also near the little rivulets which make down from the hills and mountains   it puts up many stems from the same root, some of which are partialy branched and all reclining.   the berry is attatched seperately by a long peduncle to the stem from which they hang pendant underneath.   the berry is of an ovate form smooth as large as the common garden goosberry when arrived at maturity and is as black as jet, tho' the pulp is of a cimson colour.   this fruit is extreemly asced.   the leaf resembles the common goosberry in form but is reather larger and somewhat proportioned to the superior size of it's stem when compared with the common goosberry.   the stem is covered with very sharp thorns or bryers.   below the tree forks as we passed this morning I observed many collections of the mud nests of the small martin attatched to the smooth face of the limestone rocks sheltered by projections of the same rock above. Our hunters returned this evening with 6 deer 3 Otter and a musk rat.   they informed me that they had seen great numbers of Antelopes, and much sign of beaver Otter deer Elk, &c.   at 3 P. M. Capt Clark arrived very sick with a high fever on him and much fatiegued and exhausted.   he informed me that he was very sick all last night had a high fever and frequent chills & constant aking pains in all his mustles.   this morning notwithstanding his indisposition he pursued his intended rout to the middle fork about 8 miles and finding no recent sign of Indians rested about an hour and came down the middle fork to this place. Capt. C. thought himself somewhat bilious and had not had a passage for several days; I prevailed on him to take a doze of Rushes pills, which I have always found sovereign in such cases and to bath his feet in warm water and rest himself. Capt. C's indisposition was a further inducement for my remaining here a couple of days; I therefore informed the men of my intention, and they put their deer skins in the water in order to prepare them for dressing tomorrow.   we begin to feel considerable anxiety with rispect to the

Snake Indians. if we do not find them or some other nation who have horses I fear the successfull issue of our voyage will be very doubtfull or at all events much more difficult in it's accomplishment. we are now several hundred miles within the bosom of this wild and mountanous country, where game may rationally be expected shortly to become scarce and subsistence precarious without any information with rispect to the country not knowing how far these mountains continue, or wher to direct our course to pass them to advantage or intersept a navigable branch of the Columbia, or even were we on such an one the probability is that we should not find any timber within these mountains large enough for canoes if we judge from the portion of them through which we have passed. however I still hope for the best, and intend taking a tramp myself in a few days to find these yellow gentlemen if possible. my two principal consolations are that from our present position it is impossible that the S. W. fork can head with the waters of any other river but the Columbia, and that if any Indians can subsist in the form of a nation in these mountains with the means they have of acquiring food we can also subsist. Capt. C. informed me that there is a part of this bottom on the West side of the Middle fork near the plain, which appears to overflow occasionally and is stony.

Courses and distances of July 27th 1805.

N. 65° W.	½	to the center of a Stard. bend passing an Island.
South	1 ¼	to a clift of high rocks on the Stard. here the river is again confined between high and perpendicular clifts of rock.—
S. 2° E.	2 ½	to the center of a Lard. bend passing a small Island
S. 45 W.	1 ¼	to the upper point of a high clift of rocks in a Stard. opposite or a little below the entrance of the S. E. fork of the Missouri which we called *Gallitin's river*[8] in honor of Albert Gallitin Secretary of the Treasury
S. 45° W.	½	to the confluence of the middle and S. W. forks of the Missouri each 90 yds. wide; the Middle fork we called Maddison's river in honor of James Maddison the Secretary of State.—[9] and the S. W. fork we called Jefferson's River in honor that illustrious peronage Thomas Jefferson President of the United States.

N. 45° W.	¼	to the entrance of a Bayou on Stard. side
S. 30° W.	¼	to a Stard. bend.
S. 20° E.	¼	to the center of a Lard. bend where we encamped on Lard.
Miles 7		in Camp Island.—

[Clark]   *July 27th Saturday 1805*

I was verry unwell all last night with a high fever & akeing in all my bones.   my fever &c. continus, deturmind to prosue my intended rout to the middle fork, accordingly Set out in great pain across a Prarie 8 miles to the Middle   this fork is nearly as large as the North fork & appears to be more rapid, we examined and found no fresh Sign of Indians, and after resting about an hour, proceeded down to the junction thro a wide bottom which appears to be overflown every year, & maney parts Stoney this river has Several Islands and number of beaver & orter, but little timber.   we could See no fresh Sign of Indians   just above the Point I found Capt Lewis encamped haveing arrived about 2 oClock. Several Deer killed this evening. I continue to be verry unwell fever verry high; take 5 of rushes pills & bathe my feet & legs in hot water

1. The limestone belongs to the Mission Canyon or Lodgepole limestones of the Madison Group. The rocks in this area have been tilted to steep angles by faulting and folding. It was probably Biddle who drew a red vertical line through part of these geology notes.

2. The Madison range.

3. This is a monolithic outcrop of Mississippian-age limestone of the Madison Group.

4. Like other maps Lewis may have made, this apparently has not survived; the information was probably incorporated into *Atlas* map 65.

5. This site, where they remained until July 30, was apparently on later Barkers Island (not now named), between two branches of the Jefferson, northeast of the present town of Three Forks, Gallatin County, Montana, and two miles northeast of where Interstate Highway 90 crosses the Jefferson River. *Atlas* map 65; MRC map 83.

6. An old colloquial name for the mallard. Burroughs, 188–89; Holmgren, 30. It was probably Biddle who drew a red vertical line through the passages beginning with "duckanmallard" to "same rock above."

7. The swamp currant (see July 17, 1805).

8. The names the captains gave to the three forks have remained, unlike many others they bestowed. Albert Gallatin, born in Geneva, came to the United States in 1780 and settled in southwest Pennsylvania. He was secretary of the treasury under Jefferson and

Madison (1801–11), helped negotiate the Treaty of Ghent ending the War of 1812, was minister to France, 1816–23, and minister to Great Britain, 1826–27. He was active in preparations for the Lewis and Clark expedition, and devoted much of his later life to a study of the American Indians, being recognized as having made the first steps toward a systematic classification of Indian languages. Walters.

9. James Madison, one of the leading figures of the Constitutional Convention of 1787 and co-founder, with Jefferson, of the Democratic Republican Party, was Jefferson's secretary of state and president from 1809 to 1817.

Volume 4

Sources Cited

Allen (LCDM)   Allen, John L. "Lewis and Clark on the Upper
                    Missouri: Decision at the Marias." *Montana, the
                    Magazine of Western History* 21 (July 1971):
                    2–17.

Allen (PG)   ———. *Passage Through the Garden: Lewis and Clark
                    and the Image of the American Northwest.* Urbana:
                    University of Illinois Press, 1975.

Anderson (SSS)   Anderson, Irving W. "Sacajawea, Sacagawea,
                    Sakakawea?" *South Dakota History* 8 (Fall 1978):
                    303–11.

AOU   American Ornithologists' Union. *Check-list of North
                    American Birds.* 6th ed. Baltimore, Md.: Ameri-
                    can Ornithologists' Union, 1983. [AOU] in
                    brackets with numbers refers to a species item-
                    number in the book.

Appleman (LC)   Appleman, Roy E. *Lewis and Clark: Historic Places
                    Associated with Their Transcontinental Exploration
                    (1804–06).* Washington, D.C.: United States
                    Department of the Interior, National Park Ser-
                    vice, 1975.

Atlas   Moulton, Gary E., ed. *Atlas of the Lewis and Clark
                    Expedition.* Lincoln: University of Nebraska
                    Press, 1983.

Bailey   Bailey, L. H. *Manual of Cultivated Plants.* 1924.
                    Reprint. New York: Macmillan, 1971.

Barkley   Barkley, T. M., ed. *Atlas of the Flora of the Great Plains.*
                    Ames: Iowa State University Press, 1977.

Benson (HLCE)   Benson, Keith R. "Herpetology on the Lewis and
                    Clark Expedition: 1804–1806." *Herpetological
                    Review* 3 (1978): 87–91.

Benson (CUSC)   Benson, Lyman. *The Cacti of the United States and*

	Canada. Stanford, Calif.: Stanford University Press, 1982.
Booth & Wright	Booth, W. E., and J. C. Wright. *Flora of Montana, Part II*. Bozeman: Montana State University, 1959.
Burroughs	Burroughs, Raymond Darwin. *The Natural History of the Lewis and Clark Expedition*. East Lansing: Michigan State University Press, 1961.
Chuinard (OOMD)	Chuinard, Eldon G. *Only One Man Died: The Medical Aspects of the Lewis and Clark Expedition*. Glendale, Calif.: Arthur H. Clark, 1979.
Clark	Clark, William P. *The Indian Sign Language*. 1885. Reprint. Lincoln: University of Nebraska Press, 1982.
Clarke (MLCE)	Clarke, Charles G. *The Men of the Lewis and Clark Expedition: A Biographical Roster of the Fifty-one Members and a Composite Diary of their Activities from all Known Sources*. Glendale, Calif.: Arthur H. Clark, 1970.
Coues (HLC)	Coues, Elliott, ed. *History of the Expedition under the Command of Lewis and Clark. . . .* 1893. Reprint. 3 vols. New York: Dover Publications, 1965.
Criswell	Criswell, Elijah Harry. *Lewis and Clark: Linguistic Pioneers*. University of Missouri Studies, vol. 15, no. 2. Columbia: University of Missouri Press, 1940.
Cronquist et al.	Cronquist, Arthur, Arthur H. Holmgren, Noel H. Holmgren, James L. Reveal, and Patricia K. Holmgren. *Intermountain Flora: Vascular Plants of the Intermountain West, U.S.A.* Vol. 4, *Subclass Asteridae (except Asteraceae)*. New York: New York Botanical Garden, 1984.
Cutright (LCPN)	Cutright, Paul Russell. *Lewis and Clark: Pioneering Naturalists*. Urbana: University of Illinois Press, 1969.
Dorn	Dorn, Robert D. *Vascular Plants of Montana* Cheyenne, Wyo.: Mountain West Publishing, 1984.
Ewers (BRNP)	Ewers, John C. *The Blackfeet: Raiders on the Northwestern Plains*. Norman: University of Oklahoma Press, 1958.

Ewers (ILUM)   ———. *Indian Life on the Upper Missouri*. Norman: University of Oklahoma Press, 1968.

Fernald   Fernald, Merritt Lyndon. *Gray's Manual of Botany*. 8th ed. New York: D. Van Nostrand, 1970.

Flannery   Flannery, Regina. *The Gros Ventres of Montana:* Part I, *Social Life*. Washington: Catholic University of America Press, 1953.

Gilmore (SCAT)   Gilmore, Melvin R. "Some Comments on 'Aboriginal Tobaccos.'" *American Anthropologist*, n.s., 24 (October–December 1922): 480–81.

Gilmore (UPI)   ———. *Uses of Plants by the Indians of the Missouri River Region*. 1919. Reprint. Lincoln: University of Nebraska Press, 1977.

Hahn   Hahn, Barton E. *Flora of Montana: Conifers and Monocots*. Bozeman: Montana State University, 1977.

Hall   Hall, E. Raymond. *The Mammals of North America*. 2d ed. 2 vols. New York: John Wiley and Sons, 1981.

Heiser   Heiser, Charles B., Jr. *The Sunflower*. Norman: University of Oklahoma Press, 1976.

Hitchcock & Cronquist   Hitchcock, C. Leo, and Arthur Cronquist. *Flora of the Pacific Northwest: An Illustrated Manual*. Seattle: University of Washington Press, 1973.

Hodge   Hodge, Frederick Webb, ed. *Handbook of American Indians North of Mexico*. 1912. Reprint. 2 vols. St. Clair Shores, Mich.: Scholarly Press, 1968.

Holmgren   Holmgren, Virginia C. "A Glossary of Bird Names Cited by Lewis and Clark." *We Proceeded On* 10 (May 1984): 28–34.

Jackson (FLCE)   Jackson, Donald. "A Footnote to the Lewis and Clark Expedition." *Manuscripts* 24 (Winter 1972): 3–21.

Jackson (TJ)   ———. *Thomas Jefferson and the Stony Mountains: Exploring the West from Monticello*. Urbana: University of Illinois Press, 1981.

Jackson (LLC)   ———, ed. *Letters of the Lewis and Clark Expedition with Related Documents, 1783–1854*. 2d ed. 2 vols. Urbana: University of Illinois Press, 1978.

Jefferson   Jefferson, Thomas. *Notes on the State of Virginia*.

	Edited by William Peden. Chapel Hill: University of North Carolina Press, 1955.
Jones et al.	Jones, J. Knox, Jr., David H. Armstrong, Robert S. Hoffmann, and Clyde Jones. *Mammals of the Northern Great Plains*. Lincoln: University of Nebraska Press, 1983.
Kartesz & Kartesz	Kartesz, John T., and Rosemarie Kartesz. *A Synonymized Checklist of the Vascular Flora of the United States, Canada, and Greenland*. Chapel Hill: University of North Carolina Press, 1980.
Large	Large, Arlen J. "'. . . it thundered and Lightened': The Weather Observations of Lewis and Clark." *We Proceeded On* 12 (May 1986): 6–10.
Lee et al.	Lee, David S., Carter R. Gilbert, Charles H. Hocutt, Robert E. Jenkins, Don E. McAllister, and Jay R. Stauffer, Jr. *Atlas of North American Freshwater Fishes*. Raleigh: North Carolina State Museum of Natural History, 1980.
Little	Little, Elbert L., Jr. *Atlas of United States Trees*. Vol. 1, *Conifers and Important Hardwoods*. Washington, D.C.: United States Department of Agriculture, Forest Service, 1971.
Lowie (IP)	Lowie, Robert H. *Indians of the Plains*. 1954. Reprint. Lincoln: University of Nebraska Press, 1982.
McJimsey	McJimsey, George Davis. *Topographic Terms in Virginia*. New York: Columbia University Press, 1940.
MacGregor	MacGregor, James G. *Peter Fidler: Canada's Forgotten Surveyor, 1769–1822*. Toronto: McClelland and Stewart, 1966.
Mattison (GR)	Mattison, Ray H. "Report on Historic Sites in the Garrison Reservoir Area, Missouri River." *North Dakota History* 22 (January–April 1955): 5–73.
Montana Guide	*Montana: A State Guide Book*. Compiled and Written by the Federal Writers' Project of the Works Progress Administration for the State of Montana. American Guide Series. 1939. Reprint. New York: Hastings House Publishers, 1949.
Moodie & Kaye	Moodie, D. W., and Barry Kaye. "The Ac ko Mok

ki Map." *The Beaver* (Spring 1977): 4–15.

MRC Missouri River Commission. *Map of the Missouri River From Its Mouth to Three Forks, Montana, in Eighty-four Sheets.* Washington, D.C.: Missouri River Commission, 1892–95.

Nelson Nelson, Joseph S. *Fishes of the World.* New York: John Wiley, 1976.

North Dakota Guide *North Dakota: A Guide to the Northern Prairie State.* Compiled by workers of the Federal Writers' Project of the Works Progress Administration for the State of North Dakota. American Guide Series. 1938. Reprint. New York: Oxford Univesity Press, 1950.

Pendergast Pendergast, David M., ed. *Palenque: The Walker-Caddy Expedition to the Ancient City, 1839–1840.* Norman: University of Oklahoma Press, 1967.

Pennak Pennak, Robert W. *Fresh-water Invertebrates of the United States.* New York: Ronald Press, 1953.

Peterson Peterson, Harold L. *The Book of the Continental Soldier.* Harrisburg, Pa.: Stackpole Company, 1968.

Pursh Pursh, Frederick. *Flora Americae Septentrionalis.* 1814. Reprint. Braunschweig, Germany: Strauss and Cramer, 1979.

Reid & Gannon Reid, Russell, and Clell C. Gannon. "Birds and Mammals Observed by Lewis and Clark in North Dakota." *North Dakota Historical Quarterly* 1 (July 1927): 14–36.

Ronda (LCAI) Ronda, James P. *Lewis and Clark among the Indians.* Lincoln: University of Nebraska Press, 1984.

Rose Rose, Donald W. "Captain Lewis's Iron Boat: 'The Experiment.'" *We Proceeded On* 7 (May 1981): 4–7.

Saindon (RSO) Saindon, Bob. "The River Which Scolds at All Others: An Obstinate Blunder in Nomenclature." *Montana, the Magazine of Western History* 26 (July 1976): 2–7.

Shultz Shultz, Leila M. McReynolds. "Systematics and Anatomical Studies of *Artemisia* Subgenus *Tri-*

	dentatae." Ph.D. diss., Claremont Graduate School, 1983.
Steffen	Steffen, Jerome O. *William Clark: Jeffersonian Man on the Frontier.* Norman: University of Oklahoma Press, 1977.
Thwaites (LC)	Thwaites, Reuben, Gold, ed. *Original Journals of the Lewis and Clark Expedition, 1804–1806.* 8 vols. New York: Dodd, Mead, 1904–5.
Tooley	Tooley, R. V. "Aaron Arrowsmith." *The Map Collector* 9 (December 1979): 19–22.
USGS	United States Geological Survey, 30' × 60' quadrangle, 1 : 100,000 planimetric maps.
Virginia Guide	*Virginia: A Guide to the Old Dominion.* Compiled by the workers of the Writers' Program of the Works Progress Administration in the State of Virginia. American Guide Series. New York: Oxford University Press, 1940.
Walters	Walters, Raymond. *Albert Gallatin: Jeffersonian Financier and Diplomat.* Pittsburgh: University of Pittsburgh Press, 1969.
Weaver & Albertson	Weaver, J. E., and F. W. Albertson. *Grasslands of the Great Plains: Their Nature and Use.* Lincoln, Nebr.: Johnsen Publishing Co., 1956.
Welsh	Welsh, Stanley L. "Utah Flora: *Compositae (Asteraceae).*" *The Great Basin Naturalist* 43 (April 30, 1983): 179–357.
Werner et al.	Werner, Floyd G., et al. *Common Names of Insects and Related Organisms, 1982.* College Park, Md.: Entomological Society of America, 1982.
Wheeler	Wheeler, Olin D. *The Trail of Lewis and Clark, 1804–1806.* 2 vols. New York: G. P. Putnam's Sons, 1904.
Willard	Willard, John. "Discovery of the Missouri's Great Falls Inspired Meriwether Lewis." *Hoofprints* 14 (Spring–Summer 1984): 3–15.
Wood (MMA)	Wood, W. Raymond. "Lewis and Clark and Middle Missouri Archaeology." *The Quarterly Review of Archaeology* 3 (December 1982): 3–5.
Wood (SR)	———. "Slaughter River: Pishkun or Float Bison?" *We Proceeded On* 12 (May 1986): 11–14.

Index

447